DIARY OF A CHRISTIAN SOLDIER

This book offers both a meticulous reconstruction of the life of Rufus Kinsley, an ordinary New England soldier who during the Civil War became an officer in one of the nation's first and most famous black regiments, and an expertly edited transcription of Kinsley's hitherto unpublished wartime diary. Kinsley's diary sheds light on such important topics as the fall of New Orleans, the capture of Mobile Bay, and the battle for the bayou country of southwestern Louisiana. It also illuminates the workaday routines of black and white soldiers stationed behind Union lines but thoroughly immersed in the unprecedented improvisations that accompanied the social revolution that was emancipation. Kinsley's perspective is that of an often overlooked type: the absolutely dedicated evangelical abolitionist soldier who believed that the war and its consequences were divine retribution for the sin of slavery. The introductory biography places Kinsley's Civil War experience in the context of his life and times. It focuses particularly on Kinsley's life from the end of the war until his death in 1911, emphasizing an unrelenting struggle for his health, his pension, and his family's survival. It concludes that the war was the defining moment of Kinsley's life and suggests that those soldiers who came home victorious, including those who escaped enemy fire, did not necessarily return unscathed.

David C. Rankin has taught at Oberlin College and currently teaches at the University of California, Irvine. The recipient of fellowships from the American Council of Learned Societies and the Charles Warren Center at Harvard University, he is also the author of *My Passage at the New Orleans Tribune: A Memoir of the Civil War Era* as well as articles in *Perspectives in American History, Civil War History,* and *The Journal of Southern History.*

Rufus Kinsley. Courtesy of Reba Kinsley Hall.

Diary of a Christian Soldier

≋ Rufus Kinsley and the Civil War ≋

David C. Rankin
University of California, Irvine

CAMBRIDGE
UNIVERSITY PRESS

PUBLISHED BY THE PRESS SYNDICATE OF THE UNIVERSITY OF CAMBRIDGE
The Pitt Building, Trumpington Street, Cambridge, United Kingdom

CAMBRIDGE UNIVERSITY PRESS
The Edinburgh Building, Cambridge CB2 2RU, UK
40 West 20th Street, New York, NY 10011-4211, USA
477 Williamstown Road, Port Melbourne, VIC 3207, Australia
Ruiz de Alarcón 13, 28014 Madrid, Spain
Dock House, The Waterfront, Cape Town 8001, South Africa

http://www.cambridge.org

First published 2004

Printed in the United States of America

Typeface ITC New Baskerville 10/13 pt.   *System* LᴬTEX 2ε   [TB]

A catalog record for this book is available from the British Library.

Library of Congress Cataloging in Publication Data
Kinsley, Rufus, d. 1911.
Diary of a Christian soldier : Rufus Kinsley and the Civil War / [edited, and with an
introduction by] David C. Rankin.

   p. cm.
Includes bibliographical references (p.) and index.
ISBN 0-521-82334-X
1. Kinsley, Rufus, d. 1911 – Diaries.   2. United States – History – Civil War, 1861–1865 –
Personal narratives.   3. Louisiana – History – Civil War, 1861–1865 – Personal narratives.
4. United States – History – Civil War, 1861–1865 – African Americans.   5. United States.
Army – African American troops – History – 19th century.   6. Soldiers – Vermont –
Diaries.   7. Abolitionists – Vermont – Diaries.   8. United States – History – Civil War,
1861–1865 – Religious aspects – Christianity.   I. Rankin, David C.   II. Title.
E601.K555   2003
973.7'415'092 – dc21   2003055192

ISBN 0 521 82334 X hardback

TO THE MEMORY OF MY FATHER

Wilfred Warren Rankin

AND TO MY SONS

William Massey Rankin

Andrew Howe Rankin

For the day of vengeance *is* in mine heart, and the year of my redeemed is come.

Isaiah 63:4

The wail of the oppressor mingles with the wail of his victim, by reason of whose oppression the whole land groaneth, and is made desolate.

Rufus Kinsley
August 31, 1862

We have sown seeds in the past. We are reaping the harvest to-day. God is just, though his judgments be long delayed. By and by, when we learn justice, God will give us great victory. And we are beginning to learn. O yes, we *are* beginning to learn.

Rufus Kinsley
June 29, 1864

Contents

Illustrations

Preface

LIKE THOUSANDS OF AMERICANS, PAST AND PRESENT, RUFUS
Kinsley kept a diary. He began writing in his diary on November 29,
1861, the day he enlisted in the Union army. By the time of his last entry,
on August 2, 1865, he had filled two small books. The first was an eight by
six and one half inch volume bound in black leather. It has reddish clay-
colored endpapers and forty-one leaves (eighty-two faintly ruled, cream-
colored pages) sewn together with chartreuse ribbon. Kinsley filled all
but the final few pages with tidy, highly legible, black-ink prose. Slightly
larger, at 8 inches wide and 10 inches tall, the second volume also has reddish clay-colored endpapers, which serve as its front and back covers. Its
thirty-three leaves (sixty-six faintly ruled white pages) are taped together
at the spine. Kinsley filled this volume also with his handsome handwriting. Apparently, Kinsley had initially planned to use the first volume for
another purpose, for on the top line of its first page he wrote, "Society,
on motion, adjourned. Syne die," and on the second line he signed the
name "Rufus." When Kinsley next opened the volume, on November 29,
1861, he wrote in the upper right-hand half of page 3: "Diary . . . . . . By
Rufus Kinsley, of Fletcher, Vermont."[1] He then added "The Slaveholders' Rebellion" in large letters in the center of the page. By giving his
diary a title, Kinsley committed an unusual act among diarists. Kinsley's
act and the title that he selected speak volumes about the man and his
diary.

Kinsley may have started keeping a diary because he knew that within
a few weeks his regiment was scheduled to leave for the Gulf of Mexico,
and like many travelers about to visit distant lands, he wanted to keep a
record of his impressions. This impulse was doubtless reinforced by his
awareness from reading *Uncle Tom's Cabin* and other abolitionist tracts

that the Deep South was the antithesis of New England, that it was in fact, if not in name, a foreign country. And not the least of Kinsley's virtues as a diarist was his ability to make the Gulf South come alive as a distinct region of wild roses, cypress swamps, menacing alligators, quadroon concubines, restless slaves, cruel masters, and French-speaking priests.

Kinsley may also have taken up a diary simply to keep track of what happened to him during the war. He seemed to understand from the day he enlisted that he was about to embark upon a momentous journey.[2] His father, who would later write a brief history of his hometown, had taught him the importance of the past, and Kinsley's own work at a newspaper instilled in him the discipline as well as the value of keeping a daily record of events. In short, Kinsley became a kind of unofficial recorder of the war, and in the late nineteenth century he would draw upon his diary for evidence to support the pension claims of needy veterans and, as the local press noted, to establish "dates and incidents of Vermont in the Civil War."[3]

But Kinsley was not merely a tourist compiling a travelogue or a clerk keeping a chronicle. He was a soldier on assignment, and much of his diary is devoted to military matters. His journal not only describes such dramatic events as the fall of New Orleans and the capture of Mobile Bay but it also illuminates the critical war for southwestern Louisiana and speaks candidly of army life in a black regiment. These are unique contributions, for there are few eyewitness accounts of either the battle for the bayou country or the trials of the 180,000 black troops who served in the Union army.[4] Although written by a man with no military training and little formal schooling, Kinsley's account of the war is marked by a penetrating intelligence and an appreciation of the heroism as well as the absurdities of martial life. It seems fitting that Kinsley, an eminently democratic man, would use a diary, arguably the most democratic of all literary forms, to describe the nation's most democratic war.

The strictly military dimension of the war failed, however, to bring out the best in Kinsley the diarist. He offers few original insights into strategy, tactics, weapons, munitions, transportation, and the other staples of nineteenth-century warfare. This may be in part because Kinsley himself saw very little combat during the war, and he based most of what he reports about the actual fighting of the war on hearsay. He arrived at both New Orleans and Mobile Bay after the heavy fighting was over, and during much of the battle for the bayou country, he was either managing a refugee camp, running a printing press, or lying sick in a hospital. Furthermore, the tools and techniques of war held no intrinsic appeal for Kinsley; he was interested in them only insofar as they would hasten the defeat of the Confederacy and the destruction of slavery. To be sure, Kinsley was fighting for the survival of his nation, but more than a wish to preserve the political and geographical integrity of the Union inspired him to reenlist for three more years in the fall of 1863 and to proclaim that he was "'in for the war,' be it three years, or thirty. . . . " Kinsley, as he explained in his diary, was "thankful for the privilege of standing, with my life freely offered up, not for the defense of my country, merely, but for the defense of Liberty. . . . "[5]

By "Liberty" Kinsley did not mean solely the freedom of Northern whites from the tyranny of a conspiratorial "Slave Power" that for years had subverted American democracy in order to protect and expand the institution of slavery.[6] He also meant the freedom of four million black slaves from the dominion of a cruel bondage that for generations had made a mockery of the ideals embodied in the Declaration of Independence. But in Kinsley's view slavery was much more than a repudiation of the nation's founding ideals; it was an affront to God, and the Civil War was a holy crusade to redeem the soul of America. Consequently, as it turns into a vehicle for exhortation and excoriation rather than observation and explanation, Kinsley's diary sometimes reads more like a jeremiad – filled with dire prophecies and sanctifying scriptures – than a journal. Agent of a vengeful Jehovah, Kinsley showed no sympathy in his diary for unrepentant white Southerners, and at one point he even suggested that extermination might be the best policy. If nothing else, Kinsley's diary offers insight into the true believer at war, reminding us that while the Civil War may not have been a war of religion, it was for many soldiers a religious war.[7]

Condemning slavery as an unusually barbaric "crime," Kinsley maintained that genuine emancipation required freeing the minds as well as the bodies of those who had been enslaved. And like the great black abolitionist Frederick Douglass, Kinsley also believed that the destinies of the nation and of the freedmen were inseparable.[8] "In the education of the black," he wrote in his diary on September 21, 1862, "is centered my hope for the redemption of the race, and the salvation of my country." During the war Kinsley worked tirelessly to achieve both goals by serving as a commander of black troops and as a teacher of illiterate freedmen.

On New Year's Day 1863 he observed with a typical touch of sarcasm: "I suppose I have friends who would sneer at the business [of feeding and teaching runaway slaves] ... but as for myself, I am fallen so low, and my sense of the proprieties of life is so dull, that I am satisfied with my summer's work, and thank God for the opportunity of sowing seed, in this field."[9] Throughout his life, Kinsley took great pride in working for and with African Americans. Unfortunately, the historical record has left no direct evidence from blacks telling us what they thought about Kinsley or his efforts.

We do know that Kinsley did not entirely escape the pervasive racism of his time and place. Early in his diary, before he joined a black regiment, he used the words "niggers" and "darkies" once, and another time, intending to compliment an African American whom he identified as "my friend Washington," Kinsley described him as "a very intelligent man, as little like a negro as my father." But he also spoke of the fugitive slaves he taught and fed in a refugee camp outside New Orleans as "My family of negroes" and praised them as avid learners who "*never forget any thing*" and are "as keen and shrewd as a live Yankee." He saw them as active agents not passive pawns in the war, as contributing to the destruction of slavery by running away and to the defeat of the Confederacy by joining the Union army. He invariably referred to the black soldiers under his command as "men," not "boys," and he identified with them completely in 1864 when he included himself in the term "we niggers."[10] Progressive as they were, Kinsley's racial attitudes, when viewed from a modern perspective, fall somewhat short of perfection, but when compared to those of highly educated New England elites like Thomas Wentworth Higginson, John W. De Forest, and Robert Gould Shaw, who also joined or seriously considered joining black regiments during the war, Kinsley's views on race were downright radical.[11]

Infused with iconoclastic religious convictions and racial attitudes, Kinsley's diary is above all else a political document. Largely because the diary brims with self-deprecating humor, irrepressible wit, scathing sarcasm, and intense passion, we do get glimpses of Kinsley's personality, but this is not an intimate or introspective document. Social revolution, not personal revelation, is the diary's primary focus. Kinsley turned repeatedly to his journal to build his case against sin and slavery. Perhaps in the process he bolstered his confidence in an agenda that frequently had him waging war against Union as well as Confederate soldiers. But it is not obvious that Kinsley needed motivational sermons from himself or anyone else to convince him of the righteousness of his cause. Throughout the war he never wavered in his beliefs. He left the army in the summer of 1865 pretty much the same man who enlisted in it nearly four years earlier in the winter of 1861. When Kinsley returned to his diary late in life, this righteous consistency must have pleased him. Diaries tend to disabuse us of faulty, often romanticized, memories; looking back on them can be both sobering and painful. But for Kinsley, rereading his diary must have brought mostly joy and affirmation. Time had validated his views on the meaning and purpose of the war. In America's Armageddon he had fought on the side of the angels, and he had won.

Of course, Kinsley did not write his diary solely, or even primarily, for his own entertainment and edification. As Thomas Mallon concludes in his thoughtful study of diaries and their authors, "no one ever kept a diary just for himself."[12] The fact that Kinsley titled his diary – and that he gave it such a grand title – suggests that he wrote it for posterity. It was a brief arguing the purity of his mission before future generations. But it was also a story, and by all accounts Kinsley was a great storyteller.[13] He wanted us to read his story, to learn from it, and, I suspect, to admire the man who wrote it.

In the Introduction that follows, I hope to demonstrate that Rufus Kinsley is worthy of our admiration. His story is that of a young man who grew up in poverty in the virtually all-white world of northern Vermont but went on to become a crusader for black emancipation and education in the Deep South and the author of an engaging, often eloquent, account of the Civil War. In an effort to understand Kinsley, I have tried to place him in the context of his times. In the process, I pay special attention to his life before and after the war. The postwar lives of Union veterans, in particular, have long been neglected in writings about the Civil War, and through an investigation of Kinsley's life after Appomattox I hope to reveal the pathos of those forgotten years, when many veterans struggled to stay alive and retain a sense of purpose. Kinsley's story suggests that those soldiers who came home victorious, including those who escaped enemy fire, did not necessarily return unscathed.

In attempting to reconstruct Kinsley's life, I have tried not to read too much into either what Kinsley said or what he did not say, and the reality is that very little of what he actually said during his lifetime has survived. For the period prior to his enlistment in the Union army, I have been unable to find a single document written by Kinsley, and for the postwar era I have found only a few. Piecing together Kinsley's life has convinced me of how little we can truly know about the lives, let alone the motives, of most men and women who lived in the nineteenth century. I have found some comfort in the words of the eminent biologist Richard Lewontin: "Like it or not, there are a lot of questions that cannot be answered, and even more that cannot be answered exactly. There is nothing shameful in that admission."[14]

In preparing Kinsley's diary (and his few surviving Civil War letters) for publication, I have placed all editorial emendations in brackets, and most appear in italics as well. I have tried to keep these interventions to a minimum and to further reduce textual clutter by making some silent alterations in Kinsley's prose. When, for example, he inadvertently omits an "e" from "before," I have supplied it, and when he carelessly adds an "e" to "with," I have removed it. More significantly, I have regularized Kinsley's datelines, though I have left intact his practice of always identifying the Sabbath,[15] and I have standardized his spelling of Des Allemands, Thibodaux, Terrebonne, Berwick Bay, and other place names. I have also omitted words that Kinsley accidentally repeated and words that he lined through to correct a false start or an error in spelling. On a few occasions, for the sake of clarity, I have silently moved, removed, or added a comma, period, or apostrophe, but for the most part I have allowed Kinsley's often creative punctuation (and capitalization) to remain untouched. Underlined words have been rendered in italics, as have the titles of all books, periodicals, newspapers, and ships. Marginal and interlinear words and phrases made at the time of original composition have been incorporated without comment in the text at the point indicated by the author, but marginal notes added at a later date have been identified as such. And finally, I have divided Kinsley's diary into five sections and a handful of his exceptionally long letters and diary entries into two or more paragraphs.

Since the letters and especially the diary were often written under diverse and difficult circumstances – on rolling ships and windswept beaches, in crowded train depots and bustling hospitals, under the threat of an immediate enemy attack, and so forth – it is not surprising that minor errors crept into Kinsley's writings. What is amazing is the felicity and accuracy of his prose. Perhaps these unusual qualities stemmed from his previous experience as a printer working under the pressures that accompany the production of a daily newspaper, and perhaps the writings

1. Page from Kinsley diary, February 1864. Courtesy of the Vermont Historical Society.

that date from his commission in the Second Corps d'Afrique benefited from the fact that he was an officer whose daily routine required the hurried but precise writing of orders, requisitions, reports, and dispatches. Whatever the cause, Kinsley has left us an extraordinary account of the nation's greatest crisis from an often neglected perspective – that of a devout Christian soldier and a dedicated New England abolitionist.

Acknowledgments

IN WRITING RUFUS KINSLEY'S BIOGRAPHY AND EDITING HIS DIARY, I have had the assistance of many people and institutions. First among them is the late Barbara Davis Haigh of San Francisco, who nearly thirty years ago handed me a faded typescript of a Civil War diary that her father had "picked up somewhere back East." In time I learned that the original diary still existed and had been deposited in the Vermont Historical Society by Kinsley's family. Following this discovery, I made a trip to Montpelier to inspect the diary and was treated with great kindness by the society's librarian, Paul A. Carnahan, and its director, Weston A. Cate, Jr. I am grateful to the society for its cooperation in the publication of Kinsley's diary.

My initial trip to New England also resulted in a long visit and lasting friendship with Kinsley's granddaughter, Reba Kinsley Hall. In addition to taking me on a lively tour of Franklin County, where her grandfather was born and reared, Reba shared with me her photo albums, newspaper clippings, family histories, and most important, her memories. She also provided me with copies of Kinsley's Civil War diary and letters, as well as with many of the photographs reproduced in this book, and I am indebted to her for permission to publish them. It is no exaggeration to say that without the help and support of Reba Hall this manuscript would never have been completed, especially in its present form. My joy at the publication of Kinsley's diary is tempered only by my disappointment that his granddaughter, who played such a crucial role in bringing the project to fruition, did not live to see it.

For their generous assistance in locating information about Kinsley, I am indebted to the librarians and staff of the following institutions: American Antiquarian Society; Bailey-Howe Library, University of

Vermont; Bentley Historical Library, University of Michigan; Boston Athenaeum; Bostonian Society; Boston Public Library; Ellender Memorial Library, Nicholls State University; Hill Memorial Library, Louisiana State University; Historic New Orleans Collection; Houghton Library, Harvard University; Howard Tilton Memorial Library, Tulane University; Indiana Historical Society; Library of Congress; Los Angeles Federal Records Center; Main Library, University of California at Irvine; Massachusetts Historical Society; New Orleans Public Library; New York Public Library; and the Vital Records Office of the Vermont General Services Center. I am especially obligated to Mike Meier, Michael P. Musick, and the late Sara Dunlap Jackson for introducing me to the riches of the National Archives; to the late Joan Carmody for providing me with copies of several Kinsley letters; and to H. Carlton Ferguson for granting me access to Edgar Kinsley Montague's unpublished diary and other useful materials in his possession.

In exploring many of these sources I was fortunate to have the help of Betty H. White, a talented researcher who also typed Kinsley's diary, as well as several other documents, created the Kinsley genealogical chart found in the Introduction, and offered insightful observations, especially on Kinsley's health, that greatly improved the manuscript. I am also indebted to David Parson and Maudean Neill for superb research assistance, and to Ira Berlin, John Dorsey, Jeffrey Marshall, Charlene Peacock, Sherrie Pugh, Leslie Rowland, Sally Stassi, Cliff Theriot, Courtney Wright, and especially Pembroke Herbert for timely aid in the search for illustrations. J. Chase Langford of the University of California at Los Angeles produced the excellent map of the Gulf South.

For answering numerous questions raised by Kinsley's diary, I am indebted to Duane Chase, William E. Gienapp, Thomas H. O'Connor, James I. Robertson, Judith K. Schafer, and Steven E. Woodworth. Mike Hobbs of the Gulf Islands National Seashore helped me to better understand the hardships of life on Ship Island. I also learned a great deal about life in the bayou country by spending a rewarding afternoon with Glenn Conrad and Carl Brasseaux at the University of Southwestern Louisiana and a memorable evening at nearby Chretien Plantation. I have further benefited from the encouragement of Paul Kinsley, Sumner Kinsley, William Kinsley, and Patricia Packard, and from the expert editorial assistance of Camilla Knapp and Susan Greenberg at Cambridge University Press. I am particularly grateful to Lew Bateman for his faith in this project and his skill in turning my rough manuscript into a finished book. Aid of a different kind came in the form of a Fellowship from the American Council of Learned Societies.

The entire manuscript has been read and commented upon by two extraordinary historians: David Herbert Donald, who first encouraged me to publish Kinsley's diary when I was a Research Fellow in the Charles Warren Center at Harvard University, and Michael P. Johnson, who has once again proven himself to be a thoughtful critic and valued friend. The manuscript has also profited from the advice of my former colleague at Oberlin College, the late Geoffrey T. Blodgett, and my current colleagues at the University of California at Irvine, Dickson Bruce and Jon Wiener. None of these historians is, of course, responsible for any remaining errors of fact or interpretation.

For a variety of contributions to the completion of this project, I want to thank my family, especially my grandfather, an old-time Methodist minister who preached temperance with such passion in the northern California wine country that his church in Sonoma County was burned to the ground in 1914. I am convinced that knowing him helped me to better appreciate Kinsley and his lifelong battle against demon rum. I also want to thank Barbara for her critical eye and quiet inspiration; Nancy for helping identify Kinsley's biblical allusions; Sally for answering countless questions; Mike, M'Lisse, and Elizabeth for listening patiently; Will for gathering information on the Second Louisiana Corps d'Afrique; and Andy for repeatedly admonishing me to "get it over with and get a life." I want finally to thank my mother for years of encouragement, and to offer this book as a gift on her ninetieth birthday.

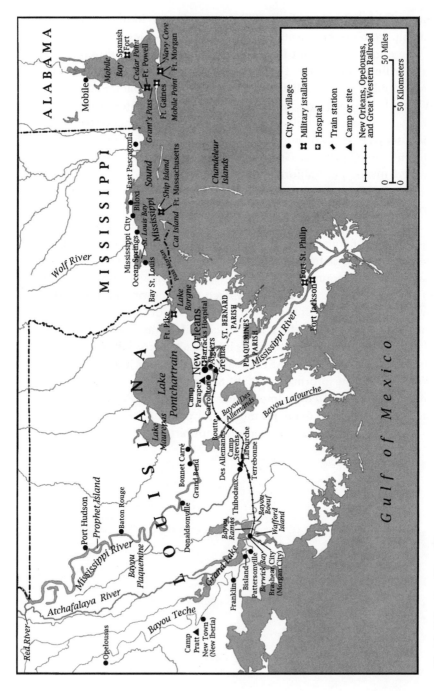

2. The Gulf South, 1862–1865.

INTRODUCTION

Rufus Kinsley and the Civil War

RUFUS KINSLEY WOULD PROBABLY NOT HAVE LIKED ROBERT
Gould Shaw, the now-famous young Civil War officer who gave
his life leading black troops into battle at Fort Wagner, South Carolina,
and whose life has been immortalized in the popular movie *Glory*, in
Augustus Saint-Gauden's magnificent sculpture on Boston Common,
and in the memorable words of the philosopher William James, who
proclaimed Shaw America's "blue-eyed child of fortune." To be sure,
Kinsley would have respected Shaw for his decision to become an officer
of black soldiers, although he would not have known that Shaw accepted
the position only out of obligation to his abolitionist mother, who called
her son's initial refusal of the commission "the bitterest disappointment
that I have ever experienced." But beyond serving as officers in black
regiments, Kinsley and Shaw had little in common. Although their lives
briefly overlapped in Boston, where Shaw was attending Harvard and
Kinsley was working on a newspaper, they were from different worlds.
Kinsley's grandfather was not one of the richest men in New England,
his family was not so wealthy that his father could retire at age thirty-
two, his mother's closest friend was not Lydia Maria Child, his childhood
playmates did not include William Lloyd Garrison's sons, his education
did not require a private academy in Switzerland, his circle of acquaintances did not encompass Harriet Beecher Stowe, James Russell Lowell,
and Nathaniel Hawthorne, and his death would not have inspired Ralph
Waldo Emerson to write a poem eulogizing his sacrifices on the altar of
freedom.[1]

But Kinsley's disdain for Shaw would not have emanated from a sense
of envy or jealousy, for that would have been a sin, and Kinsley was ever-
mindful of sin. Kinsley's ideas about what constituted sinful behavior

would, however, have played a major role in his evaluation of Shaw. To Kinsley, Shaw would have been just another example of the party-loving, cigar-smoking, "rum-sucking officers" who all too often were put in command of black troops during the Civil War. Kinsley, who stopped using racial epithets prior to becoming an officer in the Second Louisiana Corps d'Afrique, would have been disappointed that Shaw continued throughout his colonelcy in the Fifty-fourth Massachusetts to call African Americans "nigs," "niggers," and "darkeys."[2] Kinsley, who delighted in calling the freed slaves "men," would have been offended by Shaw's assertion that "they are perfectly childlike . . . and are no more responsible for their actions than so many puppies." Kinsley, who took great pleasure in ridiculing those who spoke of "slavery loving negroes," would have been outraged at Shaw's suggestion that some slaves actually loved their masters. Kinsley, who could never see beyond the barbarity of slavery, would have been appalled by Shaw's statement that the slaves of Charlestown, Virginia, were "well cared for." Kinsley, who believed that the devastation Union troops inflicted upon the Confederacy was the fulfillment of God's will, would have been utterly dumbfounded by Shaw's characterization of the destruction of Darien, South Carolina, by Yankee soldiers as "barbarous" and "distasteful." And Kinsley, who spent most of his free time teaching runaway slaves to read and write, would have been saddened by Shaw's general indifference to the fate of the freedmen. Kinsley could not abide such liberators. And probably the feeling would have been mutual, for Shaw was contemptuous of the rough Western volunteer soldiers like Kinsley who made the job of Eastern elites like himself so difficult.[3]

≈ One ≈

Although Kinsley was born in western Vermont on the other side of the Appalachian Mountains – a cultural as well as physical barrier to someone like Shaw – his ancestors were among the earliest settlers of the Massachusetts Bay Colony and lived just outside of Boston in the 1630s. His maternal great-grandfather was driven out of Sunderland, Massachusetts, for radical religious beliefs and in 1761 settled in Bennington, Vermont, where he served on the town's first board of selectmen. His maternal grandfather, Rufus Montague, was one of the original founders of the town of Fletcher, Vermont, and his paternal grandfather, Daniel Kinsley, was one of the first settlers of the adjoining town of Cambridge.

In fact, Daniel Kinsley's marriage to Lucy Montague was the first marriage recorded in Cambridge.[4] Both of Kinsley's grandfathers were among the famous "Green Mountain Boys" who fought in the Revolutionary War, and doubtless Kinsley was proud of their role in creating the Union, just as he would later take great pride in his own role in preserving it. But like most Vermonters, Kinsley was especially proud of Vermont's founding generation for writing the nation's first state constitution that prohibited slavery, and in later years he would take even greater pride in the part he played in abolishing slavery throughout the nation.[5]

Rufus Kinsley was born in Fletcher on October 9, 1831. Encompassing about twenty-four thousand acres and sitting on the southern edge of Franklin County, Fletcher is about twenty-five miles from the Canadian border. To the west is Lake Champlain, to the north Quebec, to the east the Green Mountains, and to the south the fertile Champlain Valley. Fletcher's landscape is hilly, even mountainous in places, and broken by valleys, meadows, ponds, rivers, and streams. Chartered by Governor Thomas Chittenden in 1781 and organized in 1790, Fletcher welcomed its first wave of settlers in the 1790s. These early settlers, as well as those who came later, according to Kinsley's father, were ordinary, hard-working Americans of good democratic stock. He wrote that "men of eminence are to be looked for in some other locality. But for men of solid worth, of stern integrity, men of unimpeachable character, Fletcher is by no means wanting. . . . " In fact, Ben Alva Kinsley believed that "probably, there are few towns in the State whose inhabitants are more nearly on a level, than in the town of Fletcher." By the time of Kinsley's birth, Fletcher boasted nearly eight hundred such inhabitants.[6]

Kinsley was the fourth of eight children born to Ben Alva and Catherine Montague Kinsley. Prior to Kinsley's birth, his parents and their children Guy, Lucretia, and Daniel lived in a log cabin that Kinsley's grandfather had built on the south side of Fletcher Mountain. But in the spring of 1829 the family moved into a small wooden building that Kinsley would call home for much of his childhood. "It was a very cheap structure," according to Kinsley's brother Guy, and "a sorry place for a mother and small children." It consisted of two rooms, a garret, and a stone fireplace. Instead of glass the windows were covered with raw sheepskin. There was no running water in the house; there was no tub, no sink, just a stream at the base of the hill. Over the next few years, Kinsley's father, a stonemason by trade, plastered the house, replaced the fireplace with a stove, installed a sink, and dug a well. Kinsley's two older brothers, Guy and Daniel, slept

Daniel Kinsley (1764–1828)
m. (1788)
Lucy Montague (1765–1850)

Clarissa (1788–1820) Eunice (1790–?) Hannah (1792–1884) Lucretia (1794–1871) Ben Alva (1796–1870) Elvira (1798–1859) Guy (1800–1886) Earl (1802–1867) Nancy (1804–?) Samuel (1807–1808) Chellis (1809–1901) Calista (1812–1847)

Ben Alva (1796–1870)
m. (1824)
1) Catherine Montague (1798–1849)
m. (1854)
2) Lucy Hubbard Blair (1809–1881)

Guy (1825–1921) m. (1853) Lucinda Ellsworth (1830–1889)

Lucretia (1827–1912) unm.

Daniel (1829–1923) m. (1854) Harriet Newell Mudgett (1834–1900)

Rufus (1831–1911) m. (1872) Ella Lenora Bingham (1851–1909)

Jason (1833–1903) m. (unknown)

Alonzo (1836–1911) m. (1869) Emma Brown (1849–1908)

Edgar (Montague) (1837–1914) m. (1860) 1) Louisa Sherwood (1842–1866), m. (1868) 2) Annette Blair (1848–1914)

William Lyon (1844–1901) m. (1870) Ellen Whittle (1848–1900)

Clayton Bingham (1873–1956) Benton Allen (1874–1907) Amy Leona (1876–1939) Lester Montague (1877–1949) Leroy Tyler (1879–1947) Floyd Guy (1881–1946) Chellis Alonzo (1884–1939)

3. Kinsley genealogy.

up in the garret, while he slept downstairs in a trundle bed with Lucretia and his younger brothers. By 1837 three more sons, Jason, Alonzo, and Edgar, joined an already crowded household. In the spring of 1837, a few months before Edgar's birth, Kinsley's father, who had been employed at a local brickyard, left home in search of work. He moved about fifteen miles southwest to the town of Colchester, where he found employment building factories around Winooski Falls. His earnings allowed him to send supplies home to a growing family that, according to one of his sons, he was having a "very difficult" time feeding and clothing.[7]

In the fall of the same year, however, the family suffered a devastating blow, as Kinsley's mother fell helpless to a crippling disease that left her knees swollen and stiff. Ben Alva gave up his job in Colchester, returned home, and began doing part-time agricultural labor for neighbors; the one and a half acres he owned were unfit for cultivation. That winter was grim for the family as Kinsley's mother struggled to regain her health, but she was never able to walk again and spent the rest of her life in a wheelchair. A few months after Catherine Kinsley was stricken with what her family called "inflammatory rheumatism," Kinsley's parents were forced to abandon the crude little wooden shanty they called home and farm out their children among friends and relatives. What happened to Kinsley, who was only six years old at the time of this crisis, is unknown, but in the spring of 1838 his brother Guy took a "very small bundle of clothes" and moved in with a neighbor, who paid him five dollars a month in farm produce for helping out with chores. A year later Guy returned home to help his mother and allow his father to find work in places like Colchester. In the summer of 1840 when the federal census taker visited the Kinsley household he found all the Kinsleys again living together.[8] Had he returned four years later, he would have discovered that their number had grown to ten, for on March 12, 1844, Catherine Kinsley gave birth to William, her eighth and final child. Not quite five years later, at age fifty-one, she was dead.

Kinsley, from the time he was about six years old, watched as his mother suffered stoically through the last dozen years of her life until February 15, 1849, when, in the words of her husband, "her Heavenly Father said, 'it is enough, come up higher.'" Although Ben Alva married Lucy Blair, the childless widow of an old friend, five years after Catherine's death, the Kinsley children never forgot their natural mother. Seventeen years after her demise, Kinsley's brother Jason affectionately remembered the mother "whose smiles we miss" and reassured his brothers and sister that

"A Mother's fond caress, a Mother's loving kiss," awaits each of us "When we have done / With this dark, weary world, and soar to worlds above."9

Within a year of Catherine Kinsley's death, her family had been permanently broken up. Guy had been boarding with neighbors and relatives from about 1841 until roughly 1847, when he and his brother Daniel moved to Massachusetts in search of employment. In 1850, Guy was working in Worcester County as a laborer for Amasa Walker, a "Gentleman" who owned property valued at twenty-eight thousand dollars and who by 1853 was paying Guy twenty dollars a month in wages. Daniel was working on the North Brookfield farm of Bonum Nye, a county commissioner who helped him win election in 1853 to the post of messenger of the Worcester County courts, a position Daniel held for the next fifty years. Kinsley's sixteen-year-old brother Jason was also living in Worcester County in 1850. He had apparently been entrusted to his aunt Nancy Kinsley Scott and her husband Jefferson. Kinsley's thirteen-year-old brother Edgar remained in Fletcher, but sometime prior to the summer of 1850 he had been handed over to his mother's brother Rufus Montague II and his wife Elvira. They legally adopted the boy, who thereafter was known as Edgar Kinsley Montague. Kinsley's sister Lucretia, under the thumb of a strong patriarchal father, remained at home in 1850 to take care of fourteen-year-old Alonzo and six-year-old William.10

Before long, even Kinsley's father was thinking about moving. On June 13, 1851, probably in response to his dire economic situation, Ben Alva Kinsley, who had fought in the War of 1812, applied for "bounty land" that the federal government in 1850 had set aside for "certain officers and soldiers who have been engaged in the military service of the United States." On October 1, 1853, the Pension Bureau granted him a 160-acre quarter section in Iowa; a month later his son Guy was on his way west to see whether the land was worth settling. Once there, Guy decided to stay. With the savings he had amassed during his six years as a farm laborer in Massachusetts, he purchased 240 acres of his own near the town of McGregor in Clayton County. Two years later his brother Jason also left Massachusetts for Iowa. While Guy took up farming, Jason became a teacher, but both of them called Iowa home for the remainder of their lives. Apparently encouraged by reports from his sons and eager to see his homestead in the West, Ben Alva migrated to Iowa in the late 1850s. He lived there along with his new wife Lucy and his young son William on Guy's farm for about two years before deciding to return to Fletcher in the fall of 1860.11

In returning to Fletcher, Ben Alva was moving against the tide. Most of those who left Fletcher in the 1850s never looked back. In 1850 Fletcher had 1,084 inhabitants, but by 1860 that number stood at only 916, a 16 percent decline. Most of the decline can be attributed to the out-migration of young males, like the Kinsley brothers, as is suggested by the drop in the town's ratio of males per 100 females from 104 in 1850 to 97 in 1860. These young men left what they obviously believed was a poor farming community with little opportunity. Fletcher was, to be sure, an agricultural community. According to the 1850 census nearly 90 percent of those living in Fletcher who reported an occupation identified themselves as either farmers or farm laborers, and they worked hard at raising cattle, sheep, and oxen and at producing butter, cheese, wool, sugar, wheat, corn, potatoes, and hay. Fletcher was also a poor community. In 1850 fully 90 percent of its residents reported owning no property, and the per capita wealth in real estate was a paltry $171. Even among those who reported owning property, the median value of their real estate was only $800, and 97 percent of them owned real estate valued at $1,500 or less. No wonder the Kinsleys took to heart Horace Greeley's admonition to "Go West, young man, go West."[12]

Like his father and brothers, Rufus Kinsley was also on the move. About the time of his mother's death in 1849, when he was in his late teens, Kinsley left home for St. Albans, a shire town of about eighteen hundred inhabitants that was ten miles north of Fletcher. Known for its antislavery sentiments, St. Albans was a stop on the Underground Railroad and home to some of Vermont's leading abolitionists. One was Asa O. Aldis, the first president of the Vermont Anti-Slavery Society, which had been founded in 1834 as an auxiliary to William Lloyd Garrison's American Anti-Slavery Society. Another was Lawrence Brainerd, recognized in St. Albans for his work smuggling runaway slaves into Canada and known throughout Vermont as gubernatorial candidate of both the Liberty Party and the Free Soil Party. Brainerd's cousin Joseph also resided in St. Albans. A Yale graduate, Joseph Brainerd had gained notoriety in St. Albans in the early 1830s as the man who had founded one of the county's leading newspapers, the reform-oriented *Franklin Journal.* Brainerd subsequently sold the paper to Enoch B. Whiting, who renamed it the *St. Albans Messenger* and published it without interruption for thirty-three years. It was a job as a printer's devil on Whiting's newspaper that brought Rufus Kinsley to St. Albans.[13]

Kinsley arrived in St. Albans having had very little formal education. The Fletcher common schools appear to have been adequate, although the Kinsley children did have a teacher who once hung a student by his thumbs until the boy was blue in the face. But according to family members it was not fear of corporal punishment that kept the "Kinsley urchins" from attending school regularly. First, the family simply did not have enough pants for all the boys to attend school on the same day, and, second, the family's desperate need for supplementary labor and income often determined that the children would work, at home or for a neighbor, rather than go to school. Consequently, much of Kinsley's education took place at home, in talk with his father. Ben Alva himself had virtually no regular schooling, but he was a man of genuine intellectual curiosity. Although his spelling and grammar were erratic, Kinsley's father wrote engaging letters that, given his upbringing in an oral, face-to-face, frontier culture, were remarkably literate. He also wrote an entertaining essay on Fletcher for inclusion in Vermont historian Abby Hemenway's massive five-volume study of the state's towns and counties. Subscribers to the Hemenway volumes included many of Vermont's richest and most powerful citizens, but at the head of the subscription list for Franklin County was the name of a struggling stonemason named "BEN A. KINSLEY."[14]

Kinsley's father also belonged to local literary clubs and regularly opened his home to speakers "of all religious denominations." This last activity hints at one of the Kinsleys' most fundamental beliefs, that education was useless unless it was tested and tempered within a Christian context. Thus, when Kinsley's brother Guy later remembered that "the acquisition of knowledge from books and schools in my native town was an uphill business," he immediately added that "not all knowledge is wisdom, much of it is great folly. One of the wisest men said many hundred years ago, that the fear of the Lord is the beginning of wisdom. . . . " The kind of education that Kinsley offered to freed slaves in the South during the Civil War suggests that he agreed completely with his family's assessment of the limits of a purely secular education.[15]

There was little chance that Kinsley himself would receive an education devoted entirely to worldly knowledge. He grew up in a region that had been repeatedly "burned-over" by evangelical Protestant revivals and in a family that offered compelling models of Christian piety. One such model was an uncle who served as the pastor of the Congregational Church in nearby Cambridge, a church whose founding members included several of Kinsley's ancestors. Another was his aunt Elvira Kinsley, who "loved the Bible," read it religiously, and for thirty-five years taught the children of Fletcher with "christian devotion" and "a rare modesty and humility of spirit." Still another was his grandfather Rufus Montague, who took Kinsley's entire family into his household from 1833 to 1835 and gathered them around him to pray every morning. And, finally, there was his father, himself the product of a "strict and reverent" upbringing, who not only held religious meetings in his home but also served as superintendent of the town's Sabbath school and who worked tirelessly to overcome what he perceived as insufficient religious unity and zeal among Fletcher's inhabitants. "Mr. Kinsley," a friend of Ben Alva's observed, "is a man of good judgment, deep feeling and religious principle," who "has ever taken an active interest in . . . whatever pertains to the improvement and advancement of society in general."[16]

Elaborating on his portrait of Kinsley's father, the friend noted that Ben Alva was known "for his eccentricities, originality and stern independence of thought and action, and has a vein of good humor underlying his whole character. . . . To say that he has no enemies would be to make him more than a god, or less than a man," the friend continued. "Such a character as his always gains warm friends and bitter enemies. . . . " Perhaps Kinsley was inspired by the example of his father to stand up for principle whatever the cost, for by the end of the Civil War the words offered by Ben Alva's friend perfectly described Rufus Kinsley as well as his father. Whatever the case, these were the values that Kinsley brought with him in the late 1840s when he went to work for Enoch Whiting's *St. Albans Messenger*.[17]

In 1850 the eighteen-year-old Kinsley was not only working for Whiting but also residing at the publisher's home. Others who lived under Whiting's roof included his parents, his wife and two children, an editor, three printers, and two illiterate young girls, who were probably domestics. Whiting's wife Mary was a native of the nearby town of Georgia and "one of the [county's] most estimable of women, excellent in every Christian and womanly virtue." Whiting, a native of Amherst, Massachusetts, had achieved an equally respectable position. Over the years he built a reputation as a gracious but serious gentleman of deep religious convictions and unassailable integrity. Except for Whiting's wealth – in 1850 at age thirty-four he already owned property valued at four thousand dollars – the Whiting household, marked as it was by piety and propriety, must have reminded Kinsley of home and reinforced the lessons of his youth.[18]

Work at the paper must also have reinforced the informal, eclectic education that Kinsley received at home. Billed as "A Journal of Politics,

Literature, Morals, Agriculture and General Intelligence," the *Messenger* filled its columns with poems, fiction, and essays as well as with the standard crop reports, crime notes, town council minutes, and legislative debates.[19] Perhaps it was while laying out these literary columns that Kinsley first began reading Shakespeare's plays, parts of which, along with the Bible, he committed to memory. Perhaps it was also at the *Messenger* that he picked up the smattering of Latin that appears in his diary. It is certain, however, that in setting type for the paper, Kinsley learned about words: how to spell them, shape them, and use them. He learned how to make them bold or thin, pointed or flat, piercing or dull. As a printer he came to appreciate the power of words, and as someone who was always aware of space limitations and production costs, he came to appreciate an economy and simplicity of style that would later be reflected in the lean, lucid prose of his Civil War diary.[20]

Kinsley learned about more than words and writing at the *Messenger*. The paper was full of news about politics and reform at the local, state, and national levels. It discussed the advantages of admitting California to the Union; it reported the minutes of women's rights conventions; it assessed the Vermont state legislature's budget for plank roads; it covered Franklin County temperance meetings, at which Kinsley's father – an avid prohibitionist as well as abolitionist – played an active role. The paper even addressed environmental issues, and in the process chided Vermonters for despoiling their landscape by cutting down every tree in sight and encouraged readers to "Go and plant a tree at once, then boast of having done one good deed in your life...."[21] But after Congress passed the Compromise of 1850, with its infamous Fugitive Slave Law that required Northern states to assist in the return of runaway slaves to their masters in the South, the *Messenger* was dominated by articles chronicling the growing national crisis over the institution of slavery. Like most Northern papers, the *Messenger* denounced the Fugitive Slave Law as "evil" and "unconstitutional," but it was equally vehement in denouncing those who advocated violent resistance to the law. It condemned meetings like the one held in New York City on October 10, 1850, at which "there was a great deal of talk about bowie knives and bloodshed" and about arming blacks and killing police officers who tried to enforce the law. "What right," the *Messenger* asked, "have these men to put down all law and set up anarchy? What right have they to peril the life and property of all the citizens? What right have they to go armed?"[22]

How Kinsley, who may well have set the type for this moderate anti-slavery editorial, would have answered these questions in 1850 is open to conjecture, but within a little more than a decade he would not only be defending John Brown's lawless rampage in Kansas and advocating the arming of African Americans, but he would be marching alongside black men in Louisiana, turning them into disciplined soldiers in Mississippi, and leading them into battle in Alabama. In the immediate future, however, Kinsley was on his way to Boston, that hotbed of abolitionism, where black and white radicals had long maintained that there should be no compromise with Southern slaveholders or with Northern proslavery laws and institutions.

Kinsley's departure for Boston in the early 1850s might indicate that the *Messenger*'s politics were already too conservative for his taste, or perhaps it simply indicated that Kinsley, an able and adventurous young man, wanted to pursue his career in a city that was the hub of the nation's print world as well as an exciting metropolis of nearly 150,000 inhabitants. In 1853 he was boarding at 10 Morton Place, just off Washington Street, which was known as "Newspaper Row" and was the scene of frantic, nonstop activity where the clashing of presses could be heard day and night. Kinsley worked nearby at 27 School Street as a printer for the *Massachusetts Life Boat*, a weekly temperance paper. The offices of Ticknor and Fields, the preeminent publisher of belles lettres in nineteenth-century America, were just a few doors down the street, at the corner of School and Washington Streets. Below Ticknor and Fields was the Old Corner Bookstore, which stocked foreign as well as domestic publications and was a popular meeting place for Emerson, Longfellow, Hawthorne, Julia Ward Howe, and other members of Boston's literati. Also close at 22 School Street were the offices of *The Youth's Companion*, a popular magazine aimed at nurturing the moral character of young men and women, for which Kinsley also set type during his stay in Boston.[23]

Although it might publish a literary review from time to time and it repeatedly professed an interest in "Morals, Education, Business, and General Information," the *Life Boat* was above all else a hard-core temperance paper. In early 1853 the paper boasted that it was "the only paper in Boston devoted exclusively to the cause of temperance," and claimed to have "as large a circulation as any temperance paper ever had in this State." The paper's owner and editor, Benjamin W. Williams, was also the secretary of the governing committee of the Massachusetts Temperance Society, and the society's statewide headquarters were located

ANTIQUE BUILDING, CORNER OF SCHOOL AND WASHINGTON STREETS, BOSTON.

4. Historic Boston building on the corner of School and Washington Streets that during the nineteenth century served as home to both the Old Corner Book Store and the publishers Ticknor and Fields. Courtesy of the Bostonian Society.

at the offices of the *Life Boat*. Each week the paper carefully reported the progress of temperance reform throughout New England, and then flooded its columns with sensational cautionary tales about "Dissipation and Destruction," "Robbery and Rum," "The Rumseller and His Victim in a Village Graveyard," "The Loved and Lost," and "The Poor Drunkard." Like most other reform papers, the *Life Boat* occasionally expressed its abolitionist sympathies by publishing harrowing accounts of slavery in the South, and a Fourth of July editorial observed that the Fugitive Slave Law and Southern efforts to take slaves into the Nebraska territories "should make every freeman hang his head for shame." But however brutal slavery in the South might be, the editor of the *Life Boat* maintained that "Never was there a more cruel Slavery than that imposed by the drinking system. . . . The slave trade in all its horrors, never killed, and maimed, and tortured a tithe of the number that strong drink is doing every year." Yet the odds against the paper succeeding in its war against alcohol were overwhelming, according to the editor, because Robert Gould Shaw's grandfather and other members of the "wealth and talent and respectability of Boston" were bitterly opposed to the anti-liquor laws that could put an end to "The Slavery of Drinking." Here, in this small newspaper office staffed by a handful of dedicated teetotalers, Kinsley got a taste of fighting formidable opponents in the name of principle.[24]

Kinsley worked at the *Life Boat* until August 22, 1854, when the paper ceased operation because its owner and editor Benjamin W. Williams merged his temperance sheet with the *Boston Weekly Commonwealth*, an organ of the Free Soil Party, to form the *Boston Evening Telegraph*, which appeared daily except Sunday. Williams brought Kinsley along with him to the new operation, which had its business offices at 82 Washington Street, and paid him twenty-five dollars a week. The new paper continued to advocate temperance, to attack Boston as a dangerously complacent community where "moderate drinkers . . . are thick as blackberries," and to denounce the rumseller as "an outlaw – he is a criminal, and in pursuing his business he commits a grave offense." The paper also took a strong stand against slavery. And in light of the importance Kinsley later attached to John Brown's war against the spread of slavery into the Midwest, it is perhaps worth noting that the *Telegraph* devoted considerable space to the activities of the "resolute and determined anti-Slavery men" fighting for Kansas and declared that until the "Kansas Question" is settled "we have but the form of a republic, writhing under the rule of oligarchic tyranny. . . ."[25]

Massachusetts Life Boat.

The wise enter it and are safe:—Fools remain by the wreck and perish.

DEVOTED TO TEMPERANCE, MORALS, EDUCATION, BUSINESS, AND GENERAL INFORMATION.

Volume IX.] BOSTON, MASS., WEDNESDAY, AUGUST 31, 1853. [Number 21.

R. W. WILLIAMS, EDITOR AND PROPRIETOR.

THE MASSACHUSETTS LIFE BOAT.

Will be published every WEDNESDAY morning, at One Dollar and Twenty-Five Cents, or One Dollar IN ADVANCE.

No subscriptions received for a less term than SIX MONTHS.

Boston subscribers furnished by carriers will be one and One Dollar and Twenty-Five cents.

The volume of the Life Boat will be enriched from time to time with communications from some of the best writers in this region.

Publishing Office, No. 27 SCHOOL ST.

Poetry.

For the Massachusetts Life Boat.

ONWARD AND UPWARD.

Onward and upward! tho' the way be rough,
The sky be dark above us,
The darkest cloud a silver lining hath;
There is a bow within.

Onward and upward! Was life given for sleeping?
To watch, to sit us down?
To watch, in lifeness, the moments creeping,
Each worth a princely crown?

Onward and upward! On the field of battle,
When foes push the cannon's roar,
We hear the clanging gloom, and booming steeds,
And earth is steeped in gore.

One Day's Experience in Maine.

For the Mass. Life Boat.

The morning I left Waterville, a Hotel keeper from a town in Maine, stepped up to a lawyer from a Bangor, who was standing near me, and took him aside, and in words that told him that he had just come to town...

5. Front page, *Massachusetts Life Boat*, August 31, 1853. Courtesy of the Boston Public Library.

It is also worth noting that in early 1856 the *Telegraph* harangued Kinsley's future employer, the *Boston Evening Traveller*, for suggesting that slavery was an issue in America primarily because a few fanatics had made it one for political reasons. Indignant, the *Telegraph* contended that slavery "is no paltry question about men; but a question of principles; Liberty or Slavery is the issue." Later, in 1857, when Kinsley was working there, the *Traveller* published other articles that must have upset the young idealist, who by this time was almost certainly committed to the immediate abolition of slavery. One editorial dismissed the abolitionist circle as "not larger than a fashionable hoop," another attacked Wendell Phillips for criticizing the Republican Party for promising not to interfere with slavery in the South, and yet another opposed the introduction of slaves into the nation's temperate zones on the grounds that "A free negro population is bad enough and a great injury to such a land, but as slaves they are infinitely more detrimental."[26]

At the same time that Kinsley's employers at the *Traveller* were complaining about how unpleasant it was to be around free blacks, Kinsley was seeking out black Bostonians and making forays into their community. Since at least the early 1830s with the arrival of William Lloyd Garrison and his newspaper, *The Liberator*, Boston had been home to a handful of black and white antislavery advocates and their integrated meetings. Kinsley probably attended some of these meetings and was inspired by the courageous men and women who even in Boston risked their lives and reputations by preaching immediate abolition. Kinsley knew about the meetings because the newspapers he worked for reported when and where they would be held. Perhaps Kinsley set the type in early 1856 that announced the forthcoming lyceum lecture by John Swett Rock, the brilliant physician and lawyer who would later become the first African American admitted to practice law before the United States Supreme Court. Perhaps after work Kinsley even made his way over to Tremont Temple and listened as Rock delivered an invigorating speech to an integrated audience on "The Unity of the Human Race." And perhaps it was at one of the bookfairs that often accompanied such meetings that Kinsley acquired a small leather-bound volume of religious poems that he kept for the rest of his life and inscribed with the words: "Written by a Negress."[27]

Attending a racially mixed gathering such as the one at Tremont Temple would have signaled a dramatic change in Kinsley's life, for prior to moving to Boston he had lived in a virtually all-white environment. In

1850 there was only one African American, an eighty-three-year-old mulatto laborer, living among the roughly 1,000 residents of Fletcher; there were two African Americans living among the nearly 2,000 inhabitants of St. Albans; and in all of Franklin County there were only eighty-six blacks, most of them in the city of Burlington, and they constituted less than a half of one percent of the county's 28,500 residents.[28]

In Boston, Kinsley was living in a city where there were twice as many black residents as there were residents of any color in his home town. They made up only 1 percent of the city's population, however, and most of them lived in the West End. By 1857 Kinsley also lived in the West End, boarding at a three-story redbrick house at 27 Pinckney, a narrow cobblestone street that climbed up Beacon Hill from Charles Street, past posh Louisburg Square, to the edge of the Massachusetts statehouse. Here Kinsley resided, across the street from Louisa May Alcott's former home and in the shadow of the state capitol's glistening golden dome. But not all the residents of Pinckney Street were Boston Brahmins. Pinckney was an integrated street with black and white residents, and it was situated in the Sixth Ward, which was home to 60 percent of Boston's black population. From his boardinghouse Kinsley could easily make the ten-minute walk up Beacon Hill, past the state capitol, over to the offices of the *Traveller* at 31 State Street. But he could even more quickly walk the five blocks down the north slope of Beacon Hill to the May Street African Methodist Episcopal Church, where he served as superintendent of the Sabbath school.[29]

At the time of its organization in 1818 the May Street Church had twenty-three members and no meetinghouse. Initially, the congregation met in private homes and rented halls, but in 1823 it acquired a meetinghouse of its own, a small, two-story brick building only forty feet by twenty-five. The school was on the first floor, and religious services were held on the second. By the time Kinsley joined the church in the 1850s, the congregation had grown considerably and moved to larger quarters. Among Kinsley's predecessors as superintendent of the Sabbath school was Robert Morris, the first African American to gain admission to the Massachusetts bar. Morris was an eloquent leader in campaigns to desegregate the state's public schools and a fearless defender of Anthony Burns and other fugitive slaves who were captured in Boston and were slated under federal law to be returned to the South. Through the Burns case, Morris was involved in one of the most important events in the history of American antislavery. Burns's trial in 1854 brought the human face of slavery and the unbridled power of the slavocracy home to Kinsley and the other residents of Boston with such force that they never again seriously contemplated compromise with the South.[30]

The May Street Church had a long and illustrious history not only of saving souls but also of fighting racial oppression. David Walker, the author of the revolutionary *Appeal to the Coloured Citizens of the World* (1829) and Boston's most famous black abolitionist, had been a member of the May Street Church and a close friend of its first pastor, Samuel Snowden. Walker's *Appeal* was a black jeremiad that bitterly denounced the hypocrisy of the Declaration of Independence and encouraged slaves to rise up and take their freedom by violence if necessary. Snowden, whom William Lloyd Garrison referred to as "my beloved colored brother," and his successor, the Reverend Elijah Grissom, who was himself a fugitive slave, were both members of an enduring biracial coalition that simultaneously fought segregation in Boston and slavery in the South. Under their tutelage, the May Street Church became a center of abolitionism, where clergy and lay people alike taught that slavery was a sin and that opposition to the institution, even violent opposition, was a Christian duty. At the May Street Church Kinsley learned that black men like Robert Morris, David Walker, Samuel Snowden, and Elijah Grissom were part of a long tradition of black activism that dated back to the Revolution. He learned that the tradition of radical reform in Boston was not limited to white Bostonians with names like Wendell Phillips, Charles Sumner, and William Lloyd Garrison.[31]

By working at the Sabbath school, Kinsley also got to know ordinary, working-class African Americans. Many of those he dealt with at the school were poor migrants from the South – in 1860 a quarter of Boston's black population was Southern born – and doubtless some were runaway slaves who had come to Boston in search of the promised land. The May Street Church welcomed these impoverished refugees and offered them food, clothing, and housing as well as spiritual aid. Less than a decade later, Kinsley would face a similar situation in Louisiana when he was put in charge of providing food and shelter to thousands of fugitive slaves who were pouring into Union army lines in search of something they called "freedom." One of them, who apparently had been helped by the earnest young soldier from Vermont, named her newborn "Freedom Kinsley."[32]

Sometime in 1857, probably because of familial obligations but possibly because of the Panic of 1857, which greatly disrupted the publishing industry, Kinsley quit his job at the *Traveller*, resigned his position as superintendent of the May Street Church Sabbath school, and moved back to Fletcher, where he lived with his Aunt Elvira Montague and his younger brothers Edgar and Alonzo. He found work as a farm laborer – hauling stone, uprooting stumps, repairing fences, plowing fields, planting potatoes, and so forth – but in June of 1860 he informed a census taker that he owned no real estate and no personal property. A year and a half later, on November 29, 1861, he traveled to St. Albans and enlisted in the Union army. His seventeen-year-old brother William, to whom he was deeply attached, followed in his footsteps and enlisted in the same company a few days later. A month later, in the dead of winter, the two brothers gathered up their gear and headed some one hundred miles downstate to Brattleboro, where they were mustered into Company F of the Eighth Vermont Volunteers.[33]

Other Vermonters had responded more quickly than Kinsley to Lincoln's call for volunteers to suppress Confederate insurgents after their attack on Fort Sumter in April 1861. In fact, Kinsley was not even the first in his family to sign up. When he finally enlisted, he became the third of the five sons of Ben Alva who would eventually join the Union ranks. Kinsley's brother Alonzo had enlisted in the Second Vermont Volunteers in May 1861, and his brother Jason had enlisted in the First Iowa Cavalry in June 1861. His brother William, as noted, enlisted shortly after he did, while Edgar, the fifth and final brother to sign up, joined Alonzo in the Second Vermont Volunteers in December 1863.[34]

Vermont's response to the call for troops was impressive. A small state with a shrinking population, Vermont nevertheless contributed some 32,000 soldiers to the Union war effort. One of every 10 Vermonters enlisted. Among all Vermont males, 1 of every 5 enlisted, and among those who fell within the military ages of eighteen to forty-five, 1 out of 2 volunteered. These are extraordinary figures that testify to Vermont's devotion to the Union. But the Kinsley family, in offering the army 5 of its 10 members, and 5 of its 7 military-age males, made a singular contribution to the Union cause. Indeed, their story gives new meaning to the timeworn appellation of the Civil War as a "Brothers' War." In the context of their hometown, the Kinsley record is even more striking. In Fletcher only 1 of 12 residents enlisted; among male residents, 75 out of 452 donned blue uniforms, or 1 out of 6. All but 5 of these 75 men entered the service as privates. Kinsley, who had also enlisted as a private, stood somewhat apart from his fellow fighting townsmen after his promotion to corporal, 4th class, on January 8, 1862. When later promoted to second lieutenant, he joined even more select company, for throughout the war Fletcher furnished only 3 commissioned officers, and one of them lasted less than three months.[35]

≈ Two ≈

During the first week of January 1862 the roughly one thousand men who had volunteered for the Eighth Vermont began arriving at Camp Holbrook, just outside the village of Brattleboro in southeastern Vermont. Most of Company F reported on January 8, the day Private Rufus Kinsley was promoted to corporal. Within a few days Kinsley, his brother William, and the other new recruits had settled into flimsy wooden houses that were built in sections so they could be taken apart and transported with the troops when they headed south. At Brattleboro the men of the Eighth Vermont faced a rigorous military training program, as well as two months of heavy winter snowfalls and temperatures that dipped to fifteen degrees below zero, and gradually they made the transition from undisciplined farmers to regimented soldiers.[36]

On March 6 the Eighth Vermont boarded a train at Brattleboro station and headed south down the Connecticut Valley. Late that evening they arrived at New Haven harbor, boarded the steamer *Granite State*, and started for New York City, which they reached at dawn the next morning. During a brief layover Kinsley managed to visit both Trinity Church in lower Manhattan and Plymouth Church in Brooklyn, where he heard the renowned antislavery minister Henry Ward Beecher deliver a rousing sermon. On March 10 the regiment was ready to ship out. Six companies boarded the schooner *James Hovey* and four others, including Kinsley's, boarded the *Wallace* and were towed to Staten Island, where they anchored for the night. Early the next morning they set sail for Ship Island, off the coast of Mississippi. The voyage was marked by cramped quarters, stormy seas, and sick soldiers. A private wrote from the deck of the *Wallace* that at one point "the waves were runing biger than any ten barns you ever saw" and the men were "sicker than horses." Some of the men, while leaning over the side of the ship and "vomiting as though they were going to throw their boots up," swore that "if they were back in Vermont the Union might go to the Devil."[37]

About dusk on April 5, after twenty-six days at sea, the *Wallace* cast
anchor on the leeward side of Ship Island. Virtually uninhabited since
Confederate forces abandoned it in September 1861, Ship Island had by
early April become the temporary home of some fifteen thousand Yankee
soldiers. They were under the authority of Major General Benjamin
F. Butler, who had arrived there just two weeks before Kinsley and his
regiment to assume command of the newly created Department of the
Gulf. Butler's division, which now included the Eighth Vermont, was to
support Union naval forces under the direction of Flag Officer David
G. Farragut in an amphibious attack on New Orleans, the largest city
in the Confederacy and entrepôt to the entire Mississippi Valley. Union
strategists in the nation's capital were convinced that the capture of New
Orleans and the lower Mississippi would deal a crippling blow from which
the Confederacy could never recover.[38]

Early on the morning of April 24, after nearly a week of fierce fighting,
a small flotilla of Union ships slipped past the two Confederate forts that
guarded the mouth of the Mississippi River and captured New Orleans
the next day without firing a shot. On May 1 Butler and several thousand
Union soldiers occupied the city. Six days later, after five weeks on Ship
Island, Kinsley and the rest of the Eighth Vermont boarded the *James
Hovey* and, packed "like sardines in a box," set sail for the Crescent City.
Upon reaching the mouth of the Mississippi, the *Hovey* was towed the
final eighty-five miles up the river to New Orleans by a steamer. One soldier from the regiment wrote of the slow, meandering ascent: "There is
some of the most beautiful places along on the river I ever see. The plantations all look as fresh and green the shugar cane is up about 18 inches
and you can see thousands of acres of it along side." Another soldier pronounced the trip up the Mississippi "one of excitement as every thing was
so different from any thing we had ever seen."[39]

The Eighth Vermont arrived in New Orleans in the late afternoon of
May 12 and went ashore that evening. "On approaching New Orleans,"
one private later remembered, "we found every thing as quiet as on a
Sunday morning." But after disembarking and marching a short distance
to the regiment's encampment at the Union Cotton Press on Henderson
Street between Tchoupitoulas and New Levee, that same soldier described
New Orleans as "a city full of excited people moving aimlessly about
with 'blood in their eye' and expresions [*sic*] which plainly showed they
would delight to crush us like an eggshell and throw the crumbled ruins
into the river." By publicly hanging one particularly defiant Rebel and

incarcerating others in military prisons, Butler tried to curb the barrage of threats and insults hurled at his men. To deal with the incessant taunting of Union soldiers by Confederate women, he issued on May 15 his famous General Orders No. 28, which declared that "hereafter when any female shall by word, gesture, or movement insult or show contempt for any officer or soldier of the United States she shall be regarded and held liable to be treated as a woman of the town plying her avocation." Upon learning of Butler's order young Clara Solomon, a resident of the city, rushed to her diary and wrote: "Oh! Philomen, I cannot express to you the indignation this thing awakened. . . . The cowardly wretches! to notice the insults of ladies!" Although never mentioned in Kinsley's diary, Butler's outrageous edict likely brought an approving smile to Kinsley's face. Kinsley liked incendiary language, and he had little sympathy for Confederate women, most of whom he described as inveterate Yankee haters.[40]

Two days after Butler issued the order that guaranteed his place as the most hated person in the history of New Orleans, the Eighth Vermont moved to the Mechanics' Institute, which in 1866 would be the scene of the bloodiest riot of the entire Reconstruction era. No sooner had Kinsley settled into his new quarters on Dryades Street than he was over at City Hall copying down barbaric passages from the Louisiana slave code or down at the French Market rescuing a fugitive slave "from the hands of a kidnapper." These initial encounters with the "peculiar institution" convinced Kinsley that although New Orleans boasted "splendid palaces, and parks, and gardens, . . . an ever-present curse overhangs it all."[41]

After about a month of police and provost duty, the Eighth was ordered out of the city, and on May 31 the regiment established a new camp directly across the river at the New Orleans, Opelousas, and Great Western Railroad Depot in Algiers. At the depot the Eighth set up quarters in waiting rooms, on covered platforms, and in boxcars on side tracks. Some of the men found Algiers to be "a better place" than New Orleans because "we have more air hear than we did over thear." But there were more mosquitoes too, and the men never stopped complaining about them. They also complained endlessly about guard duty, which Kinsley performed fairly regularly during his first two months at Algiers. One of the men from Company A confessed to his parents that "it makes a fellow feel a little ticklish to start out with four besides himself in a dark night and go off a mile into the tall grass and bushes whear you can't see plain ten feet ahead of you and stand thear 3 or 4 hours with the owls hooting and aligators splashing in the water." More worrisome still was the

constant fear of a surprise attack by Confederate guerrillas who controlled
most of the countryside south and west of Algiers.[42]

But the biggest problem facing Union troops at Algiers in the summer
of 1862 was the enormous influx of runaway slaves, or "contrabands" as
they were generally called, who were fleeing the plantations of southern
Louisiana by the thousands. According to an officer in Kinsley's regiment
who later wrote a history of the Eighth Vermont, those who poured into
the camp at Algiers "had very crude and indefinite notions of the great
struggle in which the nation was involved, but firmly grasped the idea
that 'Massa' Lincoln was the God-sent Moses, who was to deliver their
race from bondage, and that escape into the Union lines was the first
step on the road to freedom." In this conclusion, they were absolutely
right.[43]

The determination of thousands of slaves to defy the authority of their
masters and run to Union lines provoked several of Kinsley's superiors
to express genuine anxiety about the possibility of blacks rising up in
rebellion and turning Louisiana into another St. Domingue. On July 25,
1862, the commander of the Department of the Gulf warned that "we
shall have a negro insurrection here I fancy. If something is not done
soon, God help us all. The negroes are getting saucy. . . . " In contrast,
Kinsley, who spent a great amount of time among black fugitives, never
expressed any such fear. Instead, he actively encouraged slaves to get
saucy, to run away, and to demand their freedom.[44]

Sometimes, though, helping a runaway slave could be a dangerous
business, forcing a soldier to take a stand that might ruin his military
career. On June 25, for example, Kinsley wrote in his diary of a master
who came into camp to retrieve a fugitive slave. But instead of getting
his slave, he "got badly used, and was glad to escape with his life." In
the aftermath of this incident Lieutenant Colonel Edward M. Brown,
the second highest ranking officer in the regiment, harshly rebuked the
men for their conduct, reminding them that they "came into the service
to obey orders and not to interfere with personal property, whether in
slaves or anything else." Brown, according to regimental historian G. G.
Benedict, was one of "a number of officers and some men" who believed
that "this was no 'abolition war.'" Kinsley, on the other hand, was undoubtedly one of the men Benedict was referring to when he reported
that in response to the lieutenant colonel's reprimand "a number of
the men, expecting an order to deliver up the negro, who had been secreted in the camp, pledged themselves to protect him and to refuse

obedience to any such order, even at the cost of trial and punishment for mutiny."[45]

Fortunately, the order to "deliver up the negro" never came, and three weeks later Congress put an end to the issue of what to do with fugitive slaves. The Second Confiscation Act of July 17, 1862, declared that slaves who ran away from Rebel masters were free, and consequently the return of such slaves to their former masters was illegal. While this legislation had a salutary effect on the lives of slaves who had already escaped to Union lines, it had no impact on the treatment of slaves who remained on Louisiana's sugar plantations. A month after the act was passed, Kinsley was washing the wounds of a runaway who had come into camp with an ear cut off, a brand burnt into his body, and flesh torn by whips and dogs, wearing an iron yoke, dragging a ball and chain, and destined to die.[46]

Kinsley's commitment to the fugitives was so well known that on September 1 he was removed from the government printing office to which he had been detached for the previous two months and put in charge of the huge contraband camp that the army had set up on the outskirts of Algiers. Caring for massive numbers of destitute fugitives was, as Kinsley understood from the outset, "an arduous undertaking."[47] Over the next three months he and his brother William, who assisted in overseeing the camp, fed 4,000 to 6,000 contrabands a day and managed a makeshift hospital that ministered to the needs of some 3,000 sick men, women, and children. In a less official capacity Kinsley and his brother often attended camp worship services, and on occasion they participated in a funeral, marriage, or baptismal ceremony. But Kinsley's greatest passion was teaching at the contraband school. Benedict, in his detailed history of the Eighth Vermont, singled out only one soldier from the entire regiment for his efforts to teach the Algiers contrabands how to read, and that was Rufus Kinsley.[48]

In mid-October Kinsley learned that the contraband camp and school were to be shut down and that his "family of negroes" was to be put to work on plantations that the government had seized since the capture of New Orleans and its environs by Union forces in late April. Kinsley disapproved of these government plantations, contending that blacks would benefit more from reading books than harvesting sugar. His displeasure with the substitution of canefields for schoolhouses as the locus of contraband life was doubtless exacerbated by the fact that only a month before he had gone to his company commander and received assurances that "arrangements will be made forthwith, for putting into operation an effective and extensive system of schools for the Contrabands." Kinsley wrote in his diary that "No doubt, for the present hour, this process will *pay*, but whether, in the end, their labor will prove more profitable to the Government than the learning they would otherwise get, I seriously doubt." Kinsley's indictment of government policy as shortsighted and dollar-driven would make no difference. On October 13, two days before Kinsley's private protest, the government issued an order authorizing the Charles A. Weed Factioning Company to work the abandoned plantations in the nearby parishes of Plaquemines and St. Bernard using contraband labor that would be provided by the government. And three weeks later the government issued General Orders No. 91, which provided for the use of contraband labor on abandoned plantations to the west of New Orleans in the Lafourche district. Workers were to work ten hours a day, twenty-six days a month, and be paid ten dollars per month, less three dollars for clothing. There was to be no "cruel or corporeal punishment," but the government would "provide suitable guards and patrols to preserve order," and anyone who disobeyed instructions or refused to work could suffer "imprisonment in darkness on bread and water."[49]

By the end of November all the fugitives in Kinsley's camp, except the very sick, had been sent to work on the government's "free labor" plantations. A few day later, on December 4, Kinsley struck his tent and boarded a train for Brashear City, the western terminus of the New Orleans, Opelousas, and Great Western Railroad. A major campaign, headed by Brigadier General Godfrey T. Weitzel, commander of the Second Brigade of the First Division of the Nineteenth Army Corps, had recently secured the line to Brashear City, and the virtually deserted little village on the edge of Berwick Bay was the new headquarters of the Eighth Vermont. Union soldiers referred sarcastically to the "'Mammoth' City of Brashear" as a place where there was nothing to do, nothing to eat, and nowhere to sleep. Also one of the unhealthiest sites in the entire state of Louisiana, Brashear City was nevertheless of great strategic importance because of its location. From there transports could carry soldiers up the Atchafalaya River to Grand Lake, the northern Lafourche district, and beyond; up Bayou Teche to Opelousas, Attakapas, and other regions of western Louisiana; or down the Atchafalaya to the Gulf of Mexico and over to Galveston, Texas.[50]

Kinsley's regiment spent most of the next few months playing a deadly game of cat-and-mouse with Confederate forces that were determined to control not only Berwick Bay but also the New Orleans, Opelousas, and

Great Western Railroad. It was during this period, in a battle with the Confederate gunboat *John L. Cotton* on a bayou just above Berwick Bay, that Kinsley first came under serious enemy fire. He later remembered the frenetic nature of these times as he trudged back and forth through swamps and bayous that were infested with bloodthirsty mosquitoes, bellowing alligators, deadly snakes, and rats the size of terriers: "During Dec. 1862, and Jan. Feb. and March 1863, our Regiment, the 8th Vermont, moved very often, – from Bayou Lafourche to Berwick Bay, then back as far as Bayou Boeuf, then to Bayou Ramus, then back to Lafourche, then to Berwick Bay again; and thence, in the spring of 1863, to Port Hudson, *via* the Teche and Red rivers."[51]

But Kinsley did not accompany his regiment on the march up the Teche or at the battle for Port Hudson because of an injury he had sustained at Bayou Boeuf. The mishap occurred in February 1863 after Kinsley had been relieved of picket duty and took a nap in the cooper's shop on a plantation that his detachment was using for sleeping quarters. "The board on which I slept," he later recalled, "was not quite so long as its occupant, and when I awoke I was lying on my face with my feet projecting over the end of the board, and my left knee was in acute pain." Cyrus H. Allen, the regiment's assistant surgeon, restored what was a dislocated kneecap to its proper position, but Kinsley "had lain so long that the knee was badly swollen and painful for some weeks." He was, according to the commander of his company, "brought back to camp disabled and was for some time obliged to walk & hobble about with canes, and . . . by reason of said disability was placed on detached service by order of Genl. Weitzel." On April 9, Weitzel, who had assumed command of the Eighth Vermont in January 1863 when the regiment had been incorporated into his brigade, ordered Kinsley to remain at Brashear City, where he was to serve as printer for the Second Brigade.[52]

Assisted much of the time by his brother William, Kinsley did printing for the army until April 28 when, as he put it, "I was carried to General Hospital on Wafford's Island a little down towards the Gulf of Mexico from Berwick Bay, absolutely helpless from chronic diarrhoea." Two weeks later Kinsley weighed eighty pounds, less than half of what he had weighed in the summer of 1862. He wrote in his diary on May 17 that there was "Not flesh enough on my bones for a fly's dinner." Kinsley remained at the island hospital, where he enjoyed recuperative boating excursions with William, until June 10. Then, because of rumors of an imminent Confederate attack, the hospital was dismantled and its patients were piled into railroad cars headed for New Orleans. Amazingly, only two patients died on the way back to the Algiers depot. The eighty-mile trip, when not interrupted by frequent stops at stations along the way, was on a rickety, uneven track. It was a journey, according to one soldier, that "would make a dog sea-sick."[53]

Upon arriving in New Orleans, the sick and wounded were dispersed among several military hospitals, but Kinsley, who seemed to be on the mend, had recovered enough to secure his own lodgings across the river in Gretna. On June 25 he boasted that he weighed 106 pounds. Over the next few weeks, however, Kinsley apparently suffered a relapse, for on July 24 he was admitted to the Barracks General Hospital just below New Orleans on the east bank of the Mississippi River. The physician who initially examined him wrote "General Debility" on his bed card, but in reality Kinsley was again suffering from chronic diarrhea. Over the next three months physicians at the Barracks Hospital put Kinsley on a diet of strychnine, beer, ale, and whiskey. Somehow, the old temperance crusader never got around to mentioning these medications in either his diary or his letters home. He did get better, however, and for several weeks prior to his discharge from the hospital on October 15 Kinsley worked as a nurse in Ward One.[54]

On August 25, 1863, while Kinsley was still a patient at the Barracks Hospital, Major General Nathaniel P. Banks, who had replaced Butler as commander of the Department of the Gulf on December 16, 1862, issued a provisional commission promoting Kinsley to second lieutenant in a regiment of black soldiers.[55] Banks's action caught Kinsley by surprise. He had not applied for the commission, and for a number of reasons he did not know whether to accept it. Certainly, he was flattered by the language of Banks's commission, which began: "Reposing Special Trust and Confidence in the Loyalty, Courage, Prudence and Ability of Corpl. Rufus Kinsley of Company F 8th Vermont Vol. Infty. by virtue of the authority entrusted to me by the War-Department, I do appoint said Corpl. Rufus Kinsley 2d Lieutenant of the Second Regiment of Infty. Corps d'Afrique Volunteers, (Company 'B',) to be obeyed and respected accordingly."[56] But as Kinsley explained in his diary, he had "no ardent thirst for 'glory'" and he was not eager to wind up on the short end of a rope, which is where Confederate officials had promised to put any white Yankees who dared to serve as officers in black regiments. Moreover, as Kinsley emphasized not only in his diary but also in a letter to his sister Lucretia, he did not want to abandon his brother William. Not quite five years old when his mother died, William was the baby of the Kinsley clan, and Rufus, twelve years his senior, had kept a watchful eye over the young teenager during the year and a half they had spent together in Company F. Another source of hesitation may have been the bad reputation that black soldiers had among many of Kinsley's peers and superiors. It was, for instance, common knowledge that General Weitzel, commander of Kinsley's brigade, did not think black soldiers would fight and did not want them under his command.[57] Colonel Stephen Thomas, commander of Kinsley's regiment, made the same point in a speech he delivered to a regiment of black soldiers just before an anticipated battle with the enemy along the New Orleans, Opelousas, and Great Western Railroad. Doubting their courage, he threatened them: "[I]f one of you hesitates, I shall shoot him on the spot."[58] A private in another black regiment that was guarding the same railway charged that there were men in Kinsley's regiment who had no use for black soldiers. Unable to offer conclusive proof, he nevertheless strongly implied that in November 1862 members of the Eighth Vermont had, under the cover of darkness, fired repeatedly and indiscriminately into his regiment for an entire night.[59] Shortly before this incident Dunham Burt, a young soldier from Castleton, Vermont, who had sailed from New York to Ship Island with Kinsley on the *Wallace,* wrote home: "There is one thing which causes a great deal of dissatisfaction in this division, and that is the arming and equipping of negroes, and thus putting them on an equal footing with a white soldier." From his campsite a few miles outside of New Orleans, Burt added that "The President's [preliminary emancipation] proclamation is well received here, but we all hope that the plan will work of putting the darkeys in Florida or some other place, for we do not want any more here just at present."[60]

While some whites wanted nothing to do with black troops, others considered joining black regiments but ultimately decided against such a move for reasons that had more to do with careerism than racism. For example, Captain John W. De Forest of the Twelfth Connecticut Volunteers, who was stationed just outside of New Orleans at Camp Parapet, considered applying for a colonelcy in a black regiment but decided not to when his superior, Colonel Henry C. Deming, advised against it because of "the character of the officers" and "the nature of the service that will be assigned to the Negro troops. . . . " Even before talking to Deming, De Forest had correctly predicted that "The colored troops will probably be kept near here and used to garrison unhealthy positions; they will be called on for fatigue duty, such as making roads, building bridges and draining marshes; they will be seldom put into battle, and will afford small chance of distinction."[61] Lieutenant John C. Palfrey, an engineer who had been trained at West Point, also hoped that "negro service" might help him move up in the military hierarchy. Dispatched to the Department of the Gulf to assess and improve captured military fortifications, Palfrey spent most of his time overseeing the completion of Fort Massachusetts, a masonry structure that the federal government began building in 1858 on the west end of Ship Island. In 1863, while stationed on the island, Palfrey seriously contemplated assuming command of a black regiment, but like De Forest he was counseled against it by his superiors. Moreover, according to Palfrey, there were only a few black regiments with troops that were qualified to help him complete Fort Massachusetts, and he had no desire to command a regiment of unskilled runaway slaves. In a letter marked "*Private*," Palfrey explained to his father that such regiments "are not expected to learn much soldiering, are set digging as soon as recruited, do not stand guard & hardly handle their arms at all, and are hardly allowed to make themselves respected or respectable, and I do not feel called upon to sacrifice myself in any such way."[62]

Unlike De Forest, Kinsley was not interested in accumulating marks of "distinction" by serving in a black regiment; on more than one occasion he announced that he had "something to fight for in this war, besides promotion." And unlike Palfrey, Kinsley was ready to "sacrifice" himself for the cause; indeed, Kinsley believed that the Christian concepts of sacrifice and atonement were at the heart of the Civil War. Consequently, in deciding whether to become an officer in a black regiment, Kinsley was much more likely to follow the lead of the crusty old Vermont soldier John W. Phelps than that of two well-heeled young careerists from elite New England families. Phelps, a brigadier general in the First Vermont Volunteers, approached the status of a folk hero among his men because of his honesty, fairness, and Spartan life style. Also known for his radical abolitionism, he issued upon reaching the Gulf of Mexico in December 1861 an inflammatory proclamation calling for the immediate abolition of slavery, "a system of violence, immorality, and vice" that had turned the United States into "the disgrace of Christendom." Six months later at a camp just outside of New Orleans he began organizing fugitive slaves into military regiments that he intended to place under his command in the "great battle of Armageddon." For these actions, both of which defied official Union policy,[63] David Dixon Porter, the respected naval officer who had assisted Farragut in the capture of New Orleans, labeled Phelps "a crazy man," and Butler pronounced him "mad as a March Hare on the 'nigger question.'" Such epithets did not faze Phelps, who placed John Brown, the much maligned commander of another "army" of black and white soldiers at Harpers Ferry, "on a level with the great martyrs of the Christian world." Phelps's own martyrdom was completed when Butler ordered him to stop raising black regiments and put his fugitive slaves to work chopping down trees. Phelps responded that "while I am willing to prepare African regiments for the defense of the Government against its assailants I am not willing to become the mere slave-driver which you propose...." Phelps resigned and went home to his farm in Vermont. This was the kind of man Kinsley could admire and emulate.[64]

The men in his own regiment who had made the decision to become officers of black troops may have also influenced Kinsley as he debated accepting a commission in the Second Corps d'Afrique. One of the first of the approximately forty soldiers to move from the Eighth Vermont to a black regiment was Oscar W. Goodridge, who did so in November 1862. Kinsley and Goodridge had known each other forever; indeed, the latter's mother was working in the Kinsley household when Rufus was born. Captain Hiram E. Perkins, a St. Albans machinist, was also "well acquainted" with Kinsley before the war. Perkins had been the recruiting agent who originally convinced Kinsley to sign up for the Eighth Vermont, and he then served as the commanding officer of Kinsley's company. In April 1863 Perkins accepted a commission from Banks that promoted him to major in a black regiment. When Perkins left to take up his new position, Kinsley wrote in his diary that he was "Sorry to lose so good an officer." By the time Banks offered Kinsley his commission in the Second Corps d'Afrique, four other members of the Eighth Vermont were already officers in the very regiment Kinsley was contemplating joining. In fact it was one of these men, Augustine P. Hawley, who in early October 1863 made the thirteen-hour trip from his post on Ship Island to the Barracks Hospital in New Orleans to present Kinsley his provisional commission.[65]

Since his arrival in Louisiana, Kinsley had taken more than a passing interest in the issue of blacks fighting in the Union army. On August 24, 1862, for example, he noted in his diary: "Orders issued to arm and equip the negroes of the State." Furthermore, he had some positive first-hand knowledge of black troops, for in October 1862 the First Louisiana Native Guards had come to Algiers in preparation for a joint expedition with the Eighth Vermont aimed at repairing and opening up the New Orleans, Opelousas, and Great Western Railroad from Algiers to

6. Pickets of the First Louisiana Native Guards guarding the New Orleans, Opelousas, and Great Western Railroad. *Frank Leslie's Illustrated Newspaper*, March 7, 1863. Courtesy of the Louisiana and Lower Mississippi Valley Collections, Louisiana State University Libraries.

Brashear City. During what became a highly successful campaign, the black troops acquitted themselves well, and Kinsley wrote in his diary on October 28 that at Des Allemands, a station about thirty miles up the line, Confederate forces had fled before the advancing black and white regiments, "evidently deeming it beneath their dignity to fight negroes." Two months later, during which time the Second and Third Louisiana Native Guards had joined the First in guarding the railroad and taking control of the territory around it, Kinsley acknowledged in his diary the central role blacks were playing in the destruction of slavery.[66]

Overcoming his initial concerns about leaving his brother, drawing upon his own personal knowledge of black troops in the Lafourche district, and perhaps finding inspiration in the actions of Phelps, Goodridge, Perkins, Hawley, and some of the other Green Mountain Boys, Kinsley decided to accept the Banks commission and, in his words, "cast my lot with the Colored Soldiers, for life or death." On October 1, 1863, he wrote to Major G. Norman Lieber, acting assistant adjutant general of the Department of the Gulf, requesting "that I be discharged from my Regiment, in order that I may accept a Commission in the Corps d'Afrique."[67]

Kinsley was joining a remarkable regiment, whose roots stretched back into the peculiar history of antebellum New Orleans. On the eve of the Civil War, twenty-four thousand persons of African descent lived in the Crescent City, thirteen thousand of whom were slaves. The remaining eleven thousand were *gens de couleur libres* who, according to the free colored press, belonged to "an old population with a history and mementos of their own, warmed by patriotism, partaking of the feelings and education of the white." From 1810 to 1840 free coloreds had made up nearly a quarter of the city's total population and over a third of its free inhabitants. In fact in 1850 more free coloreds lived in the city of New Orleans than in the states of Georgia, Florida, Texas, Arkansas, Alabama, and Mississippi combined. And given the prevalence of miscegenation in antebellum New Orleans, a situation that Kinsley deplores in his diary, it is not surprising that over three-quarters of the city's free coloreds were of mixed ancestry and described in census returns as mulatto rather than black. Because of their own hard work and the advantages that often accompanied their paternity, the free coloreds established themselves as integral and influential members of the city's economy. In 1859 the New Orleans *Picayune* maintained that "As a general rule, the free colored people of Louisiana, and especially of New Orleans – the 'creole colored people,' as they style themselves – are a sober, industrious and moral class, far advanced in education and civilization." The 1860 federal census confirmed that nearly 85 percent of free colored males were artisans, professionals, or proprietors and that free colored wealth, including hundreds of slaves, stood at over two million dollars. On December 28, 1860, barely seven weeks after Lincoln, a man most Southerners considered a flaming abolitionist, was elected president, a group of free colored New Orleanians publicly declared that the members of their community had "no sympathy for Abolitionism; no love for the North, but they have plenty for Louisiana; and let the hour come, and they will be worthy sons of Louisiana." Four months later, immediately after Louisiana's own P. G. T. Beauregard ordered the bombardment of Fort Sumter, over a thousand "worthy sons" met at an old free colored schoolhouse in the Faubourg Marigny to organize military companies and offer their services to Governor Thomas O. Moore.[68]

Moore accepted the offer, and in early May he incorporated the First Native Guards into the Louisiana Militia of the Confederate States of America. Six months later over seven hundred fifty free colored soldiers marched through the streets of New Orleans in review before the governor and various military dignitaries. In late March 1862, as the threat of Yankee invasion mounted, Moore advised the Native Guards to "hold themselves prepared for such orders as may be transmitted to them" and declared that he was counting on "the loyalty of the free colored population of the city and State for the protection of their homes, their property, and . . . Southern rights from the pollution of a ruthless invader. . . . " After the capture of New Orleans, some Native Guards explained that their "loyalty" had been coerced by Confederates, but others maintained that Governor Moore had not erred in his faith in them. One former Native Guard claimed that his fellow free colored soldiers "would have fought courageously against the Federals" if a battle for New Orleans had actually taken place. He proudly pointed out that the Native Guards were still at their post on Esplanade Avenue awaiting orders when the city's white troops "had already made a long distance between themselves and the approaching Federal fleet. . . . " In similar fashion, the editors of the free colored press complained that in the face of Farragut's attack Confederate leaders had not made proper use of the Native Guards, who were itching to fight the Yankees, and asked rhetorically, "Sons devoted to our dear Louisiana, were we not ready to go to her defense?"[69]

In the months immediately following the Crescent City's capture, however, most Native Guards transferred their allegiance from the Confederacy to the Union. Commenting on this phenomenon, the distinguished Southern historian Eugene D. Genovese has observed that "During the War for Southern Independence, free colored militia units, most notably at New Orleans, offered their services to the Confederacy and then changed sides at the appropriate moment – a record which each of us may interpret for himself."[70] Although historians have had difficulty evaluating the free colored flip-flop, General Butler, in desperate need of more troops because of a growing Confederate threat to New Orleans, had no trouble figuring out what he thought about it. The Native Guards were an available source of manpower at a time when the War Department had no additional troops to send him. On August 14, 1862, three months after meeting with the former officers of the Confederate Native Guards and discovering that "in color, nay, also in conduct, they had much more the appearance of white gentlemen than some of those who have favored me with their presence claiming to be the 'chivalry of the South,'" Butler wrote to Secretary of War Edwin M. Stanton that he had "determined to use the services of the free colored men who were organized by the rebels. . . . " A week later, on August 22, he issued General Orders No. 63, which called upon the "free colored citizens" of Louisiana who had previously served in the Louisiana Native Guards to enlist in the Union army. In a letter informing Major General Henry W. Halleck that he had decided to recruit some of the free colored soldiers "who were in the Confederate service, and are now ready and desirous of doing loyal service to the Union," Butler emphasized that by enrolling only free coloreds he had "kept clear of the vexed question of arming the slaves." He further noted that his action was "fortified by precedents of a half century's standing," that General Andrew Jackson in 1815 as well as Governor Thomas Moore in 1861 had enlisted the help of free colored troops, and that, consequently, he believed that "I have done nothing of which the most fastidious member of Jefferson Davis' household political can rightfully complain. . . . "[71]

The response to Butler's call was overwhelming. Within days some eighteen hundred free men of color began drilling on the grounds of the old Touro Infirmary on Front Levee Street. On September 27, a little more than one month after the promulgation of General Orders No. 63, the First Louisiana Native Guards were mustered into the Union army. Over the next eight weeks, two more regiments, the Second and the Third Louisiana Native Guards, were also recruited and mustered into service. The regiment that would later be home to Rufus Kinsley, the Second Louisiana Native Guards, was organized on October 12, seven months before Robert Gould Shaw and the famous Fifty-fourth Massachusetts left Boston for South Carolina. A large percentage of the soldiers enlisted in the Louisiana Native Guards, but especially in the Second and Third regiments, were actually fugitive or freed slaves rather than freeborn men of color. According to one black soldier in Kinsley's regiment, "Any negro who could swear that he was free, if physically good, was accepted, and of the many thousand slave fugitives in the city from distant plantations, hundreds found their way into [the] Touro building and ultimately into

the ranks of the three regiments formed at that building." The recruitment of black troops continued under Butler's successor, Nathaniel P.
Banks, and by the end of the war Louisiana had contributed over twenty-
four thousand black soldiers to the Union army, more than any other
state in the nation.[72]

Louisiana also contributed more black officers than any other state; indeed, nearly 90 percent of the black officers who held combat positions in
the Union army belonged to either the First, Second, or Third Louisiana
Native Guards.[73] The Second, Kinsley's future home, had thirty-one black
officers before the war was over, the most of any regiment in the Union
army. But Banks, who replaced Butler in December 1862, opposed placing African Americans in command positions. To be sure, Banks would
oversee the recruitment of thousands of black soldiers during his tenure
as commander of the Department of the Gulf, and he would praise them
for their "great service in this department," even declaring that "our
victory at Port Hudson could not have been accomplished at the time
it was but for their assistance." But Banks was not a champion of black
soldiers. In need of troops, he enlisted them "as a practical and sensible
matter of business" and not "upon any dogma of equality." His opposition to blacks in the officer corps was evident almost from the moment
he arrived in New Orleans.[74] Unlike Butler, who freely appointed blacks
to officer his three Native Guard regiments, Banks believed that black
officers were a "constant embarrassment and annoyance" whose presence was "detrimental to the Service" and demoralizing to white as well
as black soldiers. In February 1863 he informed the adjutant general of
the Union army that whenever possible he intended to replace Butler's
colored officers with white ones. Then, through methods both fair and
foul, he set about creating vacancies as quickly as he could.[75]

One of Banks's most useful weeding tools was the board of examination,
which proved especially effective in depleting the black officer corps of
the Second Native Guards. In response to the prospect of taking an oral
exam that tested knowledge of military rules and regulations, a group of
black officers from the Second protested that since November 1862 they
had been either shouldering "the heaviest guard duty ever known" on the
New Orleans, Opelousas, and Great Western Railroad or "working both
day and night" building batteries, magazines, and fortifications on Ship
Island, and "consequently we have not been able to acquire that perfect
knowledge of Military [matters], that would fit us to go before a board
of examination." Noting that only black officers would have to go before

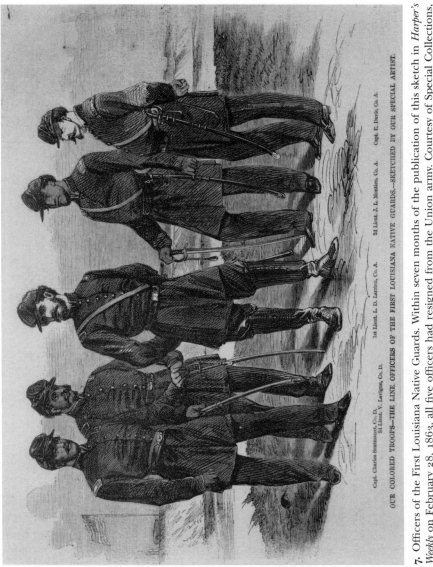

Capt. Charles Sentmanat, Co. D.   1st Lieut. L. D. Larrieu, Co. A.   2d Lieut. J. L. Montieu, Co. A.   Capt. E. Davis, Co. A.
2d Lieut. V. Lavigne, Co. D.

OUR COLORED TROOPS—THE LINE OFFICERS OF THE FIRST LOUISIANA NATIVE GUARDS.—SKETCHED BY OUR SPECIAL ARTIST.

7. Officers of the First Louisiana Native Guards. Within seven months of the publication of this sketch in *Harper's Weekly* on February 28, 1863, all five officers had resigned from the Union army. Courtesy of Special Collections, Tulane University Library.

the board, the protesters also gave voice to their suspicion that the exams were a sham in any case, "but a preliminary step to our being mustered out of the Service."[76]

During the spring and summer of 1863 numerous black officers from Kinsley's future regiment went before Banks's examining board. Some failed and were discharged, some passed but quit anyhow because of a pernicious racism they could no longer endure, and some resigned rather than undergo what they believed was an unjust and humiliating exercise. Among those weeded out were Alphonse Fleury, Jr., and Octave Rey, both French-speaking, freeborn natives of New Orleans and important figures in the struggle for equality in postwar Louisiana. Others included William B. Barrett, Robert H. Isabelle, and Ernest C. Morphy, all of whom had been free before the war and served in the Louisiana State Legislature during Reconstruction. Complaining of habitual racial prejudice, Captain E. Arnold Bertonneau also quit the Second Native Guards. A fair-skinned, blue-eyed wine merchant who was born and reared in New Orleans, Bertonneau had originally served as an officer in the Confederate Native Guards. In 1864 he and Jean Baptiste Roudanez, another French-speaking free man of color, traveled to Washington, D.C., and presented to President Lincoln a petition that was signed by a thousand free men of color and asked for the right to vote. Lincoln must have been impressed, for a day after meeting with Bertonneau and his companion he suggested to the governor of Louisiana that an upcoming constitutional convention might want to consider granting the elective franchise to those African Americans who were "very intelligent" or who had "fought gallantly in our ranks." Later elected a member of the 1868 Louisiana State Constitutional Convention, Bertonneau remained a prominent actor in the Reconstruction drama as it unfolded in postwar Louisiana.[77]

Another casualty of Banks's campaign against black officers was Francis E. Dumas, one of only two African Americans to attain the rank of major during the Civil War. A wealthy slaveholder who had been born, reared, and educated in France, Dumas originally served as an officer in the Confederate Native Guards. He cut quite a figure according to Captain De Forest of the Twelfth Connecticut Volunteers, who attended a party at the New Orleans home of Dumas's brother in late 1862. There, surrounded by fair-skinned guests who were speaking French, singing French and American songs, dancing waltzes, and dining on "a collation of cakes, confectionery, creams, ices and champagne, followed by *cafe noir*, cognac and delicious cigars," De Forest met the elegant Francis Ernest Dumas.

He had "the complexion of an Italian and features which remind one of the first Napoleon," according to De Forest, and "did not differ in air and manners from the young Frenchmen whom I used to know abroad." De Forest, future author of the brilliant Civil War novel *Miss Ravenel's Conversion from Secession to Loyalty,* knew a memorable scene when he saw one and described the party in great detail in a letter to his wife. After the war Dumas would play a key role in Louisiana politics and face a number of difficult challenges, but in the summer of 1863 he chose not to face Banks's examining board and resigned from the Second Native Guards.[78]

By the time Kinsley joined the regiment only seven of the original thirty-one black officers were left. One was P. B. S. Pinchback, who during Reconstruction became the most powerful black politician in Louisiana, serving as state legislator, lieutenant governor, acting governor, and U.S. congressman. But Pinchback, who felt isolated after scores of his fellow black officers in the three Native Guard regiments had resigned in the spring and summer of 1863 and who had himself informed Banks that he was ready to resign if "you have concluded that *none* of us are fit to command," was gone by early November 1863. A few months later Solomon Hayes also resigned "on account of the prejudices . . . against Colored Officers." By mid-August 1864 there was only one black officer left in the Second Regiment, First Lieutenant Charles S. Sauvinet. Born and reared in New Orleans, fluent in French, German, Spanish, and English, and a former officer in the Confederate Native Guards, the fair-skinned Sauvinet had somehow survived the Banks reaper. In fact by the time he was finally mustered out on July 11, 1865, Sauvinet had compiled the longest continuous service record of any black officer to serve in the Union army.[79]

Although they spent a year and a half together in the same regiment on the same small island, Kinsley never mentions Sauvinet (or most of the other black officers of the Second Regiment) in his diary. Still more perplexing is his failure to mention Banks's controversial purge of black officers. Since most of the dismissals occurred prior to his arrival on Ship Island, perhaps Kinsley did not know about them. This is possible but seems unlikely given his perspicacity and the tendency of off-duty soldiers to sit around camp and gossip. Perhaps he knew about them but did not want to admit that he had become one of Banks's replacements. There is also the possibility that Kinsley agreed with most of the expulsions and saw no particular reason to comment on the matter. After all, according to Kinsley there were many "totally incompetent" officers in the black regiments, regiments that he thought deserved "the best corps of officers in the service." Consequently, where the proud Dumas and many other black officers viewed competency exams as an indignity, Kinsley believed that such exams were "an admirable sieve" that would rid black regiments of unfit officers, whatever their race.[80] In August 1864, when two black officers with whom he had spent ten months on Ship Island failed a competency exam and were summarily cashiered, Kinsley exhibited no special sympathy for them. Instead, he wrote in his diary that "Such a sifting as this will be no loss to the service."[81]

Furthermore, Kinsley would have had a difficult time supporting many of these officers. It is hard to imagine Kinsley having much respect for Bertonneau, the former officer in the Confederate Native Guards who trafficked in demon rum, or for Pinchback, who was a hot-tempered, hard-drinking, swashbuckling opportunist. Even during his most altruistic moments, Pinchback, according to his grandson, employed "the tactics, not of an idealist and liberator, but of a bold dramatic venturer."[82] It would also have been exceedingly difficult for Kinsley to rally behind someone like Dumas. De Forest, the French-speaking man of letters, may have been impressed with the urbane Dumas and his francophone world, but it is impossible to imagine Kinsley sipping cognac and smoking cigars with a man who had once been a slaveholder and an officer in the Confederate Native Guards. Whatever the rationale for owning slaves or enlisting in the Confederate army, it would not have satisfied Kinsley, the fervid abolitionist and uncompromising Unionist who believed that "every man, not only for himself but for every other man, should love liberty more than life." The black soldiers who won Kinsley's admiration were the former fieldhands who, by fleeing slavery and joining the Union army, had indeed risked everything, including their lives, for liberty. These were the men who would pass through the eye of the needle and enter the Kingdom of God.[83]

∽ Three ∼

Kinsley was mustered in as a second lieutenant in Company B of the Second Regiment Infantry, Louisiana Corps d'Afrique, on October 27, 1863. For the next two months he served as the company's commanding officer, for which he was paid an extra twenty dollars, until Captain Lemuel

I. Winslow, another former member of the Eighth Vermont, took command. With the exception of three companies that had been detached to Fort Pike on Lake Pontchartrain, his new regiment had garrisoned Ship Island since January 12, 1863. The Second had been sent there to protect the island from enemy attack. The Confederates, who had actually occupied Ship Island during the early months of the war, were well aware of its significance.[84]

Lying roughly twelve miles off the coast of Mississippi, Ship Island was one in a chain of sixty-eight Eastern Gulf Coast barrier islands that ran northwestward along the Gulf of Mexico from Cape Sable, Florida, to Cat Island, Mississippi. Although unimproved until 1858 when the federal government began to build Fort Massachusetts on the west end, Ship Island had always been of strategic importance because of its location and protected anchorage. The island had served as the staging area for the Union's amphibious expedition up the Mississippi to New Orleans in April 1862, and it controlled access to New Orleans through Lakes Borgne and Pontchartrain. It was also a repair and refueling base for the Union ships that enforced the blockade of the Gulf Coast from the mouth of the Mississippi to Mobile Bay. Indeed, Ship Island was so important that the Union navy kept the 700-ton war sloop *Vincennes* and its crew of over one hundred fifty men docked there throughout the war to protect the anchorage.[85]

Sailors from the *Vincennes* were part of the large and diverse population that resided on or visited Ship Island during Kinsley's twenty-one-month stay in the middle of Mississippi Sound. In the fall of 1864, for instance, approximately fifteen hundred men, women, and children lived on the island. They included not only the soldiers garrisoning the island but also civilians who were employed by the Corps of Engineers to work on the construction of Fort Massachusetts, naval personnel who worked at the repair and refueling station, Union military convicts, and Confederate prisoners of war. These groups of inhabitants, whose numbers fluctuated dramatically throughout the war, were joined on the island by sailors and passengers coming ashore from visiting ships and by a floating population of black contrabands and white refugees who, often at great peril, made their way to the island in hopes of joining the Union army or catching a boat to New Orleans.[86]

Living conditions on the island were primitive. Some of the soldiers in Kinsley's regiment lived in tents and at night had only mattresses separating them from damp earth and coarse blankets protecting them from ravenous sand fleas. Other soldiers lived in roofless barracks with irregular, rough-hewn floors. A few lived in the portable wooden buildings that the Eighth Vermont had brought with them from Camp Holbrook in April 1862. Kinsley roomed in such a building until a Gulf storm blew it down in the summer of 1864. For his meals, he boarded from the beginning to the end of his stay on the island with Captain James Noyes and Noyes's wife Annie. Kinsley felt right at home in the Noyes household, not only because Mrs. Noyes kept house "in good Vermont style" but also because Captain Noyes, formerly a private in the Eighth Vermont, was a pious Wesleyan Methodist and his wife was the daughter of Orange Scott, the famous Methodist evangelist. In the 1830s Scott had waged war throughout New England against the church hierarchy for its indifference to the sin of slavery. The good fellowship accompanying the breaking of bread was enhanced in the spring of 1864 when Lieutenant Charles C. Colton, an old friend who had served with Kinsley in Company F of the Eighth Vermont, joined him in boarding with Captain and Mrs. Noyes. The table around which they all gathered for dinner was a dry goods box covered with a newspaper, and since most of the food consumed on the island had to be imported, the fare was usually bland and basic.[87]

Claim to the most extraordinary living arrangement on the island probably belonged to a black private in Kinsley's regiment. He lived in a tent with his wife, "a tidy mulatto woman" who was acknowledged as having "the nicest things of any one on this island. . . . " Her things included a chest full of bedding, "table-linen of the finest damask, chinaware and solid silver spoons, pitcher, forks, and plated table knives, etc." Both the private and his wife were the children of wealthy white planters who freed them and later left them substantial inheritances. On the eve of the war, they owned a successful business and held property valued at fifty thousand dollars.[88] Few of the men in the Second Corps d'Afrique had this kind of wealth or lived in this kind of luxury either before or during the war. To be sure, some of the approximately six hundred African American males in the regiment at the time of Kinsley's muster were light-colored hereditary free blacks who had made a good living before the war working as shoemakers, cigarmakers, coopers, carpenters, bricklayers, painters, and so forth. But the vast majority of the men in Kinsley's regiment were dark-colored, unskilled former slaves.[89] Many were among the thousands of contrabands who had fled rural plantations and claimed their freedom by entering Union lines. These men came into camp with nothing; in fact, some of them remembered Kinsley affectionately as the quartermaster who a year earlier had fed and clothed them at the Algiers contraband camp. There were also those who came into camp still wearing shackles. According to Kinsley, these men "made soldiers who hesitated not to brave the greatest dangers."[90]

Unfortunately for the men of the Second who wanted to prove their mettle in battle, the "greatest dangers" rarely included fighting Confederate soldiers. Perhaps they were lucky since, like many other black Civil War regiments, they had been equipped with obsolete firearms. In April 1864 when Adjutant General of the Union Army Lorenzo Thomas visited Ship Island, he declared the regiment "in capital order and fine drill" but expressed dismay at finding the men armed with old flintlock muskets that had been discarded by white troops. Thomas recommended "placing in their hands the best arms. The blacks will take the best care of them," he added, "and use them with effect when the necessity arises."[91]

Only twice while posted on Ship Island did men from the Second Corps d'Afrique actually engage Confederate forces. The first time was in early April 1863 when two companies from the regiment raided East Pascagoula, a small hamlet on the Mississippi coast. The misguided raid, which failed miserably, left several men dead, most of them killed when a Union gunboat fired into the retreating companies. The second engagement occurred in late August 1864 when three companies, one of them under Kinsley's command, were sent to Mobile Bay to participate in the siege of Fort Morgan. This encounter, despite Kinsley's efforts to puff it up in his diary, was also pretty forgettable. Kinsley and his men did not arrive at Fort Morgan until two days before a Confederate force, outnumbered 11 to 1, surrendered after a bombardment that lasted less than twenty-four hours. Kinsley probably experienced his "greatest danger" after the fort capitulated when a sloop on which he was sailing in Mobile Bay accidentally drifted into a minefield.[92]

Perhaps sensing that his son would not see much combat in a black regiment that was stationed on an island in the middle of Mississippi Sound, Ben Alva Kinsley in January 1864 admonished Rufus to "so discharge your duties as an officer that the cause of universal liberty may be advanced by your fidelity, if not your military skill or prowess." Kinsley's service record suggests that the dutiful son embraced the father's advice. He quickly proved himself conscientious to a fault, rising at four o'clock in the morning to begin work and typically not retiring until nightfall

after attending officer school or participating in some kind of religious
or educational activity. Six months after Kinsley received his father's letter,
a board of examiners from departmental headquarters included Kinsley
among the officers of the Second Corps d'Afrique it judged "efficient
and capable of performing the duties now assigned them" and ranked
him third in a class of twenty second lieutenants.[93]

Denied the opportunity to fight Confederates on the battlefield,
Kinsley and his men demonstrated their worth in other ways. They would
unload ships, mount guns, saw wood, build barracks, man pickets, and
master artillery as well as infantry drills. Their marching skills were truly
exceptional according to the regimental chaplain, who found dress pa-
rades a source of "pleasure and pride" as the men marched "with a step
so uniform and simultaneous, that, one would almost be inclined to believe that the whole army moved with one set of joints." Kinsley and his
men would also spend much of their time guarding prisoners. Because
of its isolation, Ship Island was an ideal location for a prison, and during
the course of the war thousands of men and a few women were incarcerated there. Arriving in April 1862, the first prisoners were Union soldiers
who had been convicted of various infractions of the military code. But
most of those incarcerated in 1862 were political prisoners, that is, they
were Confederate sympathizers or Rebel soldiers who had violated their
paroles. Most of the political prisoners had been released by the fall of
1863 when Kinsley arrived, but Union military convicts continued to arrive at the island until October 1864. Thereafter Ship Island was almost
exclusively a camp for Confederate prisoners of war.[94]

Kinsley did not miss the delicious juxtaposition of ex-slaves guarding
their former masters. The arrangement was fraught with tension as black
guards and white prisoners vied for supremacy in the vast prison pen
that was cordoned off near Fort Massachusetts. One former prisoner
complained that Confederate soldiers incarcerated at Ship Island had
endured "shocking treatment" at the hands of black guards and had
"every possible indignity heaped upon them." Hyperbole aside, this account, as well as others, leaves little doubt that the black soldiers who
guarded Confederate prisoners on Ship Island were not the faithful and
forgiving darkies conjured up by late-nineteenth-century white Southerners. Black guards repeatedly demonstrated their dominance, and when
challenged or insulted, they responded decisively. On one occasion, when
a black soldier overheard a Confederate prisoner talking about "niggers,"
he attacked the offending party with such a torrent of verbal abuse that

the officer of the guard had to intervene. On another occasion the abuse became physical when a Rebel prisoner, coming under the direct authority of black guards for the first time, called out derisively to a fellow inmate that "The bottom rail is on the top." A black guard, who took offense at the remark, responded by lunging at the taunting Confederate with his rifle, "the bayonet striking the man's hip" and leaving him grasping his wound. More deadly was the case of a black guard who shot a Confederate prisoner to death for refusing to leave a cookhouse that he had been ordered to vacate. The black private then calmly reloaded his rifle and declared: "I have killed one of the damned rebels. I'll kill another if I get a chance." Following an investigation that exonerated the guard of any wrongdoing, the post commander praised the private as "a trustworthy soldier" and reported that the shooting "has had a good effect on the surviving, undisciplined crew [of Confederate prisoners]."[95]

This incident probably registered in Kinsley's mind as another example of a growing black assertiveness, an assertiveness that Kinsley regularly notes, applauds, and encourages in his diary.[96] Kinsley might even have been sympathetic to the stance on Confederate prisoners taken by a private in another black Louisiana regiment. Recruited off a plantation a little north of Brashear City about the time the Eighth Vermont was stationed there, the black soldier spoke in the same Old Testament idiom as Kinsley. All "cut up" from whippings, the young private did not understand why Yankee soldiers took any Confederate prisoners. He asked a Union officer: "Why don't dey sweep 'em, like as with a broom? then we'll be all right, and can commence all over again. . . . The Bible says, sweep 'em with a besom. Clear the country. There is no good in any of them. . . . Kill 'em all! that is my motto."[97]

Despite this language of retribution, Confederate prisoners on Ship Island were much more likely to die of a disease than a bullet. In fact, only two of the 153 Confederate soldiers who died while confined to Ship Island were shot by black guards. The cause of death for the remainder included pneumonia, smallpox, typhoid, consumption, and phthisis, but the vast majority succumbed to dysentery and diarrhea.[98] Drinking water that came from "the seepage from barrels sunk in the sand" did not help to make Ship Island a salubrious place for the incarcerated, and neither did the fact that hundreds of prisoners arrived at the island already infected with "almost every variety of contagious, cutaneous disease." Other prisoners, according to the post surgeon, although they lived in tents only a few feet from the beach and thus had easy access to "one of the finest bathing places in the world," refused to wash regularly and died "from absolute indolence and filthiness."99

Kinsley, in contrast, went swimming in the ocean every day except Sunday, avoided contracting any contagious maladies, and enjoyed excellent health during his stay on Ship Island. In fact just a few months after leaving the hospital in New Orleans and joining his new regiment on Ship Island, the five-foot nine-inch Kinsley wrote a letter to his sister bragging that he weighed 170 pounds, 40 more than he had ever weighed at home in Vermont. Even more remarkable, Kinsley was happy as well as plump. On June 1, 1864, he wrote in his diary: "Time has passed very pleasantly. No occasion to regret that I came here." In expressing this sentiment, Kinsley distinguished himself from virtually everyone else who spent any time on Ship Island during the Civil War. In truth, he occupied a post that was probably the least desirable in the entire army.100

Ship Island was a windswept bar of drifting sand that reached seven miles in length and ranged from a quarter to three-quarters of a mile in width. With the exception of sand hummocks along the beach that occasionally rose to ten feet, the island was low-lying and flat. Only a few pines, palmettoes, and holly shrubs at the island's east end and occasional sedgy marshes interrupted the long monotonous stretch of shimmering snow-white sand that swallowed walkers up to their ankles. Violent storms often left large portions of the island underwater in the winter, and summertime typically brought drenching humidity and scorching temperatures. Flies, mosquitoes, and sand fleas were ubiquitous. A correspondent for a New York newspaper reported in 1862 that the walls of the wooden houses on Ship Island were "ornamented by a living cover of flies; reminding a person who is the unfortunate occupant that his house may move off some day by magical wings."101 In February 1865 a Union soldier from Ohio pronounced Ship Island the "most desolate looking place I ever saw." He understood perfectly why the federal government had chosen the island as a place to punish prisoners. Indeed, he thought "it would be punishment enough . . . to confine a man there without the 'Hard Labor.'"102 Another Yankee visitor described Ship Island as "a grand place for one who is disgusted with the world, but a very disagreeable place for one who has any desire to enjoy himself." John Palfrey, the West Point graduate who was stuck for a while on Ship Island overseeing the completion of Fort Massachusetts, wrote to his father that "Everything continues in status quo on this green isle of the ocean and I suppose you have long since learned to look anywhere rather than in my letters for incidents." Another Union officer, after only two and a half months on the island, ranted in his diary about government regulations that kept him stranded on this "dreary desolate sandbar," "this God-forsaken Isle."[103]

Less colorful language but no less damning depictions of life on Ship Island during Kinsley's tour of duty are found in the bureaucratic records kept by the U.S. Army. Under "Record of Events" in the monthly Regimental Returns of the Second Corps d'Afrique nothing at all is reported for the period October 1863 through May 1865 except for a notation under August 1864 that the Second had been consolidated with another black regiment. Under "Record of Events" in the regiment's Field and Staff Muster Rolls the same pattern of nothing being reported holds true for July 1864 through May 1865; for the earlier months, from November 1863 through June 1864, the usual refrain is "No changes of importance have occurred."[104]

But if life was tedious as well as harsh on Ship Island, what must it have been like on Cat Island, which is where Kinsley was sent on September 13, 1864. Named after its wild raccoons, which French explorers called *chats*, Cat Island was five miles west of Ship Island and somewhat larger. With the exception of a few poor tar and turpentine workers, the island had been uninhabited by humans until a couple hundred contrabands were sent there during the Civil War to do menial labor in return for government provisions. Unlike Ship Island, Cat Island had no fort, machine shop, refueling station, or prison camp to attract visitors or employ even modest numbers of military and civilian personnel. Cat Island was a place where one not only could get lonely, one could get killed. While stationed there, Kinsley endured devastating tropical storms. On several occasions he almost drowned while sailing to Ship Island for rations, and on more than one occasion he and his men were forced to eat rats in the absence of such rations. In short, Kinsley had been sent to a place that made Ship Island look like a vibrant, civilized metropolis.[105]

Detailed along with Kinsley to Cat Island was First Lieutenant John W. Harrison, another officer from Vermont. Their orders were to guard the island against Confederate attack and especially to procure and prepare wood for use on Ship Island.[106] By late November the two officers had about seventy soldiers, sixteen mules, and three sawmills under their command. Colonel Ernest W. Holmstedt, the post commander at Ship Island, needed firewood so that his men could cook meals and keep warm at night, and he needed finished lumber to build barracks that would protect prisoners as well as soldiers from blistering sun, driving wind, and wet sand. Although he had two sawmills on Ship Island by the summer of 1864, Holmstedt complained that he frequently could not get his hands on "a board of lumber, not even for coffins." Given over almost entirely to sand and swamp, Ship Island simply did not yield much wood of any kind. In contrast, nearly half of Cat Island consisted of heavily forested wetlands, and apparently Kinsley and his men worked hard at turning pine and oak trees into firewood and finished lumber. In January 1865 Holmstedt reported that he had "200,000 feet of lumber and over 300 cords of wood on Cat Island" ready for delivery. The problem, and it was a formidable one according to the colonel, was that he had no way of transporting the wood to Ship Island. In that same month an inspector general sent to review Holmstedt's post declared the Cat Island operation to be a total fiasco. He estimated that every cord of wood sitting on Cat Island, waiting for a nonexistent transport, cost the government a whopping two hundred fifty dollars. Not surprisingly, he recommended that the operation be shut down immediately.[107]

Again, Kinsley refused to complain about a situation that was marked by futility, boredom, danger, deprivation, and, once word got around that the men on Cat Island had been reduced to eating rats, humiliation. In fact, near the beginning of his fifth month on Cat Island, Kinsley wrote to his sister Lucretia that "Life is very far from monotonous" and "Time has passed *very* pleasantly. . . . " He even told his sister that the rats tasted "very good." He admitted that "It is a little dull to be so isolated from the world, but it may not be such a bad thing, after all." Here on Cat Island, and on Ship Island as well, one could concentrate on the little things, which of course were not really little at all, and one could contemplate, as Kinsley did in November 1864, the words of the prophet Zechariah: "Despise not the day of small things."[108]

Kinsley's words, written on an obscure little island on the periphery of the Confederacy, encourage us to reflect on what was central to the Civil War. Kinsley asks us to look beyond the occasional big battle to the little struggles that were fought every day across the entire South in small communities that experienced occupation and emancipation. Like a handful of other radical abolitionists, Kinsley understood that the destruction of slavery involved more than simply defeating Confederate soldiers on the battlefield. It also meant preparing freed slaves to participate in a democratic society, and to Kinsley that meant teaching them to read and write. On Cat Island, on Ship Island, at the contraband camp outside Algiers, and at the Sabbath school in Boston, Kinsley repeatedly demonstrated his commitment to the education of African Americans. The first thing he mentions in his diary, on his first full day on Cat Island, is building "a house at once, and a school house, also," and in his last entry about Cat Island he boasts of having built a "very good" second schoolhouse. Kinsley fervently believed that "In the education of the black is centered my hope for the redemption of the race, and the salvation of my country." From this perspective, Kinsley's labor beside the sea, which focused on the education of freed slaves, was as important as Sherman's march to the sea, which focused on the destruction of enemy soldiers. Both were essential to America's future.[109]

Recalled with his men in late February 1865, Kinsley summed up his stay on Cat Island: "Have passed the winter on Cat Island very pleasantly, and I hope with some profit to some of the men. Built two school houses, one very good, and spent much time in teaching soldiers and contraband children. Some of the soldiers who were slaves three years ago, and did not know a letter," he proudly reported, "can spell and read well all through Webster's spelling book, and are making good progress in arithmetic and geography." Two years later, a black officer who had served with Kinsley in the Second Corps d'Afrique remembered that some two hundred fugitive slaves had joined the regiment in a state of illiteracy, but left it "knowing how to read passably." In a poignant observation that Kinsley would have both affirmed and appreciated, he further recalled that as soon as the men "were free of their regular duties, they all had their books, and you could see them all day long trying to learn."[110]

During Kinsley's absence on Cat Island, Ship Island was transformed into an overcrowded detention center for Confederate prisoners of war. A steady stream of captured Rebel soldiers began arriving in October 1864, and by the time Kinsley returned in early March 1865 there were over seventeen hundred Confederate prisoners on Ship Island. As a result of the successful Union campaign to capture Mobile, there were more than four thousand Confederate soldiers incarcerated on the island by the end of April. Kinsley and his men joined in the grueling task of guarding this large, menacing population as the war slowly ground to a halt. Throughout the month of May nearly all the Confederate prisoners on Ship Island were sent to Vicksburg in exchange for Union prisoners who had been paroled by the Confederacy. On May 31 only ten prisoners remained on the island, and they were gone a week later.[111]

≋ Four ≋

In early July 1865, scarcely a month after the last Confederate prisoner left Ship Island, Kinsley decided to resign from the service. He applied to John H. Gihon, the regimental surgeon, for a medical certificate of disability upon which to base his application for an early discharge. After examining him on July 11, Gihon reported that Kinsley was suffering from an injured left knee that was "painful and produced lameness." In his opinion, Kinsley was "unfit for duty" and would remain so for at least three months. The next day Kinsley submitted his resignation "on account of 'Surgeon's certificate of disability.'" The resignation quickly worked its way up the chain of command, and on July 18, 1865, Major General E. R. S. Canby, commander of the Department of Louisiana and Texas, issued Special Orders No. 1, Extract No. 3, which granted Rufus Kinsley an honorable discharge.[112]

Since the surgeon's report stated that Kinsley would be incapacitated for three months, and his term of service expired in less than three months, the decision to accept Kinsley's resignation was routine. What was unusual about the disposition of Kinsley's application was the endorsement offered by the regiment's commanding officer, Colonel Ernest W. Holmstedt. Holmstedt wrote on the back of Kinsley's request: "for the *benefit of the service* highly recommended for approval." In plain language, Holmstedt was informing his superiors that he regarded Kinsley with disapprobation and thought the army would be better off without him. Holmstedt was not alone in this belief. Kinsley's previous commanding officer, Colonel William M. Grosvenor, despised him. Gihon, the regimental surgeon who signed his certificate of disability, disliked him and, despite Kinsley's indignant objection, stated in his official report that Kinsley had not hurt his knee "whilst in the line of duty," thereby making it impossible under existing pension laws for him to receive government disability payments for the injury.[113] Other officers filed formal complaints against Kinsley and openly declared their intention to drive him from the service. In fact, Kinsley appears to have had only one real friend among the officers stationed on Ship Island, the teetotaling Methodist, Captain James Noyes. When the other officers thought of Kinsley, they saw a moral zealot with piercing blue eyes, always watching, always weighing. Their hostility toward Kinsley perhaps helps explain why he was never promoted after his initial commission and why he was assigned the unenviable task of guarding Cat Island for six months.[114]

8. Endorsements in support of Kinsley's resignation from the Seventy-fourth United States Colored Infantry, including Colonel Ernest W. Holmstedt's recommendation that Kinsley's resignation be accepted "for the *benefit of the service*." Courtesy of the National Archives.

For his part, Kinsley was utterly contemptuous of the officers who ruled over Ship Island like the pharaohs over Egypt. On numerous occasions he lashed out at their incompetence and their hostility toward the freedmen, but what troubled him most was their complete lack of moral character. They were, according to Kinsley, a gang of "rum-sucking officers" who had forgotten their mothers and their manhood. With surviving military records revealing that every single one of the regiment's commanding officers had to face charges of improper conduct, it is easy to understand why Kinsley was so upset. To be sure, he would have admired the radical abolitionism and racial egalitarianism of the regiment's first commanding officer. But there was much about Colonel Nathan W. Daniels that would have greatly distressed Kinsley. Daniels was a free spirit who looked to clairvoyants rather than to Christ for guidance. He liked whiskey, champagne, cigars, and fast horses, and once lost five hundred dollars in a game of chance. He had an eye for pretty young women, allowing them stay with him at his quarters on Ship Island and letting them dress up in his uniform at festive parties. After sleeping with another soldier's wife, he blithely explained that if he didn't someone else would. Lieutenant Palfrey, who worked with Daniels on Ship Island, found him to be a "bad example" for his troops and "an unprincipled man . . . in a position to do a great deal of harm." The army agreed. Daniels was arrested and court-martialed for, among other things, unauthorized use of fifteen thousand feet of lumber. On August 11, 1863, just two weeks before Kinsley received his commission in the Second Corps d'Afrique, Daniels was dishonorably dismissed from the service.[115]

Lieutenant Colonel Alfred G. Hall followed Daniels as the commanding officer of the Second Corps d'Afrique. Hall's men accused him of being "drunk most of the time," and a medical report that appeared about the time Kinsley joined Hall on Ship Island pronounced him "suffering from congestion of the liver with a generally debilitated system." Like Daniels, Hall was "dishonorably dismissed" from the service.[116] Hall's successor was Colonel William M. Grosvenor. Kinsley recognized Grosvenor's skill as a drill instructor, but he had nothing else good to say about the man he described as "a genuine pro-slavery cotton-hearted negro hater." Grosvenor's blasphemous language also must have set Kinsley's teeth on edge. When a subordinate committed a minor infraction in April 1864, Grosvenor cursed at him: "By Jesus Christ, I will put you under arrest; God damn you, Sir, I will let you know that I command this Post: damn you dont say a word to me. By God you are too God damned lazy to attend to your business. . . . " A month later Grosvenor was court-martialed and dismissed from the service for keeping "a woman not his wife" in his quarters.[117]

The regiment's next and final commanding officer was Colonel Ernest W. Holmstedt.[118] Like his predecessors, Holmstedt was eventually charged with a number of transgressions. Kinsley's good friend James Noyes and others from the regiment testified that, in addition to lying, stealing, and gambling, Holmstedt had been party to an illegal liquor ring that sold beer, wine, brandy, and whiskey to Confederate prisoners as well as Union soldiers. To top things off, Holmstedt's alleged improper conduct included showing a fundamental disrespect for his black troops. According to the charges, he loudly and angrily asked First Lieutenant William C. Abbe "if he would 'believe a nigger's word in preference to a white mans,' or words to that effect, in the presence of enlisted men of his own regiment, who are all colored men."[119]

While disgusted with the regiment's commanding officers, Kinsley saved his most insulting comments for a man whose views seemed to parallel his own. Stephen A. Hodgman, the regiment's original chaplain, had himself complained that under Lieutenant Colonel Hall's leadership the regiment was "going down for the want of discipline," and like Kinsley he believed that Southern chivalry was a sham, that efforts to prove black inferiority were "puerile and ridiculous," and that black soldiers were as courageous and hardworking as any other soldiers. He further maintained that America was "*guilty*" of tolerating "the most matured system of iniquity and oppression, that devils or wicked men ever yet devised," and that the Civil War "was intended [by God] as a righteous and just judgment for the sin of slavery." But instead of making the sacrifices necessary to see this holy war through to its glorious conclusion, instead of reenlisting for the duration of the war as Kinsley did, instead of fighting corrupt commanding officers like Hall and Grosvenor whatever the consequences, Chaplain Hodgman abandoned his flock and resigned from the regiment after serving for barely a year. According to Kinsley, he "got frightened," gave up "in despair," and "ran home to his mother, where he should have stayed, instead of coming here."[120]

Kinsley made no effort to curry favor with such men. He refused to turn over runaway slaves to officers he thought abusive. He refused to sign a petition circulated by his fellow officers attesting to the good character of an officer he believed hated blacks. When ordered by his commanding officer to distribute whiskey among his men for a toast celebrating Christmas, he asked to be excused from that duty, climbed upon a barrel from which he delivered a temperance speech, and watched with satisfaction as most of his men poured their drinks into the sand. Kinsley did not worry about what his fellow officers thought of him; their disdain only affirmed the purity of his mission. Answering to a higher authority, Kinsley was not intimidated by the murmurings of mere mortals. He was guided by the gospel of Jesus Christ, who taught his followers that "Blessed are those who are persecuted for righteousness' sake, for theirs is the kingdom of heaven."[121]

Officers were not the only ones to incur Kinsley's wrath. He could also be severe in his judgment of errant enlisted men, as two episodes illustrate. The first occurred near Algiers in the summer of 1862 when a band of Confederate guerrillas ambushed some soldiers from Kinsley's regiment shortly after they had returned fifteen runaway slaves to their masters. Kinsley apparently felt little sympathy for the men who were killed and wounded in the attack. From his perspective, they were complicitous in an immoral act, and the fact that they were young soldiers following the orders of a highly respected commanding officer made no difference. Although he acknowledged that the dead and injured soldiers from his regiment looked "bad, very bad," Kinsley proceeded to note in a remarkably cold passage in his diary that "as I look at it, they were engaged in bad business." He then sanctions this hard-hearted judgment by quoting scripture: "Verily I say unto you they shall receive their reward."[122]

The second episode involved Laura S. Haviland, a prominent evangelical abolitionist who visited Ship Island and the hundreds of Union soldiers who were imprisoned there in April 1864. Upon seeing the horrendous condition of the prisoners, and learning that most of the men were guilty of minor infractions but had received outrageously harsh sentences from a notoriously vindictive judge, Sister Haviland launched what would ultimately become a successful crusade for their release.[123] Although Haviland's efforts won the enthusiastic support of both Kinsley's close friend Captain James Noyes and his bitter enemy Colonel William Grosvenor, Kinsley apparently remained indifferent to the fate of these wayward Yankees. He never wrote sympathetically about them – they are "hardened wretches" in his only vague allusion to their existence – and he never acknowledged anywhere in his diary or surviving correspondence that the prisoners he and his men were guarding most of the time were not Confederate but fellow Union soldiers. Moreover, while Kinsley praises Haviland and her good works on several occasions, he never mentions her campaign to liberate the Union soldiers incarcerated on Ship Island, although it became the focal point of her seven-day visit and achieved the status of a cause célèbre in the Department of the Gulf.[124]

Kinsley's encounter with Sister Haviland is instructive not only because it reveals the limits of his Christian charity but also because it suggests that at some level perhaps he was anxious about his role in the war. The visit of this "Godly woman, full of faith and the Holy Ghost," prompted Kinsley not to take up the cause of badly treated and unjustly imprisoned Union soldiers, but to confess that he is "not satisfied with his attainments in the divine life" and to ask that he be "remembered at a throne of grace." Given Kinsley's belief that the Civil War was a holy war and that he was a Christian soldier in the ranks of God, he may have felt some disappointment, perhaps even shame, that in the great apocalyptic struggle to abolish the sin of slavery he spent much of his time not fighting Confederate soldiers, not even guarding Confederate prisoners, but watching over the dregs of the Union army. If so, perhaps Haviland, who recognized that Kinsley was a fervent abolitionist and a man of "sterling principle," put his mind to rest, for after she "earnestly remembered" him at a season of prayer, he declared himself "greatly encouraged."[125]

If Haviland's prayers inspired Kinsley to continue in his iconoclastic ways, so did the exemplary lives of the two men he wrote about most reverently during the Civil War. One was Benjamin F. Butler, the other John Brown. Kinsley wrote to his father about Butler in late November 1864: "Next after President Lincoln's reelection we niggers hurrah loudest for General Butler." Naturally, Kinsley supported Lincoln's reelection in 1864 – the alternative was the copperhead George B. McClellan – but he also thought Lincoln a compromiser who followed a policy of pacifying traitors in the border states and who lacked the courage to follow the will of the people, who "were ripe for the extermination of traitors."[126] In contrast to Lincoln, Butler, according to Kinsley, was a man of principle who was maligned and marginalized for his righteous antislavery convictions by those who compromise with evil. As for John Brown, here was a man of pure antislavery ideals, whom Kinsley had "believed in and loved" since 1856 when the old man took up his sword against slavery in Kansas. Again the compromisers came forward, this time to discredit Brown by calling him a crazed and cold-blooded murderer. Unfazed by the charges, Brown persevered and went on to lead his famous raid on Harper's Ferry in 1859. Kinsley revered Brown because he acted upon his belief that slavery was a sin. Indeed, Kinsley was probably among those radical abolitionists who came to think of Brown's execution in terms of Christ's crucifixion. For a man like Kinsley, who regularly taught Bible-study classes while stationed on Ship Island, the example of Christ dying to make men free was always close at hand.[127]

But for Kinsley, as for his beloved John Brown, it was not the compassionate and forgiving Christ of the New Testament who sustained his personal war against slavery. Instead, the God repeatedly invoked by

Kinsley was the stern and unforgiving patriarch of the Old Testament, a vengeful Jehovah who meant to punish Southerners for the sin of slavery. Thus in January 1863, after looking out over the once lush Lafourche region of Louisiana and seeing only wasted land and deserted villages, Kinsley wrote in his diary that "The South is being burned with fire, and drowned in blood. . . . I am content. Slavery must die; and if the South insists on being buried in the same grave, I shall see in it nothing but the retributive hand of God. I thank God I live to see the day when the South is beginning to *burn*; and that it is my privilege to help kindle the fires." Two years later he compared the South to the filthy Augean stables of Greek mythology and recommended that blood rather than water be used to clean them. Only once, after describing the desolation along the Mississippi coast in June 1865, did Kinsley seem at all troubled by the unbridled joy he felt upon seeing the death and destruction Union forces had inflicted upon the South. "Do you think it is wicked?" he asked rhetorically. His answer was reassuring, and it echoed similar responses to the South's suffering offered by Wendell Phillips, Frederick Douglass, Harriet Beecher Stowe, and other ardent abolitionists: "I can't help it: I love to see it so. I see the hand of God."[128]

To Kinsley, white Southerners, by maintaining the institution of slavery, were guilty of a monstrous crime. And because of his belief that everyone had the capacity to accept Christ and combat sin, his indictment of the white South exempted no one, not even "the poorest of 'pore white trash,'" whom he dismissed as "ignorant as mules." Kinsley was confident that white Southerners would pay for their unspeakable crimes, for he had always believed in "a law of compensation," under which "all men and all nations are sure to receive, some where, some time, the exact measure of their deserts." But beyond his desire to see them severely punished, Kinsley was indifferent to the fate of white Southerners, most of whom he believed would remain forever opposed to the emancipation and education of the nation's slaves. In Kinsley's case, Lincoln's eloquent appeal to Americans in his Second Inaugural Address to bind up the nation's wounds with malice toward none and with charity for all, fell on deaf ears.[129]

Kinsley had not traveled all the way from the Canadian border to the Gulf of Mexico to save unrepentant slaveholders, any more than he had come to reform drunken officers or rehabilitate incarcerated soldiers. He had come to free the enslaved, to redeem the innocent, to spread light among those who had been kept in darkness for two hundred fifty

years. He had come to atone for what America had done to the children
of Africa, and he thanked God "for the privilege I have enjoyed of sowing
seed while soldiering in the South." Fashioning himself a savior as well as
a soldier, Kinsley invested his Civil War experience with the highest moral
purpose. He could leave the army with an abiding sense of pride in what
he had accomplished under the most difficult circumstances. Indeed, in
the coming years, his Civil War experience would be the primary source
of his identity and self-esteem. He was Lieutenant Rufus Kinsley for the
rest of his life.[130]

Kinsley's discharge papers arrived at Ship Island on July 21, 1865. Four
days later he was on a steamer bound for Mobile, where he inspected
abandoned Confederate fortifications and visited freedmen's schools before sailing to New Orleans. After nearly a month in the Crescent City, he
worked his way up the Mississippi to Cairo, Illinois. There, on August 24,
he booked passage for Boston, where he stopped long enough to look
up some old friends before heading home to Fletcher. He returned to
the same house he had lived in nearly four years earlier when he first
enlisted.[131]

Because Kinsley was not discharged from the army until the summer
of 1865, he missed his chance to participate in the grand victory parade of thousands of Union soldiers down Pennsylvania Avenue from the
Capitol to the White House on May 23, 1865. But a year later Kinsley did
participate in an extraordinary celebration of the war's end. In the final
months of 1864 the five Kinsley brothers who had enlisted in the Union
army agreed that, if they all survived the war, they would hold a family reunion in Fletcher, at their father's home. At the time these plans
were laid, Ben Kinsley's children were scattered across the nation in
Massachusetts, Maryland, Virginia, Iowa, Louisiana, and Texas. But on
April 4, 1866, barely three weeks after Kinsley's brother Jason was
mustered out of the First Iowa Cavalry, they were all in Fletcher.[132]

The reunion was a joyful occasion. Throughout the day family, friends,
and relatives exchanged social gossip, swapped war stories, and listened to speeches by Ben Kinsley, "several of the soldier boys," and the
Reverend Edwin Wheelock, a longtime family friend. The festivities
reached their peak with everyone feasting on a pan of hot sugar and
singing patriotic songs – this was probably about as rowdy as the Kinsleys
ever got. They never strayed too far from the path of righteousness. For
them the reunion was a time of reflection and thanksgiving as well as
celebration. Late that night Daniel Kinsley, one of the brothers who had

not gone off to war, wrote that "Perhaps a more remarkable family gathering never occurred than one assembled in this town today.... [W]e have this day assembled around the fireside of our aged father, (himself an old soldier), an unbroken family of seven sons and one daughter ... to make glad our hearts and to praise God for his preserving care over us."[133]

Daniel knew that the Kinsleys had been lucky – or rather blessed – and so did his father, who throughout the war was keenly aware that his sons were constantly at risk, subject to all kinds of obvious as well as unforeseen dangers. In January 1864, for example, he wrote to Rufus: "We were beginning to feel some anxiety on your account as we have not heard a word or seen a line from you for a long time, we began to fear you had been betrayed into the hands of those who threaten to wreak their vengeance dire upon all who should dare to act as officers of the bondman, or in any way assist time to put off his yoke, & there are so many changes & vicissitudes in war; that men are not always secure when they feel safe."[134] But when the war ended Rufus and his brothers were safe. They had survived deadly fevers, serious accidents, and battle wounds acquired at places like Bull Run, Cedar Creek, Brashear City, Pleasant Hill, and Petersburg. They had served a combined total of seventeen years in a war that claimed over six hundred thousand lives, and had come home to tell about it. Their collective homecoming was all the more remarkable because they returned to a state that, in relation to the number of men of military age, lost more lives in the war than any other state in the Union. One of every six Vermont soldiers died in the war, and one of every five who served with Kinsley in the Eighth Vermont never came home again.[135]

But if one purpose of the reunion was to thank God for sparing the lives of Alonzo, Jason, Edgar, William, and Rufus Kinsley, another was to give thanks for the preservation of a nation that had finally rid itself of the barbarism of slavery and embraced the principles of freedom and equality. In "Home from the War," a poem written especially for the reunion, Jason Kinsley observed:

> We can thank God to-night it hath not been in vain,
> These years of bloody strife, of weary toil and pain;
> The war, so fiercely waged, hath rent the Bondman's chain.
>
> . . . .
>
> From Slavery's blighting curse our land at last is free;
> And as it is to-night, so shall it always be,
> The land of *Equal Rights*," the "*Home of Liberty!*"[136]

In its final stanza Jason's poem, like Daniel's late-night musings, returned to the theme of family, safe at home.

> All Home at last,
> Safe Home once more,
> Our dangers past,
> Our trials o'er
> Each happy heart to-night with joyful music rings,
> A glad thanksgiving hymn to God, the King of Kings.

But things were not quite as safe and serene as Jason suggested. Two years later, the "Home" was gone. Ben Kinsley, after having lived almost his entire adult life in Fletcher, packed up his belongings and moved to Lowell, Vermont.[137] Nor were all the "trials" and "dangers past." Indeed, at the very moment Jason was proclaiming in his poem that each of the five returning soldiers "still bears aloft a strong and true right hand" to fight for "Truth and Right," Rufus Kinsley's right hand was already swollen by a debilitating disease that would plague him the rest of his life. We do not know what Rufus thought about this part of Jason's poem or about Daniel's observation that his brothers, although "war-worn, weary, and wounded," had returned "every one with body unmaimed and constitution unbroken."[138] We do know, however, that Kinsley was about to begin another, less glamorous battle for survival and dignity.

During his stopover in Boston on his way home from the war, Kinsley was offered a position as foreman of a printshop. He could not accept it, he later wrote, because "my hands were so swollen and stiff with rheumatism that I could not empty a 'stick' or pick up a handful of 'matter' without 'pi.'" The problem did not go away, and Kinsley was, in fact, never again able to unload a compositor's tray or gather up set type without spilling it. He still had the intelligence and good memory required of all successful printers, but he lacked the digital dexterity needed to pick up narrow slugs of metal type, set them in a small composing tray, and then transfer them to a shallow galley tray. "I have been *absolutely prevented* from following my usual occupation [of printer] ever since the war closed," he wrote in 1886. His brother Edgar and his aunt Elvira, with whom he lived after returning to Fletcher, confirmed that before the war he had worked regularly as a printer for at least twenty-five dollars a week, but that "since the war he has not been able to work at his trade at all. . . . " According to Edgar, when his brother arrived home in the fall of 1865, he was "all broken down," suffering from chronic diarrhea as well as from rheumatism in his knee, back, hip, and hands. His aunt emphasized that Kinsley had experienced an especially bad bout of rheumatism in the spring of 1866. "I am able to fix the date," she said, "from the fact that we had a family reunion at that time." The same reunion that inspired Jason to write his poem and Daniel to marvel at the triumphant return home of the five "unmaimed" and "unbroken" soldier brothers would later remind their Aunt Elvira just how broken down Rufus was only a year after the war ended.[139]

Unable to resume his trade as a printer, Kinsley worked as a farmhand for his brother Edgar and for other neighbors. Like most agricultural labor, the work was hard and monotonous: a day of hauling stone, a day of plowing, three days of splitting wood, four days of digging a ditch, and so forth. But on some days Kinsley was able to work only half a day according to Edgar's diary. Moreover, as Kinsley himself stated, he was on some occasions, "for several weeks at a time, unable to work at all...." A physician who treated him during one of these rheumatic "attacks" in June 1868 found him "entirely incapacitated from performing any manual labor...." According to his aunt, Kinsley never regained his health while living with her and Edgar, which he did until October 1868, when he moved to North Hero, a long sliver of an island in Lake Champlain.[140]

Why Kinsley moved to an isolated island in a desperately poor county remains a mystery. Perhaps his inability to perform the back-breaking work expected of farm laborers induced him to accept the much less physically demanding position of store clerk on North Hero. Perhaps he wanted to take advantage of the medicinal springs located on the island. Perhaps he was enticed by invitations from friends and relatives who were living there. Or perhaps the war-weary Kinsley, who had not had a day off duty during his last two years in the army, needed the peace, serenity, and soothing water views offered by this thinly populated island of six thousand heavily forested acres. For whatever reason, Kinsley took up residence in a small village on North Hero, where he worked as a clerk for sixteen months before moving back to his brother Edgar's farm in February 1870. Four months later, when interviewed by a federal census taker, Kinsley identified himself as a "farm laborer" and reported owning no property of any value. In contrast, Edgar was listed as a "farmer" with assets valued at nine thousand dollars.[141]

Kinsley may have returned to Fletcher to court Ella Lenora Bingham, who was born in Fletcher on June 8, 1851. A friend of her older brother since childhood, Kinsley probably remembered the day she was born.

In 1870 she lived on a modest farm with her father, mother, two sisters, and a brother. She accepted Kinsley's proposal, and on April 10, 1872, the twenty-year-old farm girl married the forty-year-old war veteran. After the ceremony, which was conducted by a Methodist minister in nearby Cambridge, Kinsley carried his young bride some fifty miles by handsled to the farm in Lowell where his father had settled in early 1869 and lived until his death in December 1870. Actually, Ella and Rufus had traveled to Lowell a few days before their wedding to purchase the family farm from Ben Kinsley's widow Lucy, which explains why they were listed as residents of Lowell on their wedding certificate. On April 6, 1872, Kinsley agreed to pay forty-two hundred dollars for the 275-acre parcel, which was fifteen hundred dollars less than his father had paid for it just three and a half years earlier. Lucy, who never bore any children of her own and was fond of Rufus, also accepted a small down payment and a promissory note to pay the remaining debt over the next five years. Two years later, however, Kinsley and his brother Daniel took out a new $4,000 mortgage on the home farm and paid off the remaining debt to Lucy, who renounced her claim to the place.[142]

When Rufus and Ella took possession of the farm, Lucy, who under the purchase agreement had the right to retain "the widow's homestead," was still living there. At the time of the purchase, Kinsley's brother Alonzo, his wife Emma, their two-year-old daughter Ethel, and a young female domestic were also living on the farm. In fact in June 1870 thirty-four-year-old Alonzo, who had moved to Lowell to live with his father on January 15, 1869, was listed in the census as the head of the household and the owner of real estate valued at $5,700, which was exactly how much Ben Alva had paid for the farm in 1868. But by 1875, Lucy, Alonzo, Emma, Ethel, and the domestic were gone. Kinsley's brother had left for Fletcher shortly after Rufus and Ella arrived in Lowell, and in October 1874 his stepmother had moved to Lancaster, New York, where she died in 1881.[143]

Rufus and Ella lost no time in starting a family. Every year and a half for the first seven years following their marriage, Ella gave birth to a child. Then, after a two-and-a-half-year hiatus, two more children were born over the next three years. By September 1884, twelve years after their marriage, Rufus and Ella had seven children: Clayton, Benton, Amy, Lester, Leroy, F. Guy, and Chellis. Ella's sister Emma, who served as midwife at the births, grew tired of making the long trip from Fletcher to Lowell, and took Rufus to task for having too many children. He wryly reminded her

9. Kinsley, his wife, and children, circa 1895. Front row, seated, left to right: F. Guy, Chellis, Leroy. Middle row, seated, left to right: Benton, Rufus, Amy. Back row, standing, left to right: Ella Bingham, Clayton, Lester. Courtesy Reba Kinsley Hall.

that "the Bible tells us we must multiply and replenish the earth." "I know that," she replied, "but it does not say that Rufus Kinsley has to do it all by himself."[144]

The Kinsleys raised their daughter and six sons in Lowell, a triangle-shaped township situated roughly sixteen miles from the Canadian border in the western part of Orleans County. Surrounded by lofty mountains timbered with birch, beech, maple, spruce, and hemlock, and cut through by the Missisquoi River as well as a rugged range of serpentine, Lowell offered its inhabitants scenic vistas of breathtaking beauty. But the Lowell environment also meant a short growing season, a brutal winter, and a hilly, broken landscape that was tough to farm, especially in areas where the soil consisted primarily of clay or sand. As census returns for both Orleans County and Lowell suggest, this was a hard place to make a living. Of Vermont's fourteen counties in 1870, Orleans ranked ninth in the value of farms, tenth in the value of farm products, and eleventh in the value of manufactured products. With the average resident reporting property worth $598, Orleans County also ranked eleventh in the value of real and personal estate. The figures for Lowell were even worse, with the average (or per capita) wealth standing at about $531 per resident. In the face of these findings few could be optimistic about Lowell's prospects, although at the time one sanguine resident described Lowell village, the township's economic center, as "2 stores, 1 hotel, a post-office, 2 houses for public worship, 2 starch-factories, 2 clapboard-mills, 1 grist-mill, about 30 dwellings and a chance for improvement." Population figures from later censuses indicate, however, that most took a less Pollyannaish view of Lowell's future. After growing steadily from 430 inhabitants in 1840 to about 940 when Kinsley arrived in 1872, Lowell's population leveled off. In the next thirty years it experienced a net growth of only 40 residents.[145]

Unlike thousands of other inhabitants of small Vermont towns who in the second half of the nineteenth century responded to economic stagnation and dwindling opportunity by migrating to Eastern cities or Western farms, Kinsley remained in Lowell. There, on a hilly farm of 50 acres of cultivated land, 100 acres of forest, and 125 acres of permanent meadow, pasture, and orchard, he struggled to attain self-sufficiency by raising a variety of crops and selling off small surpluses. In 1880 his crops included corn, potatoes, hay, barley, pulse, apples, and maple sugar. His livestock consisted of 1 horse, 1 pig, 4 cattle, 6 sheep, 11 chickens, and 13 milch cows, which allowed him to produce 1,600 pounds of butter. Still, the estimated value of his farm's total output in 1880 was only $635, nearly $1,100 less than it had been in 1870 when Alonzo was running the farm.[146] Clearly, Kinsley was struggling to provide for his wife and children; indeed, six years later Ella's brother bluntly declared that "the need of the family . . . is very great." A successful physician who lived in Burlington, LeRoy M. Bingham blamed the family's dire straits not on a harsh

10. Kinsley, his brothers, and sister, on the front porch of Edgar Kinsley Montague's home in Binghamville, Vermont, circa 1891. Front row, left to right: William, Rufus, Jason, Alonzo. Back row, left to right: Guy, Daniel, Lucretia, Edgar. Courtesy of Reba Kinsley Hall.

illnesses.[151] Her children, while still very young, helped out on the farm by gathering sugar, milking cows, harvesting hay, and doing other jobs that demanded hard physical labor. As teenagers they often took jobs in the village or on neighboring farms, jobs that occasionally resulted in a lost thumb, a badly lacerated hand, or, as the case of fifteen-year-old Chellis illustrates, being knocked unconscious while trying to repair an elevator in a tub factory.[152] Not surprisingly, the family's need for supplementary income took a toll on the children's formal education. Indeed, according to Kinsley's granddaughter, none of his children graduated from high school, and her father F. Guy never got beyond the eighth grade.[153]

When the oldest children came of age and moved away, they returned regularly to see their parents and help with the farm. Even after he was married and living in Boston, Clayton spent his summer vacations on the family farm. Benton, the second oldest, followed in his brother's footsteps by moving to Boston and by making regular trips back to the family homestead. When Benton died at age thirty-two, the local press described him as "a faithful son . . . whose life was an example of love and obedience."[154] Other Kinsley children appear to have delayed leaving home, perhaps so they could help with the endless round of daily chores that accompanied life on a nineteenth-century farm. Amy, Lester, and Leroy continued to live on the farm in 1900 when they were in their twenties. In 1910 twenty-nine-year-old F. Guy and twenty-six-year-old Chellis were still there taking care of their father and working his farm.[155]

Over the years, Kinsley found many reasons to be proud of his children – Lester was the center fielder on Lowell's baseball team, Clayton was an officer in a temperance society, Benton was a graduate of Burdette Business College in Boston, Amy was one of the most popular schoolteachers in Orleans County, and so forth – but probably nothing they did brought him greater satisfaction than the sacrifices they made to keep his family intact during its formative years. He knew from his own childhood that poverty could break families apart prematurely.[156]

But distant relatives and small children could do only so much, and Kinsley was fortunate to have friends and neighbors who rallied around a newcomer in need. Certainly, some of the support emanated from the friendships that his father, stepmother, and brothers had made prior to his arrival in Lowell in 1872.[157] Perhaps more important, Kinsley appears to have quickly won the respect of his fellow townspeople by establishing himself as a good neighbor, genial host, and civic-minded resident. He and Ella were known throughout the community for their hospitality, which included entertaining family, friends, and neighbors at parties and wedding receptions that featured music, games, ice cream, and cake. Given Kinsley's inquisitive mind, it is not surprising that one of his parties culminated in the formation of a study group, and it seems probable that he was active in the town lyceum, which was presided over by his brother William and debated issues such as whether "Washington was a greater man than Lincoln." As the people of Lowell got to know Rufus Kinsley, his popularity grew and eventually he was elected town moderator, a position of importance and esteem in the small towns that dotted the landscape of nineteenth-century New England.[158]

Kinsley was also integrated into Lowell society through his organizational commitments and connections. Soon after taking up residence in the tight-knit, mountain-locked little community, Kinsley joined the Baptist Church, where he taught Sunday school and was warmly welcomed into the congregation by Reverend Joseph Buzzell, an old friend from Fletcher. He was ecumenical enough, however, to attend events at the Congregational Church, where his brother William sang in the choir, and to allow the Methodists to hold picnics in his backyard.[159]

Kinsley also joined the Mount Norris Lodge of the Independent Order of Good Templars. Founded in 1852, the Good Templars were a fraternal organization that held weekly meetings featuring rituals, regalia, recitations, popular songs, religious hymns, and speeches. It featured as well the popular election of officers, and in May 1873, scarcely a year after Kinsley arrived in Lowell, the lodge's seventy-two members chose him to serve as Chief Templar.[160] The members of the Norris Lodge who elected Kinsley to their highest office were unique in their diversity. Most fraternal societies of postwar America claimed to welcome all men, but in reality were comprised primarily of middle-aged, middle-class white Protestant males, and virtually no fraternal orders admitted women except in sexsegregated auxiliaries. The Good Templars, in contrast, embraced a universalist ideology that offered full membership rights to the young, the poor, the black, and the female. Incredibly, a third of all Templars were women, and in Kinsley's lodge it was not unusual for half the elected officials to be women, and their posts included everything from assistant secretary to Chief Templar.[161]

The Templars were not, however, just a social club that provided fun and fellowship to female as well as male members. With several hundred thousand members nationwide, the Templars were also the largest temperance society in America in the decades immediately following the Civil

War. To become a member one had to promise total abstinence from alcoholic beverages. The order's primary goal was to convince everyone else to do likewise, and the Mount Norris Lodge had been saving souls "from the jaws of the fiery-demon" since 1866. Membership in the Good Templars thus allowed Kinsley to keep alive his utopian vision of a republic that was free of alcohol as well as slaves. Not surprisingly, Kinsley simultaneously pursued his dream of a dry nation in another anti-liquor league, the Lowell Temperance Society. In 1876 he was elected treasurer of the society's annual meeting; the year before he had gained notice in the local press by winning a spelling bee that concluded one of the society's largest meetings.[162]

Undoubtedly, the Vermont Templars held a special appeal for Kinsley because of their stand against lodges, predominantly in the South, that sought to deny membership to African Americans on the basis of race. The local press recognized that the Templars were about more than fellowship and temperance and that the problem of racial bigotry knew no geographical boundaries. On March 16, 1874, the editors of the *Orleans County Monitor* called upon the Good Templars of Lowell to prepare to fight the Ku Klux Klan. According to the paper, a group of men, all masked and some partially dressed in military uniforms, had brazenly ridden on horseback through the streets of nearby Newport Center in the early evening after having defiantly announced in advance their intention to do so in handbills posted around town. The article concluded: "To-arms, ye Grangers and Good Templars! 'Twas the Ku-Klux-Klan!" Perhaps the editors looked to the Templars to stop the Klan because the two men who headed the Mount Norris Lodge immediately before the unsettling incident at Newport Center were former soldiers in the war against slavery. Their names were Rufus and William Kinsley.[163]

Kinsley also joined Hazen Post, No. 74, of the Grand Army of the Republic (GAR), an association of Civil War veterans that was founded in 1866. Later remembered primarily as a special-interest lobby for aging veterans and a partisan front for the Republican Party, the GAR was initially a fraternal order that focused on providing veterans with fellowship and, in some cases, sustenance. Over the years, membership in the GAR offered Kinsley the opportunity to make new friendships and reaffirm old ones; to attend picnics and campfires; to hold a variety of offices, including that of chaplain; to represent Hazen Post, No. 74, at a massive encampment of veterans in Burlington, where according to the local press "Lieut. Kinsley was able to contribute important facts of the war" that "were greatly prized by those who are preparing a history of the place Vermont had in the great struggle"; to write moving tributes to fallen members that celebrated the "ties of comradeship" and promised to keep the departed in "sacred rememberance" [*sic*]; and to participate in Memorial Day services, at which virtually the entire village of Lowell paid homage to its surviving Civil War heroes and civilian speakers testified to their "sympathy and love for the veterans of the war."[164]

Some of that love and sympathy was directed specifically toward Rufus Kinsley, according to Lewis J. Ingalls, a member of Hazen Post, No. 74. Kinsley and Ingalls had known each other during the Civil War, when they served together in the Eighth Vermont. About 1874, a couple of years after Kinsley settled in Lowell, Ingalls began doing seasonal labor on his old comrade's farm. From that time forward, according to Ingalls, although Kinsley was "unable to do more than half an able bodied mans [*sic*] work," he got by because the people of Lowell picked him up when times were tough. Ingalls remembered that in the summer of 1883, for example, Kinsley "was laid up three months – and unable to do any work and the nabors [*sic*] turned out and planted his crop and did his haying."[165] Two of these neighbors, Andrew Richardson and Oliver Newton, confirmed Ingalls's observation. They recalled in 1890 that since his arrival in Lowell in 1872, Kinsley had "been so much of the time helpless that a large number of his neighbors have from time to time assisted him."[166]

Kinsley appreciated the support. "My neighbors have helped me splendidly," he acknowledged, "and my relatives at a distance have done for me more than I have any right to expect. ... " But even this family and community largesse was not enough. On February 2, 1886, less than a year and a half after the birth of his son Chellis had expanded his household to include a wife and seven children twelve or younger, Kinsley turned to the federal government for help. After all, he wrote, "being much of the time helpless, and none of the time able to do half work, I feel bound to ask the Government in whose service I ruined my health, to give me a pension."[167]

☙ Five ❧

Kinsley had waited twenty-one years after his discharge from the Union army to apply for a pension. In failing to make a pension claim until long after the war ended, Kinsley was typical of most Civil War veterans. Twenty years after the war ended only 17 percent of all Union veterans were enrolled as pensioners. But over the next twenty years the figure jumped from 17 percent in 1885 to 83 percent in 1905. In 1886, when Kinsley applied, there were 365,783 veterans receiving pensions that cost the government about $67 million a year. Seven years later in 1893 there were nearly a million pensioners and the federal government was spending an astounding 42 percent of its income on their benefits. Like Kinsley, many of the beneficiaries hailed from Vermont. In fact in 1900 one out of every thirty-seven residents of the state received a pension, and ten years later Vermont ranked second among the nation's 46 states in per capita pension disbursements.[168]

Kinsley knew first-hand about the pension system long before he applied. His father, stepmother, and brothers William, Jason, and Alonzo had all taken advantage of government programs for former soldiers and their widows. Moreover, whatever Kinsley had failed to learn about pensions at home, he undoubtedly learned at meetings of Hazen Post, No. 74. In its role as lobbyist, the GAR sought to improve the quality of pensions granted to its members, as well as keep its constituents abreast of the bewildering number of changes in the content and interpretation of federal pension legislation. It was probably at these local GAR meetings that Kinsley, his brother William, Lewis Ingalls, and other veterans first discussed the pros and cons of applying for a pension. For someone with Kinsley's history of self-reliance and independence, the decision to become a special pleader at the public trough must have been difficult. Moreover, to receive a pension under the narrowly conceived federal pension law of 1862, a soldier not only had to admit that he was permanently disabled, but he had to prove conclusively that the disability was a consequence of military service. Even under the much more liberal pension act of 1890, which removed the necessity of proving that one's disability was caused by the war, pensioners were seen as dependent wards of the state who could not take care of themselves. Kinsley seems to have genuinely believed that he had earned a pension by sacrificing his health in the service of his country. He may even have believed, as did the members of many small, rural GAR posts that were dominated by ordinary soldiers instead of commissioned officers, that, as saviors of the nation, all Civil War soldiers deserved an honorable *service* pension rather than a demeaning *disability* or *dependent* pension.[169]

Whatever his precise position on this issue, Kinsley, like the vast majority of Civil War pension applicants, attributed his disability to diseases contracted while in the service rather than injuries received in battle. Specifically, he complained of rheumatism and chronic diarrhea, the two diseases cited most by Civil War pension applicants as the cause of their disability. Unfortunately, pension claims alleging that diseases contracted in military service later caused disability were much more difficult for Pension Bureau officials to evaluate than straightforward claims citing, say, the loss of an eye, arm, or leg. Calling the adjudication of claims based upon disease "a field of obscurity and uncertainty," the most careful student of Civil War pensions has concluded that the more one "penetrates into the obscurities of the system the more he is apt to regard the complicated practice of the Pension Bureau as likely to achieve either the arbitrary or the absurd – and sometimes both."[170] It appears that Kinsley reached the same conclusion after his repeated appeals for an increase in benefits fell short of his expectations.

Perhaps the arbitrariness of the bureau's rulings, along with the absurdity of having to prove that he deserved a pension, explain why Kinsley (and his relatives) occasionally provided misleading and contradictory testimony in support of his application.[171] Unfortunately for the historian attempting to determine the merit of Kinsley's various claims, some of this testimony is simply impossible to reconcile with other surviving evidence. For example, Kinsley informed the bureau in 1886 that "From 1847 to the beginning of the war I worked in a printing office. . . . " But in fact he quit his printing job in Boston four years before the outbreak of war and moved back to Vermont, where he lived on his brother's farm and was listed as a "laborer" in the 1860 census. Kinsley also declared before a board of three medical examiners in April 1886 that he did not quit his occupation as a printer until 1882, when he "was obliged to give it up from the fact that his fingers were so stiff from rheumatism that he could not handle type." But this testimony is suspect because Kinsley had previously informed the bureau that he had been unable to work as a printer "ever since the war closed" and because his brother Edgar, with whom he lived upon returning home from the Gulf South in the fall of 1865, said the same thing. Moreover, with the exception of sixteen months when he clerked in a store, there is no evidence that Kinsley had any job other than farming after he returned from the war. In the 1870 U.S. census returns Kinsley appears as a "farm laborer" living in Fletcher, and in 1880 he appears as a "farmer" living in Lowell. If Kinsley still described himself as a printer in 1882, it was because he liked to think of himself as a printer, not because he actually was one.[172]

In his testimony before the three medical examiners Kinsley further declared that he began to suffer from "chronic diarrhea" in April 1863 and that it had "followed him ever since." But by the end of July 1863 Kinsley wrote that he was "in good health," and he never mentioned having diarrhea again during the war. By the end of December he stated that his weight had shot up from the roughly 80 pounds he weighed in the spring to 170 pounds, 40 more than he had ever weighed. In June 1864 he told his father that he was "in perfect health," and a month later he assured his sister that he had "not seen an unwell day for nearly a year." In November he again told his father that he was in "perfect health." He repeated this mantra, but with a slight twist, in a diary entry of June 17, 1865, only a month before his discharge: "In perfect health, except lame knee." The exception – that is, the lame left knee – would play a central role in Kinsley's efforts to prove that his postwar rheumatism had its origins in the Civil War.[173]

In his earliest correspondence with the bureau about his rheumatism, Kinsley maintained that his battle with the dreaded disease began in February 1863 when he injured his left knee while sleeping in an awkward position on a plantation near Bayou Boeuf, Louisiana. In subsequent depositions, Kinsley remained faithful to these basic facts, but offered differing accounts of what happened to him after he sustained the injury. According to one deposition that Kinsley filed with the bureau, the injury rendered him disabled for duty for only "a few days"; thereafter, he said, "I had no more trouble with it until about March 1865 when the rheumatism attacked me in my left knee. . . . " But in other testimony he claimed that the injury at Bayou Boeuf "resulted in extreme weakness and constant lameness which has followed him ever since, and that rheumatism about this time [February 1863] set in, and that he has not been free from it since." In still another deposition he claimed that from late October 1863 to the spring of 1865 he was "frequently treated" for lameness in his left knee and thereafter "treated constantly" until his discharge on July 18, 1865. Kinsley apparently offered this last version of his injury and its consequences to his physician brother-in-law as well as to the bureau. Dr. LeRoy Bingham, who had known Kinsley since childhood and prescribed medication for him from the time of his return home in 1865 until his death in 1911, declared that "From his statements, I concluded that he contracted the rheumatism while serving in the 74th U.S.C.T.s, which settled in one knee which had been injured while in the 8th Vt. Vols, and has extended to other parts of the body, as it is a rule that the rheumatism will attack a point that is weakened by a former injury." James Noyes, Kinsley's friend and comrade in the Seventy-fourth United States Colored Troops, also confirmed this version of the story in a letter stating that Kinsley "was lame from time to time during the entire term of his connection with the Regiment; and from the spring of 1865 to the time of his discharge, he was constantly very lame; so much so that field duty would have been absolutely impossible, and the Post Surgeon repeatedly offered to relieve him from duty on account of his lameness." But according to Noyes, Kinsley "declined to be relieved and went to his duty, much of the time suffering acutely [*sic*].... "[174]

Noyes was correct in stating that Post Surgeon John H. Gihon believed Kinsley's knee problem was severe. In fact Gihon believed it was so severe that on July 11, 1865, he signed off on a certificate of disability that allowed Kinsley to be discharged and go home. But unlike Noyes, Bingham, and Kinsley, Gihon did not believe that Kinsley's rheumatism stemmed from his injury at Bayou Boeuf in 1863. After examining him on July 11, Gihon concluded that Kinsley was "suffering from an injury to the left knee joint, acquired previous to his having entered the service, and not whilst in the line of duty. The wound was supposed to have been so far healed as not to be troublesome again, but exercise has rendered it painful and produced lameness."[175]

Clearly, Kinsley had his work cut out for him as he campaigned to convince the Pension Bureau that he had injured his knee in the line of duty and that the injury had brought on his rheumatism. It would have been difficult under the best of circumstances to prove that his postwar rheumatism was caused by an injury sustained a quarter century earlier, but Kinsley also had to overcome a document in his file in which the post surgeon, presumably a disinterested professional, stated that he had sustained his knee injury before the war and even intimated that the consequence of the injury was a nagging wound rather than an autoimmune disease. Furthermore, there was no mention of an injury to Kinsley's knee in any of his military records (or in his diary or letters home for that matter).[176] And perhaps the fact that Kinsley offered three different versions of what happened to his knee after the injury indicated to the bureau that this was a case of an impoverished farmer in search of additional income. Kinsley was indeed a man in need of money and a petitioner who engaged in some exaggeration, misrepresentation, and obfuscation in his fight for a pension, but I tend to believe Kinsley, his family, friends, and former comrades, who swore that his knee was healthy until he hurt it in February 1863, and to doubt the prewar dating of the injury offered by Gihon, who disliked Kinsley. The post surgeon deceived Kinsley about what he intended to identify in Kinsley's medical report as the cause of his ailing knee, and Gihon's testimony stands alone without any corroborating evidence.[177]

Current medical knowledge lends credence to Kinsley's contention that his 1863 knee injury triggered the rheumatism that by early September 1865, when he reached Boston on his way home from the war, had attacked his hands as well as his knee. In a postwar deposition Kinsley elaborated on the further spread of his disease, stating that "soon after I resigned the rheumatism extended to my left hip and my back and since that time it has extended to almost every joint in my body." Kinsley's observation, in conjunction with testimony from several physicians, leaves little doubt that Kinsley had rheumatism, but rheumatism is a catch-all term for several diseases causing inflammation or degeneration of joints, muscles, ligaments, tendons, and bursae. From our distant perspective, it is difficult to identify with certainty the type or types of rheumatism Kinsley had, but it seems likely that he suffered from both rheumatoid arthritis and fibromyalgia.[178]

Rheumatoid arthritis is an inflammatory autoimmune disease in which the body's natural defenses attack healthy joints. The results can be devastating, as is suggested by the case of Kinsley's mother, who almost certainly had rheumatoid arthritis and consequently increased the chances that her son would have it also. Monoarticular arthritis is a form of rheumatoid arthritis that in its progression resembles Kinsley's so-called rheumatism. It is a disease, according to one expert, "in which one or two joints may remain painful and swollen for several weeks to months before other joints become involved – sometimes the joint, *usually the knee*, resolves before polyarthritis ensues."[179] In Kinsley's case the knee joint did not resolve, or heal, before the disease spread to other sites, but swelling of the left knee along with some enlargement and contraction of his fingers appears to be the extent of Kinsley's deformity. Assuming Kinsley did have rheumatoid arthritis, he had a mild case compared to his mother who was wheelchair-bound at age thirty-seven; to his brother William who needed crutches in his mid-forties; to his brother Jason who also used crutches or a wheelchair to get around but by his early fifties was confined to bed much of the time and needed ropes "fastened to the ceiling" to turn himself over; and to his sons F. Guy and Chellis who were so badly crippled that they could not keep up the family farm and had to sell it in 1930.[180] The fact is that most of Kinsley's aches and pains appear to have been situated not in his joints, but in his muscles, and he was not alone in this. Indeed, he was one of countless Civil War veterans who suffered from what contemporary physicians called "muscular rheumatism," and today would probably be identified as fibromyalgia.[181]

The American Arthritis Foundation has classified fibromyalgia as a form of soft-tissue rheumatism. It is characterized by chronic and widespread pain along the skeleton in the areas of the neck, chest, back, and hips. It exhibits systemic symptoms such as extreme fatigue and non-restorative sleep patterns, and it causes exaggerated tenderness in muscles, ligaments, and tendinous attachments. Today the key to diagnosing fibromyalgia is locating "tender points" in specified areas of the body such as the lower back, thigh, abdomen, head, and hips but not the wrists, hands, and feet, which are the primary anatomic sites for rheumatoid arthritis.[182] Unfortunately, since this method of diagnosis is of recent origin and Kinsley is long gone, it is impossible to state with certainty that Kinsley had fibromyalgia, but a medical examination of Kinsley by a board of surgeons in 1892 did reveal "tenderness of the shoulder & elbow joints and of the cervical and dorsal muscles and a general muscular rheumatism."[183] Moreover, Kinsley suffered from mitral valve prolapse, irritable bowel syndrome, stomach discomfort, thoracic pain, aching joints that were not noticeably swollen, and other ailments that often appear in conjunction with fibromyalgia. Some ailments, like mitral valve abnormality, appear in conjunction with other autoimmune diseases as well, but where there is a roughly 72 percent incidence of mitral valve abnormality among fibromyalgics, there is only a 30 percent incidence of this abnormality in rheumatoid arthritis patients. Other clues found in Kinsley's diary, correspondence, and pension file also point toward the conclusion that Kinsley had fibromyalgia.[184]

Despite extensive recent research, there is no consensus on what causes fibromyalgia. There is, however, broad general agreement that it is often triggered by an autoimmune disease, trauma, or stress and that it usually hits people in their thirties or forties. In 1864 Kinsley was thirty-three years old. The evidence in Kinsley's pension file strongly suggests that he was already showing signs of rheumatoid arthritis by the time he arrived at Ship Island in late October 1863. Then, in August 1864, during the siege of Fort Morgan, he badly reinjured his left knee. By the time he left Mobile Bay, Kinsley later recalled, his knee was "worse than ever," and from that moment until his discharge in July 1865 it was often "impossible for me to walk without a cane."[185]

In addition to the single-event trauma that aggravated his rheumatic knee, Kinsley endured intense psychological stress during the campaign to capture Fort Morgan. Kinsley had no illusions about the mission. He knew it would be dangerous as well as demanding, and he made preparations for his death before leaving Ship Island for Mobile Bay. Once there, he was in the midst of an unrelenting, bone-rattling bombardment of the fort, and shortly after its surrender he spent what he called a "night of terror" drifting on Mobile Bay in a small sailboat without a keel, "expecting every minute to be blown up by a torpedo." He had virtually no food for three weeks, except the oysters he scavenged from the bottom of the bay, and complained of nearly starving to death. He also experienced severe sleep deprivation, which some researchers have linked to the onset of fibromyalgia. At the beginning of the mission he did not sleep at all for five straight days. Subsequently, he caught a little shut-eye when he could – sleeping on the ground without a tent – but basically he returned to Ship Island utterly exhausted and, as previously noted, with his left knee in a flare. In Kinsley's uncharacteristically understated words, he "had a hard time" at Mobile Bay. The conditions Kinsley endured during the siege of Fort Morgan could have caused fibromyalgia symptoms in people without a family history of rheumatism like Kinsley's. With proper rest, "normal" people would recover without any lasting ill effects; Kinsley, however, was not normal.[186]

According to depositions in his pension file, Kinsley was treated for rheumatism by the post surgeon from the time of the fall of Fort Morgan until his discharge from the army. But things could have been much worse had Kinsley's fibromyalgia gone into a full-blown flare. Indeed, in reading Kinsley's journal entries and letters, one is struck by how healthy and happy he is. Apart from the fact that Kinsley never complained much about wounds of the flesh until he needed a pension, this is probably because the conditions at Ship Island – balmy weather, vigorous exercise, regular sleeping hours, daily swimming in the warm salt waters of the Gulf, and a relatively stress-free existence – were the most ideal conditions he would ever encounter in staving off the more severe symptoms associated with fibromyalgia. Upon his leaving those conditions late in the summer of 1865, it is entirely possible that Kinsley's fibromyalgia flared up. Exercise and routine are crucial in managing fibromyalgia, but Kinsley was now traveling, sleeping irregularly, unable to swim or exercise,

and heading toward a bitter cold climate and uncertain future.[187] His decision to take up farming in northern Vermont meant that he would be
living in an environment that was driving far healthier young men away
in record numbers. The decision to become a farmer may in itself have
been a source of anxiety, for according to his granddaughter, "From all
reports, Rufus was eminently unsuited to a farming career."[188] His decision to marry and have seven children may have also exacerbated his
health problems. At the very least, he undoubtedly suffered sleep deprivation living in a small clapboard house with seven young children and
worrying about how he was going to feed and clothe them. Perhaps he
was at times haunted by the spectre of his own past, and worried that his
children, like his father's, would have to be split up and sent away in the
face of sickness and poverty. Kinsley made choices about how to live his
postwar life, and those choices had consequences. He broke virtually every rule for containing fibromyalgia, and his condition became chronic
and increasingly severe. Fibromyalgia is an excruciatingly painful illness,
comparable to rheumatoid arthritis, and can strike at any time and leave
a sufferer like Kinsley prostrate for days, weeks, or even months at a time.

Given the unpredictable and debilitating nature of his illness, Kinsley
was determined to have a pension that would help him through the tough
times. He prosecuted his claim with the same kind of passion that he had
pursued slaveholders. To put it simply: he waged a relentless war against
the Pension Bureau. In its intensity, his battle for an equitable pension
became the postwar equivalent of his battle for a Union without slaves.
In another sense, it became an extension of the Civil War, and ultimately
turned him back, into that great event of his past.

Kinsley filed his application for a pension on February 2, 1886. Ten
months later, he was still waiting for a decision on his case. Impatient,
he contacted his brother-in-law in Burlington, and together they convinced Senator George F. Edmunds of Vermont to intervene in his behalf. Edmunds asked the bureau to consider Kinsley's claim "at once
on the ground of special circumstances," as "the need of the family in
the helpless condition of the soldier is very great." Although John C.
Black, commissioner of the Pension Bureau, assured Edmunds that the
case would "be considered at an early date," Kinsley waited until April
1887 to learn that he had been awarded a pension of eight dollars per
month for hemorrhoids. Outraged that his rheumatism claim had been
completely disallowed and convinced that bureau officials had grossly
underestimated the extent of his disability as a result of the chronic

diarrhea he had contracted while in the service, Kinsley began a long and often futile round of appeals. He also fired the Washington, D.C., attorney he had hired to shepherd his case through the bureaucracy, and took over himself. His frustration shows through during an interview that occurred in 1892 when a special examiner visited Lowell to gather information about the case. When asked if he wished to introduce any more testimony, Kinsley, who by this time had endured several physical examinations and arranged for scores of letters, affidavits, and reports to be forwarded to the bureau, responded evenly: "I want you to see such witnesses as are necessary to establish the facts."[189]

To establish "the facts," Kinsley went beyond gathering the expert testimony of medical and military personnel. He enlisted a small army of friends and relatives to write in support of his application, and his campaign can be fairly described as a family and community affair.[190] One of those enlisted was Loren C. Lee, an old friend from Fletcher, who for years had been a close neighbor of Kinsley's uncle Guy and brother Edgar. Lee's deposition, which was notarized by Justice of the Peace Charles B. Parsons, who was the cousin of Kinsley's wife, declared that Kinsley,

> from the time of his return from the army in the fall of 1865, until the spring of 1872, when he left town, . . . suffered exceedingly from lameness in the left knee, hip, and back, so much so at times that he was entirely incapacitated for manual labor, and sometimes confined to his bed for weeks together. . . . He was also during all these years troubled with severe internal pains which would prostrate him and leave him absolutely helpless wherever he might happen to fall. These severe attacks would emaciate him to the last degree, and so reduce his strength as to leave him helpless for weeks after the pain had abated. Since 1872 . . . his disability has increased to such an extent that he is absolutely helpless much of the time, and when not confined to his bed he is so bad off that it is impossible for him to earn his living. His joints are swollen and distorted, and he looks like a skeleton almost.[191]

What is most intriguing about this poignant depiction of Kinsley's condition is that it was written, not by Loren Lee, but by Kinsley himself. And not only the handwriting is Kinsley's, but the words, phrases, and ideas are his as well. It is a moving self-portrait of a tired and emaciated old man who bears little resemblance to the robust young soldier that he described twenty-three years earlier as weighing 170 pounds and being "tough as a bear." Then he was helpful rather than helpless. Then he had a purpose and a profession. But the war that had propelled both an ordinary unit commander like Rutherford B. Hayes and a perennial failure like Ulysses S. Grant into the presidency had done nothing to advance Kinsley's career. Instead, according to Kinsley, the war ruined his health and ended his career as a printer. It offered him no new skills, knowledge, or confidence with which to face the future. What it did offer was memories, and one can only wonder if some evenings, late into the night, Kinsley climbed the stairs of his two-story farmhouse, opened the bureau that rested on the landing, fingered the brass buttons of the dark blue dress uniform he kept there, and drifted back to his glory days when he was engaged in a great civil war.[192]

The war looked better to Kinsley with each passing year. It became the shining as well as the defining moment of his life. He came to think – and to write – about himself in the past tense, as a Civil War soldier. The pension battle encouraged this trend, as Kinsley spent hundreds of hours recovering and reliving his Civil War experiences. Of course, he undertook this journey so that he might eke out a marginally better existence. And by 1893, when he had pretty much won on all his claims before the Pension Bureau, his past had literally become his lifeline to the present. Kinsley was no doubt grateful for the aid, but at some level mere survival must have seemed bleak fare after the heady wine of freeing the slaves and saving the nation.[193]

Even after the pension battle, Kinsley continued to live, or at least think about himself, in the past. In 1904, for example, a short biographical sketch of Kinsley appeared in *Successful Vermonters: A Modern Gazetteer of Caledonia, Essex, and Orleans Counties*. Although William H. Jeffrey compiled the volume, the style and content of the sketch leave no doubt that it was written by Kinsley. What is most striking about the essay is the centrality of Kinsley's Civil War experience; indeed, Kinsley devotes nearly three-fourths of his essay to the four years he spent in the Union army. He relates how he and fifty-nine other sharpshooters, outnumbered nearly 4 to 1, had undertaken "the hazardous enterprise of capturing [Rebel] rifle-pits," thereby saving a fleet of Union gunboats and guaranteeing "a signal Union victory"; how he had commanded a company of black troops "during the siege and bombardment of Fort Morgan"; how he had served as quartermaster to fugitive slaves and given "hundreds of them the rudiments of an education in the *face* of *Section 28* of the *statutes* of Louisiana, which, prior to the war, made such teaching a crime 'punishable by twenty years imprisonment, or *death*, at the discretion of the court.'" Here, Kinsley's (auto)biography proclaims, is a man of courage, compassion, and high moral purpose. In contrast, Kinsley's life

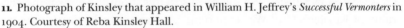

11. Photograph of Kinsley that appeared in William H. Jeffrey's *Successful Vermonters* in 1904. Courtesy of Reba Kinsley Hall.

both before and after the war receives brief and perfunctory treatment. Of the postwar years from 1866 to 1904, which made up over half of his entire life and three-fourths of his adult life, Kinsley states only that he has lived on a farm in Lowell since 1872, that he has a wife and seven children, and – back to the war – that he "is an active worker in Hazen post, No. 74, G.A.R."[194]

The other biographical sketches in *Successful Vermonters* suggest that few shared Kinsley's preoccupation with the war. Of the three Lowell residents joining Kinsley in Jeffrey's gazetteer, two failed to mention the war at all, and the third, Henry H. Newton, who served for four years in the Eighth Vermont, gave it nowhere near the attention Kinsley did. Where

71 percent of Kinsley's essay was devoted to his life as a Civil War soldier, only 34 percent of Newton's was; and where only 17 percent of Kinsley's essay was allotted to his life after the war, 52 percent of Newton's was. If one extends the analysis beyond Lowell to include all the residents of Orleans County whose lives are chronicled in Jeffrey's gazetteer, a similar pattern emerges. The vast majority did not mention the war, and of those who served in the Union army, none devoted even half of his essay to the war, and most spilled less than a quarter of their ink on the subject.[195]

The title page of *Successful Vermonters* states that the book offers biographies of men "who have won distinction in their several callings, and who have become conspicuous in the professional, business, and political world." One can only wonder why Rufus Kinsley was included in such a volume. He certainly was not "conspicuous" in the professional, business, or political world. The only explanation seems to be that Kinsley was recognized as a man of "distinction" in his "calling" as a Civil War soldier.[196]

Kinsley the Civil War soldier reappeared two years later in the *Boston Herald* in a story about his neighbor and fellow veteran of the Eighth Vermont, Lewis J. Ingalls. The recipient of the Congressional Medal of Honor for bravery during the Civil War, Ingalls was "the most fearless" soldier in Vermont's entire history, according to the *Herald.* Unfortunately for the reporter who made the long trip to Lowell to prepare a feature story on "Dare Devil Lou," Ingalls was also shy, modest, and reticent. The reporter lamented that Ingalls "will not speak of his own [wartime] deeds, and prefers not to relate any stories regarding that conflict." Fortunately, this was not true of Ingalls's neighbor, "and the story was learned through his comrade, Lieut. Rufus Kinsley of the same town." Kinsley dutifully relayed the details of Ingalls's valor under Confederate fire in southwestern Louisiana, but as the following passages from the article suggest, Kinsley was not about to miss an opportunity to remind everyone that he too was a brave Civil War soldier.

> Kinsley was born in Fletcher, Vt., Oct. 9, 1831, and his father was a hero in the war of 1812. He enlisted in company K [F] and served as corporal until 1863. He was then assigned with sharpshooters, who undertook the hazardous capture of many of the strongest rifle pits in the South. He was commissioned second lieutenant in 1863 by Maj. Gen. N. P. Banks, and was assigned to company B, 2d corp d'Afrique, a colored regiment. Because of disability caused by being wounded, he was honorably discharged July 18, 1865.[197]

12. "Lieut Rufus Kinsley" as he appeared in a feature article about his friend Lewis Ingalls in the *Boston Herald* on March 19, 1906. Courtesy of the Boston Public Library.

Like most veterans who look back on their time with Mars, Kinsley embellished his story. Hardly a sentence is free of exaggeration or distortion. His father, who served one year in the War of 1812, was apparently a competent soldier, but not a hero.[198] For one day in January 1863 Kinsley was a member of a detachment of volunteer "sharpshooters" from his regiment whose assignment was to pick soldiers off the deck of a Confederate gunboat; eventually, the detachment did attack some rifle pits, but they were far from the strongest in the South. And the immediate precipitant of Kinsley's discharge from the service was a sprained knee that he sustained while swimming in the Gulf of Mexico.[199]

But it was not simply in self-promoting vanity volumes and nostalgic newspaper retrospectives on old veterans that Kinsley presented himself as a Civil War soldier. In September 1907 he and his wife Ella appear in an obituary for their son Benton, who died unexpectedly of smallpox while working for the Standard Oil Company in China. Kinsley, in keeping with the practice of the times, probably wrote the obituary or at least provided the information upon which it was based.[200] In it Ella is identified as the daughter of Royal T. Bingham, but Rufus is not identified as the son of Ben A. Kinsley. Rather, the obituary reads: "Rufus Kinsley, the father, is a Civil War veteran." It then reports that Kinsley "kept an extensive daily memoranda of passing events, while in the service, which has been of much value in aiding the establishment of dates and incidents of Vermont in the Civil War." One can only speculate on why such an irrelevant account of the value of Kinsley's diary appeared in a notice about the tragic death of Benton Kinsley at the young age of thirty-two. Perhaps, with the death of his second-born son, Kinsley had begun to think about his own mortality, perhaps he had even come to realize that Kinsley the diarist was as important as Kinsley the soldier.[201]

Little is known about the final years of Kinsley's life, except that the Civil War kept cropping up. In the summer of 1910 a government worker visited Kinsley's farm to collect information for the Thirteenth U.S. Census. In the process of gathering all the standard data on age, sex, race, birthplace, and so forth, he learned that the seventy-eight-year-old Kinsley was living with his two youngest sons, F. Guy and Chellis, F. Guy's wife Sybil, and a hired girl named Mae Sawyer. Kinsley's wife Ella was no longer there, having died nine months earlier at the age of fifty-eight, and his brother William was no longer just down the road, having taken his own life nine years earlier.[202] An inquiry was made about the inhabitants' occupations, to which F. Guy and Chellis reported that they worked the "home farm." Kinsley responded rather vaguely that he lived off his "Own income," perhaps a reference to his hard-won pension benefits. Then, finishing up the interview, the census taker asked a question that must have stirred a mixture of indignation and pride in the old veteran. Was there anyone living on the farm, he asked, who had fought in Union *or* Confederate forces during the Civil War? Kinsley's recorded reply was a terse "Union Army," but one suspects that by the time the census taker got out the door he had heard a lot about places with exotic names like Opelousas, Atchafalaya,

13. Rufus and Ella Kinsley with their children and their spouses in front of the Lowell farmhouse in 1906. Courtesy of Reba Kinsley Hall.

and Thibodaux, and he had learned that no one who had fought for the Confederacy would ever be living on Rufus Kinsley's farm.[203]

A few months later another visitor provoked a fuller, and more revealing, reflection on the Civil War. The visitor was his daughter Amy, who was still living on her father's farm in 1900 but had since married and moved away. Kinsley had clearly planned for her visit. He had two gifts waiting for her when she arrived. They were not ordinary presents: they were his dearest possessions, symbolic links to the most meaningful period of his life. He had prepared a carefully written description of each gift. Apparently sensing that the end was near, Kinsley wanted to find someone who would preserve and appreciate his Civil War mementos. His daughter seemed a safe choice; after all, she was a schoolteacher.[204]

The first gift was a saltcellar. Writing about himself in the third person, Kinsley declared that "This salt cellar was presented to Lieut. Rufus Kinsley of Co. G. 74th U.S.C. Inf. by the valet of Gen. Page, commandant of Fort Morgan, Alabama, on the day of the surrender of the Fortress to Gen. Gordon Granger, Aug. 25, 1864, after a siege of three weeks by Negro and white troops combined." In keeping with the remarkably ceremonial nature of the presentation, Kinsley concluded with the words: "Presented to Amy L. Gelo, Jan. 21, 1911. By her father, Lieut. Kinsley."[205]

Besides a formality that suggests how seriously Kinsley took this occasion, his description is significant because of what it does not say. The saltcellar does not inspire Kinsley to reminisce about how he personally was under enemy fire at the Battle of Mobile Bay or how he had negotiated a treacherous minefield in a small skiff. Neither does it cause him to reflect on the larger military significance of the battle – that it resulted in the capture of the Confederacy's last major ocean port south of Charleston or that it produced perhaps the most memorable words in American naval history when Rear Admiral David Farragut shouted, "Damn the torpedoes! Full speed ahead!" Rather, what Kinsley chose to impress upon his daughter as most important about this great Union victory was that it had been accomplished by black and white troops working together. In 1911 when Kinsley made this observation, most Americans had forgotten, or never knew, that black Americans had played a major role in the Civil War, and those who remembered rarely placed them in the forefront of their diaries, memoirs, histories, poems, paintings, or songs.[206] Indeed, in Guilford, Vermont, John W. Phelps, who had won fame for his courageous campaign to enlist Louisiana blacks in the Union army during the war, advocated sending all black Americans back to Africa.[207]

14. The saltcellar and writing case Kinsley gave to his daughter Amy in 1911. Courtesy of Reba Kinsley Hall.

But whereas Phelps and other disillusioned reformers abandoned their idealism after the war, Kinsley, as his second gift to his daughter further demonstrates, remained proud of his. The gift was a large, dark, leather-bound writing case. "This writing case," Kinsley explained in the accompanying note, "filled with stationery and stamps, and containing a goodly number of gold dollars, was presented to Rufus Kinsley, superintendent of the May street Sunday School, Negroes, Boston, on his retirement therefrom in 1857; and was by him carried through the war for the suppression of the slaveholders' rebellion, from 1861 to 1865, where it served a very useful purpose in giving a great many hundred (late) slaves the rudiments of an education."[208] A half century after it was given to him, the case still triggered his memories of teaching former slaves in the Deep South.

But the case had been more than a portable writing desk upon which to prepare lesson plans for the freedmen. It had served also as Kinsley's link to the militant black community of Boston, to the church of Elijah

Grissom, Samuel Snowden, and David Walker. As he lugged it through the snow in Brattleboro, the swamps surrounding New Orleans, and the sands of Ship Island, the case reminded Kinsley of where he came from and what he was fighting for. The case was also, quite literally, the wellspring of his diary. It was on this writing case, given to him by African Americans, that Kinsley turned the war into words, and with the passage of time, these words, which we call his diary, became his greatest gift of all. The note Kinsley attached to the writing case leaves little doubt about how he wanted to be remembered. He was a soldier in the war to end slavery and a teacher in the struggle for equality.[209]

Five months after his daughter's visit, Rufus Kinsley was dead. He died, after a brief illness, of acute gastritis on June 11, 1911. Three days later, at a ceremony attended by Lowell's surviving Civil War veterans, he was buried in Mountain View Cemetery, overlooking the grave of his beloved brother William. Cut deep into his granite tombstone in bold capital letters were the words: "LIEUT. RUFUS KINSLEY."[210]

15. Union soldiers making diary entries and writing letters home while waiting to disembark at Ship Island. *Frank Leslie's Illustrated History of the Civil War*, 330.

The Slaveholders' Rebellion: The Diary of Rufus Kinsley

NOVEMBER 29, 1861. Enlisted at St. Albans, for the 8th Vermont Regt., for service in Butler's Brigade, designed to operate in the Gulf of Mexico, against New Orleans, Mobile, and other rebellious cities of the South.[1] Enlisted for three years, from first day of June, 1861.

DECEMBER 24, 1861. Brother Wm.,[2] having previously enlisted, joined me at St. Albans.

DECEMBER 28, 1861. Went with Wm. and Zeri Campbell[3] to Georgia, and had a most glorious visit with Uncle Chellis' folks.[4] Stayed over Sabbath.

JANUARY 4, 1862. Went home, with Wm., and spent the Sabbath. Last day at home.

JANUARY 6, 1862. Edgar[5] carried me to Essex, and on my return to St. Albans, via Georgia, stayed over night with Uncle Chellis' folks.

JANUARY 7, 1862. Elected officers: Capt. H. E. Perkins,[6] lst Lieut. D. S. Foster,[7] 2d [Lieut.], C. H. Nason.[8]

JANUARY 8, 1862. Went into encampment at Brattleboro. Was honored with office of 4th Corpl.

JANUARY 10, 1862. Wm. returned home, sick with measles.[9] On furlough of 14 days.

JANUARY 12, 1862. (Sunday) Went to church at Dr. Tyler's,[10] and attended Sabbath School. Went home to dinner with Superintendent Mead,[11] a brother of the sculptor.

JANUARY 17, 1862. Listened to a splendid lecture by "Timothy Titcomb," in the evening, and went home with Rev. N. Howe,[12] of the M[ethodist].

E[piscopal]. Church. Not being very well, and Bro. Howe having a very interesting family of daughters, I was very happy to accept an invitation to stay a week or two, until my health should improve.

JANUARY 31, 1862. Wm. returned from home, well: bringing a huge loaf of brown bread from mother, with other things good to eat. I returned to camp to stay with him, having quite recovered my health. Time passed very pleasantly and not unprofitably at Brother Howe's, and in visiting, with himself and family, the Asylum, Masonic Hall, Library, and various public institutions. Made many pleasant acquaintances.

FEBRUARY 2, 1862. (Sunday) Heard Dr. Tyler on the war. Well pleased.

FEBRUARY 9, 1862. (Sunday) Heard Bro. Colburn[13] of the Methodist persuasion.

FEBRUARY 17, 1862. Battery fired 34 rounds from their big guns, in honor of victory at Fort Donelson.[14]

FEBRUARY 18, 1862. Were mustered into the U.S. Service, for 3 years. Nothing about 1st of June.

FEBRUARY 21, 1862. Received State pay, and military glory. The first for service, and the latter by drilling a culprit at dress parade, who wore for his overcoat an empty flour barrel, properly labelled. Received a visit from several friends at the village. Very pleasant time.

FEBRUARY 28, 1862. Were paid off.[15] A large majority of the Co., (F), run the guards. Sent my trunk home to father. Wonder if I will ever see it again.

MARCH 5, 1862. Spent the night down town, with some friends. Ordered to report at 4 next morning.

MARCH 6, 1862. On reaching camp at 4 A.M., found the houses all down, and the boys nearly ready for a start, for the seat of war. At the depot I received various parcels of good things from various warm friends, some of whom I left with regret. At 10 P.M. we reached New Haven, Conn., where we took steamer *Granite State* for New York. Good bye, my father, friends, and home. Good bye, my native state. Shall I ever see your lofty hills and fertile vales, your limpid lakes and streams? I hope I may.

MARCH 7, 1862. Reached New York at 6 A.M. Passed the day on shore, with Wm. Visited the Parks, Trinity Church, Barnum's Museum, the palaces on Broadway and on some of the narrow ways, besides other places of interest.[16]

MARCH 9, 1862. (Sunday) Attended Trinity Church. In the evening, went to Brooklyn and heard H. W. Beecher preach a "live" sermon on "the times."[17]

MARCH 10, 1862, The right wing of the Regiment went on board ship *Wallace*, and the left on board the *James Hovey*, and we were towed out and anchored off Staten Island.

MARCH 11, 1862. The *Wallace* weighed anchor, and sailed for the South. Nearly all were sea-sick before night.

MARCH 13, 1862. Dead calm, and all hands dead sick. Ship surrounded by schools of porpoise, highly tickled at sight of the Yankees, who looked, in their blueish hats and blueish green coats, as they were sprawling around the decks and hanging over the rails, quite like a cargo of overgrown bull-frogs.

MARCH 14, 1862. Two men in Co. I very sick with lung fever: not likely to live long. A huge shark alongside, to save them from being buried "at the bottom of the deep blue sea;" whereat they are doubtless very grateful, if they are aware of the shark's disinterested benevolence.

MARCH 16, 1862. (Sunday) Awakened at 2 in the morning, by the howling of the tempest, and the pitching of the ship, setting me on one end, and then suddenly on the other. Moveables lashed to their places, and the sick to their berths; and soon after daylight the gale increasing to a hurricane, all hands ordered below. Many were frightened out of their wits. Before noon storm abated, hatchways raised, and all on deck again.

MARCH 17, 1862. Sailing rapid[l]y south. Saw Spanish ship: first sail seen in six days.

MARCH 18, 1862. Getting over sea-sickness a little: have had a hard time of it;[18] and have seen a sad sight this evening: – a poor old father burying his son at sea. E. L. Davis,[19] of Co. I, died at 9 1/4 p.m., and at 9 1/2 was thrown to the sharks. I pity his father. The body was wrapped in a blanket, with iron slugs tied to the feet, and slid over the side on a plank.

MARCH 22, 1862. Rough sea, and rations short. Splendid sun set at sea: such as I never saw described.

MARCH 26, 1862. Caught shark 8 feet long, with a hook. He fought like a tiger, and came near swallowing the mate; but the carpenter's ax made a bad hole in his head, after which he kept very quiet while surgeon Gale[20] dissected his body. Saw two whales.

MARCH 27, 1862. Made the Bahama Islands: first land seen for seventeen days. Islands covered with verdure, and a great variety of fruits and flowers. Saw a turtle about 5 feet long. Black fish by thousands. Full rations of water to-day. Terribly hot: most of us badly blistered.

MARCH 28, 1862. Passed the "hole in the wall."[21]

MARCH 31, 1862. Passed Key West before light, and have been in sight of it all day.

APRIL 1, 1862. Passed Tortugas. Health still improving.

APRIL 5, 1862. Made Ship Island,[22] after having sailed four weeks, with almost nothing to eat, and much of the time with only a half pint of water per day. Some base villains managed to steal a little of the filthy, stinking stuff, for which many were glad to pay 25 cents per gill. Much of the time we had a little hard bread and salt: two or three times, boiled potatoes and salt; sometimes a little meat with our "white oak chips."[23] We came to anchor at 8 p.m. off the west end of the island, near the fort.[24] Found a fleet of about forty vessels. Had heard heavy guns during the afternoon, and learned soon after anchoring that the Ship Island boys had just captured a rebel steamer that was attempting to run their blockade.

APRIL 6, 1862. (Sunday) Six of the Maine boys were drowned while bathing.

APRIL 7, 1862. Disembarked, and pitched our tents on Ship Island, in a bed of white sand, as loose as meal.[25] No floors to our tents. Found 18,000 troops on the island, and an enormous fort, mounting guns with bores as large as a flour barrel. Island nine miles long, and one-half mile wide at the west end; at the east end, two miles. East end covered with pine, and various other trees; and inhabited by alligators, and all the snakes in the catalogue; besides wild fowl in abundance. A great variety of flowers. West end, all sand.

APRIL 9, 1862. A grand review of all the troops. I was on guard, and had an excellent opportunity to witness, without participating in it.

APRIL 10, 1862. Went blackberrying. Found them plenty, and nice.

APRIL 11, 1862. Went to the east end. Saw a huge anaconda hanging over the limb of a tree. Left the vicinity on the "double quick." Helped kill an alligator.

APRIL 12, 1862. Awful thunder storm all last night. 4 men of the 31st Mass. killed by lightning.

APRIL 13, 1862. (Sunday) Heard the Chaplain's[26] first sermon to the Regiment. Wrote home. No facilities for writing, but to sit in the sand and hold my case in my lap.

APRIL 14, 1862. One of the Mass. 31st killed by the accidental discharge of a pistol.

APRIL 15, 1862. Six Regiments embarked on transports. Going somewhere.

16. Union vessels backed up on Mississippi Sound off the west end of Ship Island. The island's lighthouse and Fort Massachusetts are visible in the distance. Circa 1863. *Harper's Pictorial History of the Civil War*, 263. Courtesy of Special Collections, Bailey-Howe Library, University of Vermont.

APRIL 17, 1862. Several heavy vessels, filled with troops, and armed with big guns, left their mooring and started toward the mouth of the Mississippi. Let Fort Jackson[27] say its prayers.

APRIL 18, 1862. Heavy firing all day in the direction of Fort Jackson. Mercury 130. No water except the sea, filtered through sand.

APRIL 19, 1862. Taylor,[28] of our Co., an insane old man, cut his throat. Dr. says he will die.

APRIL 20, 1862. (Sunday) Few troops on the island. Terribly hot. Firing on the river more incessant and heavier than on any previous day. The air has become so filled with the smoke of battle that we can hardly see at all; even at this distance. No news from the Forts. Suspense is awful.

APRIL 24, 1862. Forts Jackson, and St. Phillip have fallen. Terrible slaughter on both sides. The rebels' rams and gun-boats all destroyed or captured. One of them sunk in two minutes after receiving a broadside from the *Mississippi*, carrying down all on board.[29] Our forces on their way to New Orleans.

MAY 1, 1862. The steamer *New London* captured three rebel vessels, with rich cargoes.

MAY 2, 1862. New Orleans has surrendered: the proud city; mistress of the Gulf.

MAY 6, 1862. Struck our tents, preparatory to a start for New Orleans.

MAY 7, 1862. At daylight the 8th Vt. set sail for the Crescent City.

MAY 8, 1862. At night reached the south-west pass; the principal mouth, where we rode at anchor until [*continues in next entry*]

MAY 11, 1862. The steamer *Miss.* came and towed us slowly up the stream all day. On either bank were lodged the remains of scores of rebel vessels, which had been destroyed in the fight, and fired by the rebels at New Orleans, and left to float down. Passed Forts Jackson and St. Phillip at 3 p.m. Fort Jackson badly battered. From the forts up the river, the scene presented is the most perfect picture of paradise, of which one can conceive. The levees are full of water, lifting the ship some 15 or 20 feet above the surrounding country, and the banks are covered with an infinite variety of tropical fruits and flowers; while farther back, the fields of corn, and cane, and rice, extend for miles. All the plantations are deserted by the whites, but thousands of negroes welcome us with various demonstrations of pleasure.[30] At dark, we came to anchor, and waited for day.

〰 **One** 〰

MAY 12, 1862. At daylight we were again on the move. As we reached the city, near sun-set, the levees were crowded with thousands of people from all countries, and in all costumes; some giving us a most hearty welcome, and singing Union songs; and some others demonstrating their displeasure, and singing the songs of secession. Our splendid brass band played for their benefit Yankee Doodle, Columbia, John Brown, and others. Landed and quartered in a cotton press. Slept at night, with others all the way from Ship Island, on an ordinary ladder, hung horizontally over the deck. It proved the best berth on the ship, for in the hold the air was bad, and the weather was so rainy that those lying on deck were in the water, and could not sleep; while those of us who "went to roost" on the ladder, two abreast, and wrapped our rubber blankets around us, with cartridge boxes for pillows, awoke perfectly dry. No facilities for cooking, on the ship, and nothing to eat but hard bread.

MAY 13, 1862. Looked the city over a little. Found the wharf burnt for several miles, the vandals having, on the approach of the Federal ships, rolled out millions of dollars worth of cotton, and fired it. They also burnt scores of ships and steamers, some of them just completed, and seven "rams," which were almost ready to launch. On the levee for miles up and down the river, on both sides, were mounted guns of the heaviest caliber, most of which the "chivalry" succeeded in getting into the river before they "left for parts unknown." Many of these guns had just been made at two large establishments here, which are now in our hands. We find in them thousands of shells and solid balls, of all sizes, and several unfinished cannon; besides everything for iron steamers. No expense had been spared in fortifying the city; and it was deemed impregnable; and when the events of today shall have become History, posterity will be amazed that the Crescent City, Queen of the South and mistress of the Gulf, defended by thousands of her chivalrous sons, should surrender to the despised Yankees, without striking a blow. *Sic transit gloria chivalri.*[31]

MAY 16, 1862. A rebel ship from the other side of the sea towed up. She had reached the pass, unmolested, when one of our gun-boats brought her to, and she was much astonished to learn that New Orleans had changed hands. She has on board 1800 barrels [of] powder, 5000 boxes [of] cartridges, 300 bushels [of] pepper, and many guns. The ship and cargo changed owners suddenly.

MAY 17, 1862. The Regiment removed to Mechanic[s'] Institute,[32] in the centre of the city.

MAY 20, 1862. Rice for dinner. Nothing but hard bread the last seventeen days.

[**MAY 20, 1862.** *On this date Kinsley makes the following observation on a separate sheet of paper. He explains in a marginal note added later that* These sections were copied by Rufus Kinsley, Corporal of Co. F, 8th Vt., while the regiment was in camp at Jackson Square.]

Department of the Gulf

New Orleans, La., May 20, 1862.

The following sections of the law of Louisiana and other slave states, illustrate the barbarism of slavery as it exists in the southern half of this Nation, not less forcibly, – if less eloquently – than Charles Sumner's most resonant Philippics.[33]

Sec. 28. Be it further enacted, That, whosoever shall, with the intent to produce discontent among the free colored population, or insubordination among slaves, write, print, publish or distribute anything having a tendency to produce discontent among the free colored population, or insubordination among the slaves therein, shall, on conviction, be sentenced to imprisonment at hard labor, or suffer death, at the discretion of court.

Sec. 29. Be it further enacted; That whosoever, with the intent aforesaid, shall make use of language in any public discourse, from the bar, bench, stage, the pulpit, or in any place whatsoever, or whosoever shall make use of language in private discourse or conversation, or by signs or actions have any tendency to produce discontent among the free colored population of the state, or to excite insubordination among the slaves therein, or who shall be instrumental in bringing into this state any papers, books, maps, pictures, or anything having such tendency, shall, on conviction, suffer imprisonment not less than three, nor more than twenty-one years, or death, at the discretion of court.[34]

MAY 22, 1862. The Police force of the city in revolt, and the soldiers called out to restore order, and then act as police. Our Regiment sent to the Court House and Jail, at Jackson Square.[35]

MAY 25, 1862. Attended Church at the Catholic Cathedral.[36] Splendid building, in which to enact magnificent villany. Flour $60.00 per barrel.

MAY 26, 1862. Rescued a slave from the hands of a kidnapper, at the French Market.[37]

MAY 27, 1862. Just begin to realize, from observation, the horrors of starvation. Many have starved to death, and there is nothing to eat. Men buy an ounce of bread and a half gill of "slosh," called coffee, for 50 cts., and it makes a meal.[38] Milk is fifty cts. a quart. Lean, haggard women sit on the curbstone

17. Jackson Square, where Kinsley briefly encamped in May 1862. The buildings, from left to right, are the Cabildo, St. Louis Cathedral, and the Presbytère. Circa 1850. Courtesy of the Historic New Orleans Collection, Museum/Research Center.

at the corners, with a spoonful or two of corn, on a piece of paper, for which they ask you to give a dime. They have rice, also, and oats, at the same price. Many of the rich fare little better than the poor. Hunger stands guard at every door. "Cassius"[39] is written on every face. The market is opened at two o'clock every morning, and at that hour thousands are waiting to buy the little meat there is, at 80 cts. to $1.25 per pound. Even the entrails of cattle and hogs are all washed and sold for food. The feline race is nearly extinct: starved to death: and the dogs not much better off. It is pitiable to see them.[40]

MAY 29, 1862. Have come to the conclusion that night police duty in a city that has been governed for years by thugs and assassins, is not half as pleasant as some other duties, and not very safe.[41] In the city are many splendid palaces, and parks, and gardens, with a great variety of fruits and flowers, and many statues; but an ever-present curse overhangs it all.

[**MAY 30, 1862.** *On this date Kinsley copies the following mayoral directive on a separate sheet of paper. He explains in a marginal note added later that it was* Copied from the records of the city clerk May 30, 1862, by R. Kinsley, Corporal Co. F, 8th Reg. Vt. Vol. Inf.]

State of Louisiana, Mayoralty of New Orleans

City Hall, April 24, 1858

In conformity to the provisions of Ordinance No. 3847, approved April 7, 1858, I, C. M. Waterman, Mayor, do hereby grant permission to the official members of the Coliseum Place Baptist Church in the First District of this city, to open, organize, and continue one year from this date, a church or meeting for the worship of Almighty God–for persons of color–on the Sabbath day only, from daylight till sunset: which said church shall, by this permission, and in conformity with law, be required to be wholly amenable, both as to its spiritual as well as to its temporal affairs, to the said Coliseum Place Baptist Church. This permission is granted for the establishment of a church, or meeting, on St. Mark street, between Common and Gravier; and it is understood that the Mayor reserves the right to recall or revoke it any time: and that the law of April 7, 1858, and all other laws and ordinances in relation to slaves and free persons of color, will be strictly enforced.

Signed: Chas. M. Waterman, Mayor[42]

MAY 31, 1862. New police appointed, and the Regiment returned to the Hall.[43] At night the Reg't. crossed the river in a steamer, and slept in the depot of the New Orleans, Opelousas, & Great Western R. R., at Algiers.

JUNE 1, 1862. (Sunday) Took the [railroad] cars and went west as far as Bayou Des Allemands; leaving two or three Companies at the depot to keep guard. Our Regiment is on the road, to relieve the 21st Indiana. Hope we shall not suffer as much at the hands of the rebels as they have, but presume we shall more, ~~for our field officers are not above mediocrity~~. [*This phrase has a thick line drawn through it in the original.*]

JUNE 2, 1862. Nothing to eat since Saturday morning until this (Monday) evening. We killed an ox for the planter in whose buildings we are quartered, and have had fresh beef for supper.

JUNE 3, 1862. Took a hand car, and with Wm. and Case[44] went up the road eight miles, and got sweet potatoes. We killed four alligators on the way. I tried my rifle on two of them; put a ball in the right eye of each. One of them was thirteen feet long. We ate two of them for supper. Found the flesh, when boiled, more like a chicken's breast than any thing else. Just at night the boys, having rebuilt the long bridge over the Bayou, went on to Bayou Lafourche, 20 miles further up, making 52 from New Orleans. I was left on guard, with a squad of 12 men. Wonder if the rebels will come after us.

JUNE 5, 1862. Not much to eat but alligators and blackberries: plenty of them.

Engagement with a Rebel ally

18. Union soldiers shooting a "Rebel ally." Fletcher Pratt, *Civil War in Pictures*, p. 45.

JUNE 8, 1862. Co. F ordered back to the city, and I was relieved, and returned with them.

JUNE 10, 1862. Uncle Jefferson Scott[45] came to see us: had a good visit, and Wm. and I returned with him to his ship.

JUNE 16, 1862. Our Company took the cars before light, and started to reenforce the force still at Lafourche. We found the enemy were in large force, but very careful not to get too near our Enfield rifles. At night Wm. was sent with 12 picked men across the river, in [a] skiff, to do picket duty. They killed one of the enemy. Clary and Roy hung.[46]

JUNE 17, 1862. At three o'clock this morning we were told by a negro that 300 men on horseback were tearing up the track and burning the bridge three miles below us, to cut off our retreat to New Orleans. One Company was sent up the river, another down: and our own, numbering 42 men, went direct to the burning bridge on an open car, with the engine in the rear. As soon as the enemy discovered us, they mounted their horses and broke for the woods, not waiting to see how few we were. We gave them one volley from the car, killing three, and we soon after captured three, with their horses; besides one barrel [of] powder, a pile of shot, balls, and several guns. We rebuilt the bridge, and came to the conclusion that our force was not sufficient to hold so long a road, in the heart of a country filled with guerillas. Hence we evacuated Lafourche, and returned, leaving our outposts at Bayou Des Allemands, 32 miles from New Orleans. Visited during the day several plantations; and saw enough of the horrors of slavery to make me an Abolitionist forever. On each plantation in all this section of country is a large building called a hospital, with only two rooms. In one may be seen the stocks, gnout, thumb screw, ball and chain, rings and chain, by which victims are fastened flat to the floor; and others, by which they are bound to perpendicular posts; iron yokes of different patterns, hand cuffs, whips, and other instruments of torture, for the benefit of those who had been guilty of loving liberty more than life, but had failed in their efforts to obtain the coveted boon. Verily this picture presents positive proof that the slave is happy and contented with his lot.

JUNE 19, 1862. Received two months pay: $26. Hid a negro from his master.

JUNE 22, 1862. (Sunday) Col. Thomas[47] sent a train up the road to return to their masters fifteen slaves, who had sought the protection of the Government. The train went forty miles: as far as it was deemed safe; when the negroes were turned out and ordered to report themselves to their masters. Cars had no sooner started on their return, than they were fired into by a band of guerrillas concealed in the cane-brake, and the fireman and four soldiers were killed. Several were badly wounded. Three dead bodies were

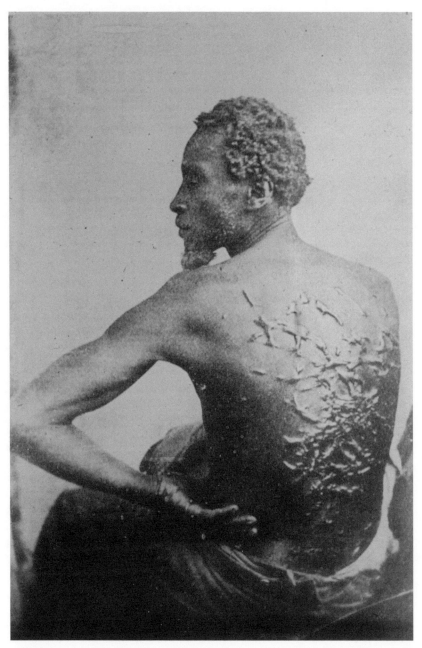

19. Photographed by a surgeon in the Union army on April 2, 1863, Gordon was a runaway slave from southern Louisiana. Courtesy of the National Archives.

left behind.[48] The dead and wounded brought in look bad, very bad; and as I look at it, they were engaged in bad business. "Verily I say unto you they shall receive their reward."[49] "Thou shalt not return him again to his master."[50]

JUNE 23, 1862. Ed. Saul,[51] a fine old Irishman, of our Co., was drowned in the Mississippi.

JUNE 25, 1862. Another hunter attempted to remove a negro from camp, but got badly used, and was glad to escape with his life. Gen. Twiggs'[52] estate confiscated.

JUNE 27, 1862. Guards fired at target. Wm. L. Kinsley best shot: carried away the bull's eye. Elisha A. Goddard[53] of our Co. died. He died well, like a good soldier.

JUNE 28, 1862. Rode into the country near 30 miles, and took dinner with a professional negro hunter, and his family. Don't envy any of them.

JULY 3, 1862. Was detailed to take an inventory of a large printing office, whose owner, J. W. Bacon,[54] has just been sent to Fort Jackson by Gen. Butler, for disloyalty. Heard the Capt. tell Col. Thomas, that in an enterprise requiring tact, skill, and cool, calculating courage, as well as great powers of endurance, Wm. was the best soldier in the Co. He is at work with me in the office, "learning the trade." We are to do a lot of Government printing.

JULY 10, 1862. Sent mother a present, by Adams Express.[55] Paid freight, $2.50.

JULY 13, 1862. Went to a Methodist church with a soldier preacher, who said he would preach to the rebel congregation in the evening if he could have a notice given out. I went to the pulpit and asked the pastor, Dr. Lee,[56] to notify his congregation that one of the Yankee Methodist preachers would preach to them at 5 p.m. He refused, saying he was a secessionist and was ready to die with the South. I intimated to him the propriety and the possible safety of complying with a request so reasonable; whereupon he gave the notice, and then preached such a sermon as would suit Jeff Davis and the devil, to a T. This evening the people got the gospel of the Golden Rule. Of course many were mad: and a very few rejoiced.

JULY 14, 1862. Went with Wm. and Uncle Jefferson, and had Daguerreotype taken.

JULY 17, 1862. Saw Wm. write [a] pass, by means of which one of the slavery loving negroes escaped from his master and found refuge with Gen. Phelps.[57] Brother Lee sent to Fort Jackson.

20. A slave who left his master's residence without written permission was subject to arrest and severe punishment. In this sketch, which appeared in *Frank Leslie's Illustrated Newspaper* on July 11, 1863, planter police examine passes just below New Orleans along the banks of the Mississippi River. Courtesy of Special Collections, Tulane University Library.

JULY 24, 1862. (Sunday) Another negro came to camp this morning, wearing a 64 pound ball, attached to his foot by a cable chain five feet long, such as is used in Vermont for hauling stone. He had traveled 40 miles. How he loved slavery. Evening: – have just filed from a negroe's neck an iron yoke weighing 13 pounds, covered with long crooked prongs, which he has worn in the swamps during the last eight days, seeking some mode of exit from the "house of bondage," which he is supposed to love so well.

AUGUST 5, 1862. Battle of Baton Rouge, Gen. Williams killed.[58]

AUGUST 6, 1862. Have just had our first hard foot march. We started at 3 a.m. yesterday, and walked in the swamps, with scarcely a halt, until 3 this a.m. We crossed several bayous which we had to bridge, or swim, and many that we had to wade, up to our waists, or necks, in mud and water. No signs of the enemy. Terribly hot: several failed up; but among them, not one of our teetotal clique, who had steadily refused all drink but water. We found no water on the route that was not warmer than blood, and covered with a green, filthy scum. Rebel ram *Arkansas* destroyed by *Essex.*[59]

AUGUST 8, 1862. Wm. had a very narrow escape while going up the road on the cars. A ball fired by a guerrilla in ambush, came very near his head.

AUGUST 23, 1862. Companies A, F, and I, took the cars at 3 a.m., and started up the road, to search for arms. One of our boys, only 18 years of age, took an old planter who had secreted his rifle and double-barreled shot gun, both loaded, and marched him to the rendezvous, compelling him to carry both guns (now empty), while he walked in the rear, with his trusty Enfield. Pretty well for a boy.

AUGUST 24, 1862. (Sunday) Attended church at the Roman Cathedral, and passed the remainder of the day in the various Cemeteries around the city. An eloquent sermon on the frailty of human life, is read in the long trenches, now covered with rank weeds, where lie myriads of men, more than thirty thousand of whom have been thus buried, without coffins, in a single summer, from the city of New Orleans. With the exception of these long trenches, into which, in time of pestilence, the dead are thrown without ceremony, all are buried in tombs on the surface of the ground; mostly in white coffins. Our soldiers, however, are buried, each in his own grave. Orders issued to arm and equip the negroes of the State.[60]

AUGUST 25, 1862. To-day, by favor of Sheriff Munday,[61] made the acquaintance of a man – one of the "chivalrous gentlemen" of the South, who is not only tolerated, but courted, and flattered, and very largely admired by the fair, and very extensively *copied* by the "sons of thunder" in this region, – who, while living with his wife, in the highest state of connubial felicity, with a

21. With its white-washed, above-ground tombs, St. Louis Cemetery II was a popular landmark among visitors to nineteenth-century New Orleans. *Frank Leslie's Illustrated Newspaper*, August 27, 1853. Courtesy of the Historic New Orleans Collection, Museum/Research Center.

family of children growing up around him, raised three daughters in less than as many years, by one of his slaves, a quadroon girl. About four years ago the quadroon girl was sold, her three daughters, as white as three Yankee girls, remaining with their father, who has since, though the youngest girl is now fifteen only, received an heir by each of them. A little while before our fleet came up the river, two of these heirs, by his own daughters, were sold. Verily slavery *is* profitable. What wonder that men are ready to die for it? What wonder that women are ready to suffer in order that it may be perpetuated, while it does them such honor? Such things sound strange to unaccustomed ears, but I am told on the best authority, that similar circumstances are to be found on almost every plantation, and in the families of merchants, lawyers, doctors, and preachers. And the moral sense of the South is such that it is looked upon as a matter of course, [a] business transaction. Well, it *is* a *coarse* business transaction. O, womanhood, how art thou fallen so low, as not to be sensitive here. How art thou despoiled of every womanly grace! No where but to Slavery can we look for the cause of a result so dehumanizing. It has been my privilege this evening to draw this picture for the benefit of a woman of large culture, and refinement, who owns a large number of slaves, and who expressed her astonishment "that a young man of such good sense and general information as I evidently possessed *could be* an Abolitionist." Much obliged for the compliment, but astonished that such a woman (Mrs. Dr. Taylor,[62] the author of several volumes of much value) could be anything but an Abolitionist. Received at the hands of Mrs. Taylor, a very dolorous letter which she had just received from my whilom friend, Rev. Dr. Lee, who is still serving the Government at Fort Jackson, with a long list of lewd fellows of the baser sort. Thank God I enlisted when I did, and where I did! Thank God for the opportunity of preaching Abolitionism to slaveholders, and to slaves: of making men dissatisfied with the condition they are in; because, until dissatisfied with their present state, they can never be led to a better.

AUGUST 26, 1862. Released another negro from his iron yoke, and ball and chain, with which he had traveled 18 miles. His ear had been cut off, to mark him, and he had been well branded with the hot iron. His flesh was badly lacerated with the whip, and torn by dogs; but he escaped, and I have just dressed his wounds with sweet oil. There is little hope that he will live.[63]

AUGUST 27, 1862. Companies A and I, with two Companies of Cavalry,[64] have gone to bring in the loose property on the old Gen. Taylor plantation; now owned by his son Richard,[65] who holds a Col's. commission in the rebel army.

AUGUST 30, 1862. Expedition returned from Taylor's farm, thirty miles up the river, bringing 1500 head of cattle, one-half of which were wild, just from

EMANCIPATED SLAVES.

Brought from Louisiana by Col. Geo. H. Hanks. The Children are from the Schools established by order of Maj. Gen. Banks.

WILSON CHINN.   MARY JOHNSON.   ROBERT WHITEHEAD.
     CHAS. TAYLOR. AUGUSTA BROUJEY.   ISAAC WHITE. REBECCA HUGER.   ROSINA DOWNS.

Entered according to Act of Congress, in the year 1863, by PHILIP BACON, in the Clerk's Office of the United States for the Southern District of New-York.

Photographed by M. H. Kimball, 477 Broadway, N.Y.

22. Evidence of the miscegenation and physical abuse that Kinsley believed characterized slavery in Louisiana is found in this 1863 photograph of emancipated slaves. Note that the forehead of former slave Wilson Chinn is branded with the initials of the Louisiana sugar planter Valsin B. Marmillion. Courtesy of the Library Company of Philadelphia.

Texas, and designed for the larder of the rebels at Camp Pratt;[66] 1200 horses, mules and negroes, and pigs and chickens enough to stock Vermont.

AUGUST 31, 1862. (Sunday) Have been at Church, and visited the Italian Cemetery. Terribly hot. The last two months have been passed mostly in the printing office. Have spent considerable time examining the public works of the city, and the splendid gardens and plantations of the adjacent country. This country is rich beyond comprehension, in material resources, but an air of gloom at present overshadows everything. Desolation reigns supreme. Hunger stands guard at every door. Starving women, who have rolled in wealth, creep forth from their princely palaces, earned for them by the victims of their tyranny, to receive at the hands of charity the Government pittance of which Gen. Butler is made the almoner; while their husbands and sons, their brothers and lovers, are in arms against the Government by whose charity they are furnished with the means of subsistence. The wail of the oppressor mingles with the wail of his victim, by reason of whose oppression the whole land groaneth, and is made desolate. Our streets are filled with the maimed, who have escaped with their lives from the sanguinary battles in which the blood of their fellows has crimsoned the turbid waters of the Mississippi, and enriched the soil on its banks. Sad, and desolate, and fearful as it is, this is a picture on which I love to look. I thank God this hour is upon us, and that I live to see it. It is come quicker than I thought, and more than I dreamed is my guerdon. The Nation is gathering in her harvest. Thank God for the harvest time: Yes, thank God; notwithstanding the terrible harvest we gather; – a nation of graves, and rivers of blood. But, it is the legitimate fruit of the seed we have sown. There is in physical and in social life, and in moral and political life as well, a law of compensation, so accurately adjusted by Infinite wisdom, that no action or purpose can fail to receive its reward. God grant that to us the Spring-time may come again soon, and that we may have wisdom, and courage, to sow such seed as shall bear to us National honor and permanent peace.

SEPTEMBER 1, 1862. A new leaf turned over recently by the Commandant of the Department has brought hundreds of Contrabands into the lines of the 8th Vermont, and I am detailed, with Wm., and O. F. Bellows,[67] from Fairfax, to take care of them. It looks like an arduous undertaking.[68]

SEPTEMBER 4, 1862. Our train came in from Boutte this afternoon, bringing 18 killed, and a large number wounded. A sad loss to the Regiment. The rebels had turned the "switch" at Boutte, and then lay in ambush, hoping to capture the train. Their first fire nearly emptied the cars, which were open platforms, and killed every man but one connected with the battery which was on the train; but the engineer escaped, and L. J. Ingalls,[69] from Hydepark, seeing the condition of the switch, leaped from the train and righted it, and then regained the rear car, and the train came down with the dead and wounded that did not fall off as they were shot. Ingalls received four balls while adjusting the switch, one [of] them through his neck, but his wounds are none of them dangerous. D. Sanford, of our Co., can not recover.[70] A sad sight, so many dead and wounded, shot down without an instant's notice.

SEPTEMBER 5, 1862. The seven Companies here, with a detachment of Nim's Battery,[71] took the train this a.m. and started for the west end of the road, hoping to rescue the prisoners taken yesterday, and save our three Companies at Bayou Des Allemands. When near the scene of action, we were thrown from the track. One man killed, 12 badly wounded, and half a dozen cars smashed fine enough for "oven wood." By the time we had got the track clear it was night, and we returned to the city. The 21st Indiana, who went up the river in a transport, to cooperate with us, were a little more successful, and have just returned with 13 of our wounded, taken by them from the rebels; but they bring word that our entire force at Des Allemands, Cos. E, G, and K, with battery detachments from the other Cos., are taken prisoners.[72]

SEPTEMBER 6, 1862. Caring for the Contrabands again after the very narrow escape yesterday, in which the car that I was on was stripped from its wheels, badly demolished, and thrown upon a pile of several demolished cars which preceded it. Strange as it seems, only one on our car was seriously injured. As soon as I got out of the rubbish, I passed to the front, where I saw four cool fellows seated on the ground in the shade of a broken car, wholly absorbed in a game of Eucher;[73] while men more *human* were pulling the dead and wounded from the ruins. Verily, thought I, those men will gamble for the estate on their dead fathers' coffins.

SEPTEMBER 7, 1862. Attended church to-day at the Swedenborgian Temple. Terribly hot day: Mercury at 132. First child born in our camp, christened: "Freedom Kinsley."

SEPTEMBER 9, 1862. Gen. Taylor threatens to shoot some of our men, taken on the 4th. Gen. Butler's reply stops it.[74]

SEPTEMBER 10, 1862. Went to the office and printed the alphabet on letters six inches long, designed to give the darkies the rudiments of an education. About 3000 of them in camp. Attended negro funeral. Wm. officiated, in good Uncle Guy[75] style.

SEPTEMBER 15, 1862. First school to-day. Hung the alphabet, tacked to a board, against the shady side of a building, where all hands could see it, and at the end of an hour several hundred had learned half a dozen of the letters.

[**SEPTEMBER 19, 1862.** *On this date Kinsley writes the following letter to his brother Daniel. He adds in a marginal note:* Tell Lucre[76] I've made most diligent inquiry for Mr. Greenwood,[77] and can hear nothing of him.]

New Orleans, La., Sept. 19, 1862

Daniel:[78]

I received a letter from you some time ago, one from Lucretia a little
while later. Glad you had a pleasant visit in Vt. Assure you the summer
has passed very pleasantly with me. We are in constant excitement day
and night, and I have business enough to keep me out of mischief. The
rebels are around us on every side, and we occasionally lose a few men,
and sometimes we kill a few of them. Of late we have had some serious
skirmishing, and our Regiment has lost heavily. Three weeks ago yesterday
we lost in killed, wounded and prisoners, 300 men. It leaves a large hole
in the Regiment. Only one man in our Co. was killed, and but few were
wounded. Only a battery detatchment [*sic*] from our Co. was engaged. The
enemy, 1500 strong, were hid in the cane brake, not more than five yards
from the track, and as the train (which was made up of open, flat bottomed
cars) approached, they discharged their pieces with deadly effect, leaving
scarcely a man on the train. The engineer's cab was literally shot away from
around him, but he stood at his post and came out unharmed, though his
hat was partly shot away, and his coat was full of holes. He was obliged to
run the train very slowly, supposing, of course, they had disengaged a rail
somewhere in the vicinity, to throw the train off the track. When he reached
the "switch," a few rods from where they first fired, he discovered they had
half turned it. Very pleasant dilemma, indeed; only a dozen men left alive,
every man but one in the battery either killed or so badly wounded as
to be helpless, surrounded by 1500 blood-thirsty guerillas, and the train
just ready to leap to destruction between the two tracks! Discovering the
dilemma just in time, Lewis Ingalls, from Hydepark, jumped from the car
and adjusted the switch, little dreaming that he could regain his place, but
hoping to save the few left alive. The bullets flew round him like hail; but
he sprang for the train, and reached the rear car just in time to escape.
The frame of the switch was literally shot away, but he received only four
wounds. One ball entered near the thorax and passed out at the back of
the neck. Otherwise, his wounds are not serious. When you hear the trump
of fame sounding the name of some great General, who had secured for
himself some safe place, where he could see his soldiers capture a city, or
win a battle, just you remember Lewis Ingalls, will you?

Next morning after the fray, we went up with re-enforcements, hoping
to release the prisoners and recover the bodies of our dead; but the fates
were, seemingly, against us. When near the scene of the previous day's
carnage, (about 18 miles from camp) our train was thrown from the track,
and half a dozen cars broken fine enough for "oven wood." Only one man
was killed, – Many were wounded, some very seriously. The car on which
I stood was stripped from the wheels, and pushed entirely over a mass of

mangled men and broken cars, and when we stopped, one end was some 15 feet higher than the other. Not a man of our Co. was killed, and only one wounded. We formed in line of battle at once, supposing of course the enemy had thrown us from the track, and were waiting in readiness to gobble us up.[79] No enemy appeared, however, and we cleared the track and started for home, leaving the force which went up the river to cooperate with us, to do the best they could. They succe[e]ded in rescuing about 20 of our wounded, who were left with a small guard; but the force had fled toward Texas, with all the uninjured prisoners except two, whom they hung. We have heard nothing of them since.

We have over 4000 contrabands in our Regiment. O. F. Bellows of Fairfax, your brother Wm. and I have the care of them all. Bellows attends to the lodgings, and Wm. and I draw all the rations, and see them cooked (all in one place) and given out to each family. We are very busy; Never had better health.

As ever,

R. Kinsley

SEPTEMBER 21, 1862. (Sunday) A large class, numbering several hundred, have learned the entire alphabet, and Col. Thomas has just given me the assurance that arrangements will be made forthwith, for putting into operation an effective and extensive system of schools for the Contrabands. In the education of the black is centered my hope for the redemption of the race, and the salvation of my country. Attended the Contraband church: heard one of the original sermons, and several of the original hymns.

SEPTEMBER 25, 1862. Over 6000 negroes to feed, and furnish with lodgings. Heaps of the little ones sick. All the buildings on a large plantation near by used for hospital. Dying pretty fast. Plenty of business for three of us.

SEPTEMBER 26, 1862. Negroes still coming, on foot and in carts, drawn by oxen and mules, bringing poultry and pigs, and the little furniture they possess. Most of them as ignorant of letters as the mules they drive; but as keen and shrewd as a live Yankee. From them the key of knowledge has been taken away, and the fact has a wonderful tendency to quicken as many as two of the senses, at least.

SEPTEMBER 28, 1862. (Sunday) At church again with the Contrabands. Most of them know more Scripture than half the Yankees, notwithstanding they can not read a word. But, they *never forget any thing.*

SEPTEMBER 29, 1862. Have been impressed with an idea of the wonderful sameness of slavery, everywhere. Barbarism, when brought in contact with civilization in the great commercial marts, and on the thoroughfares of trade and travel, becomes of necessity civilized, in a measure at least; although the change may be, perhaps, imperceptible to itself. But the barbarism of slavery is so far removed from every other crime, and the perpetrators of the barbarism understand so well the fatal effect of contact with civilization, that all the senses are constantly on the alert to guard against its influence. Hence, here in the metropolis [of New Orleans] I see the thumb and first two fingers cut from the right hand of a slave woman who had learned to write, and she sold to work on a plantation; – as in the Red River country, or Lafourche, I see the left ear cut from a slave whose sense of hearing was a little too acute.

OCTOBER 3, 1862. President Lincoln's Emancipation Proclamation received: delivered on the 24th of last month. Thank God, the word has at last been spoken. Light begins to break through. Let the sons of earth rejoice. Sing paeans to Liberty. Let tyranny die.[80]

OCTOBER 15, 1862. The Proclamation, or something else, has turned our proposed schools into working parties; and the negroes are to be removed as fast as possible, to make sugar on the confiscated plantations.[81] No doubt, for the present hour, this process will *pay*; but whether, in the end, their labor will prove more profitable to the Government than the learning they would otherwise get, I seriously question. Many of the slaves are quite as light as their owners, and have quite as clear a sense of the proprieties of life. Now and then one who is sensitive, refined, and educated. To this latter class Slavery is intolerable. I have seen only one, well educated. She is a young woman of great beauty, exceedingly sensitive, light complexion, blue eyes, brown hair, and looks for all the world like Mrs. Marks.[82] She brought to camp her books, music, drawing, painting, canaries, and a thousand things in which women of culture take delight. When I asked what could have induced one so highly favored as she seemed to have been, to leave her home, where she was surrounded with all the luxuries of life, and treated with the utmost kindness, she replied that while her condition was vastly different from that of most slaves, it was none the less painful. Her state was the same as theirs; and until their status was changed, she could have no hope that hers would be different. Hence it was natural that she should be with them. While she was at home, the fact that she was educated, debarred her from all intercourse with slaves. While her master treated her very kindly – much too kindly for her mistress' peace of mind – she was really a prisoner. God pity such as these. Those who are not more sensitive than mules, can bear it.

OCTOBER 16, 1862. Am just reminded that on the 9th, I entered upon a new year. Multiplicity of business must excuse my neglect to honor the day with a thought as it passed. It is hot, muggy weather. Most ladies wear only one garment, and that is quite apt to leave the figure at least pa[r]tially nude. But then, lots of little niggers are to be seen entirely nude, and if white folks copy their easy *habits*, especially when cotton and calico are scarce, and hoops are not to be had, it is not to be wondered at.

OCTOBER 17, 1862. Have just returned from a splendid evening ride with several "lubley cullerd gals." Received an order this p.m. from Gen. Butler, for a lot of female help at the Division Hospital; and this evening I harnessed the horse that Wm. and I have had for our own use during the season, and took over a load of the best ones, that is, the best looking ones I could find. I have not taken the *fair* sex out to ride before, since I was a young man. It almost makes me feel that the Benedictine wreath might not illy grace my bachelor brow. Our hospitals are filled with thousands of legless and armless victims, and others, afflicted with all the ills that flesh is heir to.

OCTOBER 18, 1862. Attended a review of Gen. Weitzel's Brigade.[83]

OCTOBER 20, 1862. Gen. Butler orders tenants to pay no more rent to disloyal landlords.[84]

OCTOBER 24, 1862. Received four months pay: $52.00. Gave $50.00 of it to the Chaplain, to send to father by Adams' Express. Expect to start for Texas to-morrow, by railroad, and drive the rebels before us, or capture them as we go. The First Regiment of Native Guards (colored) are to go with us; and Gen. Weitzel, with his whole Brigade, has gone up the Mississippi, to come down the Lafourche and meet us at the crossing.[85]

OCTOBER 25, 1862. Received orders this morning to stay and take care of the Contrabands. Not ambitious of military glory, nor anxious to die; so I am quite resigned to my fate; but should be very glad to be with Wm. He goes to the fight. Harnessed the horse and took Corp'l. Tillotson[86] down the river a few miles, to see the country and get some oranges, pecans, and other things, to send home by him to father. A good fellow: sorry to have him leave. Our wing of the expedition started at sunset, on a train of 38 cars. A cold, north wind prevails: the first cool breeze we have had since we crossed the Gulf Stream last March.

OCTOBER 26, 1862. (Sunday) Lonesome enough. No body in camp but the negroes, and their numbers are rapidly decreasing: only about 4,000 now. Wm. is gone.

OCTOBER 27, 1862. Carried Corp'l. Tillotson, with his things, to the steamer, and at night saw him start for home. Frost this morning. The "heated term" is evidently passed. As yet, we see no signs of the sere and yellow leaf: and there is quite as large a variety of flowers as in the spring-time and summer. The Northern troops have stood the heat remarkably well. Notwithstanding the persistent prayers of pious proslavery preachers, Providence has postponed the pestilence, and the people have enjoyed unusual health.[87] I have never been so well, or so heavy, as during the past summer: have drank nothing but rain water, very warm, with the wigglers strained out, have eaten *very little* but bread and milk, have bathed invariably once a day, befor[e] light in the morning, and usually just before going to bed at night; have labored during the past three months and more, 15 to 18 hours a day, besides falling into line two or three times a week in the night, at the call of the "long roll." Have not had the Dr. since I left Vermont, and have been unwell only once, and then for a few days only, during the past fortnight. Received every attention at the hands of friends with whom I had become acquainted down town, Mr. Irwin and wife,[88] formerly of Boston; and my friend Washington, a very intelligent man, as little like a negro as my father, who was owned by old Gen. Taylor, furnished me with an abundance of wild game, chickens, eggs, and so forth. Kind offices, especially at the hands of citizens, who do their deeds of charity at the risk of future proscription, and with the certainty of present ostracism, are very gratefully received.

OCTOBER 28, 1862. Learned to-day that Gen. Weitzel encountered the enemy yesterday on the Lafourche, and after a desperate engagement, in which he lost 40 or 50 killed, he succeeded, by a splendid bayonet charge, in driving the enemy from his entrenchments, capturing four hundred prisoners, fifteen cannon, and several hundred stands of small arms. The route [*sic*] was complete. The enemy escaped by taking the cars at Lafourche crossing, and are off for Berwick Bay. Col. McPheeters, of the Crescent City Regiment, in command of the rebel forces, was killed, besides many other officers and men. The rebels in their flight burned the village of Lafourche, and fired the bridge, but the pursuit was so close, they were compelled to leave, and our boys extinguished the flames before material damage was done.[89] The train brings word also that the 8th Vermont, with the 4th Mass. Battery, and the Colored Regiment, have to-day advanced on Des Allemands, and captured the place, without firing a gun. On their approach, the rebels abandoned their defenses, deserted their heavy guns, and fled in the direction of Vicksburg, evidently deeming it beneath their dignity to fight negroes.[90] They burned every building in the village, and the bridge crossing the bayou: about 300 feet long: a splendid bridge which we built last summer after they had burned it once before. Our boys opened two graves, in which they found the bodies of seven of our men, belonging to Co. E, who were captured by the rebels on the fourth of last month, and a little while after the capture were led out to the two graves, and shot, one at a time, falling into the grave as they were killed. They had enlisted here in New Orleans, and of course their captors must have revenge.[91]

NOVEMBER 2, 1862. (Sunday) Wm. came to town: glad to see him alive and well. The boys have completed the bridge at Des Allemands, and gone on to Lafourche.[92] Wm. is detailed, with others, to repair the telegraph line, which is down all the way, and the wire sunk in the bayous. It has been a cold week: three frosty mornings; but it is hot again now, and the people say we have had our winter, and shall get no more cold weather.

NOVEMBER 3, 1862. Wm. went back to work on the wire. Rebel steamer *Segur* captured at Berwick Bay.[93]

NOVEMBER 6, 1862. Our comrades taken at Des Allemands in Sept., released on parole, and sent down from Vicksburg under a flag of truce. Five of them were detained at Vicksburg, four died, seven were shot.[94]

NOVEMBER 7, 1862. An ammunition train that left here this morning, to supply our boys up the road, was blown up at Lafourche, killing 15 men and one negro woman. Two lieutenants of the 8th New Hampshire, sat smoking in a car that contained two tons of powder, and a large quantity of shells and balls, besides infantry cartridges, when the explosion took place. Six cars were demolished, and the engine and tender scattered to the four winds of heaven. Three of our Reg. killed, and Lieut. Nason, of our Co., slightly wounded.[95]

NOVEMBER 14, 1862. Paroled prisoners sent to Ship Island, to wait until exchanged. They take it rather hard: but *some folks* think they should not have surrendered.[96]

NOVEMBER 19, 1862. Another visit from Wm., who says they have got the telegraph in good order clear through to Berwick Bay. The rebels in their flight had burned all the railroad bridges but the one over Lafourche. The 8th Vermont built an excellent bridge, 634 feet long, over Bayou Boeuf, a deep stream, traversed by the heaviest steamers, in four days time, carrying all their timber and iron from this city, 74 miles.

NOVEMBER 24, 1862. Wm's. box came, from home, containing a variety of valuables.

NOVEMBER 25, 1862. Went over the road on a special lightning train, to assist telegraph operator, in repairing wire broken somewhere in the vicinity of the enemy. Rode on the engine. An exciting ride.

NOVEMBER 26, 1862. In the evening, with the assistance of Wm. and Elder Blake,[97] arrested two of the 9th Conn. Vols. who were robbing the Contrabands.

NOVEMBER 27, 1862. Rescued, with the help of my trusty pistol, a slave woman from the hands of a kidnapper. In the afternoon enjoyed a pleasant wagon ride up the river some 25 miles. Feel sensibly the lack of facilities for social enjoyment and mental and moral improvement.

NOVEMBER 29, 1862. A year in the service, and still alive and *well*. Well satisfied with my year's work.

NOVEMBER 30, 1862. The sick in hospital removed to the Bay (Berwick) and everybody belonging to the Regiment ordered to report there forthwith. My family of negroes are all at work on plantations confiscated to the Government, except about two hundred sick, left at their hospital, in the care of Dr. Wood. I have passed three months with them very pleasantly, and I have good reason to hope, not unprofitably. Duties have been very arduous. Wm[.] and I have had the care of all the rations, have seen them properly cooked and divided, each one receiving his share; we have attended to the wants of the sick, to the burying of the dead, and to the marrying of those connubially inclined. During most of the time we have fed from 4000, to 6,400; have had over 3000 different ones in hospital, have buried over 250, have had not quite 100 births, and have married a few score. I am well satisfied, that with all his degradation and wretchedness, the slave enjoys life far better than his owner can. Slavery of necessity robs the slave master of every incident which has a tendency to make it a pleasant thing to live on the earth.

 Two

DECEMBER 4, 1862. Struck my tent this morning, and took the ten o'clock train for Brashear City, on Berwick Bay, which is now the headquarters of the 8th Vermont: 80 miles west of New Orleans. Left Wm. to come up to-morrow. The Bay is connected with the Gulf of Mexico, and the salt water tides come in regularly. It must be a healthy city.[98]

DECEMBER 5, 1862. Put up our tent, and made a good floor, and furnished the "house" well, with things the rebels left behind them when they fled, on the approach of our troops. At night Wm. came up from New Orleans. Orders issued allowing registered enemies to leave the lines.

DECEMBER 7, 1862. On guard to-day, the first time in five months.

DECEMBER 11, 1862. Received from Col. Thomas a detail, requiring me to go to New Orleans and vicinity, and arrest deserters, Clemens,[99] bass drummer, and Decker,[100] a private.

DECEMBER 12, 1862. Found the deserters in the ranks of the Regular Artillery, having been enlisted several days. Their Commander refused to deliver them up, on our Col's. Order, and I went to Gen. Butler, who, in view of the fact that they had deserted from their Regiment, issued an order to their Commandant to deliver them up, notwithstanding they had enlisted in the Regulars. Lodged them in jail over night, and passed the evening very pleasantly with friends up town: a family of real anti-slavery Unionists. Stayed all night, and "went to bed," the first time for almost a year.

DECEMBER 13, 1862. Returned to Brashear City with the deserters.

DECEMBER 15, 1862. Went back to New Orleans after another deserter, Dr. Graves,[101] of Co. B, who has been gone nearly a month. Found Gen. Banks[102] had just reached the city with 30,000 soldiers in his train.

DECEMBER 16, 1862. Was in at Gen. Butler's Headquarters when the "little iron man of Waltham" [Banks] came in to relieve the man of many orders [Butler], of his command.

DECEMBER 17, 1862. Went up to Carrollton, and Camp Parapet,[103] in search of Graves. Saw most of the artillery and infantry, from both places, and from New Orleans, also, leaving for Vicksburg. Large numbers of the new troops are disembarking.

DECEMBER 20, 1862. Have searched the city thoroughly during the week, in uniform, and in planter's dress; and returned to Brashear City to-night without the Dr. Think he has gone back to Canada. Found all the gardens between New Orleans and Carrol[l]ton in the dress of early spring: in some of them corn, peas, lettuce, etc., were just springing up; and others were but just planted: but in all there is a great variety of fruits and flowers, many species of which are cultivated the year round. Winter weather here is better adapted to the cultivation of many kinds of flowers, and some varieties of fruit, than the extreme heat of summer.

DECEMBER 21, 1862. Find our troops here at the Bay very pleasantly located. Our land force is small: only the 8th Vermont, 21st Indiana, and a section of the 4th. Mass. Battery; but we have four gun boats here in the Bay, and the rebels have only one; but she can run in less water than our boats notwithstanding she is iron clad.[104] The bay here is one mile wide. A little farther up, not more than fifty rods. The rebels occupy the other side, and hardly a day passes but our pickets are fired at. None of us killed yet, although some of our clothes have been wounded. We have killed several of them across the Bay, distant a full mile.

DECEMBER 24, 1862. Gen. Banks' Proclamation issued: an excellent paper. If the disloyal people feel the ponderous weight of the law settling itself down upon them, let them take their necks out from under it, by becoming obedient.[105]

DECEMBER 28, 1862. (Sunday) On guard. The pickets captured and brought in a rebel lieutenant. Some of our boys escaped narrowly.

JANUARY 1, 1863. The grey old year is gone. With limping feet and silver hair, and failing voice, has gone! and with the year, what privileges have gone; what opportunities are beyond the reach of what multitudes of men. With an earnest heart, and with desires reaching beyond the circumscribed limits of geographical distinctions, I wish the world a "Happy New Year," and wish the race had not placed themselves in such position as to make it impossible for them to be happy; – until they change their relation to law. Am conscious of many things to be thankful for: – thankful for the privilege of standing, with my life freely offered up, not for the defense of country, merely, but for the defense of Liberty; thankful that God makes it my privilege to bring to the work perfect health, and a strong frame; thankful for the privilege of hearing from and thinking of home, and friends; thankful for such large hope that the temple of slavery is doomed to fall, even though it be destroyed by poor blind Samson,[106] and black at that; thankful that I live in a country able to withstand shocks that would have scattered all the other nations of the earth to the four winds of heaven; thankful that my situation, even in the army, is so pleasant as it is; thankful that our Co. is the healthiest in the Regiment, thanks to the wise counsel of our officers, who have had experience before; thankful that our officers are the smartest and best in the Regiment, and that the Col. understands it, quite as well as the men; thankful that my father and friends take so much pains to write frequent and interesting letters, correspondence covering almost the entire ground of the soldiers' facilities for the enjoyment of the amenities and courtesies of social life; thankful that the law of compensation metes out with exact justice the rewards of men, and of nations; thankful that I live to see the first day of January, 1863, but at the same time wait with anxious solicitude to hear from the President;[107] thankful that King Cotton is dethroned, and that I see in the desolation, and wide-spread ruin, and terrible starvation, and in the ceaseless wail of wretchedness that is heard all over the South, simply "the reward of their doings;"[108] thankful that I am "in for the war," be it three years, or thirty; so be God's mercy spares my life and health; thankful for the hope of returning, *some time*, to the pursuits of peace, with the *cause* of the war buried so deep that when, in the ages yet to be, it may be asked, "where is slavery?" Oblivion shall answer from the depths of hell, "The prey is mine."

How differently dies the year from what we ever saw before. As the bells in our city towers strike twelve, we see him borne gently away with silver hair and failing voice, on the balmy breeze, redolent of rose and violet, of magnolia and orange blossoms. Hitherto [in New England] we have seen him shriveled into nothingness by the chilling breath of old Boreas,[109] hiding him from mortal sight, under piles of ice and snow.

I suppose I have friends who would sneer at the business which has occupied my attention during the summer and autumn, and who would be glad of an opportunity to place themselves in the same category with the worthy ladies, and pious preachers of the Crescent City, who deem it woman-like and "chivalrous," to scoff at our noble dead – who, in defense of the Nation's life, have given their blood to crimson the waters of the Mississippi, or to enrich the soil on its banks – as they are being borne to their long home; but as for myself, I am fallen so low, and my sense of the proprieties of life is so dull, that I am satisfied with my summer's work, and thank God for the opportunity of sowing seed, in this field.

JANUARY 4, 1863. Chaplain preached his second sermon to the Regiment. On picket guard, and did not hear him. Very hot day. Terrible thunder storm all last night. No body slept a wink. Several houses demolished in the city. Enemy in sight all day.

JANUARY 7, 1863. Picket shot one of the enemy, and killed him instantly. Brought in the body.

JANUARY 9, 1863. Left Brashear City, and were placed in Gen. Weitzel's Brigade, on the Lafourche. Ten Regiments in the Brigade, besides lots of artillery, and cavalry.

JANUARY 11, 1863. (Sunday) The entire Brigade moved Back to Berwick Bay. After the *Cotton*.

JANUARY 13, 1863. The Brigade crossed the Bay, eight Regiments infantry, 21 pieces artillery, and a small body of cavalry. Marched on Patterson[ville], eight miles up [the Atchafalaya River], which place the rebels evacuated on our approach, and took shelter under cover of their gun boat *Cotton*, a few miles further up, supported also by a heavy land battery. Here they made a stand, and the battle waxed hot, until darkness put an end to the contest for the day. The two armies slept on the field, under arms. The 8th Vt. bivouacked in a cane field. Our Co. was on picket. It rained all night. At daylight we were called in from picket, and Col. Thomas read an order from Gen. Weitzel, calling for sixty sure shots to volunteer from the Regiment, to go and pick off the gunners from the *Cotton*. Eleven volunteered from Co. F, myself among the number. While volunteers were stepping out, the battle commenced a mile or so up the stream, and our regiment, preceded by the sharpshooters, marched on board a gun boat and crossed the Bay, where the Regiment landed, and we "sharpshooters," weak and breakfastless, went up to the blockade on the gun boat. By sunrise we reached the scene of action, where we found the other three gun boats in the midst of a terrific contest. Solid shot and shells from the big guns of the *Cotton*, and the rebels' land batteries were shivering timbers, and bursting on every side. We found the *Calhoun*, our most efficient boat, hard aground, and her Capt. told us there was a long line of rifle pits on the other shore, from which the enemy's sharpshooters had killed Commodore Buchanan, and were picking off all the gunners; and he gave us orders to land and capture the rifle pits, at every hazard, as the only means of saving the fleet.

We were not long in leaving that boat, and had but just stepped on shore when she was riddled with a shower of iron and lead. After firing a few shots we charged on the rifle pits, and took 37 prisoners and 45 guns, with ammunition. We found 100 rifle pits, occupied by 150 of the enemy's sharpshooters; but our numbers were so few that most of them made their escape. *Cotton* by this time badly disabled, and backing off up the Bay, which, for some miles along here is only 400 to 1000 feet wide. Our party deployed as skirmishers, and followed her, with Col. Thomas and the Regiment at supporting distance in the rear. When near the *Cotton*, a rebel battery on the other side, before undiscovered, under cover of which the *Cotton* lay, opened upon us with vigor, filling the air with bursting bombs and solid shot, which mowed the cane on every side. The Bay intervening between us and the battery, so we could not charge upon it, we were obliged to retreat under cover of our gun boats, which we found trying to remove the obstructions from the channel.

During the engagement to-day the rebels discharged a torpedo previously sunk at the blockade, which came within about six feet of making an end of the *Grey Cloud*. Her consort was shivered into a thousand pieces, and she was entirely submerged; by a sheet of water which filled the air. Search was made and another wire found, which led to a second "infernal machine,"[110] sunk in 40 feet of water, which, on being taken up, was found to contain 125 pounds powder. Action ceased, and we have bivouacked on the field, supperless, in a drenching rain. Lots of splendid buildings burned during the day by bursting shells, but the loss of life very small: less than 100 on our side. Buried rebels in their own pits.[111]

JANUARY 15, 1863. We were startled from our very pleasant dreams at three this morning, by an explosion, which proved to be the *Cotton*, which had burned to her magazine and then blew up. The end of our expedition being thus accomplished, we returned to Brashear City, the sharpshooters of the 8th being honored with a passage on one of the gun boats. Artillery and cavalry all safely crossed to the home side of the Bay soon after midnight, and we camped on the ground again, with no food since morning. Rained all day. Not a man in our Reg. killed or wounded: some escaped narrowly.

JANUARY 16, 1863. Most of the Brigade returned to Camp Stevens,[112] on the Lafourche; our Regiment with the rest. Reached camp at midnight, and after supper went to bed (that is, laid on the ground) in tents, without our equipments on. We expect to move on Vicksburg at once.

JANUARY 21, 1863. Very pleasant spring like day. Walked up the river a few miles through the very pleasant village of Thibodaux. Most splendid church, and surrounding scenery, I ever saw. Wild flowers in the church yard: the first I have seen looking like home. A profusion of yellow dandelions, daisies, and all kinds of wild violets and roses. But, with all the beauty of this lovely place, the *curse* is here. The South is being burned with fire, and drowned in blood. Her villages are desolate, her lands, the richest in the world, laid waste, the wings of commerce idle, all her interests, material, social, political, tied to the hideous monster – Slavery – which is marching with rapid strides to its death.[113] Strange they are so infatuated they will not sever the connection. Well, let them hang together. I am content. Slavery must die; and if the South insists on being buried in the same grave, I shall see in it nothing but the retributive hand of God. I thank God I live to see the day when the South is beginning to *burn*; and that it is my privilege to help kindle the fires. Not because I love to look on scenes of desolation, burning villages, and starving women and children, but because I love liberty, and hate slavery. I thank God my love of liberty is so large that it gives me courage to face the enemy without trembling.

JANUARY 23, 1863. Order making Major Dillingham Lt. Col.,[114] read on dress parade. Also promoting Capt. Grout to Major.[115]

JANUARY 25, 1863. Chaplain preached his third sermon to the Regiment, from 2d chap. of Genesis. A most excellent sermon, in which he took the true ground, in regard to the temptations incident to a soldier's life; claiming that the soldier in camp, or in the field, is subject to no temptations but such as are common to men.

JANUARY 30, 1863. Zeri Campbell (discharged) left the hospital, and started for home.[116]

FEBRUARY 1, 1863. (Sunday) Listened to an excellent sermon by Chaplain Williams. The Regiment is formed in divisions, and stands in the open air during service. The band furnishes excellent music, and the boys sing well.

FEBRUARY 13, 1863. A negro hung here at the jail, for the crime of rape.

FEBRUARY 15, 1863. (Sunday) Went to the Catholic Church at the village. Sermon in French. Congregation mostly women: almost every one dressed in mourning. Many wear white for mourning, which in this hot country, looks better than black. Excessively hot day.

23. A view of Thibodaux, Louisiana, from across Bayou Lafourche. Watercolor by Alfred R. Waud, 1866. Courtesy of the Historic New Orleans Collection, Museum/Research Center.

24. Built in 1847, St. Joseph's was the only Catholic church in Thibodaux at the time of Kinsley's visit. Courtesy of the Allen J. Ellender Archives, Ellender Memorial Library, Nicholls State University.

FEBRUARY 16, 1863. On guard to-day: home guard.

FEBRUARY 17, 1863. Attended a Catholic funeral this morning, at the Church in Thibodaux, and afterward attended as witness, the Court-Martial of Wm. A. Decker, whom I arrested in New Orleans last Dec. for desertion. Very wet, and mud three feet deep.

FEBRUARY 18, 1863. Attended at the Court House in Thibodaux, the Court Martial of G. Clemens, arrested for desertion. Received a copy of the Worcester (Mass.) *Palladium,* by which I learn of the death, by dip[h]theria, of one of the prettiest little girls in New England: my brother Daniel's second child, Fanny Amelia. She died Jan. 27, aged 5 years: too young to feel the storms of life, but not too young to be a very good girl.[117] [*Newspaper clipping inserted here which reads:* "of dip[h]theria, yesterday morning, Fanny Amelia, second daughter of Daniel Kinsley, aged 5 years 5 mos."] God has gathered one of his fairest flowers to the garden of life.

FEBRUARY 20, 1863. On picket guard. Very fine day. No body killed. Enjoyed the odors of spring, the singing of birds, and retrospective day dreams of home. How strong are the influences which bind one to the home of his youth. No combination of vicissitudes can alienate. "Let me go to my home," – when peace shall again smile upon us, with tyranny dead: until then, let me walk through carnage and blood, and let the horrors of war be my familiar friends, and let them not depart from me.

FEBRUARY 22, 1863. (Sunday) Attended Catholic church at Thibodaux. First Sunday in Lent. Enough holy water sprinkled to drown a Yankee congregation; but the residents of these Louisiana swamps are amphibious, and stood it like ducks in a shower. After service perambulated the village with four or five of the porgies.[118] Gardens are filled with all the delicacies of early spring, designed to please the epicurean tastes of our luxurious livers. Fruit trees in blossom.

FEBRUARY 23, 1863. Struck our tents before light, and marched in the cool of the morning to the Terrebonne R. R. station, a distance of five miles, and took the cars for Berwick Bay, leaving one battery of six guns and one cavalry Co. to bring up the rear. The rest of the Brigade had previously moved to the Bay. Glad enough to get back here, where we are higher than the water. At Lafourche the river was a number of feet higher than our heads, and confined within levees, like the Mississippi. Ground was very wet, and much of the time covered with water. We have here at the Bay, a nice dry camp ground, very pleasantly located, close on the shore.[119] The enemy have been heavily reenforced on the Teche, a few miles above us, and evidently intend to test our strength. They have another boat out,[120] to take the place of the

25. Union soldiers march along a bayou road lined with moss-draped cypress trees in the spring of 1863. *Battles and Leaders of the Civil War*, III, 591.

Cotton, which we destroyed the other day. I enjoyed the ride hither very much. With the exception of two miles, the entire distance from Terrebonne to this place (28 miles) is an unbroken swamp, covered with a dense growth of large cypress trees; and from the top of the cars where many of us stood, we saw hundreds of huge alligators, and large numbers of turtles, and a great variety of snakes, lying on large logs just above the surface of the water. We shot several, and *shot at* a great many. Woods vocal with birds.

FEBRUARY 24, 1863. We met with a very serious loss last night, at about twelve o'clock. The gun boat *Grey Cloud*, which was up the Teche on picket, ran against a "snag," and started at once for her mooring at this wharf, leaking badly. She had just reached this point, when she sunk, not more than twenty feet from shore, carrying down a number of men, 7, and all her heavy rifled cannon.[121] We are building a fort and fortifying extensively at the confluence of the Teche and Atchafalaya, with the Bay.

FEBRUARY 27, 1863. Rebels from the other side fired into us, but retreated on the approach of our gun boats. Detachments from the 8th Vt. detailed to do picket duty on the gun boats. The look out at the mast head stands in an iron sentry box, to protect him from the enemy's rifles as the boat flies back and forth.

MARCH 1, 1863. (Sunday) No service: Chaplain gone to Vermont.

MARCH 3, 1863. On guard. Pleasant day.

MARCH 5, 1863. Police duty occupied one hour; after which I spent the day up the river at the fort, and at the quarters of the several batteries, where they were shooting at targets, with shot and shells. Returned by the Cavalry quarters, where they were jumping their horses over fences and ditches. Splendid riding.

MARCH 6, 1863. Several of the enemy came in and gave themselves up, and a number of prisoners taken by our pickets. Four more eight inch guns brought up from New Orleans, for the fort. The bow gun, a splendid Parrott,[122] removed from the wreck of the *Grey Cloud* by the use of diving bells. The gun comes out in perfect order.

MARCH 8, 1863. (Sunday) Excessively hot. Very quiet in camp. Nothing to be seen, or heard, save the tramp, tramp, tramp, of the ever watchful sentinel, on his "beat."

MARCH 10, 1863. A small body of rebel Cavalry came down on the opposite side of the Bay. A shell from one of our batteries killed two of the advance party, with their horses, and the remainder "changed their base."

MARCH 12, 1863. Several more guns taken up from the *Grey Cloud* (*Kinsman*).

MARCH 13, 1863. On guard. One of our batteries, with a small infantry force had a slight skirmish with the enemy's cavalry and infantry. The rebels retreated, leaving three killed and several wounded. No loss on our side.

MARCH 18, 1863. Went with the Co. and one other, and a body of Cavalry, across the Bay and chased a body of rebel cavalry ten miles, and returned, bringing seven prisoners with their horses and arms. The enemy lost several killed. Our only loss was four horses, shot under their riders.

MARCH 19, 1863. The enemy fired into our flag of truce boat, which went over to carry paroled prisoners.

MARCH 20, 1863. One of Gen. Weitzel's "boys" returned this afternoon from the enemy's country, whither he had been in the guise of "poor white trash," to enlist in the Confederate service; but he was *so very "poor"* (non compos mentis), that his patriotic desire to serve the Confederacy was treated with contempt; and he was advised to "apply to the Yankees, who needed just such men as himself." He deemed the advice good, and acted upon it with all the haste that discretion would allow; and there is no question that his timely arrival has saved the entire Brigade from annihilation. As soon as darkness became visible, the great guns were removed from our fort, and everything was silently put on board the cars (115 in number), and at daylight on the morning of the [*continues in next entry*]

MARCH 21, 1863. 21st, we were here at Bayou Boeuf, waiting with open arms to receive a rebel flotilla which is on its way hither from Red River, by way of Grand Lake, with the object of burning the R.R. bridge at this point, and attacking us in the rear at Brashear City, while the forces on the Teche were to engage us in front. A very nice little plan; only the sleepless vigilance of Gen. Weitzel, who sometimes sees farther into the enemy's country than they dream, has made it expedient for them to postpone it. We still hold Brashear City, (distant seven miles) with gun boats.

MARCH 22, 1863. (Sunday) Very pleasant day; but not a very pleasant camp ground. Tents are pitched in a cane field. Ground not very dry. Cane 18 inches high, and just hoed out. Blackberries ripe, and very plenty.

MARCH 23, 1863. At one this morning the camp was fired into by a band of mounted rangers who had stolen down on the opposite side of the bayou, under cover of darkness. No body hurt: balls went over. When the line was dismissed our Company was ordered on board a gun boat, for service in Berwick Bay. We went on board at daylight, in the midst of a terrific thunder storm, which kept the boat at her moorings during the day, and all night. Everybody wet, hungry, and sleepy.

MARCH 24, 1863. At sunrise we steamed around into the Bay, and have been cruising all day, hoping to find some of the rebel fighting craft, which possess such astonishing facilities for keeping out of range of our gun boats.

MARCH 25, 1863. Stayed on gun boat last night, at the entrance of the Teche into the Bay. Relieved this morning from the gun boat, and stayed in depot all day. Got our rations at night, which we should have had last Sunday.

MARCH 26, 1863. Captured, on the other side of the Bay, a Texan Ranger, mounted on the smartest little horse in the world. Regiment returned at night to Bayou Boeuf. Ground covered with water. Large numbers sick.

MARCH 28, 1863. Our best gun boat, the *Diana*, taken by the rebels on the Teche, near Pattersonville, after a sharp engagement, in which her Capt.

(Peterson) and ten men were killed, some 25 wounded, and 98 taken prisoners. Two Cos. of rebel Cavalry were entirely destroyed by the *Diana* before her surrender.[123]

MARCH 29, 1863. (Sunday) Our Co. took cars for Bayou Ramus [Ramos], to guard R.R. bridge.

APRIL 1, 1863. Co. returned to Bayou Boeuf, had little to eat but blackberries for three days.

APRIL 2, 1863. The Brigade marched in the cool of the evening, to Berwick Bay: eleven miles between the two camp grounds. Baggage to follow by boat. Cars occupied in bringing hither 30,000 troops from New Orleans, recently from Baton Rouge, which city is now held by colored soldiers alone.[124]

APRIL 3, 1863. Have just had an addition to our artillery force, of twelve 32 pounder Parrott guns, rifled. Each gun is drawn by eight mules: and same number to each caisson.

APRIL 4, 1863. The enemy came down on the opposite side of the Bay; but a few shells from our long guns scattered them. They are taking the engines from all the sugar houses in the country, to cast into cannon.

APRIL 9, 1863. Our Regiment, with many others, crossed the Bay, for a move into the enemy's country, up the Teche. Detailed, myself, from headquarters, to remain behind, as Brigade printer.[125] The boys had some skirmishing and brought in 100 nice mules. No lives lost.

APRIL 10, 1863. Rebel battery of 12 guns withdrew toward Pattersonville.

APRIL 11, 1863. Our forces, 50 or 60,000 strong, moved toward the enemy; the 8th Vermont occupying the right of the advance column. The enemy after slight resistance, abandoned their outer line of defenses, below Pattersonville, and fell back to their strong hold above the village. None killed on our side, and but few of the enemy. Our Captain has just left us. He is now Major of the 1st Reg. Native Guards.[126] Sorry to lose so good an officer.

APRIL 12, 1863. (Sunday) The firing has been heavy all day, up the Teche, at Pattersonville. Our heavy guns have battered the enemy's fort without effect.

APRIL 13, 1863. This morning the 8th Vermont and 75th N.Y. charged the fort, and captured all the guns, losing only 30 men, killed.[127] Wm. was brought back this morning, sick. Was sick when he left, and ought not to have gone. Took him to hospital.

APRIL 14, 1863. Two gun boats and a transport came down this morning, having captured the rebel ram, *Queen of the West,* or rather destroyed her, and captured her commander, the notorious Fuller, with several other officers, and 72 men.[128] 49 were killed on the *Queen*, but not a man injured on our side. Another transport is just down, from Franklin, with a load of prisoners taken there to-day. She brings some of our wounded.

APRIL 15, 1863. Rebel steamer *Cornie*,[129] captured yesterday near Franklin, with 200 badly wounded rebels on board, has just come in, bringing the poor fellows, many of them now dead. Our boys had an encounter with the *Diana* yesterday. She soon went to the bottom, with most of her crew; whereupon the rebels fired their remaining boats, and evacuated Franklin.[130] Gen. Grover had succeeded in gaining their rear, and with a terribly destructive discharge of artillery, he ordered a halt. The slain were piled in heaps, and 1500 laid down their arms and surrendered. Capt. Simms was captured, with the rebels' best battery, and a large number of field pieces. The escaped rebels are on the way toward Texas, hotly pursued. Simms, or Semmes, is a son of the Capt. of the *Alabama* (290).[131]

APRIL 16, 1863. Transport came in with about 200 of our own wounded. 14 died on the way down from Franklin. They have been removed to the cars, and will reach New Orleans by morning. Not a woman in all this city to bring them water, or make them tea or toast. In fact, no bread, "no nothing." The poor fellows have been furnished each with a hard cracker, and they will have business till they reach the city. Another transport in from Franklin, with 200 rebel prisoners, who are to lie on the wharf over night, and visit New Orleans to-morrow. Gen. Banks' troops quartered in the rebel salt country (New Town) last night, which place the rebels made no attempt to defend. He is pressing them hotly: is already more than 100 miles from here.[132]

APRIL 18, 1863. Wm. succeeded in getting discharged from the hospital, but was obliged to be carried back before night. Another transport from Franklin, with 270 rebel prisoners. Not more than 15 in the whole number dressed in uniform. Many have women's blankets, shawls, petticoats, and calico bedquilts, rigged into coats. Some have hats, many none. One would think they had been robbing negro quarters which had been deserted since the last century, and had come out as escort to the Calathumpians.[133]

APRIL 19, 1863. (Sunday) Splendid thunder storm all day. Large quantity of rain. Not very well: getting weak, from diarrhoea which comes of drinking shocking bad water.

APRIL 20, 1863. A cargo of 200 prisoners, among them some Indians, brought down from Franklin. Another steamer, loaded with rebel camp equipage, and several heavy guns, taken from their fortifications.

APRIL 21, 1863. Considerable fasting, and a little soda cracker, have checked my umbilical difficulty, and my health is much improved. Wm. returned from hospital again. Reckon he will stay out this time. He seems much improved. Our gun boats are up these interminable bayous, within forty miles of Red River, and will doubtless join Com. Farragut soon, as Gen. Banks expects to meet a portion of the Yazoo expedition in a few days, on Red River.[134] A few rebel prisoners brought down to-day (60).

APRIL 22, 1863. A few hundred horses and mules, captured by Gen. Banks, came in.

APRIL 23, 1863. Met this evening in the Depot, one old fellow disciple of Faust, named Turner,[135] who "served his time" with me in Boston. He is in the 4th Mass. A glorious good fellow.

APRIL 24, 1863. Wm. commenced work with me in the office. My health perfect now. 35 prisoners came down.

APRIL 26, 1863. (Sunday) Webster, of 16th N. H.,[136] died on gallery in front of our office very suddenly, while talking with a companion. 179 prisoners brought down.

APRIL 28, 1863. Went into hospital, pretty hard sick with diarrhoea.

MAY 2, 1863. G. W. Scribner[137] of our Co. died, in the same ward with me. About 500 sick and wounded in hospital. We are dying at the rate of 8 to 12 a day. Congregational Chaplain from Me. brought in books and papers.

MAY 3, 1863. (Sunday) Very pleasant day. A Dutchman died so quietly that those next to him did not know he was worse, until he was found cold.

MAY 5, 1863. Think my health improving somewhat, but am not able to sit up at all. Wm. came to see me, and made a good visit. He has received an official detail to work in the printing office. He brings word also that he has definite information from Frank Scott, that he was conscripted by the rebels about six months ago.

MAY 6, 1863. Gen. Ullman[n] is here at the Bay, for the purpose of raising eighteen Regiments of colored soldiers.[138]

MAY 10, 1863. Health still improving: *very* slowly. A very pleasant Sabbath.

MAY 12, 1863. Find life in hospital much more pleasant than I supposed it could be. Wants all supplied by the kindest hands, and every effort put forth to make us comfortable; still many grumble, and act like fools: and kill themselves by imprudence, eating forbidden food which they steal.

MAY 16, 1863. Received a nice lot of letters from my very kind cousins in Georgia [Vt.].

MAY 17, 1863. Wm. came again, and stayed until night. Enjoyed the visit with him very much. Health still improving, very perceptibly; although not able to stand alone yet. Not flesh enough on my bones for a fly's dinner. Very pleasant Sabbath.

MAY 24, 1863. (Sunday) Have expected Wm. all day, but he has not been over. Think he must be busy with some pressing [print] "job." Have walked a few rods, and find my strength returning.

MAY 26, 1863. Another visit from Wm. He was in New Orleans Sunday. Went down Saturday to get an addition to his stock of printing materials.

MAY 28, 1863. A lot of boys are at work putting floors in our tents, to keep us off the wet ground when it rains. Good thing: tip top. I was sleepless last night. Listened to the bombardment of Port Hudson, which was kept up all night, and all the forenoon to-day.[139] It is sufficiently irksome to be idle at such a time as this; but somehow I am quite content to lie here and let Government take care of me until I shall regain my strength and muscle, weakened and wasted away with the wearying work of war.

MAY 29, 1863. Surgeon Allen,[140] of the 8th Vt. sent for by telegraph from Port Hudson, to assist in caring for the wounded. Cannonading incessant all day.

MAY 30, 1863. Am very much improved in health; in fact am quite well, so the Dr. says, but it will be some time before I regain my full strength. Dr. has put me into one of the Wards, to give medicine and fodder to the sick, with injunctions to sleep nights and not work more than six hours a day, until I am fit for duty, and then he will let me return to the office.

MAY 31, 1863. (Sunday) Mr. Tillotson[141] tells me that while at Brashear City yesterday morning, he saw Wm. (who had got released from the printing office) on board the cars, on his way to Port Hudson, via New Orleans. Since writing this last sentence Wm. has been over to see me. Found he was to be left, with others to nurse the sick at N. O., and returned to office.

JUNE 2, 1863. An artillery battle was kept up all night by the rebels on the other side of the Bay, and our forces on this side. Have not learned the result, but presume little damage was done to either party, distance being too great.

JUNE 3, 1863. Learn that the rebels captured several attendants at our hospital on the other side of the Bay, in the fight above, but were driven off with considerable slaughter.[142] Excessively hot to-day. Avery died.[143]

JUNE 5, 1863. Wm. came over with his boat, and gave me a very pleasant sail.[144]

JUNE 7, 1863. (Sunday) Very pleasant day. Wm. came again with his boat, and we sailed to the upper end of the island, some four miles, stopping occasionally by the way to gather blackberries which hung temptingly over the water, and easy of access from the boat. Landed at the end of the island, and attended negro meeting. One sermon by a white soldier, one by a negro field hand. Both good. Singing beyond all description: inciting first to tears, then to shouts: original, and full of power, whether of pathos, of warning, or of exultation. Sailed back in the cool of the evening, enjoying the consciousness that the day had been well spent, and very pleasantly. Am glad Wm. comes over so often. This plantation is long, and half the negroes have their quarters at each end, which saves travel. A field of corn on the island several miles long, just in condition to roast.

JUNE 8, 1863. Another visit from Wm., and another sail. Find they have a wonderful tendency to increase my strength. Rowed under the shade of some large water oaks, and hanging our clothes on the limbs, between the snakes, plunged over the side of the boat, and had a good old fashioned time. Lively work dodging alligators.

JUNE 9, 1863. Adam Armstrong, 53d Mass.[145] died suddenly, as scores have died here, without a moment's warning: some while going to or from their meals, or while walking out for exercise. Several have died in their beds so quietly as not to attract the attention of their attendants, or even of those lying nearest them. Don't understand it. Got orders in the evening to have the entire hospital ready to move to New Orleans at 5 o'clock in the morning. Cause, guerrillas are around firing into hospitals and unprotected hamlets, and we are without adequate protection, and they want our medicines and stores.

JUNE 11, 1863. Sick train reached New Orleans terminus of the road last evening, only two dying on the way, and *rested* in the cars until this morning. To-day we have got them comfortably located in the several city hospitals. I purpose to look the city over a little before going back to the printing office at Berwick Bay.

JUNE 12, 1863. Went to the Barracks on business,[146] and found Case, whom I supposed dead, in a feeble condition, and expecting to start for home in a few days, discharged. Don't think he will live to see Vt. I begin to feel the effects of over much exercise, and heat, in removing the hospital; and ward-master Sheldon, as completely "fagged out" as myself, has got leave of absence, and we are to rusticate a few days, or weeks, possibly, with some friends in Algiers,

26. Parade grounds and residential quarters at the New Orleans Barracks, circa 1895. Courtesy of the Historic New Orleans Collection, Museum/Research Center.

and Gretna. Hear of a number of our Co. killed at Port Hudson.[147] O how I wish I could be with them.

JUNE 14, 1863. We passed the day very pleasantly with Father Washington and his family, and in the cool of the evening enjoyed an excursion down the coast,[148] very much.

JUNE 15, 1863. "Billeted" ourselves on the family of James S. Thomas,[149] a loyal machinist of Gretna, hoping, by proper diet, gentle exercise, pure air, and the assiduous care of Mrs. Thomas and her daughters, to be fit for duty soon.

JUNE 17, 1863. Wm. came down from the Bay yesterday, and returned to-day.

JUNE 19, 1863. Wm. down again, from the Bay. My health improving.

JUNE 21, 1863. We learned that a band of 2000 guerrillas last night burned four of our steamers on Bayou Plaquemine, and the R.R. bridges above us, over the rivers Des Allemands and Lafourche.[150] A train has gone up the road this morning to reconnoiter. Wm. is on board, expecting a fight.

JUNE 23, 1863. Wm. returned this morning with the assurance that the steamers were burned, but that the attempt on the bridges proved abortive. The rebels however tore up some of the track beyond Lafourche bridge, and so the train he was on could get no farther than the river, which place it reached just in time to witness a renewal of the attack on the bridge Sunday evening. The bridge was defended by a force of 400, with several pieces of artillery. Our forces held their fire until the enemy, 2000 strong, with artillery, were within forty feet of their line, when they opened a storm which covered the ground with slain. They soon rallied and renewed the attack, but met the same warm reception as before. The third time they rallied, and pressed to the very mouths of our cannon and demanded their surrender; whereupon they were run through with our bayonets. They finally retired from the field, leaving nine of our men killed, and only twice that number wounded; while Wm. says he counted one hundred and eighteen slain rebels near the bridge the next morning, and there were 43 a little distance off.[151] Every shot from the enemy's cannons went several feet too high. Mr. Sheldon, well rested and in good condition again, leaves to-day for Port Hudson and Wm., being unable to get back to the Bay, remains to wait on me – and – Miss Thomas. Dare say I shall get little of his attention.

JUNE 24, 1863. Our forces at Lafourche, learning that the enemy had marched on Berwick Bay, capturing all our forces there, some 1200, burned the bridge and retired to New Orleans. By this surrender of the Bay (*a surprise*) we lose all the tents and camp equipage of some thirty of the Regiments that went up the Teche, besides a number of heavy guns, piles of ammunition, commissary and quartermaster's stores, and the knapsacks with their contents, belonging to the men. The place was taken without firing a gun, and only three of our men escaped: the quartermaster, provost marshal, and his clerk. They got on board the transport before she swung off, and reached New Orleans by the Gulf of Mexico. Wm.'s things all gone.[152]

JUNE 25, 1863. Went into a store and stood on the scales. Weigh 106 pounds: 63 less than before I was sick. Am now some 25 or 30 pounds heavier than six weeks ago, and still gaining.

JUNE 26, 1863. Passed the day very pleasantly at the residence of Mr. Morton.[153] Most persons expect an immediate attack on New Orleans. Small force here now. These guerrilla raids have frightened several thousand negroes that Gen. Banks had hired out to slaveholders, from their work, and they are flocking to New Orleans in droves. Hope that slaveholders will be left to pick up their own help, and the Government will employ the negroes in more legitimate business than raising corn to support the rebellion.

JUNE 27, 1863. Rained hard all day, and I kept quiet, in doors. Begin to feel quite strong & well.

JUNE 28, 1863. (Sunday) Dined with Mr. Yale, formerly from New York; for years past an overseer on a plantation, but now retired from business. None of the "plantation manners" about him, but thoroughly imbued with plantation principles. Great excitement in town all day: most persons apprehensive that the enemy were coming down the road to attack New Orleans.[154] No one killed.

JUNE 29, 1863. Wm. commenced at the Barracks: on night watch.

JUNE 30, 1863. Went to New Orleans in the afternoon. Stayed over night at St. Louis Hospital.

JULY 1, 1863. Went down to the Barracks to send some things home to father by Case. Found he died very suddenly Monday noon, 29th.[155] Wm. in the enjoyment of excellent health.

JULY 2, 1863. Returned to Gretna and got my clothing, to leave in the city while I go to Port Hudson to get a number of Descriptive Lists signed. Excessively hot. Wrote to father, and Mr. Janes of Georgia.[156]

JULY 3, 1863. The *Iberville*, on which I was to have gone to Port Hudson, was towed back this evening, having been disabled 70 miles up the river, by seven shells from rebel batteries on the banks, one of which entered her steam chest. Two men killed, and six wounded.[157]

JULY 4, 1863. Celebrated the "Glorious Fourth" by staying in doors and keeping comfortable, and wondering how men could be so jubilant, and the country still so sick. Things in this Department have never looked so dark as now; but I hope our case is near the "turning point," and that in a few days Drs. Banks and Grant may make us convalescent.[158] When the sun was getting low, a friend treated me to a "buggy ride" down the coast a dozen miles. Returned just in time to witness the grand demonstration on Canal street. It seems a heartless mockery. I must wait for the close of the war, and for a free country, before I get jubilant over the "Fourth."

JULY 5, 1863. Passed the day with Wm. at the Barracks. Stayed all night.

JULY 7, 1863. Glorious news from Vicksburg. Pemberton surrendered on the 4th with 31,000 prisoners, 208 guns, and 50,000 new Enfield rifles, in boxes, besides all the small arms in use by the prisoners. Port Hudson must fall soon.[159]

JULY 8, 1863. Started for Port Hudson on board the *North America*.

JULY 9, 1863. Reached Great Bend this morning. Found three rebel batteries of 30 guns on the levee, and, having a cargo of ammunition for Gen. Banks on board, we deemed it prudent to drop back to "Bonnet Carrie," where we waited until night for a gun boat. No gun boat making its appearance, we put on board our steamer and two others that were waiting there for convoy, over 2,000 negroes who had fled thither from the "*Government*" plantations, on the approach of the guerrillas, and returned to New Orleans, reaching our wharf at midnight.

JULY 10, 1863. Gun boats came down this morning, bringing official intelligence that Port Hudson fell into our hands yesterday, with 5,000 prisoners, 50 heavy guns, and all the small arms.[160] The river is at last open.

JULY 11, 1863. Learned that Widow McGarry,[161] who says she was to have been married to Sergt. Case soon, has removed his body from the hospital yard, placed it in a metallic case, and deposited it in her family tomb, in New Orleans.

JULY 12, 1863. Passed the day with Wm. at the Barracks. Find him pleasantly situated writing for the Dr.

JULY 13, 1863. Gen. Weitzel's Brigade came down the river and fought a desperate battle with the rebels at Donaldsonville and Great Bend, whipping them gloriously.[162]

JULY 14, 1863. Went up the R.R. to Gretna. Glorious news from Gens. Meade, Dix, and Rosencrans [*sic*].[163]

JULY 15, 1863. Returned to New Orleans, and am writing in Wm.'s room at Barracks. Our forces are rebuilding the bridges between here and Berwick Bay.[164]

JULY 16, 1863. Steamboat in from St. Louis. Great rejoicing. Incredulous secesh begin to believe that Vicksburg has fallen; or, rather, been redeemed.

JULY 17, 1863. Several steamboats in from the upper Mississippi. Provisions have a *downward* tendency, and prices must soon be lower. Some of our nine months men are on their way home up the river.

JULY 19, 1863. (Sunday) Very pleasant. Passed the day in writing to father, and others. Not much church service in the State this year. Secesh preachers are digging trenches for the Government, and Army Chaplains are home for their health. I find I am near the last leaf [of this volume]. Wish I could be assured that the work of war is as nearly done. But, dear as are the associations of home, strongly as I am drawn to the pursuits of peace, I would not see again the face of my friends until I have seen the end of the war. I cannot

27. Among those who fought in the battle for Port Hudson were these members of the Corps d'Afrique. Courtesy of the National Archives.

fill this page without expressing my gratitude to God for the mercy that has
preserved my life in the midst of battle, and while passing through other
scenes of danger, in which many have lost their lives. I am thankful that I
enlisted in the Eighth Vermont; thankful for the privilege I have enjoyed of
sowing seed while soldiering in the South; thankful that it is my privilege to
assist in gathering home the harvest of the year, even though the hands of
the reapers are red with blood; thankful for the hope that the light of Liberty
is soon to shine in this "house of bondage," from which hitherto the hand of
the oppressor has hidden the key of knowledge. [*The first volume of the diary
ends here.*]

[**JULY 29, 1863.** *On this date Kinsley writes the following letter to his friend Charles
Bingham.*]

New Orleans, La., July 29, 1863

My good friend Bingham:[165]

I received your very welcome letter of May 17, a long time ago; and,
contrary to my usual custom, I have delayed a long time to acknowledge it.
My anxiety to hear from my friends induces me to answer my letters with
little delay; but I have been sick some this spring myself, as well as you; and
when able to work, I have been very busy. I am at present writing at the
Barracks; because, though in good health, I am not yet strong enough for
duty in the field, and the rebels "gobbled up" my printing office at Berwick
Bay. I am sorry you are sick, and obliged to be idle while your companions
in arms are engaged in the work of war.[166] To a person capable of such
sentiments as you express in your letter, it must be irksome enough; but,
being sick, you are fortunate, I think, very fortunate, in the privilege of
being cared for at home. Of this, however, it is now too late for me to tell
you any thing. You have learned the lesson for yourself. O, how many hours,
when I was very sick last spring, I lay and thought of my mother,[167] and
my Aunt Elvira,[168] and your mother,[169] and a number of other mothers
in Fletcher, and of some who are not mothers yet, but who hope to be by
and by; and how ardently I wished I might fall in to their hands, during
sickness, at least, if no longer. I am very glad to learn that your health is
so much improved. There is no care like mother care; no love like mother
love, eh, Charley? and how quick we are to learn this lesson when the hand
of affliction falls heavy on our heads; and how readily we forget it, too many
of us, when in the pride of strength we fancy ourselves a little independent.

I hope your health is quite restored now, and I hope the war will be at
an end before you have an opportunity to reenlist. I think it might, if the
Grand Army, which has kept everything "quiet on the Potomac" during the
last two years, would insist on having a military man to lead them into battle.

It looks a little strange to us here, in the light of our own recent victories, that Lee was permitted to escape from the trap in which he seemed to be fairly caught.[170] You have read the papers, and have learned how the rebels captured Brashear City, when our troops were nearly all withdrawn to fill the place of the slain at Port Hudson. We have just recaptured the City, with *twenty* prisoners; and the R.R. bridges are being built between this city and that for the fourth time since we took New Orleans. Sometimes the rebs. have burned them, sometimes we. Altogether, we are a *little* proud of our exploits in the Department, and very glad to see the numerous steamers here from the upper rivers.

Now Charley, I am very glad you have written me, and sorry the reply has been so long delayed. I have this favor to ask: don't wait, as I have done, before you write again. Doubtless your haying is nearly done. Tell me all about it: who works for you, out doors: especially *in doors*; tell me who works for everybody, and how everybody does. How is Huldah?[171] Tell her I hope to see her when the war is over. How is uncle Medad, and the boys?[172] Who has Sam. Royce married?[173] Who else is to be married before the army boys get home? Not many three years men in this Department will see New England again. Some Companies in our Regiment have now less than a score of men; and by a year from next February we shall be not more than a handful. Our Company has been very fortunate: but few killed, and few sent home sick. Only five have died; among them Bona. Case. His body has been taken up and embalmed with widow's tears, and then placed in a metallic case and deposited in a tomb. Requiescat in pace. What is Jerome doing?[174] How is Monroe now?[175]

For your comfort, Charley, forget not this: that if you cannot serve your country in the field, you may serve her as efficiently by a useful life at home.

Your friend,
R. Kinsley

∼ Three ∼

[*Kinsley opens the second volume of his diary ten weeks after closing the first. At the outset he locates himself at the* Barracks, U.S. Genl. Hospital, New Orleans, La.]

SEPTEMBER 27, 1863. Received from Col. A. G. Hall,[176] 2d Reg. Inf. C. d. A.,[177] Ship Island, Miss., official notice that Maj. Gen'l. Banks had sent to his care a commission for me as 2d Lieut. in his Regiment, with the request that I would accept a discharge from the 8th Vermont, in order to accept it. This is altogether unexpected, never having made application for Commission. Duly thankful to the General, but have no ardent thirst for "glory," and not

28. The surgeon's building and surrounding wards at the Barracks General Hospital in New Orleans during the Civil War. Courtesy of the Jackson Barracks Military Library.

ambitious to run my neck into Jeff. Davis' halter by holding Commission in negro Regiment.[178] Don't like to leave William, either. Hardly know what to do.

OCTOBER 2, 1863. An Orderly from Gen. Banks brought me my discharge from the 8th Vermont.[179]

OCTOBER 5, 1863. Capt. Hawley,[180] from Ship Island, brought my Commission. I have determined to accept it, and cast my lot with the Colored Soldiers, for life or death. Feel no little regret at leaving the place. Have a few warm friends here: among them, Chaplain Andrus, from Michigan, the only pious Chaplain I have seen during two years of war.[181] Doubtless there are many, but in this Department they are like the visits of angels. My experience in hospital has been very pleasant, notwithstanding the constant succession of sad scenes – suffering from sickness, ghastly wounds, and many deaths daily.[182] I have learned to cherish the highest respect for a few of the ladies of New Orleans; but I am amazed when I think how very few. Seven or eight hundred, or perhaps two or three thousand Union soldiers, bruised and mangled in yesterday's battle are brought to the hospital, and a "baker's dozen," possibly a full score, of the ladies of this hospitable city, are abundant in labors, night and day, and lavish in expenditure, for their relief. When the ladies are

United States of America.

HEADQUARTERS, DEPARTMENT OF THE GULF.

PROVISIONAL COMMISSION.

No. _401_

Reposing Special Trust and Confidence in the Loyalty, Courage, Prudence and Ability of _Corpl. Rufus Kinsley_ of _Company K 8th Vermont Vol. Infty_ by virtue of the authority entrusted to me by the War-Department, I do appoint said _Corpl. Rufus Kinsley 2d Lieutenant_ of the _Second_ Regiment of _Infty. Corps d'Afrique_ Volunteers, (Company _B_ ,) to be obeyed and respected accordingly.

This Commission to remain in force until the pleasure of the President of the United States be made known in this behalf.

Given at New-Orleans, This _Twenty fifth_ day of _August_ in the year One Thousand Eight Hundred and Sixty-Three.

N. P. Banks

Major General Commanding.

By the General Commanding:

G. Norman Lieber
Acting Assistant Adjutant General.

29. Kinsley's provisional commission, signed by Major General N. P. Banks, as second lieutenant in the Second Corps d'Afrique. Courtesy of the Vermont Historical Society.

139

appealed to, "the hospital is not a fit place for ladies to visit." The next day, perhaps, the Confederate wounded are brought in, and immediately the hospitals are besieged by thousands of the dear creatures, loyal and true, ready to move heaven and earth to evince their sympathy for suffering humanity; but they never forget to inquire for the wards occupied by the Confederates. Surgeons in charge have had the good sense to receive their wines and cordials, jellies and jams, and issue them at their own option, whereat *Mesdames* have been greatly disgusted.

OCTOBER 10, 1863. Turned over my command to William, and left him Chief Nurse in Ward One, of the best General Hospital in the United States; best, because most favorably situated. Started for Ship Island to get papers necessary for being mustered.

OCTOBER 11, 1863. Reached Ship Island, and engaged board with Capt. James Noyes and wife, from Vermont.[183]

OCTOBER 20, 1863. Returned to New Orleans to be mustered in.

OCTOBER 27, 1863. Have just been mustered into service as 2d Lieut. Have [had] a pleasant visit with William. Find him in good health, and doing well. Return to Ship Island to-morrow.

OCTOBER 29, 1863. Reported to Col. Hall for duty, and was assigned to the Command of Co. B, 2nd Inf. C. d. Afrique, Ship Island, Miss.

NOVEMBER 10, 1863. On duty as Officer of the Day. Find myself acquiring knowledge of an officer's duties more readily than I expected. Find among the soldiers many that I used to feed, and teach, at Algiers. This fact furnishes ample introduction to the good graces of my Company. I am very sensible that it is a great help to me.

DECEMBER 20, 1863. A new Colonel in Command of the Regiment, Wm. M. Grosvenor,[184] from Connecticut, a genuine pro-slavery cotton-hearted negro hater. This is not a good place for him. Col. Hall transferred to a N.Y. Reg. at Bonnet Carrie.[185]

DECEMBER 25, 1863. Christmas. I committed a mortal sin (in the Colonel's eye), by asking to be excused from furnishing my Company with whiskey, on which to celebrate the day. An order had been issued to draw on the Commissary for a gill for each man in the Regiment. I drew the whiskey, stood on the barrel and delivered a temperance lecture, and then issued to the men. Very few drank. The sand soaked up the surplus.

DECEMBER 26, 1863. A general drunk all night last night, among the officers. Only one sober in the Regiment, besides myself: Capt. James Noyes, of Co. D., a staunch teetotaller. Think myself very fortunate in being able to board with him, instead of being obliged to sit at a table covered with intoxicating liquors, and surrounded by drunken officers. Verily drunkenness is the bane of the service.[186] Many men who never drank at home, and who had no difficulty in resisting the temptation while *in the ranks* of the army, no sooner pocket their Commission, than they become drunken, because it will not do at all to reproach other officers by refusing to drink with them. I have seen many painful illustrations of this. I have had occasion many times to board gunboats and other vessels in the naval service, and never, without being invited to drink. Have never yet accepted an invitation, and probably never shall.

[**DECEMBER 27, 1863.** *On this date Kinsley writes the following letter to his sister Lucretia.*]

Ship Island, Miss., Dec. 27, 1863

Dear Sister:

It *seems* a long time since I wrote you last. It cannot really be so, I am sure. It is Sunday evening. Do you think I can do better than sit and think about you? or, do you think I had better busy myself with some subject that I am better acquainted with? You will not be surprised that I write from this *home* of political and social sinners – Butler's Botany Bay[187] – where are gathered several hundred of the "Chivalry," from New Orleans and vicinity, among whom may be found mayors, merchants, ministers; bootblacks, bankers, brokers, and women; all (except the women) chained together in gangs of convenient size, and kept out of mischief by being constantly employed in the study and practice of the fine arts; the branches to which most attention is given, being the pounding of bricks, and mixing of mortar, for use in the construction of a large fort, now nearly completed.[188] My term of service is three years, commencing Aug. 25, 1863. I was very unwilling to leave William, but after mature deliberation, I concluded it best to accept the papers very unexpectedly sent me by Gen. Banks. On reaching Ship Island, early in October, I was assigned to the command of Co. B, whose Captain is Chief of Ordinance in New Orleans. Three Companies in our Regiment, mine among them, combine the artillery and infantry practice. I have visited New Orleans on business several times since I came here; stayed with William at the Hospital several nights.

Would you know of my facilities for making myself comfortable here? Very pleasantly situated, indeed. I board with Capt. Noyes, a teacher from Newbury Seminary, Vermont. He has his wife here, (as have several officers – wish I was one of the *several*) and they "keep-house" in good Vermont style. We occupy the houses that the 8th Vermont brought from Brattleboro, and left here on the Island when we went up to New Orleans. We have a number of nice hogs, (one of which will die soon) plenty of turkeys, chickens, and eggs, Irish and sweet potatoes, buckwheat cakes, etc., besides fruit ad infinitum. Notwithstanding my duties are not light, good living and congenial employment keep me in good condition. I weigh one hundred and seventy pounds: forty more than I ever weighed in the North; and William weighs only seventeen pounds less than I; so you see something is good for us both. May be it's the climate. We have Sundays here, and preaching or prayer meeting every evening during the week. Our Chaplain has given us up in despair, and left us to hardness of heart and blindness of mind. He got frightened, and ran home to his mother, where he should have stayed, instead of coming here; but we have a soldier in the Regiment who cannot read a word, that can preach to shame half the D.D.'s.[189] in New England; and he is so well acquainted with the Holy Ghost that His appearance does not frighten him out of his propriety. He preached today a funeral sermon from these words: "The wages of sin is death; but the gift of God is eternal life, through Jesus Christ our Lord."[190] "China," (I think it was) was sung at the grave, with such effect as nothing but the pathos peculiar to the negro's melody can give it. The man buried was from my Company. He was on one of the gun boats in a heavy storm, two weeks ago yesterday, and was lost overboard. His body washed ashore to-day.

I have given out several hundred books, furnished by an old friend from Boston. There are very few men in the Regiment who do not know the alphabet. Many read and write well. Some study arithmetic and geography.

I have always had an idea that there is a law of compensation; that Infinite Wisdom adjusts the matter, and that all men and all nations are sure to receive, some where, some time, the exact measure of their deserts. I have no noubt [sic] that justice will be done me yet, before I die; – or afterward. An illustration of this idea is found in the fact that we have men here at hard labor, over whom are placed, as guards, men formerly owned by them. Colloquy between the parties is often very entertaining, and to me, the picture presented is very instructive.

Didn't your geography tell large stories about storms on the Gulf of Mexico? A big storm swept over us last night and this forenoon. Houses blown down, and tents, occupied by one of the Regiments just from Washington, blown into the sea. We expect a call to take Mobile soon. Sis, please write me, and direct to

Lieut. Kinsley
Co. B, 2d Infantry Corps d' Afrique

JANUARY 1, 1864. Very cold for this latitude. Large numbers of Refugees from Secessia constantly arriving, on their way to New Orleans. Capt. Noyes being Provost Marshal, has to search them, and provide for their wants while waiting for transportation. This gives us a good opportunity to become acquainted with a great variety of characters. Most of them are the poorest kind of "pore white trash," quite as ignorant as mules, and with less common sense. Some of them belong to the chivalry, and bring thousands of dollars in gold. Many of this latter class left our lines some time since, as Registered Enemies, under Gen. Butler's Order.[191] They think they can live with Gen. Banks. Rather a doubtful compliment to Mr. Banks.

JANUARY 6, 1864. L. I. Winslow,[192] 8th Vermont, commissioned as Capt., and assigned to Co. B. Turned over property to him, and feel somewhat relieved of responsibility.[193]

JANUARY 24, 1864. Steamer brings news of Gen. Butler's pinching the rebs. in Virginia. Wish he were here.

JANUARY 26, 1864. Have cold winter. Several hard frosts. Spring is here now: fine and warm for some time: quite like July in New England.

FEBRUARY 4, 1864. Regiment inspected by Maj. General Reynolds[194] and Staff. After which, Battallion [*sic*] Drill. The General thinks it the best drilled Reg. in the Department. I think he is right. Our Colonel is the best drill master I ever saw, and he has kept the officers to their studies diligently; requiring recitations every evening.

FEBRUARY 5, 1864. After the General left last evening Adjutant Burchmore[195] got the rumsucking officers together, and a general drunk ensued. Near neighbors were unable to sleep. Several officers were carried home by the colored soldiers, among "the wee sma' hours beyont the twal:"[196] Burchmore belongs to the Boston Custom House Cottonocracy,[197] and of course loves me as ardently as he hates a "nigger." He has declared his purpose to shove me out of the Regiment. He may succeed.

FEBRUARY 14, 1864. (Sunday) Heard the Chaplain of the 2d U.S.C.T. preach to the prisoners.[198] An admirable sermon.

FEBRUARY 19, 1864. Admiral Farragut visited the island. He thinks our fort destined to be one of the best in the country.[199] He is going up the [Mississippi] Sound to see if he can get through Grant's Pass into Mobile Bay. The 2d U.S.C.T. embarked for Key West.

FEBRUARY 21, 1864. (Sunday) Admiral Farragut has gone up the Sound with the *Hartford* and several other gun boats, and we hear that Gen. Sherman is moving on Mobile with 30,000.[200]

FEBRUARY 27, 1864. We have heard the gunboats pounding away at Grant's Pass for several days; but it is all in vain. The water is so shoal they cannot get near. If we ever take Mobile we shall have to run the gauntlet of Forts Morgan and Gaines, the most hazardous undertaking of the war, the Bay being literally alive with torpedoes, and the channel so obstructed that vessels must pass close under the walls of the forts.

MARCH 1, 1864. One of the balmy breezes that are not uncommon in this latitude has just driven on shore here a vessel of the largest class, and a number of smaller crafts, several of which have gone to pieces. Three steamers have succeeded, after much difficulty, in making fast to the ship, but the waves run so high they can give but little help. The ship must go to pieces.

MARCH 3, 1864. Have just read the memoir of Adjutant Stearns,[201] from the Senior Class in Amherst College. He was killed at Newbern, N.C., March 8th, 1862. A most noble soldier, and worthy Christian; the like of which the country can ill afford to lose. Many such have been offered, a costly sacrifice, to save the country, and with the country, Justice. Thank God for the strong assurance that the sacrifice cannot be in vain.

MARCH 6, 1864. After inspection, attended church: negro preacher: good sermon: fine singing, and plenty of it.

MARCH 9, 1864. Great storm: rain and wind: hailstones three inches in diameter: one large building blown down, and several unroofed. U.S. Sloop of War *Vincennes* lost two of her cables and anchors and came near going to pieces.

MARCH 15, 1864. All our troops returning from the vicinity of Mobile; the move being simply a *feint* to cover the real move, which is against Texas; by way of Red River.[202] I hope he [Gen. Banks] may succeed as well as in his operations against Port Hudson, by way of the Teche and Red River, last year; but am satisfied that he will need a much larger force, on a much smaller number of cotton transports.

MARCH 20, 1864. (Sunday) Officer of the Guard to-day. Searched the premises of the night watchman at the fort. He is charged with having sold whiskey to soldiers and sailors. Found his "den" under the floor of his tent, all the planks of which, except one, were spiked down. A general assortment of soldiers' clothing, taken in exchange for drinks. Stock confiscated.

MARCH 21, 1864. Another big storm.

MARCH 25, 1864. Storm abated. Island has been nearly covered with water. These big blows have raised high waves, and made most magnificent bathing for expert swimmers.

MARCH 28, 1864. Lieut. Trask[203] dismissed [from] the service for neglect of duty while on guard.

MARCH 31, 1864. My old friend Corp. Colton,[204] of the Eighth Vermont, has come, with a 1st Lieutenant's Commission, and is assigned to the Co. with me. He is to board with me at Capt. Noyes'. Think we may have a pleasant time. He is one of the very few men who will not be likely to forget his manhood, or his mother, and engage in drunken broils with the majority of officers, simply because that sort are a majority. I am glad he has come: he is a good man, and I am sure he has back-bone enough to resist the importunities of his fellow officers who will constantly besiege him to worship with them at the shrine of Bacchus.[205]

APRIL 2, 1864. The steamer brought a sawmill, with which we are to saw our own lumber. She brought also, from New Orleans, a "steamboat,"[206] for Col. Grosvenor's benefit. He seems to forget that he may perhaps return to civil life again some time. Hope his folly may be the means of "starting" him from a position which he cannot fill worthily, with all his ability (and it is great), while he holds that "the negro has no rights that white men are bound to respect." It is reported that Banks has captured Shreveport.[207] No particulars. A young man named Lewis, came in skiff from Mobile. Represents himself to be in the secret service of the Government. Have satisfied myself that he *is* in the secret service of the rebel government. He is to be sent to the city under guard.

APRIL 6, 1864. Regiment received by Adjutant General Thomas,[208] after which Battallion [*sic*] Drill. We did not drill [as] well as usual. The men never did better; but some of the officers thought they were at school, with lessons half learned, and the Superintendent in. Of course they were "afraid." The General made a very instructive and appropriate speech; complimenting the Regiment on its proficiency.[209]

APRIL 8, 1864. Two ladies, Mrs. Laura S. Haviland (of world wide renown as an Abolitionist, engaged for years in the noble work of assisting slaves from the house of bondage to the land of freedom, in the prosecution of which work she has spent thousands of dollars and been several times imprisoned in Southern States) and Mrs. Backus, agents of the Michigan Freedmen's Association, have reached the island to-day.[210] They are to stay a few days with Capt. Noyes. They are old acquaintances of Mrs. Noyes' father, Rev. Orange Scott.[211]

APRIL 10, 1864. (Sunday) Mrs. Haviland preached to the soldiers: a discourse well adapted to win souls to Christ. Most of the officers in tears. Verily she is a Godly woman, full of faith and the Holy Ghost: aye, *full.* I never listened to a more simple, and at the same time, more powerful, sermon. In the afternoon the women talked to and prayed with the prisoners; a gang of about 200; sent here for a variety of offenses; some for a few years, some for life. How the hardened wretches wept, under the power of the gospel, from the lips of a holy woman.[212]

APRIL 12, 1864. Borrowed the Colonel's boat, and went with Capt. Noyes and wife, and Sisters Haviland and Backus, to the graveyard, and from there to the east end of the island. Never enjoyed a pleasanter excursion.[213]

APRIL 14, 1864. The ladies left today for home. In coming down, they stopped at all our stations on the [Mississippi] river, and went inland in many places. Lt. Abbe[214] from N.Y. City arrived.

APRIL 15, 1864. Adjutant Burchmore has preferred charges against Col. Grosvenor.[215] Both officers a disgrace to the service. Think they will manage to get themselves out, without my assistance. Hope so, most certainly.

APRIL 16, 1864. News of bloody battle at Grand Ecore, on the 6th, 7th, 8th, and 9th. Terrible slaughter on both sides; Gen. Banks victorious in the end; so the papers *say*; but I am too well acquainted with the tone of the press. I am satisfied that our army has been destroyed.[216]

APRIL 18, 1864. News of the capture of Fort Pillow, by Forrest, and his massacre and burning of the colored soldiers and their officers.[217] "Vengeance is mine; I will repay saith the Lord."[218]

APRIL 19, 1864. Two blockad[e] runners and a number of prisoners captured in the Sound by our gun boat.

APRIL 21, 1864. Two hundred Contrabands arrived at Cat Island from Prophet's Island.[219] They are to cut wood and saw lumber.

APRIL 26, 1864. Col. Grosvenor ordered to New Orleans in arrest. Received a Bible, and other good books, from Sisters Haviland & Backus.

APRIL 30, 1864. Nearly every officer in the Reg. gone to New Orleans on the Col's. Court Martial. Every officer except myself and two others signed a paper setting forth the Col's. virtues, and his high sense of honor, and his ability, etc., designed to influence the Court. I have the pleasing assurance that when the Col. comes to see this list of names, and finds that mine is not among them, he will make this island too hot to hold me, after he gets back. Perhaps he will. If so, it will be time for me to go to work then. Lieut. Col. Hall in command of the Regiment.[220]

MAY 14, 1864. Officers returned from Court Martial. Col. G. pleaded guilty to the charge of keeping a "steamboat" in his quarters.[221] Mrs. Noyes brought back a fine Piano. Dr. Gihon attempted to shoot Lieut. Foster.[222]

MAY 25, 1864. Plenty of bad news from rebel sources. New Orleans is going to fall into their hands again sure.

MAY 28, 1864. Paid to April 30. Glad to get it.

MAY 29, 1864. (Sunday) Called on by Provost Marshal [Noyes] to investigate a case of theft.

[**MAY 29, 1864.** *On this date Kinsley writes the following letter to his father.*]

Ship Island, Miss., May 29, 1864

Dear father:

It is a fine Sabbath morning. I have just inspected my Company and will occupy a little of the early morning, while not oppressively hot, in lessening, by one, at least, the file of unanswered letters that have accumulated on my desk to the number of a "baker's dozen." I received yours of the 17th ult., some time ago, but have neglected to write you, for good reason. I have not been idle. All our line officers but four, and *all* the Field and Staff, have been in New Orleans some time on Court Martial, and it has left me on guard every other day and night, besides which I have had considerable Company business to do, being left alone, for the time being. Lieut. Colton is permanently detached for duty with the Louisiana Board of Education. (You know I always have some good excuse for my delinquencies.) I am sorry to learn that mother is in ill health. Is she better now? I thank you for your invitation to visit you this summer. I wonder if you understand how glad I would be to visit home again? O, home! home! I am weary with watching the work of war, and long for a little rest. Only a little. Still, being in full strength, and perfect health, I hardly think I should receive an affirmative response to an application for furlough; because, though I have re-enlisted for three years, I am in a Colored Regiment, and it is held that Officers in such Regiments cannot be absent from their commands, except on Surgeons' certificates of disability, without detriment to the interests of the service. So I shall have to wait for my furlough until the end of the war; unless I get sick again, like I did last year. How long shall I have to wait? Most persons in civil life *seem* to think, and have from the beginning, "about three months," or "six at the outside." I have not so read history. I do not so understand the temper, or the resources of this people. I think this rebellion will test the energies of the Republic for years to come.

I am glad Edgar is so well suited with his work.[223] I received one of his letters the other day, enclosed in one from Alma.[224] I should like to hear from him now, since the Great Battle.[225] We have received no account yet of the fight, save what we get in Southern papers, brought to us by refugees, on their way to New Orleans. They make Grant's loss about eighty thousand, with near a score of Generals killed: and they claim a great victory for Johns[t]on over Sherman. They say also that Banks is captured on Red River, with all his force, except five thousand; but we hear indirectly from New Orleans that Banks has made his escape, and is on his way to New Orleans. We learned a long time ago not to put much confidence in Southern papers; and we don't know what to believe. We have been without communication for some time. If Gen. Banks and his army are destroyed, I think his policy may justly be held responsible; or the policy of the Government, which he has sought to carry out. It is the *policy*, at any rate, whoever may be responsible for it.[226] My opinion, however, may be worth as little as Confederate promises to pay. In the beginning of Gen. Banks' administration here, I had no sympathy with his entertainment of Committees whose constituents were in arms against the Government, and since that time I have had no sympathy with or confidence in the power for good, of the hideous abortion, christened "State Government," whose seed was germinated in those conferences; while at the same time it is notorious that ninety-nine one-hundredths of the population are as bitterly hostile to the Union as they ever were. "It will have a powerful effect for good in Europe," say its friends. Do they think Europe is blind? I have yet to learn that life can be produced by dressing a skeleton in clothes; or, that ever, any where, any permanent good can result from presenting false appearances, however fair. Our Constitutional Convention has done many good things, I know. It has made slavery forever impossible in the State of Louisiana. The Convention is composed largely of men from New England, who never saw Louisiana until our fleet entered the mouth of the Mississippi River two years ago last month; and if the military forever were withdrawn from New Orleans for six hours, the members of the Convention, now in session there, would be sent to heaven in a hurry by their so-styled constituents, the *loyal* people. I know what the Union sentiment of New Orleans is.[227]

Do you think this the bluest letter I have ever written you? May be it is: but I don't feel very blue. Somehow, whatever reverses may come, I am sure that Justice, calm and stern and strong, is making rapid increase in the lengths of her strides through this land, and the time is coming when Tyranny shall hide from the light of her face, and seek a place for its deeds, where the sun never shines. Thank God for this hope, so full of strength.

I believe I gave you, some time ago, an idea of my business. It is still the same, and I am still content. We have had our saw mill running about three weeks. Since it commenced we have put up from its work one building 100 feet by 42, and several smaller ones, all complete, except shingles, which are brought from N. Orleans. We also run another saw mill on Cat Island, eight miles distant. We have just received several thousand tons of hewn granite from New England, for the Fort, which will be finished in about eighteen months.

30. A school in Louisiana for the instruction of black soldiers and fugitive slaves built under the direction of a Yankee officer in the Corps d'Afrique. Circa 1863. Courtesy of the Chicago Historical Society.

I expect to go to New Orleans by the next boat, if the next boat ever comes, to get more school books for the "boys." Many men in this Regiment need Geography, Arithmetic, and Grammar, who, two years ago, could not tell A from B. It is wonderful, the earnestness with which they seek after knowledge; and every where, all over the state, almost every Yankee soldier has a class of Contrabands or colored soldiers.[228] What a work is being wrought! How many hands, all through the North, are tireless in their labor of love, for those who are surrounded by the perils of war, and for a race just struggling into the assumption of the responsibility of freemen. Two old ladies from Michigan have recently visited us. They were sent by the Michigan Christian Commission, and visited all the hospitals and contraband camps, from Chicago to Ship Island. They distributed thousands of garments, and thousands of dollars worth of table fixings to the sick and suffering. How much good is done; how many lives saved by the women of the loyal North, whose energies are so largely devoted to this work; and how much gratitude is expressed by those whom the fortunes of war compel to receive their aid.[229]

Our Regiment has no Chaplain, no schoolmaster; but we have plenty of preaching, and plenty of teaching. A colored preacher from New Orleans came down and baptised in the sea eleven of our soldiers, and two of their wives, the other Sunday. I get plenty of good reading, and a great variety. The old ladies who were here sent me a Bible from New Orleans, and somebody sends me the *Independent, Zion's Herald, N.Y. Tribune, Atlantic Monthly, Harper,* and now and then others.[230] We have nice long days in this latitude: up at four, Battalion drill at five, tattoo at quarter past nine. I take a swim every morning (except Sunday) before drill, with most of the Officers. I have never yet been swimming, or boating, or fishing, on Sunday. I wouldn't like you to hear of my being drowned on Sunday, while at play, or taken by a shark. I was very near furnishing a shark with breakfast one morning last week. We were but a short distance from the end of the wharf, in eighteen feet of water, when I, being farther out than the others, excited the appetite of the ravenous man-eater, who at once evinced his anxiety for an intimate acquaintance. I made for the wharf, and was so fortunate as to reach it in time to give a fisherman on the wharf opportunity to throw his gig. He failed to strike the creature, but frightened him away. Before we left the wharf we saw a desperate fight between the shark and a school of porpoise. The shark was vanquished after a fight of about two hours duration. Many sharks are taken here at this season of the year, and the east end of the island is covered with alligators and turtles. The turtle furnishes excellent meat, and the eggs, which are found in bushels, are quite as good as hen's eggs. [*This letter continues on June 5, 1864.*]

JUNE 1, 1864. Good news from Grant and Sherman. Have attended a school for officers during the winter and spring, with the design of perfecting ourselves in drill. We have had, in Col. Grosvenor, a most efficient instructor, and have made some improvement, I think.[231] The schools are at an end, and I hope his connection with the Regiment is at an end. In addition to school every evening, we have had officers drill, Battallion [*sic*] drill, and Company drill daily; and I have had Company business and Boards of Survey to attend to, besides instructing as many of the soldiers as my time would allow, in the rudiments of an education. Have been very busy. Time has passed very pleasantly. No occasion to regret that I came here. Nice warm weather. Splendid bathing.

JUNE 3, 1864. It has been a stormy, windy day. At noon, with no special object in view, I picked up all my things about the house, and packed them away in my trunk, and then stepped across the street to get a book to read. Had just got the book, and was considering whether to go back, or sit down and read where I was, when my house came down with a crash, smashing bedsteads, tables, and everything else. This reminds me of father's letter just received cautioning me to remember that my house is built on the sand.[232]

[**JUNE 5, 1864.** *On this date Kinsley continues the letter to his father that he began on May 29, 1864.*]

Sunday, June 5, 1864

I left this [letter] last Sabbath to go to church. I wish you could hear our colored preacher. It is a nice sunny day. Rather a warm sun, it is true; but very nice breeze gives large comfort. What a pleasant time of year to go to church in your country; early June. When I think of your facilities for useful enjoyment, and remember that I am tied to this burning sand island, or in some other equally pleasant place harnessed to the war, I feel inclined to wish that the war might end. I think there are many men alive now, who must be killed before the war can die; and that the courage needed just now is courage to kill, rather than courage to die.

A serious accident came very near me last Friday afternoon. I sat in the house alone, making Clothing Receipt Rolls, when it began to rain, and I packed my Sunday clothes in my chest and went into Capt. Dauchy's house,[233] "right opposite," to get a book he had borrowed. I had just shut his door, when a hurricane struck *our* house, and it came down with a crash, smashing timbers, furniture, crockery, and a lot of extra rifles and other Company property stored in the chamber. The desk containing Co. books and papers was slightly injured only, but papers were well wet, and so was everything else. My chest is new, just made by one of the soldiers, the joints all glued, making it water tight; and my things were not injured. My blanket is out drying now. It was a rough storm: torrents of rain. A large ship that had just discharged her cargo of granite, dragged her anchor a long distance, and was driven ashore; but the wind changed soon, and she got off, with assistance from gunboats. Mr. Reynolds, Superintendent of the Fort, was out in his sail boat, with two or three assistants, after eggs. We have not heard from him yet. I pity his wife. She stands on the gallery most of the time, crying, and looking off in the direction where we saw him last, a few hours before the storm came on. We are not done with it yet. The sun shines now, but thunder is heavy off south, and the clouds are black and angry. It may come in an hour. The waves breaking on the beach are magnificent. I am in comfortable quarters, with Lieut. Abby [*sic*], recently from N.Y. City.

Did I tell you that Mrs. Noyes has a very nice piano? She has the best one I ever saw, I think. It was manufactured in Paris, at a cost of one thousand dollars. It was confiscated from Madame Secesh in New Orleans, and Mrs. Noyes bought it for $225.00. She plays well, and several of the Officers sing, so we get music, even here; and music of the right sort. They give us the *old* tunes, and in good style.

Let's see, – it is early June; Alonzo's time is out. I wonder if William's time is out; or, if he has to serve until the 18th of next February.[234] Do you know?

What are the prospects for "crops?" Are you going to raise enough to keep
the Army at work, and hunger from your own doors? If not, send us half
rations and we will be content. How is uncle Guy now? Who weeds mother's
posey beds? How many chickens has she? How does the old cow do? Has
Charlie Bingham got right smart?[235] I suppose uncle Tyler's little girls[236]
are grown up to womanhood by this time, aren't they? How is uncle Medad?
What is Albert doing?[237] How is Susan Fleming?[238] My compliments to her,
if you please, and uncle John,[239] and the boys. Does uncle John get out
this summer? How is Aunt Junia?[240] Tell Sister Case[241] I am constantly on
the *qui vive*, and *can't get off*. [*This letter continues on June 8, 1864.*]

JUNE 6, 1864. The body of Q[uarter]. M[aster]. Sergt. Fleming,[242] who committed suicide four weeks since, was found behind a pile of rubbish in the
Q. M. Storehouse. Bad smell. Have received authentic information of the
death of our "secret service" friend, Lewis, who, after getting what information he could in New Orleans, returned to the Confederacy and organized in Mobile a band of Pirates, taking possession of a launch, with which
they designed to capture one of our gun boats by strategy. He was killed
instantly, by the accidental discharge of his own pistol, just as they were captured. Col. Hall has issued an order prohibiting gambling among officers
and men.

JUNE 8, 1864. Col. Grosvenor has been dismissed [from] the service, by
sentence of Gen. Court Martial.[243] Col. Fellows, of the 2d which left here
some time since for Key West, has just died of Yellow Fever. Also Chaplain
Schneider, and many of the line officers.[244] Some of them were noble men.
My "boy," Sam. Evans, some fifty years of age, who has taken care of me ever
since I have been here, has left for the city. A fine old gentleman, with much
better sense than a majority of white men in the South.

[**JUNE 8, 1864.** *On this date Kinsley concludes the letter to his father that he began
on May 29, 1864.*]

Wednesday, June 8

Steamer from New Orleans just in, bringing your letter of May 22, with
Cousin Samantha's,[245] and others, besides lots of papers, with abundance
of news, which you have had a long time now, as I discover by your letter.
Several of our Officers have returned from the city, but the Colonel is left
behind, dismissed [from] the service for keeping in his quarters a woman
not his wife, and for using improper language to one of his officers. Lieut.
Col. Hall is in command. The steamer returns at once. Tell Samantha I am
very glad to hear from her, and to learn that she is taking care of my father
and mother. I will write her soon. I am in perfect health. God bless you all.

R. Kinsley

JUNE 10, 1864. A meeting of officers to make arrangements for celebrating the glorious fourth. Don't care a fig about it myself. Don't want to see any attempts made to celebrate the Fourth, until the war is ended.

JUNE 15, 1864. The Regiment has been supplied with new arms and equipments.[246] Rather warm weather. Have been chased ashore by a shark, while bathing. Have had considerable sport hunting turtles, for a month or two; they are found here at this season in great numbers. Most of them weigh from three to five hundred pounds each. They come on shore in the night, to deposit their eggs in the sand. A turtle deposits two or three hundred eggs in a night, and leaves them to their fate.

JUNE 25, 1864. Left, at 9 p.m., for New Orleans, in charge of a large number of refugees. Col. Hall on board. Pleasant trip. Notified by Col. Hall that he had sent my name to Headquarters for promotion, and had got reply that the Colored Regiments were to be consolidated,[247] and no changes would be made meantime. Am not anxious for promotion. Should shoulder my musket with the greatest pleasure, and reenlist in my old Regiment, if dismissed here. Have something to fight for in this war, besides promotion.

JUNE 26, 1864. (Sunday) Reached New Orleans just in time to dispose of my Refugees in season to attend church. Heard Dr. Newman,[248] Methodist, recently from New York City. His subject was – "Judas: his treason." He assured a very large audience of New Orleans quondam slaveholders, that in all the world's history there had never been until now a parallel for the treason of Judas. The honor of furnishing a parallel to his stupendous crime, was reserved for the American slaveholders of the Nineteenth Century. It was perhaps quite as severe a sermon as I ever listened to. It created great excitement. I certainly expected to see him shot in the desk. He is evidently becoming very popular among the loyal. The churches here need a preacher with a backbone.

JUNE 29, 1864. News of desperate, bloody battles in Virginia. We have sown seeds in the past. We are reaping the harvest to-day. God is just, though his judgments be long delayed. By and by, when we learn justice, God will give us great victory. And we are beginning to learn. O yes, we *are* beginning to learn.

[**JULY 2, 1864.** *On this date Kinsley writes the following letter to his brother Daniel.*]

New Orleans, La., July 2, 1864

Dear brother:

I received your letter of the __ult. some time last month. I am glad to hear from you again, after so long waiting. I wonder if you have written me before, since I joined the army. I guess not, but I may have forgotten. I am glad to learn that you are so pleasantly situated; that you are in good health;

that your salary has been raised, and that you have not been obliged to go
to the war; for I think your father has sent about as many boys as can reason-
ably be expected of one man, and some must stay at home, or who would
feed and clothe the army?[249] Of course there are thousands whose duty it
is to stay at home. I thought duty called me to the field. I have thought so
every hour since. I think so now no less than when I started. I suppose all
the boys except Edgar and myself have had furlough this spring. I think I
should know how to enjoy a furlough this summer, myself; if the war were
ended. I hope I may not be obliged, from any cause, to accept a furlough
until such time. If not, I think I shall be pretty sure of steady employment
for at least a quarter of a century.

I left Ship Island a week ago today, with a cargo of Refugees, from Mobile and vicinity, and am here weather bound, or rather war bound, for the
steamer has been withdrawn temporarily, and is transporting troops. The
city is in a bit of excitement just now, on account of Dick Taylor's promise
to be here on the Fourth to help us celebrate. He is moving against us in
large force; but we expect he will stop in season to save himself, as he did
last year, when he came within eight miles. Vigorous efforts are being made
to tender him a warm reception. In fact, we hope to compel him to honor
us with his presence, whether he will or not.[250] Night before last, mounted
patrols were stationed on all the avenues leading from the city, and no
horses were allowed to leave. In the morning, after all the market teams
from the adjacent country had reached the city, a simultaneous descent
was made on the equine family, and everything suitable set to drilling the
Cavalry tactics. All the livery stables, and all private stables except Doctors',
were cleaned out; and meat carts, milk carts, hay carts, fruit carts, melon
carts, pleasure carts, corn carts, coal carts, cabbage carts, all carts, were
left standing in the streets. Today, many of them are moving slowly behind
little mules too small for Government use. About 3000 horses were thus
obtained. Secesh is mad, but mum.

Our Constitutional Convention is still in session here. They will soon
present for the people's acceptance, a paper of which the most rabid
Massachusetts Abolitionist could hardly complain.[251] But, the Convention
might as well be convened in Patagonia as here. If it were an expression of
the sentiments of the People, well; but it is not. The Convention is composed largely of men who never saw Louisiana until we came up the river
two years ago and more; and if their constituents, *the loyal people*, could get
inside the lines, they would hang every member of the Convention, without
waiting to consult the paper on which they have labored so assiduously for
some months, to see if it were Constitutional.

We have preachers here from the North. I heard Dr. Newman, from New
York, last Sabbath. They have never had much Gospel in the South: plenty

of bosh. Slavery, such as has cursed this country, could never live under the Gospel of Christ. Our soldiers are learning fast. There are very few in our Reg. that do not read, many write well, and are studying arithmetic, geography, grammar. Our Reg. is changed to 74th U. S. Inf. (C.)

Good by,
R. Kinsley

JULY 3, 1864. (Sunday) Attended Dr. Newman's church again to-day. Very many officers present; among them Gens. Banks, Grant, Sickels[252] and others.

JULY 4, 1864. This is the anniversary of our independence; and we are going to celebrate the day, with our soil drenched in the best blood of the nation, mingled with the worst, and still drinking more and more. About five thousand of Gen. Banks' splendid army of fifty thousand have escaped from Red River, and we are all going to have a good time celebrating the 4th. I have heard Michael Hahn,[253] a young Dutch-Irish pettifogger, who was made Governor by Gen. Banks a while since, for a consideration, deliver an oration peculiarly appropriate to the day. Two years ago he stood on the same platform and presented a Crescent City Regiment with a battle flag. In the course of his remarks on that occasion, he said he "hoped the Regiment would carry the flag through rivers of Yankee blood, and plant it in triumph on the Yankee Capitol; and if he had two legs instead of one, he would go with it." Nobody believes he [is now] any less a rebel than he was then; but policy, O policy, thou art a jewel, no less than consistency.

Also heard Gen. Sickels [sic]: and in the afternoon went with Mrs. Taylor, Alice, and some others, to the Barracks, where we heard Dr. Newman, Major Chase,[254] and others, and had a splendid dinner. Returned at dark, and passed a pleasant evening at Mrs. Taylor's, with Colton, who has been in the city some time, on duty with the Board of Education. Visited several fine schools for the colored children during the past week.

JULY 5, 1864. Saw the 8th Vermont embark for the army of the Potomac, with the entire Nineteenth Army Corps.[255] Sorry I could not have been in town when William was back here from Vermont. The Regiment is in fine condition. Has not looked so well for two years.

[**JULY 7, 1864.** *On this date Kinsley writes the following letter to his sister Lucretia.*]

New Orleans, La., July 7, 1864

Dear Sister:

I have just received your letter of the 21st ult. I am very glad to hear from you, and very happy to be able to give you information of my whereabouts. I left Ship Island on the 25th of last month, in charge of a steamer load of Refugees and Prisoners, from Mobile and vicinity. I reached this city next day (Sunday) just in season to hear Dr. Newman, from New York, in the Carondelet street M[ethodist]. E[piscopal]. Church, from these words: "My Lord and my God."[256] He seemed to think the South had never had any God but their slaves, and slavery's father, the devil. I heard him last Sunday from the words, "Judas, betrayest thou the Son of Man with a kiss?"[257] I had never imagined how a traitor looked, until I saw, or listened to the Dr's. word picture of Judas, and [Benedict] Arnold. And when he left us all staring at the picture he had made, he had the temerity to tell us that every word he had said of the character of Judas and Arnold was strictly applicable to the traitors of New Orleans, and other Southern cities, who, having thrown the country into war, were too cowardly to play the part of men, and take the field, but were content to accept the protection of the Government whose benignant sway they had sought to destroy by treason fouler than was ever born of hell. I expected to see him shot down in the pulpit; and I think that nothing but the previous vigilance of the soldiers, in disarming the people, saved his life. Your correspondent, Mrs. Taylor, gave me an introduction to him on the Fourth [of July], and after the Oration, by Gen. Sickles, which was delivered at eight in the morning, we made the tour of the city, and passed the day pleasantly. We attended another celebration a few miles below the city, at the Barracks Hospital, toward evening. The Dr. spoke very felicitously to about 1500 sick and wounded soldiers, and a large number of invited guests.

If I had time, I would tell you something about Mrs. Taylor. Inasmuch as I have not, I will send you her face, with one of her sons, and you can form your own opinion of her. She is a woman of large literary note; and although during the winter previous to our occupancy of New Orleans her house was surrounded many times by a mob of hundreds of "chivalrous gentlemen," with a worthy Judge (now a good Union man) at their head, though her property was destroyed, her oldest son taken by force and compelled into the ranks of the rebels, though a son of the above named Judge sought her life by firing a rifle bullet through her window in the night as she was carrying medicine to her sick husband, because she had said to him he would some time be ashamed of his treason, though her house was often searched for evidence on which to hang her as a "Yankee," she slept under the "stars and stripes" every night. She is the first woman that I got acquainted with after we reached the city; and a nobler woman I never knew. Her husband is a doctor; (M.D.) but since we have "run the machine" he has been employed by the Government in the City Treasury. Mrs. Taylor is principal of the best school in the city,[258] with a salary of $1200 a year, and she spends it all, and her husband's salary, for the sick and wounded soldiers of the Union. She thinks somebody else must take care of dilapidated rebs. She visits the hospitals every day in the year, and has for more than two years, and carries any amount of such things as are better than the Dr's. poisons for sick men. I shall never cease to be thankful for care that I received at her hands last year, when sick. She told me the other day when I came to town, that she had written you, on Washburne's account, but had heard nothing from you. When I got your letter last night I told her you had written, but could give her no information concerning your brother Rufus. I was a little ashamed, sis, I confess; but made a scape goat of the mail department, with pretty good grace.

I have had a good visit with the 8th Vermont. They left yesterday with an expedition 30,000 strong, to operate against Mobile.[259] I am going to start for Ship Island to-night. We are mounting some splendid guns there, running two saw mills, and doing a heap of work. Wm. has been here and gone back home, and I did not see him. We have nice warm weather, but it don't trouble me. I am "tough as a bear." I have not seen an unwell day for nearly a year. Good by. Love to Guy and Lucinda.[260]

R. Kinsley

JULY 10, 1864. (Sunday) Reached Ship Island today per schooner *Henry Latour.* Had a very pleasant trip. Find a new Colonel here, named Holmstedt;[261] a genuine Dutchman. Has been here a week. Most of the officers speak ill of him. Judge by this that I shall like him much. The celebration on the island was postponed. The officers had a drunk at night.

JULY 14, 1864. News of the destruction of the pirate *Alabama,* Capt. Semmes, who was captured last year on Berwick Bay, while in command of the *Queen of the West.* The *Alabama* was sunk by the *Kearsarge,* Capt. Winslow, of Roxbury, Mass.[262] Gen. Grant has demanded the surrender of Petersburg. Presume he will have to pound them out, or starve them out. They are bound to come out.

JULY 18, 1864. *Clyde* in, with orders to be ready for the Board of Examiners who are coming in a few days to decide who are the most efficient officers in this and the Regiment at Fort Pike.[263] The two are to be consolidated, and the surplus officers sent home. Wonder if I will go. Most of us are a little anxious. The question is, who are able to answer Gen. Canby's[264] requirements in the matter. Think I know who some of the "outs" will be.

JULY 19, 1864. Col. Holmstedt to-day confiscated $3,000 worth of liquors, brought by the sutler. The best was turned over to the hospital. The most was turned out on the sand. No wonder the officers don't like the new Colonel.[265]

JULY 20, 1864. Capt. Noyes' brother,[266] a young man, Lieut. in his Company, has contracted the habit of drinking, of late, and to-day the Capt. found him dead drunk. He went to the Lieut's. room, where he found an entire case of choice wine, which he took out and broke every bottle. Of course there is a pleasant family fight; but the Capt. has General Orders, the Col., common decency, Justice, and Lieut. Kinsley on his side, and says to the boys, "go ahead with your charges." They won't do it.

JULY 23, 1864. (Sunday) Attended church: colored man preached well. Thirteen were baptised a while since: two women. The steamer is in this evening, with the Board of examiners.

JULY 26, 1864. Have been before the "Board." Thought I should rather go "before the mast," at least three years;[267] especially as the Board was composed in part of Regular Army officers;[268] but I came out with flying colors; sails all set. Can't tell, though, whether I passed a successful examination or not.[269] Am very certain that my "friend" Adj. Burchmore did not.

JULY 28, 1864. The Board have finished their examination, and left to-day. Begin to see indications of a genuine attempt to capture Mobile. Think the blow will be struck within a month.

JULY 31, 1864. (Sunday) One of Ericcson's [*sic*] double turreted "Monitors" came in to-day, and lies at anchor.[270] Rather a formidable looking craft. Her deck, along the outer edge rises about six inches above the water. In the centre it is a little higher, giving the floor a slight convexity. This floor, or deck, is made of huge iron slabs, six inches thick fastened in the most substantial manner. The turrets are iron, fifteen inches thick. They carry guns just about large enough to take in a flour barrel. No ordnance can ever harm such a vessel. She cannot be hit at right angles. Not a man on board is exposed. The chivalry have filled Mobile Bay with torpedoes, and they may destroy these monitors. Nothing else can.

AUGUST 4, 1864. Never knew wind higher than today. Saw mill blown down, and several small vessels blown ashore. Heard of the safe arrival home of Mrs. Haviland and Mrs. Backus. Read a very interesting report of their expedition.

AUGUST 6, 1864. All hail, Farragut! Hurrah for the bravest and wisest Sea Captain that ever lived! Admiral David G. Farragut's peer is not found in all the world's history of Naval warfare.[271] He has just run the gauntlet between Forts Morgan and Gaines, captured most of the rebel fleet in Mobile Bay: taken, among other formidable vessels of war, the famous ram *Tennessee*, with the rebel Commodore, Buchanan, on board, mortally wounded.[272] We lost one of our best Monitors, blown up by a torpedo, and one wooden gunboat. The Admiral went through standing in the rigging of the *Hartford*, above the smoke, where he could direct movements to the best advantage. Our loss was large, on several of the wooden ships, and Capt. Craven, with one hundred and eight brave men, went down with the Monitor.[273] The forts can now be starved into surrender, if it proves impossible to take them by assault or bombardment. There is said to be no work in the country more formidable than Fort Morgan. It is thought that Fort Gaines may be compelled to surrender soon; but that the Navies of the world might bombard Morgan for a century without doing the least damage. Time will tell; and it is possible that 20 inch Dahlgrens[274] and 20 inch Mortars, requiring seventy-five pounds of powder for a charge, and throwing shot of 465 lbs. weight, may have a tendency to shake Fort Morgan from her foundation.

AUGUST 8, 1864. Steamer to-day brings news of Sherman's success at Atlanta, Ga., which place he now holds.[275] Victory crowns the right. Secession totters to its fall.

AUGUST 9, 1864. News to-day of the surrender of Fort Gaines, to General Granger, with near 1000 prisoners.[276] Our officers represent the *Tennessee* to be the most formidable vessel afloat. The Stars and Stripes smile upon her now. That's where the laugh comes in. The rebs must begin to see the point of the joke by and by.

AUGUST 15, 1864. *Savory*[277] in from New Orleans with the official report of the Examining Board, by which we learn our destiny. The Field Officers of our Reg., Col. Holmstedt, Lt. Col. Hall, and Major C. C. Pike,[278] are retained. My "friend" Adjutant Burchmore leaves, which saves me the trouble of preferring charges against him.[279] My rank is No. 3 in a class of 20 Second Lieutenants. Captains Nichols, Villeverde, and Hawley,[280] also 1st. Lieuts. Clark and Martin,[281] and a string of 2d Lieuts., are "left out in the cold." Such a sifting as this will be no loss to the service. Many have been Commissioned who were totally incompetent, and not fit in any sense for the position. Not alone of the Colored troops is this true. I know many officers in white Regiments who would be rejected by our Examining Boards without ceremony. Colored troops should have the best corps of officers in the service; and the Examining Board is an admirable sieve.

AUGUST 19, 1864. The officers mustered out, except Lieuts. Lewis and Sanders,[282] whose accounts would not settle, left for New Orleans, and private life. Should not feel flattered if I were obliged to leave in this way. Should much rather be dismissed for doing some act of justice, against orders.

❧ Four ❧

AUGUST 20, 1864. (Saturday) A change has "at last come o'er the spirit of our dreams."[283] The steamer *St. Charles* came in at noon, with an order from Gen. Canby requiring our Commandant to send three of his five Companies (no more could be spared from the post) to report to Gen. Granger at Mobile Point, to lead a storming party in an assault on Fort Morgan. Capt. Noyes has been designated to command the detachment, and Co. H., Capt. Winslow, Co. I, Lieut. Abbe, and Co. G, Lieut. Kinsley, commanding, are ordered to be on board in thirty minutes. It is an easy matter for me: I have no wife to weep her eyes away if I should fall; no children dependent on me for bread; not one among the sons or daughters of men, will miss me much if I never return. I pity Capt. Noyes. He has his wife here: young, timid, far from home, in the army, on a desolate island, unaccustomed to self-reliance, it is hard for him to leave her, on *such* a mission, and under such circumstances: much to do, and no time to do it. I feel compelled to leave some things with her to be sent to father in case I fall. Hot day; almost unendurably hot; but we may find it hotter before we get through with it. Good by Ship Island, till after the fall of Fort Morgan and Mobile.

AUGUST 28, 1864. (Sunday) Fort Morgan, Ala. Have been very busy during the last few days, and have had no time to write; will go back a little. On the 19th was officer of the guard at Ship Island. On the 20th started for this place in command of Co. G; on steamer all night; no sleep. Passed Fort Morgan soon after light Sunday morning, 21st, without drawing their fire. Steamed up to our fleet, the iron clads of which lie close under the walls of the Fort, and keep her two hundred heavy guns as silent as the tomb. Some of our wooden ships give evidence of having suffered severely in running the gauntlet on the 5th. The *Hartford* is riddled like a sieve from stem to stern. We disembarked at Navy Cove, five miles above the Fort, and I was kept busy with my Company during the day and most of the night discharging powder, shot and shells, from steamers at the wharf. At dark the fort opened upon us with heavy Blakely guns, all of whose shots fell short of us. They used one Whitworth gun, furnished by our neutral British friends.[284] This was elevated too much, and every shot went over our heads. The day passed, and also the night, and I was not reminded that it had been Sabbath, until near light. They kept up a vigorous fire until light, when we opened upon them for the first time, with sixteen mortars, and a large number of heavy Navy guns, removed from the vessels and planted close under the walls, and an occasional salute from the Monitors, whereupon they deserted their guns and took refuge in their bomb proof casemates, where they seemed quite content to allow us to do all the shooting. Not one of their heavy guns was fired after we opened the play. About nine in the evening (Monday, 22nd), our bursting shells set their Citadel on fire, which furnished a brilliant light for us to work by during the entire night. The fire spread, and before morning two magazines were blown up, sending high in air immense masses of timber and brick work.

31. Fort Morgan after its surrender on August 23, 1864. *Harper's Pictorial History of the Civil War*, 747.

In the middle of the night signals of distress were displayed from the parapet, whereupon our fire ceased, and they were summoned to surrender, but Gen. Page[285] replied: "*Never!* we will burn first, with our fort!" Gen. Granger told him he could have his choice; but one or the other must be done immediately. He signalled to resume the fire, with all possible energy, and our guns, which had been silent about ten minutes, reopened with such vigor as to keep from six to a dozen shells constantly in the air. Our mortars were so near, and so skillfully planted, that not one of them missed a shot during the day or night. By daylight, Tuesday morning 23d, the "fire" had become so hot that Gen. Page was obliged to display the white flag and surrender. My Company was on the line of sharpshooters during the night, about sixty yards from the walls of the fort.[286] The engineer corps were constantly digging nearer and nearer, and in eighteen hours more we would have had five or six tons of powder under the walls of the fort, which would have lifted them out. This may safely be regarded as the most remarkable bombardment on record. An impregnable Fortress, mounting two hundred of the best guns in use, besieged by a party who dug through the sand a distance of four miles, with a loss of only one or two killed, and half a dozen wounded, surrendering after a bombardment of 24 hours, during which it had lost only one man killed, according to Gen. Page, and had not fired a single gun.[287] It has been ascertained, however, that they lost largely, and threw many mangled bodies into the burning Citadel. The stench of burning flesh during the night was terrible, and we were at a loss to conjecture what they were burning. Six hundred surrendered, among them Mrs. Page, the wife of the Gen. Commanding. His servant gave me a "salt-cellar" from Gen. Page's table, and some peacock's feathers from the mantel; the only "relics" I have preserved.

Tuesday afternoon I was sent to get Commissary Stores with a flat-bottomed sloop, with no center board. I set some Naval officers on board their boats, and looked the fleet over a little, and then took my stores aboard and started;

32. The saltcellar from General Page's table. Courtesy of the Vermont Historical Society.

but the wind had changed and we were driven a long distance up toward Mobile, expecting every minute to be blown up by a torpedo.[288] Worked hard all night, trying to make land. Made the shore about eleven o'clock in the morning, five miles from camp, hands blistered with work, faces blistered by the sun, and nearly dead with thirst. This the fifth night without "a wink" of sleep. Towed our boat up "home," threw myself down in the shade of a pine bush, and slept. Our steamers are searching the Bay for torpedoes. About seven hundred have already been taken up, and towed on shore. They are exploded by our artillerists. It has been very hot, night and day. We have no tents, and not much "bush" here for shade.

SEPTEMBER 10, 1864. Embarked at seven o'clock p.m., for Ship Island. Have been nearly starved most of the time during our stay here at the Fort. Have lived mostly on oysters gathered by wading in water up to our necks. The Commissary Department has been short of supplies.

SEPTEMBER 11, 1864. (Sunday) Ship Island. Reached home at two o'clock this morning. Everybody glad to get back.

SEPTEMBER 13, 1864. Received an order from Col. Holmstedt, in obedience to Special Order from Headquarters of the Department, detailing me in command of a party of forty men for guard duty on Cat Island.

SEPTEMBER 15, 1864. Cat Island, Miss. Reached this place yesterday evening. Have thrown out pickets five miles from camp west, and three miles north. Think the winter may pass very pleasantly. Have a very comfortable tent, but am going to build me a house at once, and a school house, also.

OCTOBER 3, 1864. Oscar W. Goodrich[289] is here, running one of the saw mills: boards with me. A little colored boy cooks for us. We have got into our new house: the men are much interested in their studies.

OCTOBER 9, 1864. Thirty-four years old to-day. Went to the west end of the island and took supper with Mrs. [*sic*] Burroughs, an old sea Captain, who lives here with his wife and five children. Pleasant evening. Think I must be growing old, but cannot realize it at all. Mrs. Burroughs would hardly believe me more than 21.

OCTOBER 24, 1864. Made the rounds yesterday on board a fractious mule, that thought me better able to walk than he was to carry me. He failed to shake me off, and so swelled up and broke his girth, and while I lay at full length in the sand, stood and "laughed" at me. I tied the saddle on with a rope that would not break, so the brute compressed himself and slipped it over his head. Third time I succeeded in making it "stick," and in "sticking" the mule till he was glad to carry me the rounds so as to get rid of me.

NOVEMBER 17, 1864. Started to make the rounds, or rather to visit the pickets at the west end last night, in my sail boat. Breeze stiff from the north. About four miles out broke the mast even with the deck. Have for my crew skillful sailors, and we were soon under sail again, but glad to get back to port without being driven out to sea. Left the pickets to visit themselves.

NOVEMBER 20, 1864. Received thirty more men from Ship Island, for fatigue: making seventy in all. Some more mules, also; making sixteen, all told. Received two more negroes from Wolf River.[290] They will join the Regiment on Ship Island. Glad to see them escape, of their own free will, without the aid of the Federal army. Two men less for the rebs., and two more for the Union. "Despise not the day of small things."[291]

[**NOVEMBER 27, 1864.** *On this date Kinsley writes the following letter to his father.*]

Cat Island, Miss., Nov. 27, 1864

Dear father:

I was at Ship Island the other day, and got your letter of the 16th ult., with one from Samantha, and some others. The steamer last evening brought me letters from Daniel and Harriet,[292] Edgar and William; by all of which letters I learn many things new to me: that your land in the West is sold; that a "Literary Circle" sheds the light of Letters over the benighted inhabitants of my native town; that Edgar is doing well; that the Yellow Fever rages in this Department; that Alonzo is on the river, "watching calves;" that the Literary Circle is really a very fine thing, in the opinion of a disinterested spectator, fully competent to judge; that William is at home on furlough, wounded; that Jason[293] has been promoted; &c. &c. &c. Not much bad news, perhaps not any. William's wound may be good fortune, rather than ill. I hope the ball has been removed before this time. One of those Minnies in an elbow or knee joint is always in the way.[294]

I am glad Samantha is with you. If the Country were at peace, and you were not constantly anxious lest some of your boys should show the rebs the bottoms of their feet, or in some other way disgrace themselves, and be dismissed [from] the service, I don't see why you might not pass the winter pleasantly enough. I wish I had some of your facilities for making life pass pleasantly. We have here no literary entertainments, no social intercourse, *nothing* that will answer for mental fabulum. I believe I must be getting very rough and uncivilized. I need the meliorating influences of the "Circle" fostered by Harmons[295] Classic lore. Let Boston look out for her laurels, or she will soon cease to be the "Hub" of the literary universe. Is the Athens of America on the move to the mountains? What else does Harm. do? anything? Why don't the girls send him out to General Grant? [*This letter continues on November 29, 1864.*]

[**NOVEMBER 29, 1864.** *On this date Kinsley concludes the letter to his father that he began on November 27, 1864.*]

Tuesday evening, Nov. 29

I have just returned from Ship Island again, with your letter of the 13th inst., and William's of the 14th. I am glad you are so well provided for, and that, after all the dangers to which they have been exposed, two or three of your boys are spared to make the blessings of life enjoyable, with the assistance of two or three of their cousins in calico. Dear me, how I would like to be at home a little while; but duty keeps me here, and I can afford to wait for the close of the war: then, I think, I should know how to enjoy a furlough. Mother expects me home, you say, and thinks that is the reason that I do not write; but you attribute my silence to some other cause. What, pray? Do you think I have fallen into the hands of the enemy? or, do you suppose I was sent to my long home from Mobile Bay? I passed one "night of terror" on that Bay, such as I hope I may not be called on to endure again. I was in command of a small party transporting munitions to one of the "Monitors," using a small sloop. We had our centre board carried away early in the evening, and drifted around among the rebel torpedoes, at the mercy of the wind and waves, until near noon next day. We saved ourselves from being driven into the hands of the rebels above Cedar Point, by tearing out some of the planks from the inside of the boat and hewing them down so that we could use them for oars, lashing them to the sides with rope that had kept our sail in place. I suppose Providence saved us from destruction by torpedoes, many of which were taken up in that vicinity a few days afterward, just after the surrender of Fort Morgan. We worked hard all night, and during the forenoon, and thought ourselves well-nigh dead with thirst when we got back to the Fleet, and were furnished with water from the *Chickasaw.* I presume I should have tested the strength of a rope, without much ceremony, if I had drifted ashore with my Company of negro soldiers. Glad I didn't do it.

Please write me at once about Jason. You have heard, doubtless, by this time, more definitely. You may ask mother not to look for a visit from me until next summer, and not to look then with more than one eye, for I enlisted last fall for three years from the first day of October, 1863; and Government seems inclined to make the "nigger officers" earn their money. I am encouraged to hope, however, by an officer who has influence at Headquarters, that he can obtain a furlough for me next summer, in the event of our being all on duty here as at present.

With regard to financial matters, I do not feel disposed to dictate, nor even to suggest. If you have the means at your disposal, it seems fit that you should fill up the measure of your days pretty much as you see is best. I have to say for myself only this: that, exposed as I am to the perils of war, liable to be left helpless, dependent, at any time, through disease, or wounds, it is an ever present satisfaction to know that you have a home for me, and that I should be taken care of in case of accident. I don't know but some of the girls may think I had better look somewhere else, rather than to my aged parents, for a place of refuge; but somehow I feel more strongly drawn toward my father's fireside than to any other place I have seen, and I do not think it too much for me to assume that I should be quite welcome to keep Bachelor's Hall there, provided, always, that I were to hold myself to good behavior. I do not think I have given any one reason to infer that it was my purpose to remain permanently in the army. I have thought, and still think, it is quite probable that I may feel inclined to do a soldier's duty during this war, if I should be able; but somehow I fail to find the attraction that some seem to see in "the pomp and circumstance of glorious war." The "glory" may be a big thing, but I can't see it; and, save when its power is wielded to promote the ends of Justice, the picture of war is any thing but pleasant to me. I do not think that I was made for a holiday soldier. But you know it has never been my habit to look very far ahead, at least not since I was about twenty years of age; and when the war ends, I may possibly decide on arms as a profession. Time enough to think of that when the time comes. The end is not yet. Meantime use the money that I have sent home, and any that I may possibly send hereafter, (if the paymaster ever comes) as your judgment shall dictate.

Doubtless you have read Gen. Butler in New York. I have, and have read the speech to an audience fully competent to appreciate it. Next after President Lincoln's reelection we niggers hurrah loudest for General Butler.[296]

Six of the rebel officers confined at Ship Island (among them Col. Anderson,[297] who was in command at Fort Gaines) made an attempt to escape the other night. They cut the chain that fastened a skiff belonging to the Light House, and under cover of a thick fog, pulled for the Confederacy; but a vigilant sentinel heard the plash of an oar in the water and alarmed the camp. The Colonel started with his launch and one from the Sloop of War *Vincennes*, and the chivalrous gentlemen were very soon in close quarters inside the "Dead Line."[298]

You will be glad to learn that I enjoy perfect health. I have as much business as I can attend to: better than idleness. Please express to Sister Rood and Sister Riggs[299] my thanks for copies of the *Era* and the *Cultivator*, – I know how to appreciate their kindness, – And oblige your son.

Rufus Kinsley

DECEMBER 10, 1864. Was obliged to prefer charges against one of my men, and send him to Ship Island for trial: assault, with intent to kill, and threatening to shoot an engineer in the Q. M. Department.

[**DECEMBER 11, 1864.** *On this date Kinsley writes his brother Daniel the following letter.*]

Ship Island, Miss., Dec. 11, 1864

Dear Brother:

I am thankful that it is my privilege to acknowledge the receipt of letters from yourself and Harriet, written about the middle of October, (I think.) My writing case is on Cat Island, and I have forgotten the exact date. It is not material, however. I received the letters with no small measure of thankfulness; but I have *not* received the paper of which you spoke. Perhaps I feel more than usually thankful that it is my privilege to write you this Sabbath morning, because of recent peril, and very narrow escape. I believe I have already told you that I am stationed on Cat Island, in command of a Detachment of 70 men, doing guard duty, and of late sawing lumber for Government use. In the absence of a steamer, I have to supply my men with rations, and my team with forage, from Ship Island, by means of a sail boat, which carries, in addition to her sail, eight heavy oars. This is rather a stormy coast, you know; and the navigation of small craft is sometimes rather unsafe; but we must have something to eat, so I started last Thursday to sail across, (near 20 miles) but we had no sooner rounded the cape than a north-wester carried away our mast, and we were thankful to get back home (six miles) with the use of oars. We tried it again the next morning (the wind having abated somewhat) and were near our harbor on the north side of Ship Island, when a heavy storm struck us, and we lowered sail at once and drifted under the lee of the island, where we were obliged to pull vigorously for a number of hours, to prevent being dashed in pieces by the breakers. The rain poured upon us piteously most of the time, and when it did not rain the wind kept the air so full of spray that we could see the fort and light house on the island but a little of the time, though not more than a mile or two distant. We were constantly taking in water, and sometimes the men were thrown from their places by the violence of the waves, and nearly washed overboard. We made the pier just before dark, and were pulled up with ropes, one at [a] time; but we had not three seconds to spare, for those of us who were taken up last stood in the water waist deep, and the last man was hardly out when the boat went to the bottom and was dashed to pieces. This is the second boat I have lost since I have been on Cat Island – three months. I suppose my men are "living on the country" now; that is, eating fish and oysters, alligators and birds; and they will have to do so until the storm abates, of which there are at present no indications. We have a steamer in waiting, but she is old, and dares not venture out in such weather as this. The sun shines to-day, but the wind is very high, and the heavy, ponderous waves beat the shore furiously. The sight is grand, and so is the sound. The picture as seen from my window is much more attractive than it was Friday afternoon, when I had a *near* view.

I am building quite a city on Cat Island. I have six carpenters at work on buildings for the men, and am going to build a school house next. I have orders to draw on the Quartermaster's Department for everything I need; but there are some things that the Q. M. cannot supply me with. I need a school ma'am very much; that is, the men in my command, and the children in the Contraband Colony need one. Can't you send some one to supply the deficiency?

You have had "Thanksgiving Day" and so have we, since I wrote you last. The Col. sent means for us to have a good thankful time, and the then recent news contributed more largely still; and, with roast coon, alligator stew, oysters, fish, crabs, duck, in the shape of chicken pie, and speeches and music, we had a very pleasant time. I am glad you have so much to be thankful for, and glad you know so well to be thankful for it. I never had so much to be thankful for as I have now. A great curse is being removed. A remedy is being applied, for the cure of a stupendous wrong. I know the medicine is hard to take, and the effects are terrible; but I had rather see the Nation die under vigorous treatment, than see her drift quietly and smoothly into the death of despotism, with none to give life for her salvation.

The rebs. talk of arming their slaves. The quicker the better. But it is too late for them, and I am afraid they will not do it.

Good by, Write soon, and oblige you brother,
Rufus Kinsley

[**DECEMBER 18, 1864.** *On this date Kinsley writes the following letter to his father.*]

Cat Island, Miss., Dec. 18, 1864

Dear father:

Your letter of the 21st ult., with Cousin Augusta's,[300] reached me at Ship Island the other day, just after I had posted one to Samantha giving an account of my then recent shipwreck. Two or three days afterward the storm abated, and the Col. staffed a steamer on its way to Mobile Bay, and returned me to my command, with rations and forage. Mr. Goodrich had borrowed for the men, from a steamer lying in our harbor, and unable to get away on account of the storm, all that could be spared, but I found them well nigh starved. The Col. came over with me, bringing his wife and daughter. When supper was ready, we took our oysters all from one mess pan, and ate slapjacks and molasses with the use of only two plates, and drank coffee from two cups. The women thought I needed more dishes.

I am very glad you are so smart at home, and glad you are so well satisfied with the result of the election. You "regret that I should find so little cause for joy, in the triumph of right principles." I do not quite understand you, father. From what premises do you draw your inference? You must have misunderstood me somewhere, I think. I could have voted for Mr. Lincoln with very great pleasure, if I had been favored with an opportunity. I did receive the intelligence of his election with most profound thanksgiving to God; and it gave me much larger satisfaction, and inspired me with stronger hope for the future of my country, than would the knowledge of the fall of Richmond and destruction of Lee's army. I think, however, that I may possibly incline a very little toward radicalism, in some of my views; or, perhaps, more properly, to what would have been deemed radicalism a few years ago. I always believed that every man, not only for himself but for every other man, should love liberty more than life. Ever since the hour that he presented a practical illustration of this idea in the then inchoate State, Kansas, I have believed in and loved John Brown. This is radical; or *was*. I have never believed in the President's policy of pacificating traitors in Tennessee, thinking thereby to secure strength to the Government; or in Kentucky either, or Louisiana.[301] I never believed in a few Yankees from New England getting together in New Orleans under the protection of Federal bayonets, and voting Louisiana back into the Union, while nineteen-twentieths of her sons were in arms, sworn to destroy the Union, or die in the last ditch. A very cute "Yankee trick," tis true; but I question its utility. I have believed, and do still, that the People – (thank God for the power of the People) – were ripe for the extermination of traitors, and the overthrow of rebellion and her accursed mother, Slavery, with the first shot fired at Fort Sumpter [*sic*]. I think the President was a little afraid to trust the People to follow the leadings of the "Divinity that shapes our ends, rough hew them how we will."[302] Still, somehow, I have so much more confidence in the President's wisdom, and honesty, than I have in my own, that I receive the news of his reelection with the deepest satisfaction, and feel a great sense of relief from oppressive anxiety. Thank God for the prospect that lies before us. [*This letter continues on December 30, 1864.*]

DECEMBER 29, 1864. Wrecked my surf boat at Ship Island, while after rations: obliged to borrow a launch, of Capt. Green[e],[303] of the *Vincennes*. He has a good one, recently captured from the Johnnies in Bay St. Louis. She carried, when captured, one 12 p'dr. gun.

[**DECEMBER 30, 1864.** *On this date Kinsley concludes the letter to his father that he began on December 18, 1864.*]

Dec. 30

In tip top health. No time to write. Steamer from Ship Island going at once.

Rufus Kinsley
2nd Lieut. 74th U.S.C.I.

JANUARY 1, 1865. Another year, so soon. Time flies. Never so fast before. Never much more pleasantly. Have never been more busy than during these last three months and a half. Have recently completed a new school house, larger and much more convenient than the old one. Also a dwelling house, large enough to accommodate a family; and Mr. Burroughs has to-day left his log house in the woods, and moved in with me. Think it will be pleasant to have a woman cook for me. Mr. Goodrich has left, rather unceremoniously. It is said he has left his wife, in Lowell, Vt. *He* says she has left him.[304] He has married at Berwick Bay. I do not envy him.

JANUARY 7, 1865. Two more men (yes, I like that word), from my friend Scarborough. They had been stolen from their master by the rebel Cavalry, and were being taken to work on the fortifications. Quartermaster here sought to compel them to remain on the island and work for him. They came to me for counsel, and were soon "stowed" on the steamer *Brown*, which was loading at my wharf. I thought it might be well to go myself, and when we reached the Quartermaster's camp he came on board and searched us, but the negroes could not be found. On reaching the wharf at Ship Island, however, they were all ready to go ashore. The Col. has enlisted them. The Q. M. will never be able to forgive me.[305]

[**JANUARY 22, 1865.** *On this date Kinsley writes the following letter to his sister Lucretia.*]

Cat Island, Miss., Jan. 22nd, 1865

Dear Sister:

It is Sabbath. It is very rainy, but very warm: indeed, terribly hot. We have had south wind for some days, and I think it comes from the warmest place there is. The musquitoes [*sic*] annoy me much. Otherwise, I am very comfortably situated: too comfortably situated for a soldier. Do you think I can do better than acknowledge your very pleasant letter of the 25th ult.? I guess not. I have forgotten when I wrote you last. Did I write from this place? or from Ship Island? or Fort Morgan? It don't matter. I am here now, and have been since the 14th of September. I have had 70 soldiers, (detailed from the Reg't. on Ship Island,) most of the time. Time has passed *very* pleasantly, but I cannot say that I have improved it as well as I might have done. I am guarding the island against apprehended attacks by rebel launches from Pearl and Wolf Rivers: running three steam saw mills, also. I have put up five good frame buildings for quarters, and one, 22 by 26 feet, for a school house; in one corner of which is my office. Life is very far from monotonous: always something to keep me busy. Ship Island is my base of supplies. The winter season is stormy, and I have been nearly lost several times, in crossing. I have had two boat[s] totally wrecked. One was the best surf boat on the coast; the other, lost about the middle of December, was an excellent launch, recently captured from the rebs. I was after subsistence stores, and when near Ship Island was struck by a hurricane which filled our boat with water, and dashed her to pieces. We were on the windward side of the island, and were all rescued, by the help of those on shore. I had the mast of another boat carried away one night, while going out to visit the pickets. Two or three nights ago the lightning struck and shivered into fragments a large pine tree that stood sixteen feet from my door, and at the same time, a splendid oak that stood only seven feet from the door. So you see the elements are not less dangerous than "the enemy." Perhaps both are held in the hand of the "Divinity that shapes our ends, rough hew them how we will."

Do you know, Lucretia, I am rather glad you are teaching school? Perhaps you are employed there as usefully as you could be in the South; but somehow it seems to me that these colored people *must* be taught by somebody; and there are several vacant school districts in this Department, where "school maam wanted," *might be* posted up, if it is not. I almost think I shall have to remain in the South after the war is ended. But who can tell what shall be, at the end of the war? or *who* shall be?

I wish you would tell me a little more about Jason. The last I heard of him before, was by a letter from father received Dec. 10, which stated that Phebe Hopkins supposed he had been killed. Wherein is he more pleasantly situated than heretofore? What is he doing?[306] What is the news out in the world? I have had communication with Ship Island only once since the tenth of Dec., and I got no news then. The island was almost covered with water a few days since. We expected a flood like that of August, 1860; but the danger is past. We have been short of rations some of the time, and, when unable to catch fish, oysters and alligators, on account of the weather, have been obliged to resort to rats, and acorns, both of which are found here in great abundance. The rats live mostly on acorns, and are very good.

My buildings are pleasantly situated in a live oak grove, a few rods from the water. One of the boys (a soldier) can spell almost every word in *Webster's Elementary*, and many of them are getting on finely in reading, spelling, writing, arithmetic, and geography.

It is a little dull to be so isolated from the world, but it may not be a bad thing, after all. I am certain it is good for every man in the army to have enough to do.

Aren't you afraid of Indians?[307] The guerrillas gobble up school maams in Louisiana. I know of some who will be hard to tame. It is quite probable they may be hanged. Perhaps they had better be. I almost envy them. Not quite, though. I am in the best health, and enjoy life very much. Good by. Love to Guy and family.

R. Kinsley

JANUARY 24, 1865. Waited several days for storm to abate, so we could sail the launch to Ship Island for rations. Men nearly starved, and we started day before yesterday, but were driven back, and came near being swamped. Tried again yesterday, with twenty men on board. Got on very well till we were within a mile or two of the island, when we were obliged to bail constantly, and the air was so full of spray that we could not see the buildings, and had to steer by the sound of the breakers on the beach. We made the mile in about three hours; none too quick, for those of us who were taken out last stood in the water waist deep, and the last man was hardly on the wharf, when the boat went down, and was a total wreck. I settled with Capt. Green[e] for the loss of the boat, very easily. He told me to be thankful that I did not go down with her, and whenever I needed another, to let him know. It had cost him nothing but the capture, and its loss had saved the trouble of selling it. The storm having abated somewhat to-day, two steamers that were in the Ship Island harbor waiting for a calm, ventured out, to assist each other if necessary, and brought us back, with our rations.

JANUARY 25, 1865. Three small boats that came ashore last night were lost in trying to get back to the steamers, which have been hunting for them all day. Two have been found, one at Chandeliers, 30 miles distant, the other at Pass Marian light[house], about 12 miles.

FEBRUARY 3, 1865. Was requested by Quartermaster to arrest one of his hands. Complied with his request, in obedience to General Orders from Department Headquarters, knowing, as I did, that the man was anxious to be arrested, that he might obtain justice.

FEBRUARY 5, 1865. Requested by Q. M. to bring his "nigger up to his quarters, and tie him up by the thumbs until he should submit to terms." I was obliged to deprive myself of the privilege of doing him that favor.

FEBRUARY 6, 1865. Received peremptory orders to bring the man, as requested yesterday, with notice that a refusal on my part would cost me my Commission. I was very happy to refuse, in accordance with General Orders from Dep't. Hd. Qrs. Complaint, will be made, but I do not fear the result.

FEBRUARY 12, 1865. (Sunday) Three more men from my friend Scarborough. They are to join the Regiment.

FEBRUARY 19, 1865. (Sunday) Found one of my men at daylight this morning, in the house of one of the "poor white trash," into which he had broken during the night, armed with his musket, an axe, and a bowie knife. He had committed an assault and battery. "In prime thrust," disarmed him instanter, and I placed him under guard.

FEBRUARY 21, 1865. Found a body on the beach, dressed in sailor's clothes, but swollen as large as a barrel, and somewhat decomposed. No papers about the person, by which to identify it. Thirty-five dollars and a dime in one of the pockets, which must be preserved for his friends, if I can find who they are. Got some of the men, and buried the body as deep as we could, with no coffin.

FEBRUARY 22, 1865. Quartermaster's complaint returned to me from Head-quarters, with an endorsement approving my course.

FEBRUARY 23, 1865. Found the body buried on the 21st, dug out by the dogs, and nearly eaten up. Buried the bones, and covered with timber.

FEBRUARY 28, 1865. Have been out of rations for two weeks, and water so rough that we could not get any. A steamer has been lying here near two weeks, with over a hundred men, and almost nothing to eat. Water so high we have been unable to get oysters, and lived on one gill of corn a day for each person, until all was gone; then we resorted to rats and acorns. Killed two or three alligators, which furnished a treat. Have been over today, and got rations, and also orders to break camp as soon as may be; to send the saw mills and lumber to Ship Island, and leave Cat Island to the tar and turpentine men.

MARCH 6, 1865. At Ship Island again, for duty; which will be to guard rebel prisoners, of whom we have several hundred. Have passed the winter on Cat Island very pleasantly, and I hope with some profit to some of the men. Built two school houses, one very good, and spent much time in teaching soldiers and contraband children. Some of the soldiers who were slaves three years ago, and did not know a letter, can spell and read well all through Webster's spelling book, and are making good progress in arithmetic and geography. The fact that slavery keeps them in ignorance, teaches them that learning is of the first importance.

MARCH 15, 1865. Start for New Orleans to-day, with Capt. Noyes' Company Fund, to buy things for the Co.

MARCH 22, 1865. Returned to Ship Island, and went on duty as Officer of the Guard at Camp Dixie.[308]

MARCH 25, 1865. Appointed as Recorder of a Court to investigate the circumstances attending the shooting of a rebel prisoner by one of the guard. Found the reb. refused to obey orders, and exonerated the guard.

APRIL 7, 1865. Ordered to investigate and report upon a complaint made by one of the officers confined in the camp of rebel prisoners, of abuse by the guard. Found the complaint unfounded. The officer refused to do the police work required of him, and the guard, who was formerly owned by the officer, used the means necessary to compel him to work. This lesson he had doubtless learned on the plantation of the contumacious officer.

MAY 3, 1865. Am going to New Orleans to-day with Capt. Noyes and his wife. We mean to look the country over a little, and visit some of the battle grounds of the Eighth Vermont. I hope to get twelve months pay. I have also to attend two cases of Court Martial of soldiers who were found sleeping on posts adjoining each other, at the same time. They have been on guard every other day the last two or three months (and so have I), and I shall put in a plea in mitigation of sentence.

MAY 10, 1865. Back again from New Orleans. Spent some time visiting the colored schools in the city. Found several New England schoolma'ams, doing for their country a nobler and braver work than has been done on the bloody battlefields of the war. They have in the State, 240 teachers, with 15,000 colored scholars in attendance daily. Some teachers in the back parishes have been captured by guerrillas, but the schools are spreading, and are destined to save the Nation.[309]

[**MAY 10, 1865.** *On this date Kinsley writes the following letter to his brother William.*]

New Orleans, La., May 10th 1865

Dear brother William:

Your very welcome letter of the 15th ult. from Washington, reached me in good time. I was glad to learn that you had passed the ordeal, and that you came out alive, though "severely wounded," the papers say. The loss of an eye, and a broken head, and a ruined arm, don't seem to trouble you much if I may judge from the tone of your letters. Well, I commend your philosophy. I think you may well be cheerful, and thankful, and happy in view of the past, the present, and the prospects for the future.

I have been in town since the 3rd on Court Martial: am going to start for the island this evening. Time has passed very pleasantly. Mother Taylor's family are quite well. Johnny returned from the North months ago. They all regret your wounds, and are an[x]ious you should come and visit them until you are able to go to the front again. I visited Mother Taylor's school (Girl's High School) two or three times, and a dozen of fifteen of the Colored Schools. Gen. Banks and I made some tremendous speeches, I tell you. I board while here with Mrs. Lee, who figures so favorably in Parton's *Butler*.[310] I'll have some stories to tell you if I get home next fall; but they won't flow from my pen. Dr. Taylor still holds to his "hobby." Alice is getting to be quite a beauty; and she is the most sensible woman I have seen in the South, except her mother. I incline to think that Colton[311] will take her North with him when he goes. I believe you heard Mrs. Taylor exclaim, in holy horror, about three years ago, "What! Corporal; I hope you are not an Abolitionist, are you?" Do you remember the conversation that followed? Yesterady [*sic*] she asked me to make application to the Board for a Colored School for Alice; and she says that when her services are no longer needed in the hospitals, she shall give up her school, (with a salary of $1800 a year) and take a Colored School herself. I know several ladies in this city whose elevation to the cause of education for the negro has cost them the same price that Widow McGeary was obliged to pay for her devotion to Bona Case; viz: social ostracism, and exclusion from home. Whenever one of these female colored school teachers gets into a street car, straightway all the fools in the car get out, and wait in the rain, or sun, for the next car. Most of the girls evince the true Yankee school ma'am grit. I witnessed an encounter the other evening between one of them and Madame Secesh with several useless daughters, the recent owner of a fine stock of niggers. The house was soon cleaned out. Most of the teachers are from New England.

I saw Mr. Andrus up town the other day. He expressed regret that you had ceased to correspond with "the little Chaplain:" said his family would be pleased to have the correspondence renewed. I afterward took a half dozen New England schoolma'ams, and two or three New Orleans ditto, and went down to see the "little Chaplain." The evening passed very pleasantly. Alfred is Chief Clerk. All those buildings that the rebs burned and "blew up," east of the wall, have been rebuilt; and a fine chapel in addition. They have six hundred of our wounded from Mobile. Five hundred more are on their way there from Mobile, in hospital steamer; all wounded.

New Orleans is heavily draped in black crape. I understand it to be a sign that New Orleans mourns because the assassin's knife failed to reach the heart of Johnson, and Seward, and Stanton.[312] I do not question that ninety-nine out of every hundred of those (in this city) whose houses wear a semblance of sorrow would rejoice with exceeding great joy if the plot had been fully carried out. Very few of those who have lost their slaves will cease to hate the Emancipation Proclamation and the Common School System, while they live. One of them had the courtesy two or three days since, to assure me that as a United States officer, she entertained for me the highest possible respect; but if she had a son capable of holding such sentiments as I had just expressed with regard to labor, by white men, and the education of black men, she would cut his throat with her own hand, to save the family name from disgrace. These words were said to me by a woman who owned, three years ago, a number of slaves who were the sons and daughters of her own husband; and they were of about the same age as her own children. Verily the Augean stables need to be cleansed with blood.

I return to the island this evening. We expect to be ordered to Mississippi City in a few days, to keep returning rebs. on their good behavior. Take good care of your wounds, write me the news, and look out for me next October.

Rufus Kinsley

MAY 12, 1865. The prisoners taken at the capture of Mobile, have increased the number on our hands to over 5000, notwithstanding all we have sent away for exchange and parole.[313]

MAY 27, 1865. Confederate prisoners all sent to Vicksburg.[314] Great relief to us. Our duties have been heavy.

JUNE 2, 1865. Sprained my left knee severely while bathing with the officers. It is swollen, and painful, but I think I shall not have to be excused from duty.[315] On duty as Officer of the Day. Wish I were at home. Have been anxious to leave the service ever since the end of the war. Military is no business for me in time of peace. Should resign at once and go home, but my Captain is anxious to remain until October and be mustered out, and he is not quite willing that I should leave him.

JUNE 7, 1865. Have had a very pleasant excursion to the rebel shore, or main land, with Col. Holmstedt and his wife and their protege, Capt. Noyes and his wife. Stayed over night at Biloxi. Found the villages entirely deserted by the negroes, and mostly by the whites. They were starved out during the war. Desolation reigns. Do you think it is wicked? I can't help it: I love to see it so. I see the hand of God.

JUNE 10, 1865. Plenty of fine melons in our garden: they are just in prime order. Weather warm. Mercury, in shade, from 108 to 110 degrees since the 3d of May.

JUNE 17, 1865. Able to attend to all duties except drill. Too lame for that. Officer of the Day to-day. In perfect health, except lame knee.

JUNE 26, 1865. All the officers summoned to Headquarters to make arrangements for doing honor to the coming Fourth. A committee has been appointed to go to New Orleans to get lager beer, whiskey, and wines, fireworks and guests. I think we shall have a regular Dutch drunk, and Capt. Noyes and myself will be the only two sober officers on the island. Hope the steamer will get back too late.

JULY 4, 1865. To-day for the first time in its history, does the old Liberty Bell in Independence Hall speak the truth. To-day for the first time since I began to think for myself do I exult, and rejoice, and thank God for the return of this anniversary. How much of hollow hypocrisy has characterised our rejoicing on this anniversary in the years that are past. I think I have never indulged in much of it myself. To-day I am thankful. To-day I am ready to beat my sword into a plowshare. And I think I'll do it, too. I can afford to retire from the field of Mars. I cannot afford to spend any more time here. Have passed the day very pleasantly, and the evening too, with Capt. Noyes and his wife, reading Henry Ward Beecher, and Redpath's *John Brown*,[316] and listening to Mrs. Noyes' piano. The officers are having a grand revel. Not one of them except Capt. Noyes, who has stayed at home with his wife, and myself is sober.

JULY 5, 1865. Steamer *J. M. Brown* arrived from Mobile, with our heavy Parrott guns which were taken there to assist the city in its surrender.

JULY 8, 1865. All the officers (except Capt. Noyes and myself) with their wives, have gone to Ocean Springs on Steamer *Brown*, for a grand ball. I am on duty as officer of the Day.

JULY 9, 1865. (Sunday) *Brown* got back at 9 A.M. Everybody cross, nobody fit for duty, and I am Officer of the Day again.

JULY 12, 1865. I have to-day tendered my resignation, based on Surgeon Gihon's certificate that my knee is so lame that I cannot be fit for duty before the middle of October, at which time I would be liable to muster out on account of expiration of term of service. The Colonel has approved it, and I hope to be on my way home soon.

[**JULY 12, 1865.** *On this date Kinsley submitted the following letter of resignation to Brevet Lieutenant Colonel J. Schuyler Crosby, the Acting Assistant Adjunct General of the Department of the Gulf.*]

Ship Island, Miss.
July 12th 1865

Sir:

I have the honor herewith to tender my resignation as 2nd lieutenant in Co "G" 74th Regt, U.S. Cold Infty, on account of "Surgeon's certificate of disability."

As my term of service expires within three months – the time specified in the certificate of disibility [*sic*] – I trust this will meet the favorable consideration of the commanding General.

I certify, on honor, that I am not indebted to the United States on any account whatever, and that I am not responsible for any Govt property, and that I was last paid by Major Reese to include the 30th day of April 1865.

> Very respectfully, your obdt servt,
> Rufus Kinsley
> 2nd Lieut Co. "G" 74th U.S.C.I.[317]

JULY 14, 1865. Officer of the Day to-day. My resignation has started for the city on a schooner.

JULY 21, 1865. Officer of the Day yesterday. Before I was relieved this morning, the steamer came in, bringing my discharge from service, as follows:

> Headquarters Department of Louisiana & Texas,
> New Orleans, July 18, 1865.

Special Orders, No. 1.

The following named officers having tendered their resignation, based on Surgeon's certificate of disability, are hereby honorably discharged [from] the military service of the United States, subject to the approval of the President, on condition that they shall receive no final payment until they have satisfied the Pay Department that they are not indebted to the Government. 2d Lieut. Rufus Kinsley, 74th U. S. C. Infantry.

> By order of Major General E. R. S. Canby;
> J. Schuyler Crosby, Brevet Lt. Col. A. D. C. A. A. Gen'l.
> Official: Nathaniel Burbank, 1st Lieut. A. A. Gen'l.

JULY 22, 1865. Capt. Noyes has tendered his resignation, based on his wife's ill health.[318] I am to wait for its acceptance, so that we can go home together.

JULY 30, 1865. New Orleans, La. Left Ship Island on the 25th at two in the morning for Mobile. Stopped at Forts Powell, Gaines and Morgan, and reached Mobile a[t] one p.m. Spent two or three days visiting the fortifications, colored schools, public buildings, etc. The schools in Alabama are in their infancy. In Mobile they have been open four weeks. In the Alabama Medical College are now six female teachers from Illinois and Connecticut, giving to six hundred boys and girls, all colored, their charter of manhood and womanhood. There are other schools in the churches, in which about nine hundred of the freed children are taking to themselves the strength and knowledge which shall enable them by and by to bear with becoming reverence, and with credit to themselves and honor to the country, the burdens of freedom. Mobile is ill at ease. Mobile is rebellious. Mobile cannot sit calmly, and with quiet dignity, and see the Common School System of the North thrust into her vitals. It is inimical to the interests of aristocracy. But

Ship Island, Miss
July 12th 1865

Sir:

I have the honor herewith to tender my resignation as 2nd Lieutenant in Co. G, 74th Regt, U.S. Cold Infty on account of "Surgeon's certificate of disability"

As my term of service expires within three months — the time specified in the certificate of disibility — I trust this will meet the favorable consideration of the commanding General.

I certify, on honor, that I am not indebted to the United States on any account whatever, and that I am not responsible for any Govt property. and that I was last paid by Major Reese to include the 30th day of April 1865

Very respectfully, your obdt servt
Rufus Kinsley
2nd Lieut Co. G 74th U.S.C.I.

1st Lt. Col. J. Schuyler Crosby
A.D.C. Acting Ass't Adjt Genl.
Dept of the Gulf

33. Kinsley's resignation from the Seventy-fourth United States Colored Infantry. Courtesy of the National Archives.

the arm of the Government is long; the Federal bayonet is potent, and Mobile must submit, with the best grace she can command.[319] The Government has finished off rooms in the College, to be used for parlor, kitchen, and sleeping, by the teachers; and Secessia has been obliged to furnish them in the best style. These schools are supported by a tax on the property of those who a few months ago owned the scholars. The defenses of the city on the west side of the Bay were very extensive and elaborate. Millions of property were destroyed, and millions of material used up, in preparing to defend the city from assault by what was supposed the only feasible route. Our forces made a detour to the east, across the Bay, and the works were abandoned without firing a gun; and on the fall of Spanish Fort the City itself was evacuated.

AUGUST 1, 1865. I have presented to Gen. Canby, through his A[ssistant]. A[djunct]. G[eneral]., an earnest recommendation from Col. Holmstedt, in favor of the acceptance of Capt. Noyes' resignation; but for some reason, his paper has not yet reached the General's hands.

AUGUST 2, 1865. I have secured from Gen. Canby an order for transportation, and am all ready to leave; but shall wait a few days to hear from Capt. Noyes.[320]

Notes

Preface

1. Sometime after he moved to Lowell, Vt., in 1872, Kinsley added "Lowell," in blue ink between "Fletcher," and "Vermont." Kinsley's two-volume diary is in the Rufus Kinsley Papers, Research Library, Vermont Historical Society (Barre, Vt.).

2. Apparently, nothing else in Kinsley's life, either before or after the war, moved him to keep a daily account of his experiences. Reba Kinsley Hall, who was born and reared on her grandfather's Lowell farm, informs me that, to the best of her knowledge, Kinsley never kept another diary and, with the exception of a few Civil War letters, left no papers of any consequence. Reba Kinsley Hall to the author, February 13, 1983.

3. *Burlington (Vt.) Free Press and Times,* September 9, 1907.

4. Most of the sustained and significant first-hand accounts of the war in southwestern Louisiana and of daily life in a black regiment are listed in William F. Messner, *Freedmen and the Ideology of Free Labor: Louisiana, 1862–1865* (Lafayette: University of Southwestern Louisiana, 1978), 195–98; David C. Edmonds, *Yankee Autumn in Acadiana: A Narrative of the Great Texas Overland Expedition through Southwestern Louisiana, October-December 1863* (Lafayette, La.: Acadiana Press, 1979), 472–75; James M. McPherson, ed., *The Negro's Civil War: How American Negroes Felt and Acted During the War for the Union* (New York: Random House, 1965), 345–49; and Ira Berlin, Joseph P. Reidy, and Leslie S. Rowland, eds., *Freedom's Soldiers: The Black Military Experience in the Civil War* (Cambridge: Cambridge University Press, 1998), 181–84.

5. Rufus Kinsley, *The Slaveholders' Rebellion,* January 1, 1863. This and all subsequent references to Kinsley's diary are to the version published here. Kinsley's diary offers strong support for historian James M. McPherson's argument that ideological commitments played a crucial role in motivating Union soldiers to see the war through to its conclusion. But Kinsley's diary provides little evidence in support of the view that comradeship and peer pressure kept soldiers in the field fighting. For a thoughtful discussion of these issues, see McPherson, *For Cause and Comrades: Why Men Fought in the Civil War* (New York: Oxford University Press, 1997).

6. On the ability of slaveholding interests to dominate the federal government from the creation of the Constitution to the outbreak of the Civil War, see Leonard L. Richards, *The Slave Power: The Free North and Southern Domination, 1780–1860* (Baton Rouge: Louisiana State University Press, 2000), and Don E. Fehrenbacher, *The Slaveholding Republic: An Account of the United States Government's Relations to Slavery,* completed and ed. Ward M. McAfee (New York: Oxford University Press, 2001).

7. Like many evangelical Protestants, Kinsley assumed that no honest Christian could be a slaveholder, much less believe slavery was a divinely sanctioned institution. He never understood that a strong scriptural defense of slavery not only existed but provided the moral foundation for the worldview of many slaveholders. On the role of religion in the war against slavery and the Confederacy, see Mark A. Noll, "The Bible and Slavery," in Randall M. Miller, Harry S. Stout, and Charles Reagan Wilson, eds., *Religion and the American Civil War* (New York: Oxford University Press, 1998), 43–73; Eugene D. Genovese, "Religion in the Collapse of the American Union," in ibid., 74–88; James H. Moorhead, *American Apocalypse: Yankee Protestants and the Civil War, 1860–1869* (New Haven, Conn.: Yale University Press, 1978); Lewis Perry, *Radical Abolitionism: Anarchy and the Government of God in Antislavery Thought* (Ithaca, N.Y.: Cornell University Press, 1973); and Steven E. Woodworth, *While God Is Marching On: The Religious World of Civil War Soldiers* (Lawrence: University Press of Kansas, 2001).

8. Kinsley, *The Slaveholders' Rebellion,* September 29, 1862. Kinsley and Douglass also agreed on how best to describe the Civil War. Seven months after Kinsley titled his diary "The Slaveholders' Rebellion," Douglass chose the same title for his Fourth of July speech at Himrods Corners, N.Y. Philip S. Foner, ed., *The Life and Writings of Frederick Douglass,* 4 vols. (New York: International Press, 1950–55), III, 244–46.

9. Kinsley, *The Slaveholders' Rebellion,* January 1, 1863.

10. Ibid., September 10, 26, 28, October 16, 27, November 30, 1862, November 29, 1864.

11. Born in Cambridge, Mass., into the family of the bursar of Harvard College, Higginson was a Harvard-educated clergyman and a militant abolitionist. In November 1862 he was appointed colonel of the first officially organized black Civil War regiment, the First South Carolina Vols. In his famous memoir about officering a black regiment, Higginson referred to African Americans as "barbarians," a "mysterious race of grown-up children," and members of a race that was "simple," "docile," "childish," "affectionate, enthusiastic, grotesque, and dramatic." Higginson, *Army Life in a Black Regiment* (1869; reprint, Boston: Beacon Press, 1962), 4, 8, 16–17, 18, 52, 66. A captain in the Twelfth Connecticut Vols., De Forest decided in 1862 to apply for a commission in a black Louisiana regiment but was later talked out of it by a superior officer. The author of numerous novels and travelogues, De Forest was a bookish young man from a prominent New Haven, Conn., family. He was too sickly as a youth to attend Yale, so instead advanced his education by traveling abroad. Before the war he wrote a book depicting Native Americans as uncivilized savages, and during the Civil War he used terms such as "a fat and dirty nigger," "a blubber-lipped loafer," and "a sly and

slippery darkey" to describe African Americans. John William De Forest, *A Volunteer's Adventures: A Union Captain's Record of the Civil War*, ed. James H. Croushore (New Haven, Conn.: Yale University Press, 1946), 50–51, 77, 97; Edmund Wilson, *Patriotic Gore: Studies in the Literature of the American Civil War* (1962; corrected ed., New York: Oxford University Press, 1966), 670–71. Shaw, who after his death would become the most famous white officer of a black regiment during the Civil War, is discussed in the Introduction. For a discussion of nineteenth-century racial attitudes, which demonstrates that Kinsley lived in an era when popular belief as well as scientific learning almost universally pronounced blacks innately inferior to whites, see George M. Frederickson, *The Black Image in the White Mind: The Debate on Afro-American Character and Destiny, 1817–1914* (New York: Harper & Row, 1971), esp. chaps. 2–6.

12. Thomas Mallon, *A Book of One's Own: People and Their Diaries* (New York: Ticknor & Fields, 1984), xvi.

13. Laura S. Haviland, *A Woman's Life Work: Including Thirty Years' Service on the Underground Railroad and in the War* (Grand Rapids, Mich.: S. B. Shaw, 1881), 328; Reba Kinsley Hall, telephone conversation with the author, September 2, 2000.

14. Richard Lewontin, *It Ain't Necessarily So: The Dream of the Human Genome and Other Illusions* (New York: New York Review of Books, 2000), 269.

15. Kinsley was not alone among Union soldiers in seeking ways to honor the Sabbath and thereby keep alive a sacred tradition that reached back thousands of years. Woodworth, *While God Is Marching On*, 78–83.

Introduction

1. On the life of Robert Gould Shaw, see Peter Burchard, *One Gallant Rush: Robert Gould Shaw and His Brave Black Regiment* (New York: St. Martin's Press, 1965); Marion W. Smith, *Beacon Hill's Colonel Robert Gould Shaw* (New York: Carlton Press, 1986); and Russell Duncan, ed., *Blue-Eyed Child of Fortune: The Civil War Letters of Colonel Robert Gould Shaw* (Athens: University of Georgia Press, 1992). The quotations are from Duncan, *Blue-Eyed Child*, 25, 56.

2. Duncan, *Blue-Eyed Child*, 18, 283, 289–90, 292, 293, 299, 305, 355, 359, 360, 373. Shaw finally stopped using the words "nig" and "nigger," but just two weeks before his death he was still calling African Americans "darkeys." It is inconceivable that Kinsley would have sat around, as Shaw did, with his fellow officers and laughed at racist jokes about "niggers." Ibid., 289–90, 373. For a general discussion of the prevalence of racism among white officers and the often strained relationship between white officers and black soldiers, see Howard C. Westwood, *Black Troops, White Commanders, and Freedmen During the Civil War* (Carbondale: Southern Illinois University Press, 1992); and Joseph T. Glatthaar, *Forged in Battle: The Civil War Alliance of Black Soldiers and White Officers* (New York: The Free Press, 1990).

3. Duncan, *Blue-Eyed Child*, 360, 344, 18, 378, 349n, 16, 308.

4. George W. Montague, comp., *History and Genealogy of the Montague Family of America . . .* (Amherst, Mass.: Press of J. E. Williams, 1886), 323; Ellery B. Crane, ed., *Historic Homes and Institutions and Genealogical and Personal Memoirs of Worcester*

County, Massachusetts, with a History of Worcester Society of Antiquity, 4 vols. (New York: The Lewis Publishing Company, 1907), I, 248–50; Eleanor W. Ballway, ed., *A Genealogical Study of Some Families Who Came to Fletcher, Vt., before 1850 and of a Few of Their Descendants* (Burlington, Vt.: Vantage Press, 1981), 1, 40, 52. The marriage of Daniel Kinsley and Lucy Montague in 1788 was one of several Kinsley-Montague marriages. In 1824 Ben Alva Kinsley married his maternal cousin Catherine Montague. Rufus Kinsley was their son.

5. On the radical decision of Vermont's founders to outlaw slavery, see Michael A. Bellesiles, *Revolutionary Outlaws: Ethan Allen and the Struggle for Independence on the Early American Frontier* (Charlottesville: University of Virginia Press, 1993), 139–40. For evidence of the limits of antislavery in early Vermont, see Joanne Pope Melish, *Disowning Slavery: Gradual Emancipation and "Race" in New England, 1780–1860* (Ithaca, N.Y.: Cornell University Press, 1998), esp. 64; J. Kevin Graffagnino, "Vermont Attitudes Toward Slavery: The Need for a Closer Look," *Vermont History*, 45 (Winter 1977), 31–34; John Myers, "The Beginning of Antislavery Agencies in Vermont, 1832–1836," ibid., 36 (Summer 1968), 126–41.

6. Zadock Thompson, *History of Vermont, Natural, Civil, and Statistical...* (Burlington, Vt.: Chauncey Goodrich, 1842), pt. 1, chap. 1, pt. 3, p. 72; Lewis Cass Aldrich, *History of Franklin and Grand Isle Counties, Vermont* (Syracuse, N.Y.: D. Mason & Co., 1891), 19–23, 541–43; Ben A. Kinsley, "Fletcher," in Abby M. Hemenway, ed., *The Vermont Historical Gazetteer: A Magazine, Embracing a History of Each Town, Civil, Ecclesiastical, Biographical and Military*, 5 vols. (Burlington, Vt.: A. M. Hemenway, 1868–91), II, 202, 203. On the singularly tenacious commitment of frontier communities in postrevolutionary Vermont to the creation of a tolerant, democratic, and egalitarian society, see Randolph A. Roth, *The Democratic Dilemma: Religion, Reform, and the Social Order in the Connecticut River Valley of Vermont, 1791–1850* (New York: Cambridge University Press, 1987).

7. Guy Kinsley, "An Account of a Few Incidents of My Early Life." This memoir by Rufus Kinsley's brother was written in 1910 and later privately printed in an unpaginated booklet by his children. In it Guy Kinsley notes that "it was very difficult for father and mother to feed and keep us comfortably clothed. The only source of income was father's labor, and although he was industrious and able to do almost any kind of work, wages were very low and paid in such farm produce as we could eat or wear, or worse still, an order on a country store." He added, quite accurately judging from contemporary federal census returns, that "Really, our neighbors for whom we worked were but little better off than we." This booklet, which is in the possession of Reba Kinsley Hall, was later reprinted with omissions in Eleanor W. Ballway, ed., *A History of Fletcher, Vermont* (Burlington, Vt.: Printed by George Little Press for the Town of Fletcher, Vermont, 1976), 3–5.

8. Guy Kinsley, "An Account of a Few Incidents," unpaginated. The names of family members, other than the head of household, are not provided in the 1840 federal manuscript census returns, but in the 1840 returns Ben Alva's household is listed as consisting of seven males and two females whose reported ages correspond to those of the Kinsleys. Ben Alva is listed as employed in agriculture.

Manuscript Census Returns, Sixth Census of the United States, 1840, microcopy 704, roll 542, p. 308.

9. Guy Kinsley, "An Account of a Few Incidents," unpaginated; Ben A. Kinsley, "Fletcher," 213; Daniel Kinsley, "Letter from Vermont," *Worcester (Mass.) Palladium,* April 18, 1866; Catherine Kinsley death certificate, February 15, 1849, State of Vermont, Vital Records, General Services Center (Middlesex, Vt.) (cited hereinafter as Vital Records). The records of birth, death, and marriage are available on microfilm at the General Services Center. They are not identified individually by frame number, but are organized alphabetically by surname within time categories (e.g., 1760–1870, 1871–1908, 1909–41, etc.).

10. Manuscript Census Returns, Seventh Census of the United States, 1850, microcopy 432 (cited hereinafter as 1850 Manuscript Census), roll 343, pp. 9, 26, 34, roll 924, p. 1; Crane, *Historic Homes,* I, 250. In 1850, Emerson Safford, a twenty-six-year-old merchant who was Catherine Kinsley's nephew, was also boarding with Ben Alva, who was listed in the federal census as a farmer. Once Lucretia got away, she apparently made herself scarce. In a letter from Ben Alva Kinsley to Lucretia Kinsley on February 14, 1864, the father wrote to his daughter: "I hardly know where to direct this letter but think I will direct it to Worcester & if you are not there it [will] be directed to you. Hope you will write soon as convenient & let me know where & how you are, & how the folks are where you live, & when you are coming home...." In the late nineteenth century Lucretia, who never married, was living with her brother Daniel and his family in Worcester, Mass. In 1900 seventy-year-old Daniel, who owned his home in Worcester outright, was still listed in the census as "messenger (court)." Rufus Kinsley Papers (cited hereinafter as Kinsley Papers), Vermont Historical Society (Barre, Vt.) (cited hereinafter as VHS); Manuscript Census Returns, Twelfth Census of the United States, 1900, microcopy T623 (cited hereinafter as 1900 Manuscript Census), roll 695, p. 7A of Worcester City returns. My portrayal of Ben Alva Kinsley as a stern taskmaster who kept close watch over Lucretia as long as she lived under his roof is based upon numerous conversations with his great-granddaughter Reba Kinsley Hall.

11. Ben Alva Kinsley Pension, Records of the Veterans Administration, Record Group 15, National Archives (Washington, D.C.) (cited hereinafter as Pension); Guy Kinsley obituary in undated and unknown newspaper in possession of Reba Kinsley Hall; Jason W. Kinsley obituary in undated and unknown newspaper in possession of Reba Kinsley Hall; Vermont Land Records, General Services Center (Middlesex, Vt.), microfilm no. 7174, IX, 408, X, 66, 130, XI, 104; Manuscript Census Returns, Eighth Census of the United States, 1860, microcopy 653 (cited hereinafter as 1860 Manuscript Census), roll 315, p. 123; Edgar Kinsley Montague Diary, November 21, 1860. (Edgar Kinsley Montague's diary, which is cited hereinafter as Montague Diary, is in the possession of H. Carlton Ferguson of Fairfield, Vt. I am indebted to Mr. Ferguson for sharing the diary with me.) Guy Kinsley also had his wife and children and his brother Jason, who was listed in the census as a common school teacher, living on his farm in 1860. Jason reported no wealth, but Guy reported real and personal estate valued at

$4,000. Ten years later Guy had increased his holdings to $6,307, whereas Jason, now working as an insurance agent and boarding with a family in Monona, Iowa, still reported no wealth of any kind. Manuscript Census Returns, Ninth Census of the United States, 1870, microcopy 593 (cited hereinafter as 1870 Manuscript Census), roll 383, pp. 259, 435.

12. The preceding figures have been derived from data collected in the 1850 Manuscript Census, roll 924, and the 1860 Manuscript Census, roll 1321. The entire county of Franklin suffered a net loss in population during the 1850s, and Fletcher continued to lose population in the 1860s. Francis A. Walker, *The Statistics of the Population of the United States . . .* (Washington, D.C.: Government Printing Office, 1872), 68, 277. For a good discussion of the way in which climate, topography, economic decline, and population growth left thousands of ambitious young Vermonters no alternative but emigration in the decades immediately preceding the Civil War, see Lewis D. Stilwell, *Migration from Vermont* (1948; reprint, Montpelier: Vermont Historical Society and Rutland, Vt.: Academy Books, [1983]), esp. chaps. 6–9. Kinsley's father believed that Fletcher was "best adapted to grazing" because the township was hilly and much of its soil was stony and sterile. Ben A. Kinsley, "Fletcher," 202, 203.

13. *Burlington (Vt.) Free Press and Times*, April 4, 1898; Hemenway, *Gazetteer*, II, 331; Wilbur H. Siebert, *Vermont's Anti-Slavery and Underground Railroad Record* (1937; reprint, New York: Negro Universities Press, 1969), 25, 43–44, 86–88; Lucy A. Brainard, *The Genealogy of the Brainerd-Brainard Family in America: 1649–1908*, 3 vols. ([Hartford, Conn.]: Hartford Press, 1908), vol. II, pt. 1, pp. 53, 67, 68, 71, 98, 108, 109.

14. Guy Kinsley, "An Account of a Few Incidents," unpaginated; Reba Kinsley Hall, telephone conversation with author, April 3, 1992; Ben A. Kinsley, "Fletcher," 214; Hemenway, *Gazetteer*, II, 1193. Writing about the people of Fletcher, but perhaps thinking of himself, Ben Alva observed in 1868 that "although none of its [Fletcher's] inhabitants are collegians, there is a good degree of general intelligence among the people, a commendable zeal in the cause of education." Ben A. Kinsley, "Fletcher," 202.

15. Ben A. Kinsley to Rufus Kinsley, January 28, 1864, and Ben A. Kinsley to Lucretia Kinsley, February 14, 1864, Kinsley Papers; Guy Kinsley, "An Account of a Few Incidents," unpaginated.

16. Guy Kinsley, "An Account of a Few Incidents," unpaginated; Ben A. Kinsley, "Fletcher," 208–11, 214.

17. Ben A. Kinsley, "Fletcher," 208–11, 214.

18. 1850 Manuscript Census, roll 924, p. 80; *Burlington (Vt.) Free Press and Times*, March 4, 1876, April 4, 1898. Whiting's piety is suggested by the words with which he concluded his father's obituary in 1858: "Blessed are the dead which die in the Lord." *St. Albans Messenger*, April 14, 1858.

19. *St. Albans Messenger*, December 20, 1849–January 8, 1851.

20. During the war Kinsley's printing skills also allowed him to escape some of the dangers and drudgery of army life by serving as the official printer of his brigade and to help runaway slaves learn their ABCs by printing an oversized alphabet that could be hung on classroom walls. Rufus Kinsley, *The Slaveholders'*

Rebellion, April 9, 1863, July 3, September 10, 1862. This and all subsequent references to Kinsley's diary are to the version published here.

21. *St. Albans Messenger,* May 2, 16, January 17, February 28, 1850. Vermont, which in 1852 passed a statewide law prohibiting the drinking of alcoholic beverages, was a hotbed of reform, especially temperance and abolition, prior to the Civil War. For an old but still valuable account of reform movements in antebellum Vermont, see David M. Ludlum, *Social Ferment in Vermont, 1791–1850* (New York: Columbia University Press, 1939). Also insightful on the religious revivals that swept through antebellum Vermont and often sparked reformist activities is Jeffrey Potash's case study of Addison County, *Vermont's Burned-Over District: Patterns of Community Development and Religious Activity, 1761–1850* (Brooklyn, N.Y.: Carlson, 1991), and T. D. Seymour Bassett's more general study, *The Gods of the Hills: Piety and Society in Nineteenth-Century Vermont* (Montpelier: Vermont Historical Society, 2000), chaps. 2–5.

22. *St. Albans Messenger,* February 28, October 17, 1850. On October 24, 1850, the paper again expressed its fear of the "ultraism and fanaticism" that was sweeping through parts of the North, and counseled its readers to "live up to the [fugitive slave] law while it is a law, but repeal it as soon as possible." For a brief but brilliant discussion of the Compromise of 1850 and its consequences, see David M. Potter, *The Impending Crisis, 1848–1861* (New York: Harper & Row, 1976), chaps. 5–6.

23. *Boston Directory, for the Year 1853, City Record, a General Directory of the Citizens, and a Business Directory* (Boston: Geo. Adams, 1853), 165, 297, 363; Albert P. Langtry, *Metropolitan Boston,* 2 vols. (New York: Lewis Historical Publishing Company, 1929), vol. II, chap. 2; Walter Muir Whitehill, *Boston: A Topographical History* (Cambridge: Harvard University Press, 1968), 31, 218–19; Michael Winship, *American Literary Publishing in the Mid-Nineteenth Century: The Business of Ticknor and Fields* (Cambridge: Cambridge University Press, 1995), 7, 21. On *The Youth's Companion,* which announced on its masthead of May 11, 1854, that it was "A Family Paper, Devoted to Piety, Morality, Brotherly Love – No Sectarianism, No Controversy," see Frank L. Mott, *A History of American Magazines, 1850–1865* (Cambridge: Harvard University Press, 1967), 262–66. I have been unable to find Kinsley (or anyone else) listed as a printer for *The Youth's Companion* in surviving issues of the magazine or in contemporaneous Boston city directories. My conclusion that he worked for this important magazine is based primarily on family lore conveyed in Reba Kinsley Hall, letter to the author, November 19, 1981.

24. *Massachusetts Life Boat,* August 15, 1, 1854, March 9, April 6, October 19, 1853, April 11, July 11, 4, 1854, February 23, 9, 1853. That the parallels between slavery and drinking were evident to Kinsley is suggested by the language and metaphors of an undated poem in his handwriting entitled, "Before and Behind! Before and Behind!" The openly didactic poem describes the sinful world that the heartless rum seller has created behind the grogshop door, where "Drunkenness brews its woes, / Bodies and souls enslaving," and from which the drunkard seeks escape to sobriety, so "The chain that bound me shall bind me no more." Kinsley Papers. Temperance was a springboard into abolitionism for many New Englanders, including William Lloyd Garrison, who prior to editing *The Liberator*

ran a fiery temperance newspaper that sought the immediate and total abolition of drinking in America. Henry Mayer, *All on Fire: William Lloyd Garrison and the Abolition of Slavery* (New York: St. Martin's Press, 1998), 48–50. On the temperance movement in Massachusetts, see Robert L. Hampel's fine study *Temperance and Prohibition in Massachusetts, 1813–1852* (Ann Arbor, Mich.: UMI Research Press, 1982). On the role of printers and other skilled artisans in the Boston anti-liquor campaign beginning in the 1830s, see Jill Siegel Dodd, "The Working Classes and the Temperance Movement in Antebellum Boston," *Labor History*, 19 (Fall 1978), 510–31.

25. *Boston Evening Telegraph*, September 27, 1854, January 4, March 22, November 24, 1856. On the temperance issue, see also October 30, November 1, 6, December 16, 1854, May 30, June 2, 1855. On the battle for Kansas, see also July 21, December 5, 11, 1855, November 26, 1856. While working at the *Telegraph*, Kinsley boarded at 54 Harvard Street, near the corner of Washington Street, close to the *Telegraph*'s business offices and in the heart of the city's publishing district. *Boston Directory, for the Year 1855, City Record, a General Directory of the Citizens, and a Business Directory* (Boston: Geo. Adams, 1855), 176.

26. *Boston Evening Telegraph*, January 5, 1856; *Boston Evening Traveller*, September 7, January 16, February 27, 1857.

27. Donald M. Jacobs, ed., *Courage and Conscience: Black and White Abolitionists in Boston* (Bloomington: Published for the Boston Athenaeum by Indiana University Press, 1993); *Boston Evening Telegraph*, January 1, 1856; James O. Horton and Lois E. Horton, *Black Bostonians: Family Life and Community Struggle in the Antebellum North* (New York: Holmes & Meier, 1979), 59–61; George A. Levesque, *Black Boston: African American Life and Culture in Urban America, 1750–1860* (New York: Garland, 1994), 112–14. On the inside of the front cover of Helen M. Johnson, *Poems* (Boston: J. V. Himes, 1855), Kinsley wrote, "Rufus Kingsley [*sic*], May 17, 1857." This volume, which is in the possession of Patricia Packard, was kindly brought to my attention by William Kinsley. Kinsley was apparently misinformed about Helen M. Johnson's race, or he had learned something about her ancestry, perhaps from members of the May Street African Methodist Episcopal Church, that even her publisher, biographer, and brother-in-law John Muir Orrock did not know, or did not reveal. See Rev. J. M. Orrock, *Canadian Wild Flowers: Selections from the Writings of Miss Helen M. Johnson* (Boston: J. M. Orrock, 1884), 9–34.

In addition to probably attending integrated abolitionist meetings, Kinsley clearly read widely in the biracial abolitionist literature circulating in Boston in the 1850s. Indeed, the sarcastic descriptions of happy slaves and chivalrous slaveholders in Kinsley's diary are striking examples of the rhetorical style found in issue after issue of Garrison's *Liberator*. One suspects that Kinsley read and was influenced by such memorable Garrison editorials as "Southern Degradation," which appeared on September 19, 1856, while Kinsley was living in Boston. In it Garrison commented on Southern slaveholders' contention that the Atlantic slave trade was a benevolent institution that allowed the Christian South "to civilize the ignorant and enlighten the superstitious." Employing the sarcasm for which he was famous, Garrison asked, "Why then prohibit the African slave trade, under such a penalty [as death for piracy]? Why not give unlimited encouragement to it? Why not let Christian philanthropy be as broad as the Atlantic, and Africa be depopulated afresh? . . . Is not this the command of Christ – 'Go ye into all Africa, and seize as many of its wretched inhabitants as ye can by fraud and violence, that they may be taken to slaveholding America, where my gospel is proclaimed!'" This editorial is quoted in William E. Cain, ed., *William Lloyd Garrison and the Fight against Slavery: Selections from "The Liberator"* (Boston: Bedford Books, 1995), 146–47.

28. Walker, *Statistics of the Population of the United States*, 68, 277; 1850 Manuscript Census, roll 924, p. 13.

29. Horton and Horton, *Black Bostonians*, 2–5; Adelaide M. Cromwell, "The Black Presence in the West End of Boston, 1800–1864: A Demographic Map," in Jacobs, *Courage and Conscience*, 162–66; *Boston Directory, for the Year 1857, Embracing the City Record, a General Directory of the Citizens, and a Business Directory* (Boston: George Adams, 1857), 205. Despite its increasingly popular and integrated abolitionist movement, Boston in the 1850s was the most residentially segregated city in the North. Elizabeth H. Pleck, *Black Migration and Poverty: Boston, 1865–1900* (New York: Academic Press, 1979), 32.

30. [Abel Bowen,] *Bowen's Picture of Boston, or the Citizen's and Stranger's Guide to the Metropolis of Massachusetts, and Its Environs* (Boston: Otis, Broaders & Company, 1838), 137–38; Roy E. Finkenbine, "Boston's Black Churches: Institutional Centers of the Antislavery Movement," in Jacobs, *Courage and Conscience*, 172, 183; Horton and Horton, *Black Bostonians*, 55–57, 101, 105, 108, 117; Donald M. Jacobs, "A History of the Boston Negro From the Revolution to the Civil War" (Ph.D. diss., Boston University, 1968), 286; Albert J. von Frank, *The Trials of Anthony Burns: Freedom and Slavery in Emerson's Boston* (Cambridge: Harvard University Press, 1998), 42–45.

31. My discussion of the May Street African Methodist Episcopal Church's struggle for equality relies on the following works: Horton and Horton, *Black Bostonians*, chap. 4; Levesque, *Black Boston*, chap. 8; Donald M. Jacobs, "David Walker and William Lloyd Garrison: Racial Cooperation and the Shaping of Boston Abolition," in Jacobs, *Courage and Conscience*, chap. 1; and esp. Finkenbine, "Boston's Black Churches," in ibid., chap. 8. Helpful information on the May Street Church and its Sabbath school may also be found in Daniel A. Payne, *History of the African Methodist Episcopal Church*, ed. Rev. C. S. Smith (Nashville, Tenn.: Publishing House of the A.M.E. Sunday-School Union, 1891), and in James Mudge, *History of the New England Conference of the Methodist Episcopal Church, 1796–1910* (Boston: New England Conference, 1910). On David Walker, Samuel Snowden, and the May Street Church, see Peter P. Hinks, *To Awaken My Afflicted Brethren: David Walker and the Problem of Antebellum Slave Resistance* (University Park: Pennsylvania State University Press, 1997), 76–79.

32. Horton and Horton, *Black Bostonians*, 7; Kinsley, *The Slaveholders' Rebellion*, September 7, 1862. On the role of black churches in general, and the May Street Church in particular, in assisting fugitive slaves in antebellum Boston, see Oliver Horton, *Free People of Color: Inside the African American Community* (Washington, D.C.: Smithsonian Institution Press, 1993), chap. 1; and Levesque, *Black Boston*, 291.

33. 1860 Manuscript Census, roll 1321, p. 10; Edgar Kinsley Montague deposition, January 28, 1892, in Rufus Kinsley Pension; Montague Diary, April 23, 27, 30, May 8, 1860, November 14, 1861. The last Boston directory in which Kinsley appeared was *Boston Directory, for the Year 1857*, 205. In the 1860 census Kinsley was listed as a "Laborer" with no personal or real estate. His brother Edgar was recorded as a "Farmer" with $3,264 in personal and real estate. It may be that Kinsley's decision to leave Boston and return home to Fletcher was precipitated by his father's decision to move to Iowa and the death in 1857 of Rufus Montague, his brother Edgar's adoptive father.

34. Alonzo Kinsley, Jason W. Kinsley, Rufus Kinsley, William L. Kinsley, and Edgar K. Montague Compiled Military Service Records, Records of the Adjutant General's Office, 1780s–1917, Record Group 94, National Archives (Washington, D.C.) (cited hereinafter as Compiled Military Service Record). I am including Edgar Kinsley Montague, although adopted by his uncle Rufus Montague, along with Guy, Daniel, and Lucretia Kinsley, as a member of the Ben Alva Kinsley family.

35. The figures for Vermont are calculated from Jos. C. G. Kennedy, *Preliminary Report on the Eighth Census. 1860* (Washington, D.C.: Government Printing Office, 1862), 135; and G. G. Benedict, *Vermont in the Civil War: A History of the Part Taken by the Vermont Soldiers and Sailors in the War for the Union, 1861–5*, 2 vols. (Burlington, Vt.: Free Press Assoc., 1886 and 1888), II, 799. The figures for Fletcher are calculated from Hemenway, *Gazetteer*, II, 412–14, 452; and the 1860 Manuscript Census, roll 1321, pp. 255–75.

36. In reconstructing the history of Kinsley's company and regiment during the first year and a half of the war, I have relied heavily on Rufus Kinsley Compiled Military Service Record; the Record of Events for Co. C, D, E, and F of the Eighth Vermont (unfortunately the records for Co. F are sketchy for the period prior to the campaign against Port Hudson when Kinsley was still an active member of the regiment), in Compiled Records Showing Service of Military Units in Volunteer Union Organizations, National Archives (cited hereinafter as Compiled Records of Military Units), microcopy 594, roll 192; Benedict, *Vermont in the Civil War*, vol. II, chap. 22; George N. Carpenter, *History of the Eighth Regiment, Vermont Volunteers, 1861–1865* (Boston: Deland & Barta, 1886), pts. I-III; and Holman D. Jordan, Jr., "The Eighth Regiment of Vermont Volunteers in the Lafourche Country, 1862–1863," *Vermont History*, 31 (April 1963), 106–16.

37. Ezra Harvey Brown to Dear Brother & Sister, March 18 [1862], in Civil War Letters of Ezra Harvey Brown, microfilm no. 188, VHS (cited hereinafter as Brown Letters).

38. On the capture and occupation of New Orleans, see Chester C. Hearn, *The Capture of New Orleans, 1862* (Baton Rouge: Louisiana State University Press, 1995); Gerald M. Capers, *Occupied City: New Orleans under the Federals, 1862–1865* ([Lexington]: University of Kentucky Press, 1965).

39. Ezra Brown to Dear Father & Mother, May 14, 1862, Brown Letters; Charles S. Cooper, "Reminiscences," an undated and unpaginated manuscript in the Vermont Historical Society (cited hereinafter as Cooper, "Reminiscences"). Many years earlier John H. B. Latrobe, son of the noted architect Benjamin Henry

Latrobe and a brilliant young attorney, painter, and architect in his own right, expressed the same kind of awe and wonder as did the uneducated corporal Ezra Brown as Latrobe journeyed up the Mississippi River to New Orleans: "On either side of us the sugar plantations were now seen extending from the river to the marsh or swamp in the rear and presenting the most beautiful appearance that I ever saw in any species of cultivation. The green was so vivid, the foliage so dense, and the light wind waving it to and from marked it with the varying shadows that rolled after one another like waves upon a sea." Latrobe concluded his observation on a more somber note, one that would be repeated by Kinsley in his diary: "The melancholy recollection however that the many were labouring for the one in the very worst form of servitude – negro slavery, destroyed the zest with which I would otherwise have enjoyed the new scene before me." Samuel Wilson, Jr., ed., *Southern Travels: Journal of John H. B. Latrobe, 1834* (New Orleans: Historic New Orleans Collection, 1986), 38–39.

40. Cooper, "Reminiscences"; *The War of the Rebellion: A Compilation of the Official Records of the Union and Confederate Armies*, 128 vols. (Washington, D.C.: Government Printing Office, 1880–1901), series 1 (cited hereinafter as *War of the Rebellion*; all references are to series 1 unless otherwise noted), XV, 426; Elliott Ashkenazi, ed., *The Civil War Diary of Clara Solomon: Growing Up in New Orleans, 1861–1862* (Baton Rouge: Louisiana State University Press, 1995), 369–70. Solomon's diary offers a detailed account of the ways in which many white women of New Orleans responded to Yankee occupation. It also helps explain why Kinsley viewed most of the city's white women as unrepentant Confederates. In the same paragraph in which she condemns General Orders No. 28, Solomon writes: "Endeavored to kill as few mosquitoes as possible. For two reasons, the first being that we should be polluted by being touched by 'Yankee blood', & secondly each one increases the number & aids in biting & tormenting them." Ibid., 343–438 (quotation on 370).

41. Kinsley, *The Slaveholders' Rebellion*, May 20, 26, 29, 1862.

42. Ezra Brown to Dear Father and Mother, July 2, September 21, 1862, Brown Letters. Situated in Orleans Parish, but not annexed by the City of New Orleans until 1870, Algiers was an old river town whose economy revolved around shipyards, warehouses, and ironworks. Throughout the war Confederate guerrillas would continue to terrorize much of southwestern Louisiana, raiding the Lafourche district, for example, as late as April 1865. Beyond the garrisoned city of New Orleans, in what one historian has called a "no-man's-land" of shadow warfare, Union soldiers were repeatedly subjected to "the threat of sudden death at the hands of unseen assassins." John D. Winters, *The Civil War in Louisiana* (Baton Rouge: Louisiana State University Press, 1963), 411; Stephen V. Ash, *When the Yankees Came: Conflict and Chaos in the Occupied South, 1861–1865* (Chapel Hill: University of North Carolina Press, 1995), 63, 76–107.

43. Carpenter, *Eighth Regiment*, 41. John L. Barstow, another officer in Kinsley's regiment, wrote to his parents on May 18, 1862, about the response to Union occupation offered by African Americans that he encountered in New Orleans: "I, in common with the other officers am called *Massar Linkum*, 20 times a day – they say 'God bless you, we're glad you come' etc." Quoted in Jeffrey D. Marshall,

ed., *A War of the People: Vermont Civil War Letters* (Hanover, N.H.: University Press of New England, 1999), 79.

44. Benjamin F. Butler to Dear Sarah, July 25, 1862, in Jessie Ames Marshall, comp., *Private and Official Correspondence of Gen. Benjamin F. Butler During the Period of the Civil War*, 5 vols. ([Norwood, Mass.: The Plimpton Press], 1917), II, 109. On August 6, 1862, Brigadier General John W. Phelps warned Butler that "Society here is on the verge of dissolution" and that the "African . . . threatens to be a fearful element of ruin and disaster. . . ." Three months later Brigadier General Godfrey T. Weitzel informed Butler that he feared a "servile insurrection" in the Lafourche region. Phelps to B. F. Butler, August [6], 1862, in Marshall, *Correspondence of Gen. Benjamin F. Butler*, II, 157; Weitzel to Major George C. Strong, November 5, 1862, in *War of the Rebellion*, XV, 171–72. Union officials were not the only ones worried about a slave insurrection. In May 1862 the young New Orleans resident Clara Solomon wrote in her diary that "I fear more from the negroes than Yankees & an insurrection is my continual horror," and a year later Brigadier General W. H. Emory wrote from New Orleans: "The forced emigration and the enlistment of negroes in the parishes declared slave by the President's proclamation, have made the population here very unsettled." Ashkenazi, *Civil War Diary*, 355; Emory to Major General N. P. Banks, May 20, 1863, in *War of the Rebellion*, vol. XXVI, pt. 1, p. 497.

45. Kinsley, *The Slaveholders' Rebellion*, June 25, 1862; Carpenter, *Eighth Regiment*, 43; Benedict, *Vermont in the Civil War*, II, 91.

46. Kinsley, *The Slaveholders' Rebellion*, August 26, 1862. On the application of the Second Confiscation Act in Louisiana, see William F. Messner, *Freedmen and the Ideology of Free Labor: Louisiana, 1862–1865* (Lafayette: University of Southwestern Louisiana, 1978), 18–20.

47. Kinsley, *The Slaveholders' Rebellion*, September 1, 1862. The observations of C. S. Cooper, a private from the Eighth Vermont Vols., however culture-bound and tinted with stereotypes, nevertheless hint at the difficulty of Kinsley's task: "They [the contraband] occupide [*sic*] the old cotton ware houses on the bank of the [Mississippi] river and numbered several thousand. To the uninnitiated [*sic*] the sights and sounds as you strolled through their quarters would have been a novelty. The younger children were perfectly nude or were only partially covered by an old shirt, the older ones might have secured in addition a ragged pair of pants. On stepping in to the right, you might have joined in and had a regular plantation break-down with an indefinite number to spat the juber [Cooper probably means "pat juba," which is to pat one's hands, thighs, or knees in time with the juba dance]. To the left, they might have been having a prayer meeting, which to a stranger might have seamed [*sic*] like a squad of the first party having a fandango on a little different plan, each going for themselves, seeing which could jump the highest, shout the loudest, and create the most confusion generally. A little farther on and you find some butting their heads together like a couple of bucks, perhaps for fun, but if for a genuine fight, you will thank your stars you are not between them. In the next corner among the din and confusion, you may find the sick and dying or the dead." Cooper, "Reminiscences."

48. Kinsley, *The Slaveholders' Rebellion*, esp. September 21, November 30, 1862; Benedict, *Vermont in the Civil War*, II, 92. A third private from Co. F, Osman F. Bellows, was also ordered to help with the contraband population, but Kinsley seems to have shouldered most of the work. William Kinsley's contribution ended on October 25 when he joined the rest of the regiment on an expedition designed to open the New Orleans, Opelousas, and Great Western Railroad as far west as Brashear City, and Bellows's duties were limited to procuring housing. This latter task was not always easy to accomplish, however. On September 3, 1862, Stephen Thomas, commander of the regiment, wrote to Butler that "The report of a want of protection for the Negroes is correct, and I have been trying to-day to secure suitable shelter for them, but they have come in upon me so fast I have found it very difficult." Marshall, *Correspondence of Gen. Benjamin F. Butler*, II, 244.

49. Kinsley, *The Slaveholders' Rebellion*, September 21, October 15, 1862; C. Peter Ripley, *Slaves and Freedmen in Civil War Louisiana* (Baton Rouge: Louisiana State University Press, 1976), 44–45; *War of the Rebellion*, XV, 592–95. The primary architect of the policy that Kinsley was criticizing was none other than Benjamin F. Butler, a man Kinsley never tired of praising for his radical idealism. In setting the contrabands to work on government plantations, Butler hoped to bring fresh revenues to the government, relieve the army of an enormous financial burden, and gain control of an increasingly restless black population. He was not upset that his policies also allowed his brother and his brother's business partner Charles Weed to make a fortune leasing government plantations. The government plantations established under Butler, and continued under his successor Nathaniel P. Banks, were plagued throughout the remainder of the war by incompetence, graft, and conflict between planters and laborers. One historian has concluded that "few, if any, of the black workers . . . profitted at all from the program's operation." Paul K. Eiss, "A Share in the Land: Freedpeople and the Government of Labour in Southern Louisiana, 1862–65," *Slavery and Abolition*, 19 (April 1998), 46–89; John C. Rodrigue, *Reconstruction in the Cane Fields: From Slavery to Free Labor in Louisiana's Sugar Parishes, 1862–1880* (Baton Rouge: Louisiana State University Press, 2001), chap. 2; Messner, *Freedmen and the Ideology of Free Labor*, chap. 3 (quotation on 40).

50. S. C. Bishop to Dear Mother, September 25, 1863, Civil War Letters of Sylvester C. Bishop, Indiana Historical Society (Indianapolis, Ind.); Lawrence Van Alstyne, *Diary of an Enlisted Man* (New Haven, Conn.: Tuttle, Morehouse & Taylor Company, 1910), 186; [Henry Warren Howe], *Passages from the Life of Henry Warren Howe, Consisting of Diary and Letters Written During the Civil War, 1861–1865* (Lowell, Mass.: Courier-Citizen Co., 1899), 144.

51. Kinsley means Bayou Ramos. Rufus Kinsley to Sir, March 20, 1886, Rufus Kinsley Pension. For the reaction of other soldiers to the region's wildlife, including its alligators that bellowed "all night like bulls of Bashan" and "snakes as big as any in Barnum's menagerie," see J. N. Kidwell to Dear Mother, October 2, 1863, Ross-Kidwell Papers, Indiana Historical Society (Indianapolis, Ind.); John William De Forest, *A Volunteer's Adventures: A Union Captain's Record of the Civil War*, ed. James H. Croushore (New Haven, Conn.: Yale University Press, 1946),

81; Van Alstyne, *Diary of an Enlisted Man*, 196. Also helpful in situating Kinsley at this time is Arthur W. Bergeron, Jr., "The Lafourche Country in the Civil War," in Philip D. Uzee, ed., *The Lafourche Country: The People and the Land* (Lafayette: University of Southwestern Louisiana, 1985), 198–206.

52. Hiram E. Perkins affidavit, June 17, 1887, Rufus Kinsley Pension; Rufus Kinsley Compiled Military Service Record. Weitzel may have learned through the army grapevine that Kinsley was a skilled printer. In July and August 1862, while stationed at Algiers, Kinsley had worked in a confiscated Confederate print shop, taking inventory, setting up government publications, and teaching the trade to his brother William.

53. Rufus Kinsley to Sir, March 20, 1886, Rufus Kinsley Pension; an Iowa soldier quoted in David C. Edmonds, *Yankee Autumn in Acadiana: A Narrative of the Great Texas Overland Expedition through Southwestern Louisiana, October-December 1863* (Lafayette, La.: Acadiana Press, 1979), 9.

54. Rufus Kinsley to Sir, March 20, 1886, Report on Rufus Kinsley dated November 12, 1886, by the War Department, Surgeon General's Office, Record and Pension Division, Rufus Kinsley Pension; Kinsley, *The Slaveholders' Rebellion*, June 25, October 10, 1863.

55. Unbeknownst to Kinsley, he was originally recommended to Banks for the position of First Lieutenant in Co. H of the Second Corps d'Afrique on April 20, 1863, by the regiment's commanding officer, Colonel Nathan W. Daniels. Had Kinsley received this appointment, he would have replaced First Lieutenant Octave Rey, who had resigned in March 1863 and was from one of the oldest and most respected free colored creole families in New Orleans. For some reason Banks did not act upon Daniels's recommendation. It was not until August 25, 1863, when Lieutenant Colonel Alfred G. Hall was in command of the Second Corps d'Afrique, that Banks commissioned Kinsley to replace P. O. Dapremont, another free man of color, who in July 1863 had resigned his position as second lieutenant in Co. B. C. P. Weaver, *Thank God My Regiment an African One: The Civil War Diary of Colonel Nathan W. Daniels* (Baton Rouge: Louisiana State University Press, 1998), 94; Rodolphe Lucien Desdunes, *Our People and Our History: A Tribute to the Creole People of Color in Memory of the Great Men They Have Given Us and of the Good Works They Have Accomplished*, trans. and ed. Sister Dorothea Olga McCants (1911; Baton Rouge: Louisiana State University Press, 1973), 114–20; Rufus Kinsley Compiled Military Service Record; P. O. Dapremont Compiled Military Service Record.

56. Provisional Commission, in Kinsley Papers. The Second Regiment Infantry, Corps d'Afrique, was originally organized in New Orleans on October 12, 1862, as the Second Regiment, Louisiana Native Guards. Its designation was changed to the Second Regiment, Corps d'Afrique, on June 6, 1863, and to the Seventy-fourth Regiment, United States Colored Infantry (USCI), on April 6, 1864. *Official Army Register of the Volunteer Force of the United States Army for the Years 1861, '62, '63, '64, '65*, 8 vols. (Washington, D.C.: Adjutant General's Office, 1865–67) (cited herein after as *OAR*), VIII, 248.

57. Weitzel to Major George C. Strong, November 5, 1862, Major George C. Strong to Brigadier General Weitzel, November 6, 1862, *War of the Rebellion*, XV,

171, 164. Weitzel also feared that the mere presence of colored troops in the Lafourche district would provoke a slave uprising, for which he did not want to be responsible. Others maintained that black troops recruited and organized in Louisiana would be a source of order rather than anarchy. General Phelps in a letter to Butler on August 2, 1862, reported he had recently consulted with several groups of free colored New Orleanians who wanted to (and soon would) raise "one or two regiments of volunteers from their class of the population for the defence of the government and good order. . . ." Later Major B. Rush Plumly would dismiss as ridiculous the idea that Louisiana's black troops would incite the slaves to rebel. He assured Secretary of the Treasury Salmon P. Chase that "These men understand the philosophy of this thing. They would suppress an insurrection [of slaves] as they would this Rebellion." Plumly to Chase, July 4, 1863, Salmon P. Chase Papers, Manuscript Division, Library of Congress (Washington, D.C.).

58. The Thomas quotation is from Carpenter, *Eighth Regiment*, 70. Sergeant Major Carpenter was a member of Thomas's noncommissioned staff at the time of Thomas's threat.

59. Joseph T. Wilson, *Black Phalanx: A History of the Negro Soldiers of the United States in the Wars of 1775–1812, 1861–'65* (Hartford, Conn.: American Publishing Company, 1890), 199n. This was not the last time that a member of the Seventy-fourth USCI would charge that his regiment had come under "friendly fire" from white Union forces; see Donald E. Everett, "Free People of Color in New Orleans, 1803–1865" (Ph.D. diss., Tulane University, 1952), 308–09.

60. Dunham Burt to the *Rutland (Vt.) Herald*, October 22, 1862, reprinted in Donald H. Wickman, ed., *Letters to Vermont: From Her Civil War Soldier Correspondents to the Home Press*, 2 vols. ([Bennington, Vt.]: Images from the Past, 1998), II, 47–49.

61. James G. Hollandsworth, *The Louisiana Native Guards: The Black Military Experience During the Civil War* (Baton Rouge: Louisiana State University Press, 1995), 19, has garbled this conversation between De Forest and Deming, attributing statements by both Deming and De Forest to Benjamin F. Butler. See De Forest, *A Volunteer's Adventures*, 50–51.

62. Palfrey to John G. Palfrey, October 18, 1863, John Gorham Palfrey Family Papers, Letters to John Gorham Palfrey, bMS Am 1704 (678), Houghton Library, Harvard University (Cambridge, Mass.); this and all subsequent quotations from the Palfrey Family Papers are published by permission of Houghton Library, Harvard University. While both De Forest and Palfrey were driven by careerist and professional considerations in deciding against joining a black regiment, they were also undoubtedly eased toward such a conclusion by prevailing racial attitudes. Palfrey, for example, was under the direct command of an officer who despised blacks, and he himself was opposed to having any black officers under his command. Like many other white soldiers, Palfrey simply assumed that black officers were unqualified for their posts, and he resented being placed on an equal or lesser footing with them. In a letter to his father, a leading New England abolitionist, Palfrey described boarding railroad cars in Algiers that were filled with officers from Butler's Louisiana Native Guards: "I am a pretty good Abolitionist,

and not usually a stickler for rank, but it was not a pleasant reflection that these black & yellow men who very likely could not sign their names, so far outranked me after all my hard service in the Academy [at West Point] and out for nine years." Palfrey was even offended by black soldiers marching in the same review with white soldiers. Such mingling, in his opinion, "was way too much of a good thing. They ought to be kept by themselves." Palfrey to John G. Palfrey, December 28, 1862, January 25, 1863, Palfrey Family Papers.

Kinsley might have ended up under the command of John Palfrey if Palfrey had succeeded in his efforts to gain control of "one of Gen. Butler's old Regiments composed of free men and mechanics" or if Palfrey had accepted the colonelcy of the Second Louisiana Native Guards that Banks reputedly offered him. Palfrey to John G. Palfrey, October 18, August 16, 1863, Palfrey Family Papers.

63. At the time of Phelps's "Proclamation to the Loyal Citizens of the Southwest," Lincoln, as commander in chief, was dismissing federal officials who tried to turn the war for the Union into a war against slavery, and he did not formally move toward the recruitment of black soldiers until early 1863, although his secretary of war officially authorized the enlistment of black soldiers in South Carolina in late August 1862. Dudley Taylor Cornish, *The Sable Arm: Negro Troops in the Union Army, 1861–1865* (1956; reprint, New York: W. W. Norton & Company, 1966), 22–24, 33–55, 80–81.

64. William F. Messner, "General John Wolcott Phelps and Conservative Reform in Nineteenth Century America," *Vermont History*, 53 (Winter 1985), 26–28; John McClaughry, "John Wolcott Phelps: The Civil War General Who Became a Forgotten Presidential Candidate in 1880," ibid., 38 (Autumn 1970), 267–71; Phelps to Captain R. S. Davis, June 16, July 30, 31, 1862, Butler to Phelps, August 2, 1862, *War of the Rebellion*, XV, 488, 489, 535, 536. Phelps and Kinsley were of a piece in their reverence for Brown and hatred for Confederates. De Forest describes Phelps as a soldier who "clutches with delight at every chance of humiliating slaveholders and Rebels" and who "hates the Rebels bitterly, not so much because they are rebellious as because they are slaveholders. . . ." De Forest, *A Volunteer's Adventures*, 10, 22.

65. Peck, *Revised Roster*, 717–21; Oscar W. Goodridge (also known as Oscar W. Goodrich) Compiled Military Service Record; Betsey Goodridge affidavit, April 16, 1889, Hiram E. Perkins deposition, January 14, 1892, Rufus Kinsley Pension; 1860 Manuscript Census, roll 1321, p. 54; Kinsley, *The Slaveholders' Rebellion*, April 11, 1863. The Eighth Vermont Vols. had ties to the Second Regiment, Corps d'Afrique, that went back to the black regiment's very beginnings. William S. Peabody and Elijah K. Prouty were among the first members of the regiment, which was mustered into service in October 1862 as the Second Regiment, Louisiana Native Guards. Three other members of the Eighth Vermont Vols. joined the Second Regiment, Corps d'Afrique, after Kinsley did. One of them, Charles C. Colton, was an "old friend" of Kinsley's who had also been a member of Co. F. Not surprisingly, when Colton joined the Second Regiment, Corps d'Afrique, he boarded with Kinsley and James Noyes, another former private in the Eighth Vermont Vols. who had been transferred to the black Second in December 1862 and promoted to captain in September 1863. Muster Rolls

and Rosters of the Seventy-fourth USCI (e.g., muster rolls of October 12, 1862, and officer roster of October 14, 1864), in Regimental Papers, Seventy-fourth USCI, Records of the Adjutant General's Office, 1780s–1917, Record Group 94, National Archives (cited hereinafter as Regimental Papers, Seventy-fourth USCI); James Noyes Compiled Military Service Record; Hollandsworth, *Louisiana Native Guards*, 25n.

66. Kinsley, *The Slaveholders' Rebellion*, August 24, October 28, 1862, January 1, 1863. Ordered to remain in Algiers and oversee the contraband camp, Kinsley did not join the First Louisiana Native Guards on the march up the railroad, but he was in Algiers when they arrived on October 25 (he was also there when the Second and Third Louisiana Native Guards passed through on their way up the railroad to help in the campaign to drive Rebel forces from the Lafourche district), and after December 4 he undoubtedly had numerous encounters with black troops as he moved back and forth from Algiers to Brashear City on the New Orleans, Opelousas, and Great Western Railroad. The Eighth Vermont Vols. and the First Regiment, Louisiana Native Guards, were consolidated under the command of Colonel Stephen Thomas of the Eighth Vermont during the expedition up the railroad that began in late October. For their role in guarding and repairing the railroad, the black troops received considerable praise. According to General Butler they did their job "as well as any soldiers can," and another observer stated that "They have done well, and accomplished all that has been given them to do." Benjamin F. Butler to Salmon P. Chase, November 14, 1862, George S. Denison to Salmon P. Chase, November 14, 1862, in Marshall, *Correspondence of Gen. Benjamin F. Butler*, II, 425, 427. See also Mary F. Berry, "Negro Troops in Blue and Gray: The Louisiana Native Guard, 1861–1863," *Louisiana History*, 8 (1967), 178–181; Hollandsworth, *Louisiana Native Guards*, 32–45.

67. Kinsley, *The Slaveholders' Rebellion*, October 5, 1863; Kinsley to G. Norman Lieber, October 1, 1863, in Rufus Kinsley Compiled Military Service Record.

68. *New Orleans Tribune*, December 29, 1864; *New Orleans Picayune*, July 16, 1859; *New Orleans Daily Delta*, December 28, 1860; David C. Rankin, "The Impact of the Civil War on the Free Colored Community of New Orleans," *Perspectives in American History*, 11 (1977–78), 380–87. In 1860 when over three-quarters of free coloreds were mulattoes, less than a quarter of all slaves were. The correlation between phenotype and legal status was also high at the state level, where 81.3 percent of free coloreds in 1860 were mulattoes but only 9.8 percent of slaves were. David C. Rankin, "The Tannenbaum Thesis Reconsidered: Slavery and Race Relations in Antebellum Louisiana," *Southern Studies*, 18 (Spring 1979), 21.

69. *War of the Rebellion*, XV, 556–57; Everett, "Free Persons of Color," 270; U.S. House of Representatives, 39th Cong., 2nd sess., Report No. 16, *Report of the Select Committee on the New Orleans Riots* (Washington, D.C.: Government Printing Office, 1867), 124–26; *Boston Liberator*, April 15, 1864; Ex-Native Guard to the Editor, September 29, 1862, quoted in *New Orleans L'Union*, October 1, 1862 (my translation of this letter is from the *New York Times*, November 5, 1862; all other translations are by the author); *New Orleans L'Union*, December 30, 1862, May 5, 1863. John L. Lewis, commanding general of the Louisiana Militia at the time

of Farragut's attack, echoed the free colored editors of *L'Union* in 1866 when he testified before a congressional committee that the free coloreds were loyal to the Confederate cause and that he himself had "reviewed a regiment of colored men in the city of New Orleans, and they were ready to fight for us if we had brought them into requisition." *New Orleans Riots*, 320.

70. Eugene D. Genovese, "The Slave States of North America," in David W. Cohen and Jack P. Greene, eds., *Neither Slave Nor Free: The Freedmen of African Descent in the Slave Societies of the New World* (Baltimore: Johns Hopkins University Press, 1972), 274. My discussion of the free colored Confederate troops draws upon Everett, "Free Persons of Color," 268–76; Berry, "Negro Troops in Blue and Gray," 165–70; Hollandsworth, *Louisiana Native Guards*, 1–11. Free colored Native Guard regiments were also raised in rural Louisiana parishes such as Plaquemines and Natchitoches. It would be a mistake to assume that all Confederate Native Guards transferred their allegiance to the Union in the wake of Yankee invasion and occupation. Such a transfer never happened in Natchitoches. In the case of New Orleans, there is no systematic study of what percentage of the soldiers who served in the Confederate Native Guards later served in the Union Native Guards, but Hollandsworth points out that only 30 percent of the black officers in the Confederate Native Guards later became officers in the Union Native Guards. One of them, Henry L. Rey, on October 15, 1862, scolded his fellow free colored New Orleanians who had failed to free their slaves or enlist in the Union army. He addressed them as "MY TARDY COMPATRIOTS" and asked, "Men of my race, when will you comprehend that in living in the same errors as your oppressors you retard the march of progress, which would bring with it a social and political amelioration for you?" Everett, "Free Persons of Color," 269; Gary B. Mills, "Patriotism Frustrated: The Native Guards of Confederate Natchitoches," *Louisiana History*, 18 (Fall 1977), 437–51; Hollandsworth, *Louisiana Native Guards*, 25; Rankin, "Impact of the Civil War," where Rey is quoted on 388. See also Stephen J. Ochs, *A Black Patriot and a White Priest: André Cailloux and Claude Paschal Maistre in Civil War New Orleans* (Baton Rouge: Louisiana State University Press, 2000), chap. 3.

71. Butler to E. M. Stanton, May 25, August 14, 1862, General Orders No. 63, August 22, 1862, Butler to Major General H. W. Halleck, August 27, 1862, all in *War of the Rebellion*, XV, 442, 549, 555–57.

72. *OAR*, VIII, 246, 248, 250, 313; Wilson, *Black Phalanx*, 195; Ira Berlin, Joseph P. Reidy, and Leslie S. Rowland, eds., *Freedom: A Documentary History of Emancipation, 1861–1867*, series 2: *The Black Military Experience* (Cambridge: Cambridge University Press, 1982), 12. All told, nearly 179,000 African American soldiers served in the Union army during the Civil War. My discussion of those who served in Louisiana rests heavily on Everett, "Free Persons of Color," chaps. 8–9; Berry, "Negro Troops in Blue and Gray," 165–90; Messner, *Freedmen and the Ideology of Free Labor*, chaps. 2, 7; Manoj K. Joshi and Joseph P. Reidy, "'To Come Forward and Aid in Putting Down This Unholy Rebellion': The Officers of Louisiana's Free Black Native Guard During the Civil War Era," *Southern Studies*, 21 (Fall 1982), 326–42; Howard C. Westwood, "Benjamin Butler's Enlistment of Black Troops in

New Orleans in 1862," *Louisiana History*, 26 (Winter 1985), 5–22; Hollandsworth, *Louisiana Native Guards*.

73. According to the lists provided by Berlin, *Black Military Experience*, 310n–311n, and Hollandsworth, *Louisiana Native Guards*, 119–24, there were 87 black combat officers and 21 black noncombat officers (chaplains and surgeons) who served in black regiments of the Union army during the Civil War. Historians have had a difficult time compiling an accurate list of these 108 black commissioned officers. Hollandsworth's list, the latest and most reliable for Louisiana, is nevertheless plagued by errors. He offers two different spellings for the names of Solomon Hayes and Louis Duqueminy Larrieu (neither correct), and he misspells the names of Paul Poree and Charles S. Sauvinet. Unlike Wilson, *Black Phalanx*, 176, and Berlin et al., *Black Military Experience*, 310n, Hollandsworth knows that Kinsley is white. But despite citing Kinsley's manuscript diary, Hollandsworth has him hailing "from Boston." Hollandsworth, *Louisiana Native Guards*, 114, 120, 75, 121, 16n, 122, 32n, 124. A half century ago, in his pioneering study of the Union fighting man, Bell Irvin Wiley identified Kinsley as a white soldier from Vermont who upon becoming an officer in a black regiment "devoted himself unstintedly to making good soldiers and good citizens out of his men and to increasing his fitness to command them." *The Life of Billy Yank: The Common Soldier of the Union* (1952; reprint, Baton Rouge: Louisiana State University Press, 1978), 121–22.

74. N. P. Banks to Abraham Lincoln, August 17, 1863, and General Orders No. 40, May 1, 1863, quoted in *War of the Rebellion*, vol. XXVI, pt. 1, pp. 688–89, and XV, 717. In General Orders No. 40 Banks supported his call for black recruits by stating that "The Government makes use of mules, horses, uneducated and educated white men, in the defense of its institutions. Why should not the negro contribute . . . ?"

75. Berlin et al., *Black Military Experience*, 305–06 and 316, where Banks's letter of February 12, 1863, informing Lorenzo Thomas that he intended to replace black officers is printed. The colored officers that Butler appointed and Banks sought to remove were almost entirely either captains, first lieutenants, or second lieutenants, that is, commissioned company, or line, officers. About the time that the Second Regiment, Louisiana Native Guards, was mustered into service, all but two of the commissioned company officers were black; the exceptions were Second Lieutenant William S. Peabody of Co. A and First Lieutenant Elijah K. Prouty of Co. H, who soon became the regiment's adjutant. All but two of the commissioned regimental, or staff, officers were white; the exceptions were Quartermaster Charles St. Albin Sauvinet and Major Francis E. Dumas. Muster Rolls and Rosters, Regimental Papers, Seventy-fourth USCI; Charles S. Sauvinet Compiled Military Service Record; Francis Ernest Dumas Pension.

76. Captain P. B. S. Pinchback and others to Major General N. P. Banks, [March 2, 1863], quoted in Berlin et al., *Black Military Experience*, 321. The difficulty of these exams is hard to determine. Hollandsworth in his history of the Louisiana Native Guards suggests that the exams were demanding and evaluated by an examining board applying "the highest standards." Banks's assistant adjutant general, Richard B. Irwin, contends, on the other hand, that black officers

were administered "the most rudimentary examination." Even if Irwin's assessment is closer to the truth than Hollandsworth's, the exams may have been particularly daunting to the free colored officers because virtually none of them had any previous military training and many of them were French speakers who knew English only as a second language. As will be noted later, white officers in Louisiana's black Civil War regiments also went before boards of examination, failed, and were drummed out of the service. Hollandsworth, *Louisiana Native Guards*, 72; Richard B. Irwin, *History of the Nineteenth Army Corps* (New York: G. P. Putnam's Sons, 1892), 50.

77. Alphonse Fleurry, Octave Rey, William B. Barrett, Robert H. Isabelle, and E. Arnold Bertonneau Pensions; David C. Rankin, "The Politics of Caste: Free Colored Leadership in New Orleans During the Civil War," in Robert R. Macdonald, John R. Kemp, and Edward F. Haas, eds., *Louisiana's Black Heritage* (New Orleans: Louisiana State Museum, 1979), 139, 141, 144, 128–29; Charles Vincent, *Black Legislators in Louisiana During Reconstruction* (Baton Rouge: Louisiana State University Press, 1976), 54, 55, 72, 119–20. Hollandsworth, *Louisiana Native Guards*, 109n, states that another member of the Second Regiment, Louisiana Native Guards, Samuel W. Ringgold, also served in the Louisiana State Legislature during Reconstruction, but it was Charles W. Ringgold who served in the Louisiana House of Representatives from 1870 to 1872. See Vincent, *Black Legislators*, 120.

78. De Forest, *A Volunteer's Adventures*, 47–48; Francis Ernest Dumas Pension; Jean-Charles Houzeau, *My Passage at the New Orleans "Tribune": A Memoir of the Civil War Era*, ed. David C. Rankin, trans. Gerard F. Denault (Baton Rouge: Louisiana State University Press, 1984), 48–55. The other African American to attain the rank of major was Martin Delany. He was not appointed until the final months of the war, and his appointment came with the understanding that he would never actually be put in command of any troops. John W. Blassingame, "The Selection of Officers and Non-Commissioned Officers of Negro Troops in the Union Army, 1863–1865," *Negro History Bulletin*, 30 (January 1967), 10.

79. Pinchback to Major General N. P. Banks, July 13, 1863, Regimental Papers, Seventy-fourth USCI; Rankin, "Impact of the Civil War," 411; Berlin et al., *Black Military Experience*, 313, 326; Charles S. Sauvinet Compiled Military Service Record; *New Orleans Riots*, 44; Hollandsworth, *Louisiana Native Guards*, 74–76. I find far-fetched Hollandsworth's suggestion that Sauvinet survived because his "light complexion made his continuation in the service more acceptable to his white associates." Fair skin did not provide protective coloration to numerous other African American officers who were driven from the service under Banks's regime. Ibid., 76.

80. The history of Louisiana's Native Guards reveals that not all black officers were fit for duty and not all white officers who supported boards of examination were racists intent upon driving black officers from the Union army. It may be worth noting in this regard that in late April 1863, Colonel Nathan W. Daniels, commanding officer of the Second Louisiana Native Guards and one of the most zealous advocates of racial egalitarianism in the entire Union army, moved to have three of his black officers dismissed from the service so he could "then select officers in whom I can place reliance." A few days later Daniels requested a board

of examination for the black officers in his regiment. Kinsley, *The Slaveholders' Rebellion*, August 15, 1864; Weaver, *Thank God My Regiment an African One*, 99, 102, 108.

81. Captain John M. Wilson to Major C. T. Christensen, August 3, 1864, Applications for Commissions and Reports of Boards of Examiners for Officers in U.S. Colored Troops, pt. 1, entry 1936, Department of the Gulf, Records of United States Army Continental Commands, 1821–1920, Record Group 393, National Archives (cited hereinafter as Department of the Gulf, Army Commands); Special Orders No. 89, August 6, 1864, Unit Record Book, Regimental Papers, Seventy-fourth USCI; Hollandsworth, *Louisiana Native Guards*, 74; Kinsley, *The Slaveholders' Rebellion*, August 15, 1864. The two black officers were Theodule A. Martin and Joseph Villeverde, both of whom had been praised by the Second's regimental commander for their "unflinching bravery" during a skirmish with enemy forces at East Pascagoula, Mississippi, in April 1863. Martin and Villeverde join Frank L. Trask as the only black officers mentioned in Kinsley's diary; in all three cases Kinsley provides the officers' surnames but does not identify them as African Americans. When Augustine P. Hawley and Charles C. Colton, two white officers who were Kinsley's former comrades in the Eighth Vermont, also failed the August 1864 exams and were booted out of the service, Kinsley exhibited no more sympathy for them than he did for Martin and Villeverde. It is also worth noting that Kinsley's unshakable belief in the demoralizing consequences of alcohol consumption would have predisposed him to doubt the competence of the six black officers still in his regiment on December 26, 1863, when he expressed his dismay that all the officers of the Seventy-fourth, except himself and Captain James Noyes, were drunk the night before. And some of the regiment's remaining black officers were Catholic, a fact that would have further dismayed a man who called St. Louis Cathedral a "Splendid building in which to enact magnificent villany." Kinsley, *The Slaveholders' Rebellion*, May 25, 1862.

82. Pinchback's grandson, the celebrated Harlem Renaissance poet Jean Toomer, is quoted in Houzeau, *My Passage*, 52n. In 1864, E. Arnold Bertonneau offered the following rationalization for his and other free coloreds' decision to join the Confederate Native Guards: "When summoned to volunteer in the defence of the State and city against Northern invasion, situated as we were, could we do otherwise than heed the warning, and volunteer in the defence of New Orleans? Could we have adopted a better policy?" There were, of course, some white and free colored Unionists living in New Orleans who fled to Europe or the North rather than support the Confederacy, and there were many others who remained in New Orleans but did not find it necessary to join the Confederate army. Bertonneau is quoted in *Boston Liberator*, April 15, 1864.

83. Kinsley, *The Slaveholders' Rebellion*, December 18, 1864. It may be that Kinsley, like numerous other visitors, both African, American and white, to New Orleans in the Civil War era, noticed the tendency of many relatively affluent, well-educated, light-colored, French-speaking, and Catholic free coloreds to view their struggle for equality as distinct from that of the predominantly impoverished, illiterate, dark-colored, English-speaking, and Protestant ex-slaves. Some hereditary free coloreds even opposed sending their children to the freedmen

schools that Kinsley believed were the key to the future for African Americans. Certainly if Kinsley ever picked up a copy of the free colored newspaper *L'Union* during his long stay in and around New Orleans, he would have been upset. There, emblazoned on the masthead of the paper's first edition, Kinsley, the radical abolitionist who believed that a Union with slavery was not worth saving, would have found Lincoln's temporizing words: "l'Union avec des esclaves, l'Union sans esclaves, – l'Union quand meme." Seven months later he would have found the paper's editors vigorously protesting the efforts of whites "to regulate us to the ranks of the brutalized slaves, to the detriment of our rights, of reason, and of fairness." During the Civil War and Reconstruction some of the officers who served in Kinsley's regiment also revealed a tendency to separate themselves from the freedmen. The petition E. Arnold Bertonneau carried to Lincoln asked for the right to vote for only those African Americans who were "born free before the rebellion." When the Union army began indiscriminately impressing persons of African descent to work on the levee at Baton Rouge, Samuel W. Ringgold complained indignantly that he and other freeborn blacks were being "placed on an equality with contrabands." And during Reconstruction Francis E. Dumas ran for lieutenant governor on a ticket headed by a former white slaveholder that Republicans denounced as reactionary and freedmen repudiated at the polls. *L'Union*, September 27, 1862, May 5, 1863; Rankin, "Politics of Caste," 129; Joshi and Reidy, "'To Come Forward,'" 340; Houzeau, *My Passage*, 48–55.

For a sample of black, white, Northern, and European visitors to New Orleans during the Civil War era who noted deep divisions between the old hereditary free coloreds and the newly freed slaves, see Edmonia G. Highgate to M. E. Strieby, February 8, 1866, Papers of the American Missionary Association, Box 58, American Missionary Association Archives, Amistad Research Center, Tulane University (New Orleans, La.); *New Orleans Tribune*, October 12, 1864; Donald E. Everett, "Demands of the New Orleans Free Colored Population for Political Equality, 1862–1865," *Louisiana Historical Quarterly*, 38 (April 1955), 54–55; Whitelaw Reid, *After the War: A Tour of the Southern States, 1865–1866* (1866; reprint, New York: Harper & Row, 1965), 243–44, 259–60; Nathan Willey, "Education of the Colored Population of Louisiana," *Harper's New Monthly Magazine*, 33 (1866), 247; Houzeau, *My Passage*, 34–36, 49–50, 55–56.

84. Kinsley remained in Co. B until July 7, 1864, when the Seventy-fourth merged with the Ninety-first Regiment, USCI, and he was transferred to Co. G of the Seventy-fourth, where he remained a second lieutenant until the end of the war. Muster-out Roll, November 14, 1865, Rufus Kinsley Compiled Military Service Record; *OAR*, VIII, 248.

85. A steady stream of schooners, transports, rams, tugs, gunboats, warships, and other military vessels anchored at Ship Island during the war to have machinery repaired and decks caulked. Most were members of the West Gulf Blockading Squadron, under the command of Rear Admiral David G. Farragut. The Ship Island machine shop was always busy, according to Farragut, because of all the "lame ducks" on Mississippi Sound with "worn-out machinery, boilers, or hulls" that required constant repair. Edwin C. Bearss, *Historic Resource Study: Ship*

Island, Harrison County, Mississippi, Gulf Islands National Seashore, Florida/Mississippi (Denver, Colo.: U.S. Department of the Interior, National Park Service, 1984), 3, 94, 115, 182, 254.

86. In December 1864 there were over eighty civilians working on the fort. Ibid., 225, 293.

87. Laura S. Haviland, *A Woman's Life Work; Including Thirty Years' Service on the Underground Railroad and in the War* (Grand Rapids, Mich.: S. B. Shaw, 1881), 327–28; Donald G. Mathews, "Orange Scott: The Methodist Evangelist as Revolutionary," in Martin Duberman, ed., *The Antislavery Vanguard: New Essays on the Abolitionists* (Princeton, N.J.: Princeton University Press, 1965), 71–101; Bearss, *Historic Resource Study*, 292; Carpenter, *Eighth Regiment*, 18.

88. Haviland, *A Woman's Life Work*, 326–28.

89. Regimental Papers, Books, and Muster Rolls and Rosters, Seventy-fourth USCI. The nature of surviving military records makes it difficult to know with absolute certainty the prewar legal status of most members of the Second Corps d'Afrique (Seventy-fourth USCI), but virtually all students of the subject have concluded that most members of the Second (and the Third) Corps d'Afrique were former slaves; see, for example, Berry, "Negro Troops in Blue and Gray," 176; Hollandsworth, *Louisiana Native Guards*, 18; and Weaver, *Thank God My Regiment an African One*, 11. An exact description of the age, birthplace, occupation, and physical appearance of the men in Kinsley's company is precluded by the absence of descriptive books in the extant records for either Co. B or Co. G of the Seventy-fourth USCI, but descriptions of the men in Co. D and Co. E are suggestive and may be found in Glatthaar, *Forged in Battle*, 270, 273, and Bearss, *Historic Resource Study*, 207–08.

90. Haviland, *A Woman's Life Work*, 328, where Kinsley is quoted. According to another white officer who served in a black regiment, some of the Louisiana fugitive slaves who joined the Union army were covered with more than shackles. "Some of them," he said, "were scarred from head to foot where they had been whipped. One man's back was nearly all one scar, as if the skin had been chopped up and left to heal in ridges. Another had scars on the back of his neck, and from that all the way to his heels every little ways; but that was not such a sight as the one with the great solid mass of ridges, from his shoulders to his hips. That beat all the anti-slavery sermons ever yet preached." Van Alstyne, *Diary of an Enlisted Man*, 213–14. Kinsley was aware that his previous record of assisting sick and destitute fugitive slaves eased his acceptance by black soldiers who had reason to view Banks's replacement officers as mere opportunists in search of a path to promotion. Kinsley, *The Slaveholders' Rebellion*, November 10, 1863.

91. Lorenzo Thomas to Colonel E. D. Townsend, April 8, 1864, in "The Negro in the Military Service of the United States, 1639–1886," Bureau of Colored Troops, National Archives (microcopy 858, roll 3, frame 2477). These old muskets, some of which burst when fired, were finally replaced with Enfield rifle-muskets in July 1864. Bearss, *Historic Resource Study*, 225.

92. Kinsley's company was doubtless chosen to assist in the siege of Fort Morgan because it had artillery as well as infantry training.

93. Ben Alva Kinsley to Rufus Kinsley, January 28, 1864, Kinsley Papers; Captain John M. Wilson to Major C. T. Christensen, August 3, 1864, Applications for Commissions and Reports of Boards of Examiners for Officers in U.S. Colored Troops, pt. 1, entry 1936, Department of the Gulf, Army Commands; Kinsley, *The Slaveholders' Rebellion*, August 15, 1864.

94. A few white and black civilians who had been convicted of larceny, rape, murder, and other major crimes were also imprisoned on Ship Island. [Chaplain Stephen A. Hodgman,] *The Nation's Sin and Punishment; or, The Hand of God Visible in the Overthrow of Slavery* (New York: American News Company, 1864), 235; Bearss, *Historic Resource Study*, 170, 271, 334–38.

95. Alden McLellan, "Vivid Reminiscences of War Times," *Confederate Veteran*, 14 (June 1906), 265; Bearss, *Historic Resource Study*, 313, 317; Ernest W. Holmstedt to Brigadier General H. W. Wessells, December 19, 1864, in *War of the Rebellion*, series 2, vol. VII, p. 1246; Richard B. Harwell, ed., *Kate: The Journal of a Confederate Nurse* (Baton Rouge: Louisiana State University Press, 1959), 250–51. The post commander's investigation took place immediately after the shooting, but three months later Kinsley reported that he had served as "Recorder of a Court" that investigated and exonerated a black private for shooting a Rebel prisoner. Kinsley, *The Slaveholders' Rebellion*, March 25, 1865.

96. When two blacks fled to Union lines in November 1864, for example, Kinsley wrote in his diary: "Glad to see them escape, of their own free will, without the aid of the Federal Army." Kinsley, *The Slaveholders' Rebellion*, November 20, 1864.

97. George H. Hepworth, *The Whip, Hoe, and Sword; or, The Gulf-Department in '63* (Boston: Walker, Wise, & Company, 1864), 191–93. The soldier's allusion is to Isaiah 14:20–23, where it is said that the Lord will sweep up Babylon, its evil rulers, and their children "with the besom of destruction." Even Hepworth, a graduate of the Harvard Divinity School who was not nearly as extreme as Kinsley on the issue of punishing the South for its sins, could bring himself to only "tamely" reprove the soldier for his chilling, vengeful words, "for I knew the fellow was more than half right."

98. McLellan, "Vivid Reminiscences," 265; Bearss, *Historic Resource Study*, 309, 298, 323. Of the 153 Confederate soldiers who died while detained on Ship Island, 53 percent succumbed to dysentery, 16 percent to diarrhea, 13 percent to pneumonia, and the remainder to a variety of ailments. Ibid., 387.

99. John H. Gihon to Colonel E. W. Holmstedt, December 22, 1864, in *War of the Rebellion*, series 2, vol. VII, pp. 1259–60.

100. Kinsley, *The Slaveholders' Rebellion*, June 1, 1864.

101. Report of General Phelps, December 5, 1861, *War of the Rebellion*, VI, 466–67; John C. Palfrey to Hannah Russell Palfrey, July 27, 1862, Palfrey Family Papers. The newspaper correspondent is quoted in Bearss, *Historic Resource Study*, 166.

102. Isaac Jackson to Dear Bro., February 2, 1865, quoted in Joseph Orville Jackson, ed., *"Some of the Boys . . .": The Civil War Letters of Isaac Jackson, 1862–1865* (Carbondale: Southern Illinois University Press, 1960), 232. Another Ohio soldier referred to Ship Island as "a bleak and uninviting place," a "kind of penal colony" that had been set down "away out in the sea, . . . [without] a tree or bush

or a semblance to anything like vegetation." Frank McGregor to My dear Susie [Brown], February 2, 1865, in Carl E. Hatch, ed., *Dearest Susie: A Civil War Infantryman's Letters to His Sweetheart* (New York: Exposition Press, 1971), 104.

103. Hepworth, *Whip, Hoe, and Sword*, 17; John C. Palfrey to John G. Palfrey, August 2, 1862, Palfrey Family Papers; Weaver, *Thank God My Regiment an African One*, 47, 63.

104. Regimental Returns, October 1863–May 1865, and Field and Staff Muster Rolls, November 1863–May 1865, Seventy-fourth USCI, Compiled Records of Military Units, National Archives (microcopy 594, roll 213).

105. Kinsley, *The Slaveholders' Rebellion*, January 22, 24, February 28, 1865.

106. Kinsley, according to Co. B muster rolls, was "On detached service at Cat Island in charge of Picket Guard," but in reality he also helped run the sawmills. First Lieutenant Harrison, a sergeant major in the Seventh Vermont Vols. until his appointment to the Seventy-fourth USCI on April 21, 1864, had been ordered to Cat Island on July 7, 1864, to serve as acting assistant quartermaster. Apparently Harrison is the quartermaster Kinsley accuses in his diary of abusing runaway slaves in early 1865. Harrison was arrested in August 1865 and later court-martialed for misconduct during his service on Cat Island. Rufus Kinsley Compiled Military Service Record; Peck, *Revised Roster*, 719; *OAR*, VIII, 248; Colonel E. W. Holmstedt to Major W[ickham] Hoffman, October 5, 1865, in the Ernest W. Holmstedt Compiled Military Service Record; John W. Harrison Compiled Military Service Record.

107. Muster Roll for November-December 1864, Rufus Kinsley Compiled Military Service Record; Ernest W. Holmstedt to Brigadier General W[illiam] Hoffman, March 1, 20, 1865, in *War of the Rebellion*, series 2, vol. VIII, pp. 323, 416–17; Ernest W. Holmstedt to Captain W. T. Hartz, December 22, 1864, in ibid., VII, 125; Ernest W. Holmstedt to Commissary General of Prisoners, January 29, 1865, in ibid., VIII, 145; Lieutenant Colonel W. D. Smith to Brigadier General T. W. Sherman, January 3, 1865, Regimental Papers, Seventy-fourth USCI.

108. Kinsley, *The Slaveholders' Rebellion*, January 22, 1865, November 20, 1864; Zechariah 4:10. The sharp decline in the number of times Kinsley wrote in his diary while stationed on Cat Island suggests that life there was "a little dull." In the twenty-four weeks that Kinsley spent on Cat Island, he made twenty-one entries in his diary, less than half the number he made in the previous twenty-four weeks.

109. Kinsley, *The Slaveholders' Rebellion*, September 15, 1864, March 6, May 10, 1865, September 21, 1862.

110. Ibid., March 6, 1865; *New Orleans Riots*, 45.

111. Prior to January 8, 1865, when the Second Ohio Battery was sent to Ship Island, Union officials worried that Ship Island was garrisoned by an insufficient number of men with inadequate firepower. One officer complained in December 1864 that Confederate prisoners on the island were "guarded by a daily detail from an aggregate force of 240 colored soldiers, without a field battery, with an unfinished fort mounting two heavy guns pointing seaward, and with an old sloop of war [the *Vincennes*] in the harbor scarcely serviceable for immediate defense."

At least the Seventy-fourth had adequate small arms, in the form of relatively new .57-caliber Enfield rifle-muskets, by the time Confederate prisoners began arriving on the island. Major General G. Granger to Lieutenant Colonel C. T. Christensen, December 10, 1864, in *War of the Rebellion*, vol. XLI, pt. 4, pp. 819–20; Bearss, *Historic Resource Study*, 224–25, 297, 323–24, 367. On May 26, 1865, at New Orleans, Lieutenant General Simon Bolivar Buckner, acting for General E. Kirby Smith, agreed to surrender the army of the Trans-Mississippi Division. A week later at Galveston, Tex., Smith officially accepted the surrender of this last significant Confederate army. Winters, *Civil War in Louisiana*, 426.

112. Rufus Kinsley Compiled Military Service Record.

113. Surgeon's Certificate of Disability, July 11, 1865, Rufus Kinsley Compiled Military Service Record; Rufus Kinsley deposition, January 12, 1892, Rufus Kinsley Pension.

114. Rufus Kinsley Compiled Military Service Record; Kinsley, *The Slaveholders' Rebellion*, December 26, 1863, February 5, April 30, July 10, 1864. The only other candidate for a genuine friend to Kinsley was Charles Colton, but unlike Noyes, who was with Kinsley for his entire tour of duty on Ship Island, Colton was on Ship Island for less than two months.

115. Weaver, *Thank God My Regiment an African One*, 132–33, 147, 148, 153, 145, 51, 124, 156, 76, 77, 88, 100, 121, 150, 134, 149, 151, 163; John C. Palfrey to John G. Palfrey, April 19, 1863, Palfrey Family Papers. Banks reinstated Daniels shortly after his discharge but ordered him to face a second court-martial. The second trial never took place, however, and the verdict of "dishonorable dismissal" that emerged from the first court-martial remained the final, official word on the career of Nathan Daniels. In his often misleading discussion of his dismissal, Daniels states that he resigned prior to the proposed second court-martial, but no letter of resignation (or of its acceptance) has been found. The historian C. P. Weaver speculates that Daniels, through an association with James Brown, an unsavory character formerly imprisoned on Ship Island, negotiated "a deal of some kind" with Banks that allowed him to avoid the second court-martial. Weaver emphasizes racism among Union officers in explaining Daniels's demise, but her own evidence and comparison with other Civil War court-martials indicate that Daniels contributed significantly to his own downfall. In any case, there is little doubt that Kinsley, who must have known about Daniels but never mentions him in his diary or letters, would not have wanted a man of such questionable character leading his regiment. Weaver, *Thank God My Regiment an African One*, 160–65, 177.

116. Ibid., 151, 121; Alfred G. Hall Compiled Military Service Record.

117. Although Grosvenor pleaded "Guilty" at his court-martial to the charge of keeping "in his quarters, a woman not his wife," President Lincoln later overturned Grosvenor's dismissal from the service "on the ground that the sentence . . . is not sustained by the evidence." Kinsley, *The Slaveholders' Rebellion*, December 20, 1863; anonymous pamphlet entitled *War Record of Col.? W. M. Grosvenor, Editor of the Missouri Democrat* (n.p., n.d.), 2–4, in the Ford Collection, New York Public Library (New York City); C. W. Foster to W. M. Grosvenor, August 8, 1864, in William M. Grosvenor Compiled Military Service Record.

118. Holmstedt served as commander of the regiment for a little over fifteen months, from late June 1864 to mid-October 1865. Among his predecessors, Daniels served as commander for roughly seven months (the last three and a half on Ship Island), from mid-October 1862 to late April 1863; Hall for about eight months, from early May to early November 1863 and again from early May to late June 1864; and Grosvenor for approximately six months, from early November 1863 to early May 1864.

119. At his best, Holmstedt was paternalistic and opportunistic in his dealings with the men of his regiment. In an open letter to the "Discharged Soldiers of the 74th USCT" that appeared in the New Orleans press in late 1865, he asked the men of the Seventy-fourth who had been slaves before the war to show their appreciation of the "freedom extended to you by a wise and liberal government." Remarkably, Holmstedt, the commander of a black regiment during the Civil War, did not understand that these men – many of whom had escaped from slavery to fight in the Union army – had earned their freedom and were anything but inert recipients of government largesse. Holmstedt counseled these men not to loaf or loiter, but to seek employment, to "work hard and faithfully," and to make binding contracts. Here Holmstedt offered all the disinterested advice one would expect from a man who was about to open an employment agency for planters and laborers at 219 Gravier Street in New Orleans. He concluded his letter: "Now, my good boys, let us shake hands and say adieu." Ernest W. Holmstedt Compiled Military Service Record; *New Orleans Daily Times*, November 26, 1865, quoted in Bearss, *Historic Resource Study*, 229–30.

120. Hodgman was mustered into the Second Louisiana Native Guards in late October 1862, was absent from Ship Island for part of the summer of 1863, and left Ship Island on a sixty-day furlough to New York at the beginning of November 1863. In applying for the furlough, Hodgman stated that he wanted to visit his elderly mother and acquire "a portable Chapel for the use of our Colored Regt, on Ship Island, as we have no building or room of any kind in which to have religious meetings. . . ." He added that a chaplain without a building could be "of little use to this Regt" during the inclement winter months. Hodgman, who had talked about leaving his post as early as August 1863, never returned from his trip to New York – in fact, went absent without leave – and ended up resigning under a cloud. His resignation, tendered in a letter to Secretary of War Edwin M. Stanton dated February 3, 1864, was accepted a few days later. Stephen A. Hodgman Compiled Military Service Record; Weaver, *Thank God My Regiment an African One*, 116; [Hodgman,] *The Nation's Sin*, 54–55, 219, 233–36, 5, 91; Kinsley, *The Slaveholders' Rebellion*, December 27, 1863.

121. Kinsley, *The Slaveholders' Rebellion*, February 5, 6, 1865, April 30, 1864, December 25, 1863; Matthew 5: 10.

122. Kinsley, *The Slaveholders' Rebellion*, June 22, 1862.

123. Others were also appalled at the treatment of prisoners at Ship Island. On January 8, 1865, for example, the Confederate nurse Kate Cumming described a Confederate prisoner who had just been released from Ship Island: "I never saw such an emaciated frame as his. He is completely prostrated from disease and starvation." Then, reflecting on the awful abuses endured by Confederate

prisoners at Ship Island, she concluded that "our sins must have been great to have deserved them." Harwell, *Journal of a Confederate Nurse*, 250, 251.

124. Kinsley, *The Slaveholders' Rebellion*, April 10, 1864; Haviland, *A Woman's Life Work*, 329–36, 357–59; Mildred E. Danforth, *A Quaker Pioneer: Laura Haviland, Superintendent of the Underground* (New York: Exposition Press, 1961), 187–200. In October 1864 an army inspector also concluded that there were Union soldiers on Ship Island who had been unjustly imprisoned and should be released and returned to duty. Whenever Kinsley refers in his diary or surviving letters to the prisoners he is guarding on Ship Island, he always identifies them as Confederate sympathizers or Confederate soldiers. Lieutenant Colonel W. D. Smith to Brigadier General J. W. Sherman, October 20, 1864, in Inspection Reports, pt. 1, entry 1827, Department of the Gulf, Army Commands.

125. Immediately after praying for Kinsley, Sister Haviland went to bed, "[l]eaving all those burdened souls with the Lord Jesus. . . ." Haviland, *A Woman's Life Work*, 327, 334.

126. Kinsley also thought that the new state government that Lincoln and Banks had created in wartime Louisiana was a "hideous abortion" and a "Yankee trick" that did not represent a fraction of the Louisiana populace and was headed by "a young Dutch-Irish pettifogger, who was made Governor by Gen. Banks a while since for a consideration. . . ." Kinsley, *The Slaveholders' Rebellion*, November 29, December 18, May 29, July 4, 1864. For a judicious treatment of Lincoln's fundamentally conservative approach to the reintegration of Southerners into the nation, see William C. Harris, *With Charity for All: Lincoln and the Restoration of the Union* ([Lexington]: University Press of Kentucky, 1997).

127. Kinsley, *The Slaveholders' Rebellion*, December 18, 1864. Both Butler and Brown fell far short of Kinsley's idealization of them. See Hans L. Trefousse, *Ben Butler: The South Called Him BEAST!* (New York: Twayne Publishers, 1957), and Stephen B. Oates, *To Purge This Land with Blood: A Biography of John Brown* (New York: Harper & Row, 1970). Abolitionist propaganda, such as James Redpath's enormously popular *The Public Life of Capt. John Brown* (1860), which Kinsley read while stationed on Ship Island, contributed to Brown's deification. See Paul Finkelman, "Manufacturing Martyrdom: The Antislavery Response to John Brown's Raid," in Paul Finkelman, ed., *His Soul Goes Marching On: Responses to John Brown and the Harpers Ferry Raid* (Charlottesville: University of Virginia Press, 1995), 41–66.

128. Kinsley, *The Slaveholders' Rebellion*, January 21, 1863, May 10, June 7, 1865. The words and images Kinsley uses to describe, and justify, the South's wartime desolation suggest a close knowledge of Old Testament prophets, especially Jeremiah. For background on the Northern response to suffering, see George M. Fredrickson, *The Inner Civil War: Northern Intellectuals and the Crisis of the Union* (New York: Harper & Row, 1965), chaps. 6–7. On the tendency to see the hand of God behind the South's suffering, see William Clebsch, "Christian Interpretations of the Civil War," *Church History*, 30 (June 1961), 212–22; James H. Moorhead, *American Apocalypse: Yankee Protestants and the Civil War, 1860–1869* (New Haven, Conn.: Yale University Press, 1978), chaps. 2–3. On Wendell Phillips, whom the *New York Daily Tribune* as late as 1877 was still calling "the apostle

of unforgiving and relentless hate," see Irving H. Bartlett, *Wendell Phillips: Brahmin Radical* (Boston: Beacon Press, 1961); on Frederick Douglass, see David W. Blight, *Frederick Douglass' Civil War: Keeping Faith in Jubilee* (Baton Rouge: Louisiana State University Press, 1989), esp. chaps. 4–5. In Stowe's case it should be noted that where Kinsley saw the "retributive hand" of an avenging Destroyer in the South's desolation, she saw the redeeming hand of a chastening Father. Charles Royster, *The Destructive War: William Tecumseh Sherman, Stonewall Jackson, and the Americans* (New York: Alfred A. Knopf, 1991), 364–65.

129. Kinsley's views resonated more with the thundering call for retributive justice found in the central passages of Lincoln's Second Inaugural Address than with the magnanimous plea for sectional reconciliation found in the final paragraph. In these passages the twenty-third president states his belief that slavery is the cause of the Civil War and that if God wills that the war should continue "until all the wealth piled by the bond-man's two hundred and fifty years of unrequited toil shall be sunk, and until every drop of blood drawn with the lash, shall be paid by another drawn with the sword, as was said three thousand years ago, so still it must be said 'the judgments of the Lord, are true and righteous altogether.'" Roy P. Basler, ed., *The Collected Works of Abraham Lincoln*, 9 vols. (New Brunswick, N.J.: Rutgers University Press, 1955), VIII, 333.

130. Kinsley, *The Slaveholders' Rebellion*, July 19, 1863. Kinsley's willingness to make excuses for black soldiers who fell asleep on guard duty stands in contrast to his refusal to excuse white soldiers who committed transgressions.

131. Travel requisition, August 24, 1865, Special Orders No. 1, Extract 3, July 18, 1865, Rufus Kinsley Compiled Military Service Record.

132. Ben A. Kinsley, "Fletcher," 213; undated Jason Kinsley obituary in unknown newspaper in possession of Reba Kinsley Hall.

133. Wheelock was a Congregational minister from neighboring Cambridge, Vt., where Ben Alva Kinsley was born and reared. He participated in many of the family's most important events; for example, in 1859 he delivered a eulogy at the funeral of Ben Alva's sister Elvira, and in 1868 he presided over the marriage of Ben Alva's son Edgar Kinsley Montague to Annette Blair (sometimes referred to as Hannah Annetta Blair). 1860 Manuscript Census, roll no. 1318, p. 116; Ben A. Kinsley, "Fletcher," 214; Edgar Kinsley Montague Pension. I am assuming Daniel Kinsley, who in 1866 lived in Worcester, Mass., with his wife and three daughters, wrote the article describing the reunion dated Fletcher, Vt., April 4, 1866, that appeared as "Letter from Vermont" in the *Worcester (Mass.) Palladium* on April 18, 1866, and with minor variations in Ben A. Kinsley, "Fletcher," 213. Kinsley's brother Edgar wrote of the reunion in his diary on April 5, 1866: "Went to Uncle Bens   Boys all home   sugar party." Montague Diary.

134. Ben A. Kinsley to Rufus Kinsley, January 28, 1864, in Kinsley Papers. Apparently, Kinsley subsequently tried to ease his father's anxiety by writing home more often. He wrote his father during the week of February 7 and again on February 13, 1864. After reading Rufus's two letters, as well as letters from Daniel, Jason, Alonzo, and Edgar that arrived in the same two-week period, Ben Alva pronounced these five sons: "All well & contented." Ben A. Kinsley to Lucretia Kinsley, February 14, 1864, in Kinsley Papers.

135. The mortality rate for soldiers from Fletcher was slightly higher than that for soldiers from the rest of Vermont. Calculated from Benedict, *Vermont in the Civil War*, I, 181, II, 790–91; and Hemenway, *Gazetteer*, II, 452.

136. This poem appears in "Letter from Vermont" in the *Worcester (Mass.) Palladium*, April 18, 1866, and, with minor variations, in Ben A. Kinsley, "Fletcher," 213.

137. In January 1869 Ben Kinsley moved to a farm in Lowell, where he died on December 6, 1870. His widow Lucy Blair Kinsley sold the farm in 1872 but remained in Lowell until October 1874, when she relocated to Lancaster, N.Y. Upon learning that Ben Alva would move from Fletcher to Lowell, one of his friends expressed surprise that he "and his excellent wife are about to leave the town where they have spent the greater portion of their lives, and form new associations among strangers. They go," he added, "amid the good wishes, but deep regrets, of those who knew them best." Guy Kinsley affidavit, November 26, 1878, Lucy Blair Kinsley Claim of Widow for Service Pension, December 12, 1878, both in Ben A. Kinsley Pension. The quotation is from Ben A. Kinsley, "Fletcher," 214.

138. Kinsley's brothers did not return from the war as unscathed as the writings of either Jason or Daniel imply. During his stint in the First Iowa Cavalry Jason spent over a year in military hospitals in Arkansas, Missouri, and Texas or at home on sick leave in Iowa. He later claimed that he never fully recovered from the "Chill Fever," "Dysentery and Bloody Flux" that he contracted in the fall of 1863 and that from the time he was mustered out of the cavalry in February 1866 he had been unable "to do any sort of work harder than light chores" and had suffered from "such severe pain" that he occasionally lost consciousness. An Iowa neighbor confirmed that "He returned from the . . . war very much broken down in health." In 1888 a nurse noted that Jason was "obliged to use a rope, fastened to the ceiling overhead, to turn himself in bed." In June 1899 he lamented that his wife was dead, his son had been killed in the Spanish-American War, and he was "all alone in the cold, wide world." At the time of his death four and a half years later, the local press described Jason as "a continuous seeker after knowledge" and an avid student of literature and educational theory. "He had," the obituary added, "his own peculiar ways, and yet a man gifted with his own store house of knowledge, he lived in a sphere of his own." Apparently Jason's "peculiar ways" included not informing his family (or the U.S. Pension Bureau until he had to) that he had a wife and son. Jason W. Kinsley Compiled Military Service Record; Declaration for Original Invalid Pension, August 30, 1879, Jason W. Kinsley to J. A. Bently, June 11, 1881, Samuel Murdock affidavit, May 14, 1884, Maggie R. McGlenn affidavit, April 24, 1888, Pension Bureau Circular Response, June 1, 1899, all in Jason W. Kinsley Pension; Peg Hefke to Reba Kinsley Hall [April 17, 1992], in the possession of Reba Kinsley Hall.

On July 21, 1861, scarcely a month after he was mustered into Co. H of the Second Vermont Vols., Alonzo Kinsley was shot in the chest at the First Battle of Bull Run. Three months later on October 20, 1861, Eli Ellinwood, who was also in Co. H, wrote home to his family in Fletcher that "Alonzo Kinsley has not been able to do much since he was wounded at Bull Run. But he now looks Bright and I hope that he will get well again for I am acquainted with no better Yo[u]ng man than he is worthy of trust anywhere or in any place." Alonzo did not get better, however. He developed serious respiratory problems and was transferred to the Invalid Corps, where he spent the rest of the war, until his discharge in June 1864, working as a nurse in Maryland military hospitals. A friend recalled that when he returned home to Fletcher in July 1864 Alonzo had "great difficulty in breathing" and could do only about half a day's work. His brother Edgar said that in 1866, the year of the family reunion, Alonzo could barely do enough work "to pay for his board" and that in 1867 "much of the time he was unable to do any work." Alonzo understood that his respiratory ailments posed a serious obstacle to "my obtaining a livelihood," and until his death in 1911 he repeatedly reminded the federal government of his Civil War "disability" and its consequences. His death certificate reported that he died of acute indigestion, general debility, and a "gunshot wound received in Civil War." Alonzo Kinsley Compiled Military Service Record; Hubbell S. Storty affidavit, May 30, 1887, R. T. Bingham and E. K. Montague joint affidavit, undated [September 1883], Alonzo Kinsley affidavit, December 28, 1880, September 5, 1883, Alonzo Kinsley to O. P. G. Clarke, undated [1890?], all in Alonzo Kinsley Pension; Alonzo Kinsley death certificate of September 5, 1911, Vital Records. The Ellinwood letter is quoted in Ballway, *A Genealogical Study*, 25.

Edgar Kinsley Montague joined the Second Vermont Vols. in December 1863. Sent immediately to the front in Virginia, he got sick and spent most of the rest of the war in hospitals in Virginia, New York, and Vermont suffering from measles, typhoid fever, diarrhea, and a chronic cough, as well as from heart, lung, and throat disease. In February 1865 he was deemed "unfit for duty" and detailed as a regimental mail carrier until July 15, 1865, when he was mustered out of the service. Upon returning home in the summer of 1865 he was, according to his brother Alonzo and his aunt Alma, in "very poor health" and "unable to do anything but light work." At the time of the family reunion he was under the care of a physician for heart and lung disease, and shortly after the reunion in the summer of 1866 he was, a neighbor noted, "in poor health, unable to perform any manual labor." Edgar never was able to work his farm by himself, and until his death in 1914 relied "almost entirely" on hired labor. Edgar Kinsley Montague Compiled Military Service Record; E. K. Montague, Alfred Riggs, Alonzo Kinsley, Alma R. Scott, and Thomas G. Ryan affidavits, undated [1889], all in Edgar Kinsley Montague Pension; Edgar K. Montague death certificate of May 21, 1914, Vital Records.

William Kinsley initially served in the Eighth Vermont with his brother Rufus. During his tour of duty in Louisiana he spent much of his time as either a patient or a nurse in military hospitals, and in February 1864 he was transferred to the Invalid Corps. Mustered out of the army in June 1864, he reenlisted in the Second Vermont Vols. in August 1864. Two months later, in Virginia at the Battle of Cedar Creek, he was shot in his left elbow, which caused his hand to go numb. Then in April 1865 during the final siege of Petersburg William received a gunshot wound over his left eye that was so severe, according to his company commander, that not only his sight but "his very life was dispaired [*sic*] of." William survived these and other serious wounds, but with impaired vision, a numb left hand, and a debilitating rheumatism that had first attacked his small five-foot six-inch frame in the final year of the war, his future looked bleak. Consequently, on December 16, 1865, just six months after he was mustered out of the army for good and only four months before the family reunion, twenty-one-year-old William applied for (and received) a pension from the U.S. government. He explained that he could "do but little" work. His brother Edgar Kinsley Montague confirmed that William had worked on a neighboring farm "from the close of the war in July 1865 till 1869 and that during the entire time . . . was troubled with rheumatism being at times entirely helpless. . . ." Though he was being treated by a physician from the time he arrived home from the war, William's health did not improve, and he was frequently confined to his home. In 1888 William complained that he was "unable to work most of the time," and by the summer of 1890 he had to use crutches to get around. In March 1901 his physician reported that William was "wholly unable to perform manual labor." Six months later he was dead. William L. Kinsley Compiled Military Service Record; Declaration for Original Invalid Pension, December 16, 1865, Surgeon's Certificate, September 9, 1873, George Buck, Jr., affidavit, February 16, 1866, Edgar K. Montague affidavit, October 12, 1886, William L. Kinsley to J. C. Black, October 27, 1886, C. B. Harding affidavit, October 23, 1886, Declaration for the Increase of an Invalid Pension, August 27, 1888 and July 25, 1890, Dr. H. H. Hill affidavit, March 4, 1901, all in William L. Kinsley Pension; William L. Kinsley death certificate of September 24, 1901, Vital Records. Unfortunately, William Kinsley's Civil War diary was destroyed in a twentieth-century fire.

139. Rufus Kinsley to Sir, March 20, 1886, E. K. Montague and Elvira Montague joint affidavit, September 18, 1886, Edgar K. Montague deposition, January 28, 1892, Elvira Montague deposition, January 28, 1892, Rufus Kinsley Pension.

140. Montague Diary, January 18, 1866, February 12, 13, 14, March 6, 1867, September 3, 26, 30, October 1, 2, 3, 1868; Rufus Kinsley to Sir, March 20, 1866, D. H. Roberts affidavit, April 16, 1886, Elvira Montague deposition, January 28, 1892, Rufus Kinsley Pension.

141. Rufus Kinsley to Sir, March 20, 1866, Rufus Kinsley Pension; 1870 Manuscript Census, roll 1620, p. 233. The all-white township of North Hero was a part of Grand Isle County, which in 1870 ranked a distant last among Vermont's fourteen counties in value of farms, farm products, manufactured products, and personal and real estate. Francis A. Walker, *A Compendium of the Ninth Census* . . . (Washington, D.C.: Government Printing Office, 1872), 351, 681, 784, 785, 843; "North Hero," in Hemenway, *Gazetteer*, II, 563–70, 477, 481–83.

142. Rufus Kinsley and Ella Bingham Marriage Certificate, Vital Records; 1870 Manuscript Census, roll 1620, p. 234; Ben A. Kinsley notice of death in Ben A. Kinsley Pension; "Declaration for Pension," February 27, 1907, Rufus Kinsley Pension; Vermont Land Records, microfilm no. 7422, VII, 338, 339, 430, VIII, 56–59, 257, 283; Montague Diary, January 18, 1869. On September 2, 1868, Ben Alva Kinsley agreed to pay Edwin Woods fifty-seven hundred dollars for the 275-acre Lowell farm that Rufus Kinsley later purchased

from Ben Alva's widow Lucy Blair Kinsley; on January 1, 1869, Ben Alva and his son Daniel Kinsley of Worcester, Mass., took out a two thousand dollar mortgage against this property. Rufus Kinsley owned the farm free and clear by 1900 according to the federal census returns. 1900 Manuscript Census, roll 1693, p. 180B.

143. 1870 Manuscript Census, roll 1620, p. 79, roll 1623, p. 4; Manuscript Census Returns, Tenth Census of the United States, 1880, microcopy T9 (cited hereinafter as 1880 Manuscript Census), roll 1346, p. 440; Lucy Kinsley notice of death, Ben A. Kinsley Pension; Lucy Hubbard Blair Kinsley tombstone, Binghamville Cemetery, Fletcher, Vt.; Alonzo Kinsley death certificate of September 5, 1911, Vital Records; Alonzo Kinsley Pension. Alonzo and his wife stayed for a few days in early January 1869 with Kinsley's brother Edgar Montague before moving to Lowell; according to Edgar, it was not until January 18 that "Uncle Bens folkes moved." See entries of January 7, 8, 13, 18, 1869, in Montague Diary. Why Lucy Blair Kinsley moved away from the farm in 1874 remains unknown. Judging from surviving Civil War correspondence, Rufus and his stepmother had a close relationship. On January 28, 1864, for example, Ben A. Kinsley wrote to Rufus Kinsley that "Your Mother [Lucy Blair] sends lots of love with the assurance of her best wishes for your welfare & happiness." Kinsley Papers. Other relationships also tied Lucy to the Kinsleys; for example, her niece Annette Blair was married to Rufus's brother Edgar. Similarly, we do not know why Alonzo left Lowell in 1872 and returned to Fletcher, where he lived for eight months before moving to Cambridge, Vt. In 1890 he moved back to Fletcher. This time he stayed until 1907, when he moved to Essex, Vt., where he died on September 5, 1911. J. & J. M. Robinson deed to Lucy Kinsley, July 24, 1875, Vermont Land Records, microfilm no. 7174, XI, 423; E. K. Montague and H. A. Blair marriage certificate of June 9, 1868, Alonzo Kinsley death certificate of September 5, 1911, Vital Records.

144. Kinsley response to Pension Bureau circular, July 4, 1898, Rufus Kinsley Pension; 1870 Manuscript Census, roll 1620, p. 79; Reba Kinsley Hall, telephone conversation with author, April 3, 1992.

145. D. Eugene Curtis, "Lowell," in Hemenway, *Gazetteer*, III, 270, 280; *Twelfth Census of the United States, Taken in the Year 1900: Population* (Washington, D.C.: U.S. Census Office, 1901), pt. 1, p. 395. The figures for Orleans County are derived from Walker, *Compendium of the Ninth Census*, 681, 784, 843. The figure for Lowell is derived from data collected in the 1870 Manuscript Census, roll 1623, pp. 191–201. Lowell remained a rugged frontier community as late as 1883, when its landscape was still dotted with rough log cabins that had originally been built by pioneer settlers in the early nineteenth century. Lowell was also a white community, although 14 percent of its population in 1870 was foreign-born. Like Fletcher and North Hero, where Kinsley lived immediately after the war, Lowell had no black residents in 1870, and only 0.1 percent of Orleans County, where Lowell was situated, was black in 1870. See "Lowell," in Hamilton Child, comp., *Gazetteer and Business Directory of Lamoille and Orleans Counties, VT., for 1883–84* (Syracuse, N.Y.: Hamilton Child, 1883), 24; and Walker, *Compendium of the Ninth Census*, 351.

146. 1870 Manuscript Census, Schedule 2, Productions of Agriculture, Lowell, Orleans County, Vt., pp. 1–2; 1880 Manuscript Census Returns, Schedule 2, Productions of Agriculture, Lowell, Orleans County, Vt., p. 1. (The Vermont agricultural schedules for both the 1870 and 1880 federal manuscript census are on microfilm at the Vermont State Library in Montpelier.) In 1883, according to Child, *Gazetteer and Business Directory*, 527, Kinsley had 500 sugar trees on his property. In 1902, according to the *Barton (Vt.) Orleans County Monitor* of April 21, 1902, he produced 875 pounds of sugar from 147 trees. Kinsley supplemented his income by renting out a tenement on his farm. See ibid., October 16, 1876, December 29, 1884, January 21, 1889. On the consequences of declining economic and demographic growth for another small Vermont town, see Hal S. Barron, *Those Who Stayed Behind: Rural Society in Nineteenth-Century New England* (New York: Cambridge University Press, 1984).

147. 1900 Manuscript Census, roll 1693, p. 180B; L. M. Bingham's statement is quoted in George F. Edmunds to J. C. Black, December 10, 1886, in possession of Reba Kinsley Hall; LeRoy M. Bingham deposition, January 30, 1892, in Rufus Kinsley Pension.

148. Rufus Kinsley to Sir, March 20, 1886, Joseph W. Buzzell affidavit, May 1, 1886, Report of Board of Examiners, April 21, 1886, Surgeon's Certificate, April 20, 1892, Homer Riggs to Sir [Commissioner of Pensions], January 31, 1891 [1892], Rufus Kinsley Pension.

149. Because of his deteriorating health, William had a hard time holding a regular job after the war. At various times he tried his hand at farmer, tub maker, cooper, mechanic, horse trainer, mill hand, pension agent, and census enumerator. In 1900, a year before his death, he was still struggling to make a living, and he was still paying off the mortgage on his Lowell farm. William Lyon Kinsley Pension Record; *Barton (Vt.) Orleans County Monitor*, February 2, 1874, June 2, 1890, December 19, 1892, July 22, 1895, September 30, 1901; 1870 Manuscript Census, roll 1623, p. 7; 1900 Manuscript Census, roll 693, p. 173B; Manuscript Census Returns, Thirteenth Census of the United States, 1910, microcopy T624 (cited hereinafter as 1910 Manuscript Census), roll 1615, p. 9B.

150. Help from nearby and distant family members would continue throughout the remainder of Kinsley's life. Visitors from afar included Kinsley's sister Lucretia and brother Daniel from Massachusetts and his brothers Jason and Guy from Iowa; visitors who lived close by included Ella's siblings – Royal, LeRoy, Leona, and Emma – all of whom resided in Vermont. Kinsley especially enjoyed the company of his older brother Guy, and the two appear to have been very much alike. When Guy died in 1921 the local press described him as an "industrious, God-fearing and country-loving" citizen whose life "exemplified uprightness of conduct." But, the reporter noted in closing, "With these sterner virtues there was about Mr. Kinsley a geniality, kindliness and a vein of fun-loving which made him the best of companions." I have found no evidence that Kinsley ever visited his siblings in Massachusetts or Iowa. He did, however, make short trips in northern Vermont to places like Barton Landing, Newport, Burlington, and Binghamville, and he once made what must have been for him a difficult trip to Boston to visit three of his sons. *Barton (Vt.) Orleans County Monitor*, March 7, 1898, May 28,

November 5, 1906, March 9, 1910, August 22, 1904; Guy Kinsley obituary in undated and unknown newspaper clipping in possession of Reba Kinsley Hall. For a sample of visits to Lowell by Rufus and Ella Kinsley's siblings, see ibid., May 28, 1894, August 2, 1897, July 29, August 5, 1901, July 14, 1902, July 27, 1903, August 8, 1904, September 4, 1905, July 2, 1906, August 26, 1907, June 14, 1911.

151. Illness and injury, often serious, seemed never to be far from the Kinsley household. See, for example, ibid., June 5, June 13, 1881, March 24, 1889, August 24, 1891, December 26, 1892, May 21, July 30, 1894, March 29, 1897, February 27, March 13, 1899, February 19, March 18, 1900, March 11, 25, 1901, October 10, 1904, February 20, 1905, March 11, 1907, March 20, 1908, March 31, September 1, December 1, 1909.

152. Ibid., July 30, 1894, August 24, 1891, September 14, 1891, December 26, 1892, March 13, 1899, February 27, 1899.

153. Reba Kinsley Hall, telephone conversation with author, August 25, 1998.

154. *Barton (Vt.) Orleans County Monitor*, September 16, 1907. On Clayton's visits home, see ibid., July 20, 1896, August 22, November 28, 1898, August 14, 1899, August 26, 1900, May 13, July 29, September 23, December 2, 1901, February 10, June 16, December 1, 1902, November 23, 1903, August 8, 1904, July 2, 1906. On Benton's visits, see ibid., December 2, 1901, June 16, December 1, 1902, July 20, 1903, August 1, 1904, July 24, 1905, July 2, August 27, 1906.

155. 1900 Manuscript Census, roll 693, p. 180B; 1910 Manuscript Census, roll 1615, p. 9B.

156. *Barton (Vt.) Orleans County Monitor*, August 23, 1897, November 14, 1887, September 16, 1907, July 20, 1903.

157. Kinsley's brother William seems to have been especially well liked and respected. While living in Lowell, he was a member and lay official in the Congregational Church, president of the Lowell Republican Club, commander of Hazen Post, No. 74, of the Grand Army of the Republic (GAR), and presiding officer of the Mount Norris Lodge of the Independent Order of Good Templars. He also served as town librarian, and when books started disappearing, he moved the collection to his home and lent books out his front door. He was elected to so many public posts, including moderator, constable, lister, auditor, and selectman, that at the time of his death the local press claimed that he had "held nearly all the town offices." He capped off his political career by representing Lowell in the state legislature in 1898. Ibid., October 13, 1884, December 27, 1897, June 2, 1890, July 16, 1888, August 11, 1873, December 12, 1887, April 7, 1890, January 8, 1900, September 30, 1901; Fred A. Howland, *Vermont Legislative Directory: Biennial Session, 1898* (Montpelier, Vt.: Vermont Watchman, 1898), 400.

158. *Barton (Vt.) Orleans County Monitor*, January 20, 1902, October 15, 1906, July 20, 1903, June 15, 1908, February 11, 1907, December 23, 1895, December 27, 1897, March 23, 1896.

159. Joseph W. Buzzell affidavit, May 1, 1886, Rufus Kinsley Pension; Howland, *Vermont Legislative Directory*, 400; *Barton (Vt.) Orleans County Monitor*, July 22, 1895.

160. *Barton (Vt.) Orleans County Monitor*, May 19, 1873. Kinsley served as Chief Templar on several other occasions, and over the years he was joined in the officer

corps of the Mount Norris Lodge by several family members, including his wife Ella, his brother William, his sister-in-law Ellen, his nephew Ross, and his son Clayton. See, for example, ibid., February 22, 1875, October 18, 1886, November 14, December 12, 1887, August 6, 1888, May 13, 1889, May 12, 1890, November 16, 1891.

161. David M. Fahey, *Temperance and Racism: John Bull, Johnny Reb, and the Good Templars* ([Lexington]: University Press of Kentucky, 1996), chap. 1. For evidence of women holding a percentage of the Mount Norris Lodge offices roughly equal to that of men, see *Barton (Vt.) Orleans County Monitor*, May 11, 1874, May 16, 1886, August 6, 1888, February 18, 1889, November 17, 1890, November 16, 1891.

162. Fahey, *Temperance and Racism*, 5, 12, 24; Curtis, "Lowell," 275, 280–81; *Barton (Vt.) Orleans County Monitor*, April 4, 1874, February 7, 1876, July 12, 1875. In addition to a spelling bee, the 1876 meeting of the Lowell Temperance Society featured a "variety of interesting literary exercises [that] enlivened the occasion." One suspects that Kinsley, with his fondness for literature and the English language, never went to these meetings solely to hear what must have become fairly predictable tirades against the evils of alcohol. Ibid., February 7, 1876.

163. Kinsley's brother William was elected chief Templar on August 6, 1873. *Barton (Vt.) Orleans County Monitor*, May 19, August 11, 1873. On the opposition of the Vermont and other northern Good Templar state organizations to a movement to keep blacks out of the Templars, see Fahey, *Temperance and Racism*, chaps. 3–4, esp. pp. 80–85.

164. *Barton (Vt.) Orleans County Monitor*, February 1, 1886, December 12, 1887, January 21, April 22, September 2, 1889, May 28, June 11, 1894, December 28, 1896. According to a reporter who interviewed Kinsley and Lewis J. Ingalls in Lowell in 1906, the two old veterans attended "every encampment of their regiment whenever it is held in the state." *Boston Herald*, March 19, 1906. On the close bonds among members of the GAR, see Stuart McConnell, *Glorious Contentment: The Grand Army of the Republic, 1865–1900* (Chapel Hill: University of North Carolina Press, 1992), esp. 52–53. Prior to the pension act of 1890, local GAR posts played a crucial role in sustaining ill and impoverished veterans. Ibid., 127–30.

165. Lewis J. Ingalls affidavit, May 1, 1886, Rufus Kinsley Pension. Apparently, Kinsley did what he could to reciprocate. For instance, in the 1880s when Ingalls was helping with Kinsley's haying, he was also applying for an increase in his Civil War pension. On February 25, 1884, Kinsley prepared an affidavit in support of Ingalls's claim. Seeking to corroborate Ingalls's contention that he was still suffering from wounds inflicted in an ambush near Algiers in 1862, Kinsley reproduced most of the September 4, 1862, entry from his diary, ending with the critical sentence: "Ingalls received four balls while adjusting the switch, one of them through his neck." Kinsley then wrote that "The above is copied verbatim et literatim from a diary that I kept during four years of service in the war." This last assertion is not entirely accurate. In copying the sentence quoted above from his diary, Kinsley made a minor error of transcription. More significantly, in his eagerness to help his helper, Kinsley omitted the last part of the sentence just quoted from his diary, which read: ". . . through his neck, but his wounds are none of them dangerous."

Lewis J. Ingalls Pension. For evidence of Kinsley's involvement with Ingalls and other veterans in the GAR, see the *Barton (Vt.) Orleans County Monitor*, February 1, 1886, December 12, 1887, January 21, April 22, 1889.

166. Andrew Richardson and Oliver Newton joint affidavit, May 27, 1890, Rufus Kinsley Pension. Both Richardson, who lived with his wife and children on a modest farm about a mile from Kinsley's place, and Newton were members of Kinsley's church and claimed to be "quite intimate with the family." Communal aid continued to flow in Kinsley's direction throughout the final decades of the nineteenth century. In 1894, when one of Kinsley's teenage boys cut a toe off while doing the haying on his father's farm, the local press reported that "The next day the neighbors turned out and finished his haying." 1870 Manuscript Census, roll 1623, p. 8; *Barton (Vt.) Orleans County Monitor*, July 30, 1894.

167. Declaration for an Original Invalid Pension, February 2, 1886, Rufus Kinsley to Sir, March 20, 1886, Rufus Kinsley Pension; 1870 Manuscript Census, roll 1623, p. 8.

168. Many of the late-nineteenth-century federal pension beneficiaries were dependent relatives of Union veterans, but none were former Confederate soldiers. The latter did not become eligible for Civil War service pensions until 1958. William H. Glasson, *Federal Military Pensions in the United States* (New York: Oxford University Press, 1918), 273, 267, 269; Theda Skocpol, *Protecting Soldiers and Mothers: The Political Origins of Social Policy in the United States* (Cambridge: Harvard University Press, 1992), 109. On the role of the Civil War pension system in transforming social welfare policy in nineteenth-century America, see Megan J. McClintock, "Civil War Pensions and the Reconstruction of Union Families," *Journal of American History*, 83 (September 1996), 456–80.

169. Ben A. Kinsley Pension; William Lyon Kinsley Pension; Jason W. Kinsley Pension; Alonzo Kinsley Pension; Lewis Ingalls, Oliver Newton, and Andrew Richardson affidavits in Rufus Kinsley Pension. On the efforts of some GAR officials to convince Congress that Civil War soldiers deserved an inclusive service pension, see McConnell, *Glorious Contentment*, chap. 5. In applying for a pension in 1886 Kinsley followed in the footsteps of his brother William, who applied in 1865, and his brothers Alonzo and Jason, who applied in 1879. His brother Edgar did not file his application until 1889. William L. Kinsley Pension, Alonzo Kinsley Pension, Jason W. Kinsley Pension, and Edgar Kinsley Montague Pension.

170. Rufus Kinsley to Sir, March 20, 1886, Rufus Kinsley Pension; Glasson, *Federal Military Pensions*, 136, 138.

171. A close reading of Kinsley's pension file casts doubt upon the supporting testimony offered by several of his relatives who were less than candid about their relationship to the applicant. Kinsley's brother Edgar Kinsley Montague and his aunt Elvira Montague claim, for example, in their joint affidavit of September 18, 1886, to have "no interest in said case" and admit only to having been "well and personally acquainted" with Kinsley for thirty years. They make these statements on an affidavit that is entitled "Testimony of Employers, Neighbors or Acquaintances of Soldier, [OTHER THAN NEAR RELATIVES.]." Nowhere in the affidavit does either mention that they are related to Kinsley, and Edgar identifies himself as "E. K. Montague." Demas Robinson, Kinsley's cousin; Royal T. Bingham, his

wife's father; Nathan R. Bingham, his wife's uncle; and Albert Parsons, his wife's cousin, also fail to mention in their affidavits that they are related to the applicant. Kinsley himself may have had a hand in these omissions and in the content of the last four affidavits because they are all in his handwriting, and they are identical. The silences and misleading statements found in some of these documents were perhaps encouraged by the somewhat cynical feeling many late-nineteenth-century Americans had about the operation and equity of the Pension Bureau bureaucracy. They may also suggest just how desperate Kinsley's condition was and how eager his relatives were to help him secure a pension. The Kinsleys had a reputation for sticking together; as Kinsley's daughter Amy later put it: "The Kinsley blood was a little thicker than most." Amy's contention seems to be supported by Edgar Kinsley Montague's testimony in other pension cases involving his siblings. In an 1886 affidavit in support of William Kinsley's pension and marked "For the testimony of EMPLOYERS or NEAR NEIGHBORS of soldier, (other than relatives)," Edgar also identifies himself only as "E. K. Montague" and fails to mention his relationship to the applicant. He does, however, offer the misleading statement that he "was acquainted" with William prior to William's enlistment in the army in 1861. In an affidavit with the same restrictive instructions that was filed in 1883 in support of Alonzo Kinsley's pension, E. K. Montague again fails to declare that he is the applicant's brother, and he disingenuously states that since the war he has "seen him as often as twice each year." Apparently, a significant number of problematic pension applications came out of Vermont. On January 10, 1876, Kinsley's local newspaper, the *Barton (Vt.) Orleans County Monitor*, reported that "the most extensive and successful pension business in Northern Vermont" had been shut down by U.S. marshals for alleged irregularities. E. K. Montague and Elvira Montague joint affidavit, September 18, 1886, and the affidavits of September 18, 1888, by Demas Robinson, Nathan R. Bingham, Royal T. Bingham, and Albert Parsons in Rufus Kinsley Pension; E. K. Montague affidavit, October 12, 1886, William L. Kinsley Pension; E. K. Montague affidavit, undated (September 1883), Alonzo Kinsley Pension. The Amy Kinsley comment was made to her niece, Reba Kinsley Hall, who conveyed it to the author in a telephone conversation on September 19, 1996.

172. Rufus Kinsley to Sir, March 20, 1886, Surgeon's Certificate, April 21, 1886, E. K. Montague and Elvira Montague joint affidavit, September 18, 1886, in Rufus Kinsley Pension; 1870 Manuscript Census, roll 1620, p. 233; 1880 Manuscript Census, roll 1346, p. 440.

173. Surgeon's Certificate, April 21, 1886, in Rufus Kinsley Pension; Kinsley, *The Slaveholders' Rebellion*, July 29, December 27, 1863, June 8, July 7, November 29, 1864, June 17, 1865. The Surgeon's Certificate states that Kinsley contracted diarrhea in the spring of 1864, but it was on April 28, 1863, that Kinsley went to the hospital "pretty hard sick with diarrhoea." Ibid., April 28, 1863.

174. Declaration for an Original Invalid Pension, February 2, 1886, Rufus Kinsley deposition, January 12, 1892, Surgeon's Certificate, April 21, 1886, Declaration for the Increase of an Invalid Pension, July 2, 1887, LeRoy M. Bingham deposition, January 30, 1892, James Noyes affidavit, August 11, 1887, Rufus Kinsley Pension.

175. Medical Certificate of Disability, July 11, 1865, in Rufus Kinsley Compiled Military Service Record.

176. In a diary entry of June 2, 1865, Kinsley does mention hurting his left knee while swimming. Kinsley, *The Slaveholders' Rebellion,* June 2, 1865.

177. Kinsley inherited his knee trouble from his own mother, Gihon told him. Kinsley responded that such a conclusion was "an injustice" and that he had never been lame before the war. Gihon then proceeded to report in his official certificate of disability that Kinsley's knee trouble was caused by a lingering antebellum wound. Rufus Kinsley deposition, January 12, 1892, Rufus Kinsley Pension.

178. Rufus Kinsley deposition, January 12, 1892, D. H. Roberts affidavit, April 16, 1886, H. H. Hill affidavit, June 4, 1890, LeRoy M. Bingham deposition, January 30, 1892, Rufus Kinsley Pension.

179. Andrei Calin, *Diagnosis and Management of Rheumatoid Arthritis* (Menlo Park, Calif.: Addison-Wesley Publishing Company, 1983), 4; Warren A. Katz, ed., *Diagnosis and Management of Rheumatic Diseases,* 2nd ed. (Philadelphia: J. B. Lippincott Company, 1988), 349, emphasis added.

180. Report of Board of Examiners, April 21, 1886, Surgeon's Certificate, October 9, 1889, Surgeon's Certificate, April 20, 1892, Rufus Kinsley Pension; Declaration for Increase of Invalid Pension, July 25, 1890, William L. Kinsley Pension; Maggie R. McGlenn affidavit, April 24, 1888, Jason W. Kinsley Pension; Reba Kinsley Hall, telephone conversation with author, August 25, 1998.

181. In the 1860s doctors typically relied on signs of joint disease to diagnose rheumatism. But during the war military physicians were baffled by many cases of chronic rheumatism that were not accompanied by any joint disease. For example, Joseph Klapp, a surgeon in a Philadelphia military hospital, "was struck with the fact that among the large number of rheumatics admitted into the military hospital . . . there was no affection of the joints; the disease was manifested by neuralgic pains." Upon examining these patients, he discovered "more or less tenderness . . . in certain parts or along the whole track of the spine" but "no perceptible swelling in any of the affected parts." Other symptoms, which mirrored many of those reported by Kinsley, included head pain, thoracic pain, abdominal pain, "excessive sensibility of the surface," "dyspepsia and diarrhoea, from an irritable condition of the stomach and bowels," "neuralgia of the legs," "wasting of the muscles," and the simulation of lung and heart disease. This new kind of rheumatism, with its especially "puzzling and annoying" afflictions of the chest and abdomen, Klapp maintained, was not the result of a debilitating arthritis that had been caused by "exposure and fatigue" or an "enfeebled condition." In a remarkably insightful speculation, he suggested that the condition might have resulted from soldiers enduring inclement weather and cold temperatures, carrying heavy packs, and receiving rations of little nutritional value.

Another leading military physician, J. J. Woodward, documented the course of muscular rheumatism and its gradual progression from a general "malaise" and "sense of soreness" to severe chronic pain that left the soldier unfit for duty, either confined to bed or hobbling about with a stick. He then, however, dismissed most of these cases as "pseudo-rheumatism," and contended (incorrectly) that many of those afflicted were actually suffering from "incipient scurvy." In a disdainful tone that modern-day fibromyalgics still encounter, Woodward described many of the remaining sufferers as "malingerers," who "whimper and even sob in an unmanly manner." Clearly, the Office of the Surgeon General was not exaggerating in 1888 when it concluded that in the "so-called muscular rheumatism" cases there was "ample room for difference of opinion in forming a diagnosis." Such differences of opinion would make it difficult for soldiers like Kinsley to prove that they had "rheumatism" and that it was "caused" by the Civil War. Divergent diagnoses also resulted in wide-ranging treatments, some of which provided "temporary relief" but in general were "unsatisfactory" and failed to produce "any permanent benefit." U.S. War Department, Office of the Surgeon General, *The Medical and Surgical History of the War of the Rebellion (1861–65)*, 3 parts (Washington, D.C.: Government Printing Office, 1870–88), pt. 3, vol. I, pp. 833–35, 843–44.

182. Harvey Moldofsky, "Sleep, Neuroimmune and Neuroendocrine Functions in Fibromyalgia and Chronic Fatigue Syndrome," *Advances in Neuroimmunology*, 5 (1995), 39–56; Daniel J. Wallace and Janice Brock Wallace, *All About Fibromyalgia* (New York: Oxford University Press, 2002), 9–12 and pt. 2; Katz, *Rheumatic Diseases*, 648, 360. On the physiological basis of chronic and abnormally severe pain among fibromyalgiacs, see Richard H. Gracely, Frank Petzke, Julie M. Wolf, and Daniel J. Clauw, "Functional Magnetic Resonance Imaging Evidence of Augmented Pain Processing in Fibromyalgia," *Arthritis and Rheumatism*, 46 (May 2002), 1333–43. Although finding specific tender points that indicate the presence of chronic widespread pain and of altered pain processing is central to identifying fibromyalgia, nonbiologic factors also play a prominent role in symptom expression in all rheumatic diseases, including the soft-tissue rheumatism known as fibromyalgia. See Leslie J. Crofford and Daniel J. Clauw, "Fibromyalgia: Where Are We a Decade After the American College of Rheumatology Classification Criteria Were Developed?" *Arthritis and Rheumatism*, 46 (May 2002), 1136–38.

183. Surgeon's Certificate, April 20, 1892, Rufus Kinsley Pension. Kinsley's personal physician had diagnosed him as "suffering from Muscular Rheumatism" in 1876. H. H. Hill affidavit, June 4, 1890, ibid.

184. Miryam Ehrlich Williamson, *Fibromyalgia: A Comprehensive Approach* (New York: Walker & Company, 1996), 89.

185. Wallace and Wallace, *Fibromyalgia*, 12–19; Rufus Kinsley to Sir, March 20, 1886, Rufus Kinsley Pension.

186. Rufus Kinsley to Sir, March 20, 1886, Rufus Kinsley Pension; Kinsley, *The Slaveholders' Rebellion*, August 20, 28, September 10, November 29, 1864; Harvey Moldofsky, Phillip Scarisbrick, Robert England, and Hugh Smythe, "Musculoskeletal Symptoms and Non-REM Sleep Disturbance in Patients with 'Fibrositis Syndrome' and Healthy Subjects," *Psychosomatic Medicine*, 37 (July–August 1975), 341–51.

187. Vermont winters must have taken a terrible toll on Kinsley's body. One February the thermometer on his brother William's farm registered forty degrees below zero. *Barton (Vt.) Orleans County Monitor*, February 25, 1896.

188. Reba Kinsley Hall, letter to the author, November 19, 1981.

189. Declaration for an Original Invalid Pension, February 2, 1886, Claimant's Statement, January 12, 1892, Rufus Kinsley Pension; George F. Edmunds to Rufus

Kinsley, December 10, 1886, George F. Edmunds to John C. Black, December 10, 1886, John C. Black to George F. Edmunds, December 14, 1886, letters in possession of Reba Kinsley Hall. Not only did Kinsley arrange to have supporting documents sent to the bureau, but he often wrote them as well, and sometimes he prepared identical affidavits for different people. Compare, for example, the affidavits of Jacob Clapper, July 2, 1888, and Joel T. Hazen, July 7, 1888, Rufus Kinsley Pension.

190. The extent to which the pension struggle was a family endeavor is graphically illustrated by a document dated February 4, 1889, and entitled "Declaration for the Increase of an Invalid Pension." In it Kinsley presents his case for an increase, his sister Lucretia and his son Clayton witness it, and his brother William notarizes it. Rufus Kinsley Pension.

191. Loren C. Lee affidavit, August 27, 1887, Rufus Kinsley Pension; F. W. Beers, *Atlas of Franklin and Grand Isle Cos., Vermont* (New York: F. W. Beers & Co., 1871), plate 39.

192. Kinsley, *The Slaveholders' Rebellion*, December 27, 1863, July 7, 1864; Reba Kinsley Hall, telephone conversation with author, April 27, 1996. On the impact of the war upon Hayes and Grant, see the excellent studies by T. Harry Williams, *Hayes of the Twenty-Third: The Civil War Volunteer Officer* (New York: Alfred A. Knopf, 1965), and William S. McFeely, *Grant: A Biography* (New York: W. W. Norton, 1981). See also Maris A. Vinovskis, ed., *Toward a Social History of the American Civil War: Exploratory Essays* (New York: Cambridge University Press, 1990).

193. In preparing his original pension application and repeated appeals, Kinsley spent an enormous amount of time writing letters, drawing up affidavits, filling out questionnaires, reading government reports, tracking down old Civil War acquaintances from New Hampshire to California, and so on. Before he had finished, Kinsley had generated a pension file containing some one hundred twenty-five pages of documents. By 1893 he had even convinced bureau officials to reverse their position and allow him compensation for the knee injury that he had always contended was sustained in the service and had triggered his rheumatism. Although this victory was largely a result of changes in pension law that made it no longer incumbent upon claimants to prove that their disabilities were caused by military service, Kinsley's tenacity, beginning with his original application, in documenting the origin of his knee injury may have played a role in the decision of bureau officials to make his payments for this specific disability retroactive to 1886. The fruit of this victory was an increase in Kinsley's monthly pension payment to twenty dollars. Rufus Kinsley Pension; Glasson, *Federal Military Pensions*, 234.

194. William H. Jeffrey, *Successful Vermonters: A Modern Gazetteer of Caledonia, Essex, and Orleans Counties* (East Burke, Vt.: Historical Publishing Company, 1904), 71–72. It is remarkable that in his autobiographical essay the only thing Kinsley mentions actually doing from 1866 to 1904 is working at Hazen Post, No. 74. We know that these postwar years also saw Kinsley participate in town government, labor for the Good Templars and the Baptists, organize reading groups, entertain friends and family, and so forth. But apparently these activities were not as important to Kinsley as was working with Civil War veterans at Hazen Post, No. 74,

and they obviously failed to provide him with the kind of mission and memories that fighting a great war against slavery did. In spite of this dissatisfaction, and in spite of his deteriorating health, Kinsley does not seem to have succumbed to the depression that afflicted some Civil War veterans. *Barton (Vt.) Orleans County Monitor,* March 23, 1896, February 11, 1907, October 15, 1906, July 22, 1895, January 20, 1902; Reba Kinsley Hall, telephone conversation with author, August 7, 1998. On the severe psychological problems that historians have found among some Civil War veterans, see, for example, Eric T. Dean, Jr., *Shook over Hell: Post-Traumatic Stress, Vietnam, and the Civil War* (Cambridge: Harvard University Press, 1997), esp. chaps. 3–7.

195. Of the 4 Lowell residents included in Jeffrey's gazetteer, only Kinsley and Newton reported serving in the Union army. Of the 236 Orleans County residents included in Jeffrey's gazetteer, 30 reported serving in the Union army. Jeffrey, *Successful Vermonters,* 1–274.

196. Ibid., title page.

197. *Boston Herald,* March 19, 1906; Office of the Adjutant General of the Army, *American Decorations: A List of Awards of the Congressional Medal of Honor, the Distinguished-Service Cross, and the Distinguished-Service Medal Awarded under Authority of the Congress of the United States, 1862–1926* (Washington, D.C.: U.S. Government Printing Office, 1927), 53.

198. Ben Alva Kinsley enlisted for one year in the Thirtieth U.S. Infantry on April 27, 1813, when he was seventeen years old. He also claimed but could offer no evidence to prove that he had served as a substitute soldier in the New York state militia for six months beginning in September 1812. Ben Alva Kinsley Pension.

199. Kinsley, who was never wounded in combat during the war, did seriously sprain his knee in early June 1865. Kinsley, *The Slaveholders' Rebellion,* January 13, 1863, June 2, 1865; James Noyes affidavit, August 11, 1887, Rufus Kinsley Pension.

200. Throughout the late nineteenth century the *Barton (Vt.) Orleans County Monitor,* for example, printed marriage, birth, and death notices for free, but charged five cents a line for obituaries. Ibid., May 19, 1873, January 18, 1891.

201. Benton Kinsley obituary, *Burlington (Vt.) Free Press and Times,* September 9, 1907. For a description of Benton Kinsley's funeral, see the *Barton (Vt.) Orleans County Monitor,* September 23, 1907.

202. Kinsley's wife Ella died of interstitial nephritis on September 13, 1909, after being ill for several months. His brother William committed suicide in September 1901. William, whose house could be seen from Rufus's farm, had been "very poorly" throughout the fall of 1900, and then on December 30 of the same year his wife Ellen died unexpectedly of a heart attack. Over the years William had weathered some tough losses, including five of his six children at birth or an early age, but according to the local press Ellen's death "was a terrible shock to her family as well as the community." The following spring William's weight dropped to 105 pounds. Sick with catarrh of the stomach, he was reportedly "in a very precarious condition." On September 24, 1901, he decided he had had enough and cut his own throat. Six days later the *Barton (Vt.) Orleans County Monitor* observed: "Our community was horrified on learning of the death by his

own hand, of our worthy townsman, Will L. Kinsley.... Mr. Kinsley had been in very poor health for a long time, and this, coupled with business troubles and the recent loss of his wife, is thought to have produced a temporary fit of insanity, during which the fatal deed was accomplished." Death certificates for Ella Bingham Kinsley, Ellen Whittle Kinsley, William Lyon Kinsley, and the children of William and Ellen Kinsley, Vital Records; *Barton (Vt.) Orleans County Monitor*, March 31, September 1, 1909, December 24, 1900, January 7, April 22, September 30, 1901.

203. 1910 Manuscript Census, roll 1615, p. 9B.

204. Amy Kinsley was the kind of person you could count on. As a child she went through an entire Vermont winter without missing a day of school. As an adult she was "well known" throughout Orleans County as "an efficient and popular teacher." *Barton (Vt.) Orleans County Monitor*, March 14, 1887, July 20, 1903; 1900 Manuscript Census, roll 693, p. 180B. Kinsley's gifts to his daughter Amy, as well as the diary he left to his oldest son Clayton, were artifacts of what the philosopher William James in 1910 called the nation's "sacred spiritual possession." These remembrances of the war, which most Americans believed were "worth more than all the blood poured out" to procure them according to James, contributed to the emergence of a new modern American nationalism at the turn of the century. John Pettegrew, "'The Soldier's Faith': Turn-of-the-century Memory of the Civil War and the Emergence of Modern American Nationalism," *Journal of Contemporary History*, 31 (January 1996), 49–73.

205. Kinsley Papers. General Richard L. Page surrendered Fort Morgan on August 23, 1864.

206. Kinsley, *The Slaveholders' Rebellion*, August 28, 1864; Chester G. Hearn, *Mobile Bay and the Mobile Campaign: The Last Great Battles of the Civil War* (Jefferson, N.C.: McFarland & Company, 1993), 91, 136. As sectional reconciliation progressed in the second half of the nineteenth century, black Americans pretty much disappeared from the nation's historical consciousness. Leading historians of the time, students and teachers at such prestigious universities as Columbia and Johns Hopkins, contributed to this trend by writing histories of the Civil War and Reconstruction that either completely ignored blacks or dismissed them as "a mass of barbarous freedmen" who belonged to "a race of men which has never of itself succeeded in subjecting passion to reason, has never, therefore, created any civilization of any kind." The quotations are from William A. Dunning, *Reconstruction, Political and Economic, 1865–1877* (New York: Harper & Brothers, 1907), 212, and John W. Burgess, *Reconstruction and the Constitution, 1866–1876* (New York: Charles Scribner's Sons, 1902), 133. James Ford Rhodes devoted only a few pages of his popular multivolume history of the Civil War era to black soldiers, and most of his discussion focused on either the Boston Brahmin Robert Gould Shaw and "his blacks" or Confederate treatment of black soldiers at Fort Pillow. *History of the United States from the Compromise of 1850 to the Final Restoration of Home Rule at the South in 1877*, 7 vols. (New York: Macmillan Company, 1906–12), IV, 332–36, V, 510–13. For a brief discussion of three important but neglected studies of black Civil War soldiers by black authors that were published prior to 1911, see Cornish, *The Sable Arm*, 316–18. On the prevailing tendency among late-nineteenth-century popular artists as well as professional historians

to sacrifice African Americans on the altar of sectional reconciliation and white supremacy, see Paul H. Buck, *The Road to Reunion, 1865–1900* (Boston: Little, Brown & Company, 1937), esp. chaps. 8–12, and W. E. Burghardt DuBois, *Black Reconstruction in America: An Essay Toward a History of the Part Which Black Folk Played in the Attempt to Reconstruct Democracy in America, 1860–1880* (New York: Harcourt, Brace & Company, 1935), chap. 17. Kinsley's reflections on the Civil War and its meaning appear even more distinctive (and admirable) given David W. Blight's conclusions in his recent prize-winning study *Race and Reunion: The Civil War in American Memory* (Cambridge: Harvard University Press, 2001). By the end of the nineteenth century, according to Blight, white Union as well as Confederate veterans had embraced sectional reconciliation and forgotten slavery, emancipation, the struggle for equality, and the contribution of African Americans to Northern victory.

207. After the war, Phelps, whom Wendell Phillips had once praised as "the only abolitionist in the regular army," turned his back on the men he had fought so hard to recruit during the war. He opposed granting black Americans the right to vote and warned that American democracy could not survive mongrelization by "beer-guzzling" Germans, "pope-worshiping" Irishmen, "cunning" Chinese, and "idle, ease-loving Africans." He even maintained that *all* Southerners were "barbarians" because "a large portion" of them were "ignorant, degraded Africans" and the rest were "perverted whites whose condition has been adapted to that of the Africans." Messner, "General John Wolcott Phelps," 17–35 (quotations on 28, 29); McClaughry, "John Wolcott Phelps," 263–90. On the estrangement of black soldiers and their white officers after the war, including the exclusion of black soldiers from veterans' organizations and celebrations, see Glatthaar, *Forged in Battle*, 256–60; McConnell, *Glorious Contentment*, 213–18; and Blight, *Race and Reunion*, 190–206, 385.

208. Kinsley Papers.

209. Kinsley's continuing identification with the war and the struggle for equality is also reflected in the documents he saved in his writing case after the war. At the time of Kinsley's death, the case contained several letters he had written home during the war and sixteen other documents. All but two of the sixteen other documents also related to Kinsley's life as a Civil War soldier, and over a third of them pertained to African Americans or to Kinsley's involvement in their struggle. They were an undated and untitled temperance poem in Kinsley's handwriting; a letter from Jonathan Ross to Kinsley offering legal advice and dated July 28, 1899; four letters sent in December 1886 either to or from U.S. Senator George F. Edmunds concerning Kinsley's Civil War pension claim; an undated note from Benjamin Woods, a fellow Civil War veteran, asking that his "funeral be conducted by my comrades of Hazen Post No. 74, G.A.R., in accordance with the Ritual of the Order"; a meticulously drafted table in Kinsley's handwriting recounting the date, place, and Union and Confederate commanders and casualties in 129 Civil War battles; an 1863 Thibodaux, La., newspaper that was printed on wallpaper; an 1863 Vicksburg, Miss., newspaper that was printed on wallpaper; an undated handbill reviewing the origins of the African Baptist Church in New Orleans; a handwritten copy Kinsley made in New Orleans on May 20, 1862, of several

repressive Louisiana slave laws; a handwritten copy Kinsley made in New Orleans on May 30, 1862, of a mayoral edict granting permission for a church "for persons of color"; Kinsley's August 1863 provisional commission in the Second Regiment Infantry, Corps d'Afrique; a copy of the oath Kinsley took in October 1863 upon being mustered into the Second Regiment Infantry, Corps d'Afrique; and an undated poem in Kinsley's handwriting entitled "1861: Port Royal." Reba Kinsley Hall, conversation with the author and inspection of writing case, Fayston, Vt., March 21, 1992. In 1900 eighty-one-year-old Benjamin Woods was a "boarder" on a farm near Kinsley's farm in Lowell. 1900 Manuscript Census, roll 693, p. 174. Kinsley probably produced the undated Table of Civil War Battles, Commanders, and Losses long after the war ended. In a note accompanying data on the Battle of Chancellorsville, Kinsley observed that "Greely" had provided a different figure for the number of Union losses. In the late nineteenth century General Adolphus Washington Greely supervised War Department publications on the Civil War. The Port Royal poem which focuses on freedom coming in late 1861 to the slaves of Port Royal, S.C., reproduces the first nine stanzas of John Greenleaf Whittier's 1862 poem "At Port Royal." John Greenleaf Whittier, *The Poetical Works of John Greenleaf Whittier*, 4 vols. (Boston: Houghton, Mifflin & Company, 1892), III, 230–33. The writing case and its contents, as well as a sword Kinsley carried during the war, are in the Kinsley Collection of the VHS. Kinsley's two Civil War uniforms have not survived. His daughter-in-law cut up one to make clothes and burned the other after moths got into it. Reba Kinsley Hall, telephone conversation with the author, August 15, 1996.

210. Newspapers that reported Kinsley's death reaffirmed his identity as a Civil War soldier. The *Barton (Vt.) Orleans County Monitor* described him simply as "a veteran of the civil war" and lamented: "Our community was saddened to learn of the death of Rufus Kinsley." In Burlington the *Free Press and Times* provided Kinsley's age but otherwise identified him only as "a veteran of the Civil War, having served in the 8th Vermont regiment." William Kinsley's tombstone makes no mention of his participation in the Civil War. Rufus Kinsley death certificate, Vital Records; Rufus Kinsley Grave Registration, VHS; *Barton (Vt.) Orleans County Monitor*, June 14, 21, 1911; *Burlington (Vt.) Free Press and Times*, June 14, 1911; Rufus and William Kinsley grave sites, Mountain View Cemetery, Lowell, Vt.

The Slaveholders' Rebellion: The Diary of Rufus Kinsley

1. On October 1, 1861, the Union War Department created the Department of New England under the command of Major General Benjamin F. Butler, who was to raise, arm, and equip troops that would operate in the Gulf South. The men who volunteered for the Eighth Vermont Volunteers knew prior to enlistment that their regiment would be a part of Butler's force. A professional politician with virtually no military experience, Butler was nevertheless a hero in much of New England because in May 1861, scarcely a month after the fall of Fort Sumter, he pronounced fugitive slaves who had escaped to Union lines under his command in tidewater Virginia "contraband of war" and, in defiance of Lincoln's statements that the government had no intention of interfering with slavery where

it existed, he refused to return such fugitives to their Confederate masters. G. G. Benedict, *Vermont in the Civil War: A History of the Part Taken by the Vermont Soldiers and Sailors in the War for the Union, 1861–5,* 2 vols. (Burlington, Vt.: Free Press Assoc., 1886 and 1888), II, 80–84; Louis S. Gerteis, *From Contraband to Freedman: Federal Policy Toward Southern Blacks, 1861–1865* (Westport, Conn.: Greenwood Press, 1973), 11–18.

2. Kinsley's youngest brother, William Lyon Kinsley (1844–1901), was only seventeen years old on December 9, 1861, when he traveled to St. Albans and enlisted in the Eighth Vermont Vols. Mustered in on February 18, 1862, as a private in Co. F, where his brother Rufus was a corporal, he was mustered out on June 22, 1864. Two months later he was mustered back into the service as a private in Co. H of the Second Vermont, where his brother Edgar Kinsley Montague was also a private. While in the Second Vermont he was wounded at the Battle of Cedar Creek on October 19, 1864, and again during the final siege of Petersburg on April 2, 1865. He was mustered out of the service at the rank of corporal on June 30, 1865. William L. Kinsley Compiled Military Service Record, Records of the Adjutant General's Office, 1780s–1917, Record Group 94, National Archives (Washington, D.C.) (cited hereinafter as Compiled Military Service Record); William L. Kinsley Pension, Records of the Veterans Administration, Record Group 15, National Archives (cited hereinafter as Pension). According to his brother Edgar, Rufus Kinsley had traveled from Fletcher to St. Albans on December 23. Edgar Kinsley Montague Diary, December 23, 1861. (Edgar Kinsley Montague's diary, which is cited hereinafter as Montague Diary, is in the possession of H. Carlton Ferguson of Fairfield, Vt. I am indebted to Mr. Ferguson for sharing the diary with me.)

3. Zeri Campbell was a twenty-one-year-old resident of East Swanton, Vt., at the time of his enlistment in the Eighth Vermont Vols. on December 3, 1861. Mustered into Co. F as a private, he was discharged on June 4, 1863. George N. Carpenter, *History of the Eighth Regiment, Vermont Volunteers, 1861–1865* (Boston: Deland & Barta, 1886), 303.

4. Chellis Kinsley (1809–1901) was Kinsley's paternal uncle. He was listed in the 1850 federal census as a forty-one-year-old farmer residing in Fletcher, Vt. His wife and five daughters were listed in the 1860 federal census as living with Giles Kinsley, a fifty-year-old mason, in Georgia, Vt. Eleanor W. Ballway, ed., *A Genealogical Study of Some Families Who Came to Fletcher, Vt. Before 1850 and of a Few of Their Descendants* (Burlington, Vt.: Vantage Press, 1981), 41; Manuscript Census Returns, Seventh Census of the United States, 1850, microcopy 432 (cited hereinafter as 1850 Manuscript Census), roll 924, p. 18; Manuscript Census Returns, Eighth Census of the United States, 1860, microcopy 653 (cited hereinafter as 1860 Manuscript Census), roll 1321, p. 24.

5. Kinsley's brother Edgar wrote in his diary on January 6, 1862: "Went to Es[s]ex with Rufus." Montague Diary. Edgar Kinsley Montague was born on June 18, 1837 (the Montague family genealogy incorrectly provides August 16, 1837, as his date of birth), the son of Ben Alva Kinsley (1796–1870) and Catherine Montague Kinsley (1798–1849). Edgar was legally adopted at a young age by his mother's brother, Rufus Montague II, and Montague's second wife,

Elvira Scott. (The Montagues and Kinsleys were closely related. Edgar's natural father was the son of Daniel Kinsley and Lucy Montague, and his adoptive father's first wife was Junia Kinsley.) During the war Edgar enlisted as a private in Co. H of the Second Vermont Vols. William L. Montague, ed., *History and Genealogy of the Montague Family of America* . . . (Amherst, Mass.: J. E. Williams, 1886), 366–67; Ballway, *A Genealogical Study*, 40–42, 52–56.

6. A native of Connecticut, Hiram Edwards Perkins (1838–1908) was a machinist living in St. Albans, Vt., with his wife and two children at the time of his commission as a captain in Co. F of the Eighth Vermont Vols. He was mustered out on April 9, 1863, to accept a position as major in the First Regiment, Louisiana Native Guards. Prior to his death from Stokes Adams disease in 1908, Perkins worked as a pension attorney and wrote several letters in support of Kinsley's appeals for pension increases. 1860 Manuscript Census, roll 1321, p. 54; Hiram E. Perkins, Grave Registration, Vermont Historical Society (cited hereinafter as VHS), Barre, Vt. (cited hereinafter as Grave Registration); Hiram E. Perkins death certificate, State of Vermont, Vital Records, General Services Center (Middlesex, Vt.) (cited hereinafter as Vital Records); Theodore S. Peck, comp., *Revised Roster of the Vermont Volunteers and Lists of Vermonters Who Served in the Army and Navy of the United States During the War of the Rebellion, 1861–66* (Montpelier, Vt.: Watchman Publishing Co., 1892), 321, 720; Hiram E. Perkins's affidavit, June 17, 1887, and deposition, January 14, 1892, Rufus Kinsley Pension.

7. Daniel S. Foster was a twenty-two-year-old resident of St. Albans at the time of his commission as a first lieutenant on January 3, 1862. Later promoted to captain, Foster was discharged from the service at the expiration of his three-year term of service on June 22, 1864. Peck, *Revised Roster*, 41; Carpenter, *Eighth Regiment*, 302.

8. Carter H. Nason was a twenty-seven-year-old resident of St. Albans at the time of his commission as a second lieutenant on January 3, 1862. Nason was dismissed from the service by order of a General Court-Martial on June 2, 1863. Peck, *Revised Roster*, 41; Carpenter, *Eighth Regiment*, 302.

9. Epidemics of mumps and measles swept through the Eighth Vermont Vols. during its encampment at Brattleboro in southeastern Vermont, and an exceptionally harsh winter also took its toll on the young volunteers. No doubt they were delighted when word came to break camp on March 4, and to leave the stark, frozen landscape of New England for the lush, semitropical climes of the Gulf of Mexico. Benedict, *Vermont in the Civil War*, II, 82.

10. A native of Vermont and the son of a state supreme court justice, George P. Tyler was a fifty-year-old Congregational minister living with his wife and daughter in Brattleboro on the eve of the war. 1860 Manuscript Census, roll 1325, p. 78; Mary R. Cabot, comp. and ed., *Annals of Brattleboro, 1681–1895*, 2 vols. (Brattleboro, Vt.: E. L. Hildreth & Co., 1921–22), I, 273, 277, 463.

11. Charles Levi Mead (1833–99) was the first superintendent of the Centre Congregational Church Sunday School in Brattleboro. At the time of his death, he was vice president of the American Missionary Association and a trustee of Hampton Agricultural Institute in Hampton, Va. His younger brother, the sculptor Larkin G. Mead, Jr. (1835–1910), was listed as a twenty-five-year-old

"artist" living at home with his father in the 1860 federal census. Larkin later moved to Italy, where he designed for the city of Springfield, Ill., his famous statue of Lincoln sitting in a chair and signing the Emancipation Proclamation. Cabot, *Annals of Brattleboro*, II, 543, 544, 718; 1860 Manuscript Census, roll 1325, p. 222; *National Cyclopaedia of American Biography*, 63 vols. (New York: James T. White & Company, 1898–1984), I, 278.

12. Born in Waterford, Vt., Rev. Nathan Howe (1792–1862) was living in Brattleboro in 1860 with his wife Clarissa Coburn and two of his three daughters, Adeline and Victoria. Nathan Howe birth certificate of December 1, 1792, and death certificate of December 6, 1862, Vital Records; 1860 Manuscript Census, roll 1325, p. 227; Gilman B. Howe, ed., *Howe Genealogies: Genealogy of John Howe of Sudbury and Marlborough, Massachusetts* (Boston: New England Historic Genealogical Society, 1929), 289.

13. Born in Lyme, N.H., Samuel Hobart Colburn (1820–1890) joined the Methodist Episcopal Conference in 1851. Prior to the close of the Civil War he served as pastor of Methodist churches in Brattleboro and several other Vermont towns. After the war he attended medical school and moved to Worcester County, Mass., where he was president of the Homeopathic Medical Society. *Minutes of the Vermont Annual Conference, of the Methodist Episcopal Church, for the Year 1851.* (Brattleboro, Vt.: J. H. Capen, 1855), 3; *Minutes of the Vermont Annual Conference of the Methodist Episcopal Church, Held at Springfield, April 21-22-23-24-25, 1870* (Montpelier, Vt.: Freeman Steam Printing House & Bindery, 1870), 44, 54; George A. Gordon and Silas R. Coburn, *Genealogy of the Descendants of Edward Colburn/Coburn* (Lowell, Mass.: Courier-Citizen Company Press, 1913), 260.

14. On February 16 Union forces captured Fort Donelson in Tennessee. In negotiating the surrender, Brigadier General Ulysses S. Grant made the famous statement that "No terms except an unconditional and immediate surrender can be accepted." The capture of Fort Donelson, along with the fall of nearby Fort Henry ten days earlier, boosted Northern morale and opened routes of invasion along the Cumberland and Tennessee Rivers that threatened to split the Confederacy in half.

15. On February 21 the enlisted men of the Eighth Vermont Vols. received seven dollars payment from the state of Vermont for their first month of service; a week later they received the rest of their monthly compensation from the U.S. government. Carpenter, *Eighth Regiment*, 22.

16. While sight-seeing in Lower Manhattan, Kinsley probably visited Battery and City Hall Parks as well as P. T. Barnum's captivating American Museum and Richard Upjohn's stirring Trinity Church.

17. Henry Ward Beecher (1813–1887), pastor of the Plymouth Congregational Church in Brooklyn, was an ardent Unionist and an eloquent champion of abolitionism. Harriet Beecher Stowe, author of the great antislavery novel *Uncle Tom's Cabin* (1852), was his sister.

18. Kinsley was not alone in his suffering. On this same date Private James F. Stoddard of Co. I, Seventh Vermont Vols., wrote to his wife that nearly everyone on board was seasick, and Ezra Harvey Brown, a corporal in Co. A, Eighth

Vermont Vols., wrote to his brother and sister from the deck of the *Wallace*. "If you ever wish to know what perfect misery is I advise you to go [on] a voyage at sea in a confounded old sailing ship, crowded in with about 600 others and be real sea sick. . . ." James F. Stoddard Letters, Manuscript Collection, VHS (cited hereinafter as Stoddard Letters); Civil War Letters of Ezra Harvey Brown, microfilm no. 188, VHS (cited hereinafter as Brown Letters).

19. Private Enos L. Davis, of Newfane, Vt., was only nineteen years old at the time of his death. His father, Private Hiram Davis, also of Newfane, was forty-four. Like Kinsley, twenty-three-year-old Ezra Brown was deeply moved by the death of this "Poor Boy." On March 19 he wrote to his brother and sister that it is "hard to die so far from home and still harder for his father (who is in the same Co) to loos [*sic*] his son within 2 weeks after leaving home to fight for his Country but we don't know who of us may be taken next." Four months after his son's death, Hiram Davis was discharged from the service. Carpenter, *Eighth Regiment*, 312; Brown Letters.

20. Born in Petersham, Mass., on May 19, 1827, George F. Gale was a prominent physician living in Brattleboro at the time of his commission as a surgeon in the Eighth Vermont Vols. on December 10, 1861. He resigned from the army on June 24, 1862, and returned to Brattleboro, where he died on April 14, 1907. George F. Gale Grave Registration; Souvenir Scrapbook, Eighth Vermont Regimental Association Papers, VHS (cited hereinafter as Souvenir Scrapbook), 160, 163; Carpenter, *Eighth Regiment*, 51–52, 286.

21. An imposing navigational landmark, Hole in the Wall is literally a massive hole in the wall of stone that juts out from the southern extremity of Great Abaco Island in the Bahamas.

22. Union forces had captured Ship Island off the coast of Mississippi on December 3, 1861. Strategically located fifty miles from Lake Pontchartrain and eighty miles from the mouth of the Mississippi River, the island served as a staging area for Butler's fifteen thousand troops as they prepared for the upcoming campaign against New Orleans.

23. The term "white oak chips" may have originated in the Eastern theater of the war where the white oak tree, known for the toughness of its wood, is plentiful. Soldiers often referred to their rocklike rations of dry bread and uncooked potatoes as "white oak chips" because they were as hard to chew as the bark of a white oak tree. I am indebted to Professor James I. Robertson, Jr., for this information.

24. Fort Massachusetts.

25. Virtually all the Union soldiers who wrote about Ship Island commented on the sand. Arriving at the island a day after Kinsley, Captain John W. De Forest of the Twelfth Connecticut Vols. called Ship Island "the sandiest region this side of the Great Sahara" and described the sand as "a dazzling white which glitters in the moonlight like snow, and by day dazzles and fatigues the eyes. . . ." De Forest concluded that a soldier's life on Ship Island "is a healthy, monotonous, stupid life, and makes one long to go somewhere, even at the risk of being shot." John William De Forest, *A Volunteer's Adventures: A Union Captain's Record of the Civil War*, ed. James H. Croushore (New Haven, Conn.: Yale University Press, 1946), 3, 7. Other Vermont soldiers described Ship Island as a "narrow bar of drifting

sand," a "dreary waste of sand," a "heap of white sand," and "the sandiest place I ever saw." C. S. Cooper, "Reminiscences," n.d., VHS; Donald H. Wickman, ed. and comp., *Letters to Vermont From Her Civil War Soldier Correspondents to the Home Press*, 2 vols. (Bennington, Vt.: Images From the Past, 1998), II, 12, 43. See also James F. Stoddard to his wife, April 25, 1862, Stoddard Letters.

26. Francis C. Williams was a thirty-seven-year-old resident of Brattleboro at the time of his commission as chaplain of the Eighth Vermont Vols. on December 20, 1861. He was discharged from the service on June 22, 1864. Carpenter, *Eighth Regiment*, 286.

27. Situated ninety miles south of New Orleans, Forts Jackson and St. Phillip guarded the mouth of the Mississippi. Recognizing the strategic importance of the river as the gateway to the entire Mississippi Valley and as a north–south highway for the rapid movement of troops and supplies, the Union high command on November 15, 1861, approved a joint army–navy operation to capture the Mississippi and its greatest port. Flag Officer David G. Farragut led the joint expedition, which began on April 18. After a week of bombarding Forts Jackson and St. Phillip, Farragut's force slipped past them early in the morning of April 24 and quickly destroyed the Confederate river fleet; on the next day Farragut captured New Orleans without firing a shot. See Chester G. Hearn, *The Capture of New Orleans, 1862* (Baton Rouge: Louisiana State University Press, 1995).

28. Private Henry W. Taylor, who at age thirty-nine was one of the oldest enlisted men in Co. F, apparently survived this incident. He died "of disease" on August 27, 1863. Carpenter, *Eighth Regiment*, 303.

29. Kinsley may be referring to the famous Confederate ram *Manassas*, which the Union warship *Mississippi* sank on April 24.

30. John De Forest, whose company sailed from Fort Jackson to New Orleans about a week earlier, used the same word, "paradise," to describe this part of southern Louisiana. He also noted that most whites seemed to have fled the plantations along the levee. The remaining blacks, he wrote to his wife on May 2, 1862, "gathered to stare at us, and when there were no whites near, they gave enthusiastic evidence of good will, dancing at us, waving hats or branches and shouting welcome. One old mauma, who spoke English and had perhaps once been 'sold down de ribber,' capered vigorously on the levee, screaming, 'Bress de Lawd! I knows dat ar flag. I knew it would come. Praise de Lawd!'" De Forest, *A Volunteer's Adventures*, 17.

31. So passes the glory of the chivalry. Kinsley and other antislavery zealots regularly and sarcastically referred to slaveholders as the "chivalry" of the South. The failure of Confederate forces to fire a shot in defense of New Orleans resulted in an official inquiry and charges of cowardice from Southerners as well as Northerners like Kinsley. Hearn, *Capture of New Orleans*, 260–65.

32. A commodious building located on Dryades Street between Canal and Commons, Mechanics' Institute was used as a barracks by numerous Federal units stationed in the city during the war. It later gained notoriety as the scene of the infamous New Orleans Riot of July 30, 1866.

33. Senator Charles Sumner of Massachusetts was one of the nation's most eloquent abolitionists.

34. These passages are, with minor discrepancies, transcriptions of sections 28 and 29 of an 1855 Louisiana statute entitled "An Act Relating to Slaves and Free Colored Persons." *Acts Passed by the Second Legislature of the State of Louisiana, at Its Second Session, Held and Begun in the Town of Baton Rouge, on the 15th January, 1855* (New Orleans: Emile La Sere, 1855), 381.

35. Laid out in the original plan of New Orleans in 1721 and known as the Place d'Armes by the French, Jackson Square was later renamed in honor of Andrew Jackson, hero of the Battle of New Orleans. The jail was located in the rear of the old Spanish Cabildo, which was completed in 1799 and served as the city hall for most of the antebellum era. The court house was located in the Presbytère, which was also begun under Spanish rule but not completed until 1813.

36. Facing Jackson Square and flanked by the Cabildo and the Presbytère, St. Louis Cathedral was the third church to occupy this site, the others having succumbed to hurricane and fire. The building Kinsley visited was built in 1794, but its facade was dramatically altered in 1851 when the structure was extensively remodeled by the famed architect J. N. B. De Poilly.

37. An arcaded structure that was designed in 1813, the French Market was just a few blocks from Jackson Square, where Kinsley was stationed.

38. A month later a person could not get even an ounce of bread, according to Clara Solomon, a young resident of the city. She wrote in her diary on July 1, 1862: "There is no bread to be had as there is no flour in the city. Truly the people have not the 'staff of life' to lean on." Elliott Ashkenazi, ed., *The Civil War Diary of Clara Solomon: Growing Up in New Orleans, 1861–1862* (Baton Rouge: Louisiana State University Press, 1995), 428.

39. "Yond Cassius has a lean and hungry look; / He thinks too much: such men are dangerous." *Julius Caesar*, act 1, scene 2, lines 194–95.

40. Two weeks before Kinsley made these observations, General Butler, commander of the Department of the Gulf, commented on the "deplorable state of destitution and hunger" in the city. He explained that Union forces had come to New Orleans to fight Rebel soldiers but instead found "only fugitive masses, runaway property-burners, a whisky-drinking mob, and starving citizens, with their wives and children. It is our duty to call back the first, to punish the second, root out the third, feed and protect the last." This last task proved exceedingly difficult, and four months later Butler warned the commander of the U.S. Army that "The condition of the people here is a very alarming one. They have literally come down to starvation. . . . I am distributing in various ways about $50,000 per month in food and more is needed." General Orders No. 25 and Butler to Major General Henry W. Halleck, September 1, 1862, *The War of the Rebellion: A Compilation of the Official Records of the Union and Confederate Armies*, 128 vols. (Washington, D.C.: Government Printing Office, 1880–1901), series 1 (cited hereinafter as *War of the Rebellion*; all references are to series 1 unless otherwise noted), XV, 425, 558.

41. Many Union soldiers, not just those serving police duty, felt vulnerable in New Orleans. For example, John L. Barstow, an adjutant in Kinsley's regiment,

informed his parents on May 18, 1862, that only Union officers traveling in pairs and "carr[y]ing revolvers and bowie knives" were allowed to go out into the city. He personally did "not go out after 8-o-clock – in the evening at all." Quoted in Jeffrey D. Marshall, ed., *A War of the People: Vermont Civil War Letters* (Hanover, N.H.: University Press of New England, 1999), 79.

42. Kinsley also preserved a printed handbill that recounted Mayor Waterman's decision in 1857 to grant the same (white) Coliseum Place Baptist Church permission "to hold Divine service for Colored persons" in four other churches. The purpose of these mayoral acts was to place black Baptists under the close supervision of white administrators. More generally, these acts were part of a trend to restrict the autonomy of free and enslaved African Americans in New Orleans in the years immediately preceding the outbreak of civil war. "African Baptist Churches – New Orleans," Rufus Kinsley Papers, VHS (cited hereinafter as Kinsley Papers); Robert C. Reinders, "The Decline of the New Orleans Free Negro in the Decades Before the Civil War," *Journal of Mississippi History*, 24 (April 1962), 88–98; H. E. Sterkx, *The Free Negro in Ante-Bellum Louisiana* (Rutherford, N.J.: Fairleigh Dickinson University Press, 1972), chap. 7.

43. Mechanics' Institute.

44. In 1860 nineteen-year-old Bonaparte J. Case was living on his father's farm in Fletcher. He enlisted in the army on December 16, 1861, and two months later was mustered into Co. F, Eighth Vermont Vols., as a sergeant. 1860 Manuscript Census, roll 1321, p. 8; Peck, *Revised Roster*, 321.

45. Jefferson Scott, who was born on April 25, 1802, was married to Kinsley's paternal aunt Nancy. His sister, Emily Scott, was married to Kinsley's paternal uncle Guy. His father, Lemuel Scott, was one of Fletcher's earliest settlers and for several years the town's representative to the Vermont State Legislature. The 1850 federal census listed Jefferson Scott as a farmer holding real estate valued at six hundred dollars and living with his wife Nancy, whom he had married on May 8, 1828, and with Kinsley's brother Jason in North Brookfield, Mass. Ballway, *A Genealogical Study*, 41; Jefferson Scott birth certificate of April 25, 1802, Jefferson Scott and Nancy Kinsley marriage certificate of May 8, 1828, Vital Records; Ben A. Kinsley, "Fletcher," in Abby M. Hemenway, ed., *The Vermont Historical Gazetteer: A Magazine, Embracing a History of Each Town, Civil, Ecclesiastical, Biographical and Military*, 5 vols. (Burlington, Vt.: A. M. Hemenway, 1868–91), II, 200–201; 1850 Manuscript Census, roll 343, p. 26.

46. William M. Clary and Stanislaus Roy were part of a network of thieves who, while posing as Union officials searching for Confederate arms, robbed private homeowners. Their scam was uncovered on June 12, Clary and Roy were tried on June 13, and they were hanged on June 16. Prior to this case, the iron rule of General Butler had been felt primarily by Confederates. The case of Clary and Roy, both of whom were Unionists, signaled that justice under Butler's regime would be impartial as well as severe. *War of the Rebellion*, XV, 477.

47. Stephen Thomas (1809–1903) served as a state legislator and judge in his native Vermont before being commissioned as a colonel in the Eighth Vermont Vols. on November 12, 1861. He was wounded on May 27, 1863, during an assault on Port Hudson, and he was awarded the Medal of Honor for bravery at the

Battle of Cedar Creek. In February 1865 he was appointed brigadier general of volunteers. After the war he returned home and was twice elected lieutenant governor of Vermont. Benedict, *Vermont in the Civil War*, II, 80–81; Ezra J. Warner, *Generals in Blue: Lives of the Union Commanders* (Baton Rouge: Louisiana State University Press, 1964), 503–04.

48. The three dead soldiers left behind for the Confederates to bury were Corporal Henry K. McClure, Corporal John W. Saunders, and Private Lowell M. Richardson. The body of Private Marshall W. Wellman was carried back to Algiers. Nine soldiers were wounded. Kinsley's account of this incident, while agreeing in particulars with the narratives offered by G. G. Benedict and George N. Carpenter in their histories of the Eighth Vermont, differs significantly in explaining the origins of the encounter. For Benedict and Carpenter, the ambush happened because Captain Henry F. Dutton of Co. H sent some soldiers to investigate a rumor that Rebel forces were tearing up train tracks. For Kinsley, thirteen soldiers and a civilian fireman were dead or wounded because Stephen Thomas, commander of the regiment, had sent his men on the immoral mission of returning runaway slaves to their masters. Benedict, *Vermont in the Civil War*, II, 93–95; Carpenter, *Eighth Regiment*, 50–51. John De Forest commented on the incident from his post just above New Orleans on June 29, 1862: "There was a little fight up the river a few days ago. A party of guerrillas ambuscaded a company of Vermonters, killed or wounded thirteen men, and scampered off. This is the only skirmish which has occurred within forty miles of here since New Orleans surrendered. I had no idea until lately what a Quakerly business war could be." *A Volunteer's Adventures*, 27–28.

49. Matthew 6:2, 5, 17. The verses Kinsley drew upon in Matthew are in keeping with his belief that the Union army was fighting for Liberty as well as Union and that, consequently, the ambushed soldiers, who were returning black fugitives to slavery, were "engaged in bad business." The verses suggest that God does not reward hypocrites whose piety consists of empty words and gestures designed for public consumption.

50. Deuteronomy 23:15. Verses 15 and 16 read: "You shall not give up to his master a slave who has escaped from his master to you; he shall dwell with you, in your midst, in the place which he shall choose within one of your towns, where it pleases him best; you shall not oppress him."

51. Private Edmund Saul was a forty-four-year-old resident of Barton, Vt., when he enlisted in the Eighth Vermont Vols. on December 6, 1861. Carpenter, *Eighth Regiment*, 303.

52. The oldest officer of the regular U.S. Army to join the Confederacy, Major General David Emanuel Twiggs (1790–1862) was also the highest-ranking general in the South when he moved to New Orleans and took command of the District of Louisiana. He died about a month after his estate was confiscated.

53. Twenty-three-year-old Private Goddard of St. Albans died "of disease" on June 26, 1862. Carpenter, *Eighth Regiment*, 303.

54. Probably A. B. Bacon of Algiers, who variously gave his occupation as editor and attorney. 1860 Manuscript Census, roll 415, p. 999; *Gardner and Wharton's New Orleans Directory for the Year 1858...* (New Orleans: E. C. Wharton's, [1858]),

28; *Gardner's New Orleans Directory for 1866...* (New Orleans: Charles Gardner, 1866), 68.

55. Founded by Alvin Adams in the 1840s, Adams Express was a successful company that competed with the U.S. postal service in delivering letters, packages, money orders, etc.

56. Probably Rev. H. T. Lee, who in 1866 listed his address as 228 Howard Street. *Gardner's New Orleans Directory for 1866*, 269.

57. A graduate of West Point, Brigadier General John W. Phelps (1813–1885) was a career army officer from 1836 until he resigned in 1859 and took up farming in Windham County, Vt. When the war broke out he rejoined the army and by the early summer of 1862 he was harboring fugitive slaves at Camp Parapet, just north of New Orleans. John W. De Forest wrote from Camp Parapet in the spring of 1862 that Phelps was "a fervid abolitionist," who "clutches with delight at every chance of humiliating slaveholders and Rebels" and who "hates the Rebels bitterly, not so much because they are rebellious as because they are slaveholders. . . ." To give his wife a sense of just how radical Phelps was, De Forest added that if the citizens of New Orleans ever felt disposed to grumble about Butler, "they have only to re-member the grim old abolitionist who commands our brigade, and their mouths are shut. General Phelps tells me that in his opinion New Orleans ought to be confiscated and brought to the hammer; also that we owe it to justice and human-ity to proclaim the immediate abolition of slavery throughout the South." 1860 Manuscript Census, roll 1325, p. 28; De Forest, *A Volunteer's Adventures*, 10, 22, 23, 32; William F. Messner, "General John Wolcott Phelps and Conservative Reform in Nineteenth Century America," *Vermont History*, 53 (Winter 1985), 17–35.

58. Brigadier General Thomas Williams (1815–1862) was shot in the chest while defending Baton Rouge against Confederate forces under the command of John C. Breckinridge. In a record he kept of Civil War battles, Kinsley commented on Williams's death: "killed – *no doubt by his own men.*" A graduate of West Point, Williams was a rigid disciplinarian who was known to drill troops in full dress when the temperature was 115 degrees. He exhibited little sympathy for the wartime deprivations suffered by his men, and they roundly hated him. Warner, *Generals in Blue*, 563–64; John D. Winters, *The Civil War in Louisiana* (Baton Rouge: Louisiana State University Press, 1963), 108–11; Table of Civil War Battles, Commanders, and Losses, Kinsley Papers.

59. An imposing Confederate ram, the *Arkansas* was 165 feet long, 35 feet wide, and wore armor of railroad iron that was 4 1/2 inches thick. At the battle for Baton Rouge on August 5, 1862, it developed engine trouble and was tied up to the bank. But neither the *Essex* nor the *Cayuga*, two Union gunboats, showed any interest in doing battle with the *Arkansas*; both were content to lob shells at the dreaded ram from more than a mile and a half away. The *Arkansas* was destroyed, not by the *Essex* or the *Cayuga*, but by its Confederate commander, who set the immobilized ram adrift and afire. It exploded while floating down the Mississippi. Winters, *Civil War*, 107, 120–21.

60. On August 14, 1862, Butler informed Secretary of War Edwin M. Stanton that "I have determined to use the services of free colored men who were

organized by the rebels into the Colored Brigade, of which we have heard so much. They are free; they have been used by our enemies, whose mouths are shut, and they will be loyal." Eight days later, he issued General Orders No. 63, which stated that "all the members of the Native Guards aforesaid and all other free colored citizens recognized by the first and late Governor and authorities of the State of Louisiana as a portion of the militia of the State who shall enlist in the volunteer service of the United States shall be duly organized by the appointment of proper officers, and accepted, paid, equipped, armed, and rationed as are other volunteer troops of the United States. . . ." It should be noted that Butler did not authorize the enlistment of fugitive slaves who would constitute an army of liberation, as Phelps requested, and he justified his action in the most pragmatic terms: he needed more soldiers. Although limited, Butler's action paved the way for him to become the first Union general successfully to organize a black regiment and to gain everlasting fame as a pioneer in the campaign to enlist African Americans in the war against slavery. *War of the Rebellion*, XV, 548–49, 556–57.

61. Probably J. W. Munday, deputy sheriff of Algiers. *Gardner's New Orleans Directory for 1867*. . . (New Orleans: Charles Gardner, 1867), 292.

62. Originally from New York, N. Maria Taylor, a teacher, and her husband Dr. John T. Taylor had lived in New Orleans since about 1850. In the 1850s the Taylors resided on Lafayette Street near the corner of Second in Gretna. Mrs. Taylor, under the pseudonym "Nellie," wrote satirical sketches for the *New Orleans Daily Delta* prior to the outbreak of civil war. U.S. House of Representatives, 39th Cong., 2nd sess., Report No. 16, *Report of the Select Committee on the New Orleans Riots* (Washington, D.C.: Government Printing Office, 1867), 392–93, 428; *Cohen's New Orleans Directory . . . for 1854* . . . (New Orleans: Office of the *Picayune*, 1854), 231; *Gardner and Wharton's New Orleans Directory for 1858*, 300; James Parton, *General Butler in New Orleans: History of the Administration of the Department of the Gulf in the Year 1862* . . . (New York: Mason Brothers, 1864), 435.

63. Kinsley's shocking descriptions of the brutal physical and sexual abuse of slaves in southern Louisiana are paralleled in accounts left by other federal officials. Special Commissioner James McKaye, after a fact-finding tour of the Lower Mississippi region, reported to Secretary of War Edwin M. Stanton in 1864 that to prevent slaves from hiding in Louisiana's impenetrable swamps masters often adopted "very inhuman measures . . . such as branding with a hot iron, splitting or cropping the ears, and compelling the suspected to wear the heavy iron collar with horns, called 'a choker.'" Colonel George H. Hanks, who served as superintendent of contrabands in the Department of the Gulf, testified that after the capture of New Orleans runaway slaves came into Union lines "scarred, wounded, and some with iron collars round [t]heir necks." And General Phelps reported that after he set up camp just outside of New Orleans in 1862 "Fugitives began to throng to our lines in large numbers. Some came loaded with chains and barbarous irons; some bleeding with birdshot wounds; many had been deeply scored with lashes, and all complained of the extinction of their moral rights." James McKaye, *The Mastership and Its Fruits: The Emancipated Slave Face to Face with His Old Master* (New York: Loyal Publication Society, 1864), 12, 17; Phelps is quoted in Parton, *General Butler*, 495–96.

64. According to the report of Colonel Stephen Thomas, the force consisted of Co. A and Co. C of the Eighth Vermont Vols. and Co. B of the Second Regiment, Massachusetts Cavalry. *War of the Rebellion*, XV, 132.

65. Richard Taylor (1826–1879), son of former president Zachary Taylor, brother-in-law of the Confederate president Jefferson Davis, graduate of Yale University, and member of the Louisiana State Legislature, had since 1851 owned a sugar plantation about seven miles outside Boutte in St. Charles Parish. A colonel in the Ninth Louisiana Infantry at the outbreak of the war, Taylor was promoted to major general on July 28, 1862, and assumed command of the District of Western Louisiana on August 20. He would later write a perceptive Civil War memoir entitled *Destruction and Reconstruction* (1879).

66. Named after John G. Pratt, a brigadier general in the Louisiana State Militia, Camp Pratt was an instructional camp located on Lake Tasse, roughly six miles northwest of New Iberia. *War of the Rebellion*, XV, 919.

67. Private Osman F. Bellows was thirty-one when he enlisted in November 1861. After his discharge from the service in June 1864, Bellows returned to Fairfax, where he is buried. Carpenter, *Eighth Regiment*, 302; O. F. Bellows Grave Registration.

68. Caring for fugitive slaves would indeed prove an "arduous undertaking." On this same date General Butler wrote to the commander of the U.S. Army that he was issuing fugitive slaves twice as many rations as he was issuing Union soldiers. The fugitives, he complained, "are now coming in by hundreds, nay thousands, almost daily.... We have with us a great number of negro women and children, barefoot and half naked. May I ask in what way, in view of the coming winter, these [people] are to be clothed?" *War of the Rebellion*, XV, 558.

69. Lewis J. Ingalls (1837–1913) was a resident of Belvidere, Vt., when he enlisted on November 2, 1861. Although he was wounded again on September 19, 1864, at the Battle of Opequon, Ingalls remained in the Eighth Vermont Vols. until June 28, 1865, when the regiment was ordered home and mustered out of service. For his heroism during the Boutte Station ambush Ingalls received the Congressional Medal of Honor. Lewis J. Ingalls Grave Registration; Peck, *Revised Roster*, 335; Lewis J. Ingalls Pension; Office of the Adjutant General of the Army, *American Decorations: A List of Awards of the Congressional Medal of Honor, the Distinguished-Service Cross, and the Distinguished-Service Medal Awarded under Authority of the Congress of the United States, 1862–1926* (Washington, D.C.: U.S. Government Printing Office, 1927), 53.

70. Kinsley is referring to Private Sanford Dewey of Co. F, who died on September 12 of the wounds he received on September 4. In a February 25, 1884, affidavit supporting a pension increase for Lewis Ingalls, Kinsley stated that after the ambush "I assisted in taking the dead and wounded to the Regimental Hospital, where Surgeon Gillett dressed the wound of Ingalls, with the others." Peck, *Revised Roster*, 322; Lewis J. Ingalls Pension. This bloody ambush definitely got the attention of the men of the Eighth Vermont. Corporal Ezra Brown in a letter to his parents on September 5, 1862, offered a detailed account of the attack, which he labeled "cold blooded murder," and Colonel Stephen Thomas, in an official

report, accused the bushwhackers of "robbing our dead, wounded, and prisoners, and committing numberless atrocious acts on them...." Brown Letters; *War of the Rebellion*, XV, 134.

71. Captain Ormand F. Nims was in command of the Second Battery, Massachusetts Light Artillery. He was discharged from the service on January 7, 1865. *Official Army Register of the Volunteer Force of the United States Army for the Years 1861, '62, '63, '64, '65*, 8 vols. (Washington, D.C.: Adjutant General's Office, 1865–67) (cited hereinafter as *OAR*), I, 140.

72. Colonel Stephen Thomas, commander of the Eighth Vermont Vols., reported that the two days of skirmishing on September 4 and 5 resulted in 9 killed, 27 wounded, and 155 missing. The Union prisoners were marched to Camp Pratt, a hundred miles away, then sent to Vicksburg, and finally paroled to Ship Island, where they waited until February 1863 to be exchanged for Confederate prisoners of war. *War of the Rebellion*, XV, 133–37; Benedict, *Vermont in the Civil War*, II, 102–04.

73. Euchre was a popular nineteenth-century card game.

74. Taylor, whose own plantation had recently been ransacked by members of the Eighth Vermont Vols., warned Butler that he would retaliate against marauding troops "as robbers rather than as soldiers." In a sarcastic (and suggestive) passage describing the pillaging bluecoats, Taylor writes: "Books, pictures, household furniture, finger rings, ear rings, breastpins and other articles of feminine adornment and wear, attest [to] the catholic taste and temper of these patriots." Butler responded on September 10 by informing Taylor that "The [Union] troops at Bayou Des Allemands were an advance post, guarding a railroad bridge, and not an expedition at all, nor were they allowed to go on any expedition...." Then, taking the offensive, Butler moved to put the slave-owning Yale graduate in his place. He stated that the actions of Taylor's soldiers were more reminiscent "of Indian than of civilized warfare," and in a particularly biting passage he declared that the tactics of Taylor's officers reminded him of those employed by the Haitian slave Toussaint L'Ouverture and "seem therefore to be not even original." Butler concluded by warning Taylor "That I will take care of, protect, and avenge the wrongs and lives of my fellow-soldiers...." Butler's response put an end to Taylor's threats, and most of the captured soldiers were later exchanged for Confederate prisoners. Richard Taylor, *Destruction and Reconstruction: Personal Experiences of the Late War* (1879; Waltham, Mass.: Blaisdell Publishing Company, 1968), 107; *War of the Rebellion*, XV, 565–67.

75. Guy Kinsley, who was born in Fletcher on May 8, 1800, was Kinsley's paternal uncle. Married to Emily Scott, he was listed in the 1850 federal census as owning personal property valued at $3,500; in 1870 his reported wealth stood at $7,150. He died on August 29, 1886, in Fletcher. Guy Kinsley birth and death certificates, Vital Records; 1850 Manuscript Census, roll 924, p. 2; Manuscript Census Returns, Ninth Census of the United States, 1870, microcopy 593 (cited hereinafter as 1870 Manuscript Census), roll 1620, p. 21.

76. Born in Fletcher on February 14, 1827, Lucretia Kinsley was Kinsley's only sister. At the writing of this letter, she resided in Worcester, Mass., which was also

home to her brother Daniel; later in the war she moved to Iowa to live with her brother Guy. After the war she returned to Worcester, where she lived with her brother Daniel and his family until her death in 1912. Ballway, *A Genealogical Study*, 41; Manuscript Census Returns, Twelfth Census of the United States, 1900, microcopy T623, roll 695, p. 7A.

77. Kinsley's sister probably had inquired about Private Fred Greenwood, a resident of Middlesex, Vt., who was killed at the skirmish on Bayou Des Allemands on September 4. Carpenter, *Eighth Regiment*, 299.

78. Born on June 13, 1829, Daniel Kinsley was one of the two Kinsley brothers who did not serve in the Civil War. About 1846 he migrated to Worcester County, Mass., where in 1853 he became messenger of the county courts, a position he held for the next fifty years. He died in Worcester, Mass., on April 1, 1923. Ballway, *A Genealogical Study*, 42; Ellery Bicknell Crane, ed., *Historic Homes and Institutions and Genealogical and Personal Memoirs of Worcester County, Massachusetts, With a History of Worcester Society of Antiquity*, 4 vols. (New York: Lewis Publishing Company, 1907), I, 250.

79. The enemy had not sabotaged Kinsley's train; the conductor had hit a cow crossing the tracks. Benedict, *Vermont in the Civil War*, II, 103.

80. Kinsley is referring to Lincoln's preliminary Emancipation Proclamation, which was dated September 22, 1862, and promised to free slaves in Confederate territory still in rebellion on January 1, 1863. Despite Kinsley's enthusiasm, Lincoln's proclamation did not free the thousands of slaves Kinsley saw every day in and around the Union-occupied city of New Orleans. He was correct, however, in assuming that Lincoln's proclamation spelled the doom of slavery.

81. It was the urgent demand for reliable labor to harvest Louisiana's sugar crop during the months of October and November that turned Kinsley's scholars into workers. The harvest season for sugarcane in Louisiana begins in late October and runs into December. Consequently, if the fall 1862 crop was not harvested immediately, it would be ruined, and neither Butler nor his superiors in Washington, D.C., wanted that to happen. Encouraged to put the fugitives swelling his contraband camps to work, Butler in late October worked out a wage agreement with sugar planters in St. Bernard and Plaquemines Parishes. In early November he advised one of his generals whose camp was overrun with fugitives to "Put them as far as possible upon plantations; use every energy to have the sugar crop made and preserved for the owners that are loyal, and for the United States where the owners are disloyal." *War of the Rebellion*, XV, 162; William F. Messner, *Freedmen and the Ideology of Free Labor: Louisiana, 1862–1865* (Lafayette: University of Southwestern Louisiana, 1978), 32–38.

82. A resident of Fletcher, Emeline Marks was a close friend of the Kinsleys. In 1854 she attended Ben Alva Kinsley's marriage to Lucy Blair. She was also treasurer of the Ladies Green Mountain Soldiers Aid Society that was founded in Fletcher during the war. Emeline Marks affidavit, November 26, 1878, Ben A. Kinsley Pension; Ben A. Kinsley to Lucretia Kinsley, February 14, 1864 (letter in possession of Reba Kinsley Hall).

83. An assistant professor of engineering at West Point prior to the Civil War, Godfrey Weitzel (1835–1884) was chief engineer of Butler's expedition against New Orleans in the spring of 1862. During the occupation he served briefly as the city's mayor, and on August 29, 1862, he was promoted to brigadier general of volunteers. His brigade, which consisted of five regiments of infantry, two batteries of artillery, and four companies of cavalry, was ordered by General Butler to advance "through Western Louisiana, for the purpose of dispersing the forces assembled there under General Richard Taylor." Warner, *Generals in Blue*, 548–49; *War of the Rebellion*, XV, 159.

84. Issued on October 17, 1862, Butler's General Orders No. 82 did not exempt tenants of disloyal landlords from paying rent. Instead, it changed the beneficiary of such payments by declaring that "All rents due or to become due by tenants of property belonging to persons not known to be loyal citizens of the United States will be paid as they become due to D.C.G. Field, esq., financial clerk of the department [of the Gulf]." *War of the Rebellion*, XV, 581.

85. On October 24, 1862, General Butler explained to Major General Henry W. Halleck, commander in chief of the U.S. Army, that "At the same time [Weitzel's brigade moves down Bayou Lafourche] I push forward a column from Algiers, consisting of the Eighth Regiment Vermont Volunteers and the First Regiment of Native Guards (colored), along the Opelousas Railroad to Thibodeaux [*sic*] and Brashear City, open the railway for the purpose of forwarding supplies to General Weitzel's expedition, and to give the loyal planters an opportunity to forward their sugar and cotton to this city." Butler had organized the First Regiment, Louisiana Native Guards, on September 27, 1862. Its designation was changed to First Regiment Infantry, Corps d'Afrique, on June 6, 1863, and to Seventy-third Regiment, United States Colored Infantry (USCI), on April 4, 1864. This expedition, under the command of Colonel Thomas of the Eighth Vermont Vols., thus witnessed the first actual service by an armed black regiment during the Civil War. *War of the Rebellion*, XV, 159; *OAR*, VIII, 246. On the Louisiana Native Guards, see James G. Hollandsworth, Jr., *The Louisiana Native Guards: The Black Military Experience During the Civil War* (Baton Rouge: Louisiana State University Press, 1995).

86. Stephen O. Tillotson of Bakersfield, Vt., was twenty-seven when he enlisted on January 6, 1862. Mustered into Co. F with Kinsley on February 18, 1862, he was discharged from the service exactly eight months later on October 18, 1862. Tillotson died in Bakersfield on December 22, 1899. Peck, *Revised Roster*, 322; Carpenter, *Eighth Regiment*, 302; Stephen O. Tillotson death certificate, Vital Records.

87. The strict enforcement of quarantine and sanitary measures by General Butler (and by his successor Major General Nathaniel P. Banks) contributed to making New Orleans a surprisingly healthy city during the Civil War. This was no small accomplishment in a city where four epidemics in the 1850s had claimed the lives of over eighteen thousand residents. See Jo Ann Carrigan, "Yankees Versus Yellow Jack in New Orleans, 1862–1866," *Civil War History*, 9 (September 1963), 248–60.

88. Probably the druggist George W. Irwin of Algiers, *Gardner's New Orleans Directory for 1866*, 230.

89. Weitzel's brigade encountered Confederate forces under the command of General Alfred Mouton, a West Point graduate, on October 27 at Georgia Landing, about two miles above Labadieville. The engagement was brief as the Confederates – outnumbered roughly 2 to 1 – quickly fled. Weitzel reported that Union casualties were 18 killed, 74 wounded, and 5 captured or missing. He reported Confederate losses at 5 killed, 17 wounded, and 208 captured but was confident that the number killed and wounded was actually higher. Among those killed was Colonel G. P. McPheeters, commander of the Crescent Regiment, who, according to General Mouton, "fell gallantly and nobly defending our sacred cause at the head of his command." Mouton's forces retreated to Berwick Bay, and then escaped across the bay on October 30 when four Yankee gunboats suddenly appeared. *War of the Rebellion*, XV, 167–80; Barnes F. Lathrop, "The Lafourche District in 1862: Invasion," *Louisiana History*, 2 (Spring 1961), 175–86. De Forest, who fought at Georgia Landing, offers a vivid account of this important battle, which he says lasted only eighty minutes, in *A Volunteer's Adventures*, chap. 4.

90. Confederate troops abandoned Des Allemands because General Mouton had ordered them to Labadieville to assist in the battle against Weitzel's brigade. He also commanded them to burn the Des Allemands Bridge and anything else they could not carry with them. He did not, however, tell them it was undignified to fight black soldiers. General Weitzel was the one worrying about black soldiers, for just a week after reporting the details of his glorious rout of Mouton's forces, he was refusing Butler's offer to become commander of the District of the Teche "because accepting the command would place me in command of all the troops in the district." Such broad authority did not appeal to Weitzel because "I cannot command those negro regiments [the First and Second Regiments, Louisiana Native Guards, that Butler had raised from the free black population of New Orleans]. The commanding general knows well my private opinions on this subject.... I cannot assume the command of such a force, and thus be responsible for its conduct. I have no confidence in the organization." Weitzel especially feared that black troops would incite the slaves to insurrection. Butler's assistant adjutant general reassured Weitzel that if the slaves revolted, "You are in no degree responsible for it. The responsibility rests upon those who have begun and carried on this war, who have stopped at no barbarity, no act of outrage, upon the citizens and troops of the United States." Butler himself sympathized with Weitzel "in the matter of negroes," but he reminded his young general that, realistically, if the thousands of slaves being freed in the wake of his march through the Lafourche district "pillage of course we cannot help it. It is one of the necessary evils following this system of labor and the rebellion as far as I can see." *War of the Rebellion*, XV, 177, 171, 165, 587.

91. Among those captured by Confederate forces at Des Allemands on September 4 were seven German privates from Co. E. They had enlisted in the Eighth Vermont Vols. in the summer of 1862. Former residents of Lafourche Parish, where they had served in the local militia, they were court-martialed by

their Confederate captors, found guilty of desertion and spying, and executed on October 23. They reportedly had to dig their own graves before they were shot. Ibid., 165; Peck, *Revised Roster*, 318–20; Benedict, *Vermont in the Civil War*, II, 104–06; Barnes F. Lathrop, "The Lafourche District in 1862: Confederate Revival," *Louisiana History*, 1 (Fall 1960), 313–15.

92. On this same day General Butler wrote to the commander in chief of the U.S. Army: "I cannot too much commend the energy of Colonel Thomas, with his regiment, the Eighth Vermont, who have in six days opened 52 miles of railroad, built nine culverts, rebuilt a bridge (burned by the enemy) 435 feet long, besides pulling up the rank grass from the track, which entirely impeded the locomotive all the way." *War of the Rebellion*, XV, 161.

93. The *A. B. Seger*, under the command of Acting Master I. C. Coons, was a small Confederate steamer. When confronted by four Union gunboats on November 1, 1862, Coons panicked. According to his commanding officer, he ignored orders to withdraw from the bay, "ignobly abandoned" his ship to the enemy, and fled. Six days later, no one knew where he was. Ibid., 184, 186; *Official Records of the Union and Confederate Navies in the War of the Rebellion*, 30 vols. (Washington, D.C.: Government Printing Office, 1894–1922), series 1, XIX, 327, 332 (cited hereinafter as *ORN*; all references are to series 1).

94. According to Benedict, *Vermont in the Civil War*, II, 102–03, at the time the prisoners were paroled to Ship Island, four of them were detained, four had died under horrible conditions at the Vicksburg prison, and the seven Germans discussed earlier had been shot.

95. Benedict, in his history of Vermont Civil War soldiers, states that the explosion killed Luther Peabody of Co. D and "severely injured" Carter H. Nason of Co. F. Ibid., 109.

96. Like Kinsley, General Butler was also distressed that Captain Edward Hall and his men had surrendered at Des Allemands without firing a shot. He declared in his official report on the incident that he could not "approve of the conduct of the picket in not holding out and making a contest, as they would have been immediately supported." *War of the Rebellion*, XV, 133.

97. Issac Blake was a fifty-eight-year-old preacher living in Derby, Vt., when he enlisted as a musician in Co. B of the Eighth Vermont Vols. on November 26, 1861. Affectionately known as "Father Blake," he served as chaplain of the Third Regiment, Louisiana Native Guards, for eight months before resigning in June 1863 because of poor health. After the war, he was one of the speakers at the inaugural meeting of the Eighth Vermont Regiment Association on October 19, 1871. Peck, *Revised Roster*, 309, 717; Carpenter, *Eighth Regiment*, 289; Benedict, *Vermont in the Civil War*, II, 137n; Souvenir Scrapbook, 1.

98. The western terminus of the New Orleans, Opelousas, and Great Western Railroad, Brashear City (now known as Morgan City) was strategically located at the head of Berwick Bay. Although it possessed "a respectable harbor," Brashear City, according to De Forest, was a "straggling, unprosperous, mouldy village" and "one of the sickliest spots in Louisiana." On another occasion De Forest wrote: "We have escaped Algiers by getting sent back to Brashear City, which

is something like being delivered out of purgatory into hades. The mosquitoes and other insects, including alligators, still form the largest part of the native population, if not the worthiest." *A Volunteer's Adventures*, 78, 79, 148, 154–55.

99. A twenty-one-year-old resident of Bakersfield at the time of his enlistment in Co. F of the Eighth Vermont Vols. on December 28, 1861, Private George Clemens was discharged and transferred to Barrett's Louisiana Cavalry on February 28, 1863. Peck, *Revised Roster*, 322; Carpenter, *Eighth Regiment*, 303.

100. A resident of Alburgh and eighteen years old when he enlisted on December 2, 1861, William A. Decker was a private in Co. F, Eighth Vermont Vols. He reached the rank of corporal before being mustered out on June 28, 1865. Decker, who would later testify in support of Kinsley's pension claims, is buried at Hope Cemetery in Georgia, Vt. Carpenter, *Eighth Regiment*, 303; Peck, *Revised Roster*, 322; William A. Decker deposition, January 29, 1892, Rufus Kinsley Pension; William A. Decker Grave Registration.

101. At the time of his enlistment on January 20, 1862, Henry Graves was a twenty-seven-year-old resident of New Orleans. He was listed as a deserter and discharged from the service on December 21, 1862. Carpenter, *Eighth Regiment*, 290.

102. Nathaniel P. Banks (1816–1894) arrived in New Orleans with twenty thousand troops on December 14 and officially relieved Butler of command of the Department of the Gulf on the 16th. A consummate politician, Banks served ten terms in Congress under five different party affiliations and in 1856 was elected Speaker of the U.S. House of Representatives after 133 ballots. He was governor of Massachusetts when Lincoln appointed him major general of volunteers in early 1861. At the time of his appointment, he had had little formal education and no experience as a field commander. Prior to replacing Butler, he had been beaten soundly in two battles with Stonewall Jackson. In the Department of the Gulf he was responsible for costly, and some thought useless, assaults on Port Hudson and for the disastrous Red River campaign of 1864. Shortly after his arrival in New Orleans, he drew the ire of antislavery leaders who found his new "free labor" plantations all too reminiscent of old slave labor plantations. Warner, *Generals in Blue*, 17–18; Peyton McCrary, *Abraham Lincoln and Reconstruction: The Louisiana Experiment* (Princeton, N.J.: Princeton University Press, 1978), chaps. 3–4; Messner, *Freedmen*, chaps. 4–6.

103. Just outside of Carrollton, which was about eight miles above New Orleans on the Mississippi, Camp Parapet had been a Confederate encampment until Farragut captured the city. Boasting a massive earthwork that was twelve feet high and stretched from the river's levee on the west to a cypress swamp on the east, Camp Parapet had been home to thousands of fugitive slaves when Phelps had his headquarters there.

104. The four Union gunboats, under the command of Lieutenant Thomas McKean Buchanan, were the *Calhoun*, *Estrella*, *Diana*, and *Colonel Kinsman* (also known as the *Grey Cloud*). They had been sent via the Gulf to Berwick Bay as part of Butler's campaign to capture General Mouton's army and cut off from the Confederacy valuable supplies of salt, sugar, beef, pork, vegetables, and cotton coming from Texas and from the bountiful bayou country of southwestern

Louisiana. The Confederate gunboat was the *J. A. Cotton*, under the command of Captain E. W. Fuller. Originally a river steamer owned by an Attakapas planter, the *Cotton* had been transformed into a formidable ironclad.

105. Banks's Proclamation, dated December 16, 1862, stated: "My instructions require me to treat as enemies those who are enemies, but I shall gladly regard as friends those who are friends. No restrictions will be placed upon the freedom of individuals which are not imperatively demanded by considerations of public safety, but while their claims will be liberally considered it is due also to them to state that all the rights of the Government will be unflinchingly maintained." Then, in a remarkable example of environmental determinism, Banks warned Confederate sympathizers that they were engaged in a futile struggle against "the imperious necessities of geographical configuration and commercial supremacy." He advised them to "reflect upon the immutable conditions which surround them. The valley of the Mississippi is the chosen seat of population, product, and power on this continent. In a few years 25,000,000 people, unsurpassed in material resources and capacity for war, will swarm upon its fertile rivers. Those who assume to set conditions on their exodus to the Gulf count upon a power not given to man. The country washed by the waters of the Ohio, the Missouri, and the Mississippi can never be permanently severed." *War of the Rebellion*, XV, 624–25.

106. The allusion is to Samson, judge of Israel, who, though blinded by his Philistine captors, pulled down their temple, killing both himself and his oppressors in the process. Judges 13–16.

107. Kinsley was anxiously awaiting word that Lincoln had in fact announced his final proclamation of emancipation on January 1, 1863. His anxiety was no doubt spurred by widespread rumors that the president might revise or revoke his preliminary proclamation of September 22, 1862. Certainly Kinsley was also worried about whether the final proclamation would apply to the occupied portions of Louisiana. His anxiety on this score may have been heightened by Banks's public address on December 24, 1862, "To the People of Louisiana," in which he (correctly) predicted that Lincoln would exempt occupied Louisiana from his final proclamation. *War of the Rebellion*, XV, 619–23; McCrary, *Abraham Lincoln*, 112–14.

108. Hosea 4:9.

109. The Greek god of the north wind.

110. Torpedo.

111. This battle actually took place on Bayou Teche, which flows into the Atchafalaya River, which in turn flows into Berwick Bay. Kinsley's account closely follows the official report of commanding general Weitzel, although the latter makes no mention of fighting on the 13th. Weitzel praises the Eighth Vermont, which in its "first time in action as a regiment, reflected the highest credit upon itself by the splendid manner in which they cleared the enemy's rifle pits on the east bank and afterward pursued them." He adds that while the entire brigade took only about 50 prisoners, the Eighth Vermont alone killed 4, wounded 3, and captured 41 enemy soldiers. His losses for the brigade as a whole were 6 killed and 27 wounded. With the battle won, Weitzel telegraphed Banks: "We have

accomplished the object of our expedition. The Confederate States gunboat Cotton is one of the things that were." *War of the Rebellion*, XV, 234-37.

112. On October 28, 1862, after routing Mouton's troops, Weitzel established this camp on Burton's plantation, about a mile below Thibodaux. A few days later he declared the country around it "as safe to travel now as Canal street." Ibid., 169, 171.

113. Two months earlier De Forest offered a similar description of conditions around Thibodaux, but he took less pleasure in the situation than Kinsley: "It is woful to see how this lately prosperous region is being laid waste. Negroes and runaway soldiers roam everywhere, foraging for provisions, breaking into and plundering the deserted houses, and destroying furniture, books and pictures in mere wantonness.... It is necessary to do something to put down the multifarious anarchy which we and the rebellion have brought upon this region." Another New England soldier, James K. Hosmer, a Harvard graduate and member of the Fifty-second Massachusetts Vols. was also overwhelmed by Thibodaux's lush natural beauty, commenting that "To go from Baton Rouge to Thibodeaux [*sic*] is like changing from the outer petals to the heart of a full-blown rose." But like Kinsley, Hosmer also saw signs of the "curse" at Thibodaux. Specifically, he noted a "hybrid population" with "throngs on throngs of mixed blood, – from deep mulattoes, up through quadroon and octoroon, to fair boys and girls with complexion just made rich and vivid with a dash of the tiger-lily. Not a pleasant or creditable story it is, – this tale of corruptness which we can read in the faces of the population...." De Forest, *A Volunteer's Adventures*, 73-75; Hosmer, *The Color-Guard: Being a Corporal's Notes of Military Service in the Nineteenth Army Corps* (Boston: Walker, Wise, & Company, 1864), 118-19.

114. The son of former governor Paul Dillingham, Charles Dillingham was originally a captain in the Second Vermont Vols., and with that regiment he participated in the first Battle of Bull Run. He was only twenty-five years old at the time of his promotion to major in the Eighth Vermont Vols. in January 1862. Following his promotion to lieutenant colonel, he commanded the Eighth during the long siege of Port Hudson. Dillingham resigned from the service on December 12, 1863, but remained active in the regiment's postwar activities. Peck, *Revised Roster*, 304; Carpenter, *Eighth Regiment*, 138-40, 286; Souvenir Scrapbook, 105.

115. Luman M. Grout (1823-1913) of Elmore, who had previously fought in the Mexican War, was commissioned as a captain in Co. A of the Eighth Vermont Vols. on November 13, 1861. Promoted to major shortly after being commended by Colonel Thomas for his "very efficient aid" during the battle of the *Cotton*, Grout resigned from the service on June 11, 1863. Following the war he joined in the activities of the Eighth Vermont Regiment Association. Souvenir Scrapbook, 116, 130, 170; Luman M. Grout Grave Registration; *War of the Rebellion*, XV, 236; Peck, *Revised Roster*, 304.

116. Campbell was discharged from the hospital, not the army.

117. Fanny Amelia Kinsley died on January 17, 1863. Crane, *Historic Homes*, I, 250.

118. A blue-spotted crimson fish found in the coastal waters of the North Atlantic.

119. Upon returning to Brashear City, De Forest also praised the new campsite: "Our campground is the finest that we have had in Louisiana. It is an old canefield seamed and humped with furrows and hillocks; but there is green grass on it, which is a delightful sight to Northern eyes; and, wonderful to relate, it is fairly dry. . . . At Thibodeaux [*sic*] the bayou was six feet higher than the adjoining land, the levees were aleak in many places, the roads were quagmires." Kinsley, De Forest, and other New Englanders gradually came to understand that water, not land, dominated the geography of southern Louisiana. One of them explained from the southwestern edge of the Lafourche district: "As Northerners know nature . . . it is land that is most exulting, bounding, as it does, into hills, standing kingly in mountains; while water, more humble, hides in glens, or flows in submissive rivers before the feet of lordly ranges. Here, however, water bears itself arrogantly, – floating sometimes above the level of the soil; sometimes just even with it, as here, where the ripples of the brimful stream threaten the clover-flowers, which are scarcely above them. . . . Water is thus haughty and encroaching; while land is a poor, cowed, second-fiddle-playing creature, – only existing, apparently, that water may have something to pour itself out over and exhibit itself upon." De Forest, *A Volunteer's Adventures*, 79; Hosmer, *The Color-Guard*, 121–22.

120. Kinsley is probably referring to the gunboat *Hart*.

121. Originally a Confederate transport, the *Grey Cloud* was captured by federal forces in the spring of 1862 and subsequently put into service as the Union gunboat *Colonel Kinsman*. Banks wrote to Major General George W. Halleck on February 28, 1863, that "the embarrassing loss" of the *Colonel Kinsman* was "equal in effect to the destruction of two battalions." *ORN*, XIX, 624–26; *War of the Rebellion*, XV, 1105–06.

122. Invented by West Point graduate Robert Parker Parrott, Parrott cannons were typically rifled, muzzle-loading, and cast iron. In addition to being used on ships, Parrott guns experienced widespread use as field and siege artillery. Heavy ordinance Parrotts, as Kinsley suggests later in his discussion of the battle for Mobile Bay, were particularly effective in knocking down masonry fortifications. Warren Ripley, *Artillery and Ammunition of the Civil War* (New York: Van Nostrand Reinhold Company, 1970), chap. 6.

123. This costly skirmish occurred because Captain Thomas Peterson disobeyed orders and took his crew joyriding up the Teche. Confederate casualties were 40 killed and wounded, while Union casualties stood at 33 killed and wounded, and 120 men and officers captured. A young diarist aboard the *Diana* described the battle: "Dead and dying strewed the decks. A plunging shot, penetrated double casemating, crashed through the pilot house and Enfield bullets perforated the iron sheathing. A fireman had one leg cut smoothly off; a boatswain's mate received a shot which tore the bones of both his legs completely out. McNally, one of the engineers, was killed by a fragment which came crushing through the engine-room from a shell which had exploded in the wheelhouse.

These strange freaks of violence were noted amid clouds of scalding steam that filled the space below, to which all living men were fleeing for shelter." The *Diana* was subsequently repaired and added to the Confederate fleet of gunboats on the Teche. *ORN*, XX, 109–12; A. J. H. Duganne, *Camps and Prisons: Twenty Months in the Department of the Gulf*, 2nd ed. (New York: J. P. Robens, 1865), 200–201; Winters, *Civil War*, 222.

124. As part of the Union strategy to open the Mississippi and cut the Confederacy in half, Banks had as his goal the capture of Port Hudson, while Ulysses S. Grant had his sights set on Vicksburg, the other remaining Confederate stronghold on the Mississippi. But before Banks could move northward up the Mississippi, he had to clear the troublesome Confederate forces out of the Teche country or New Orleans would remain vulnerable to an attack from the west. Unlike Weitzel's dash up the Teche in January 1863, which had the limited goal of destroying the *Cotton*, this was a major operation, and Banks brought in two divisions from Baton Rouge under the command of General Cuvier Grover and General William Emory. Their departure left forty-five hundred infantry, including three regiments of black troops, under the command of General Christopher Augur, to guard Baton Rouge. Hoping to capture Richard Taylor's entire army in the vicinity of Camp Bisland, Banks ordered Grover's division up Grand Lake to Franklin, just above Bisland, to cut off Taylor's line of retreat. Weitzel's brigade and Emory's division were sent up the Teche from Brashear City to engage Taylor's forces from the front, while Grover enveloped from the rear. Banks's total strength was about fifteen thousand troops, half the number Kinsley estimated. Winters, *Civil War*, 222.

125. Banks appointed Kinsley brigade printer on April 9 by Special Orders No. 92. Rufus Kinsley Compiled Military Service Record.

126. Captain Hiram E. Perkins was mustered out of the Eighth Vermont Vols. on April 9, 1863, so he could accept a promotion to major in the First Regiment, Louisiana Native Guards. Peck, *Revised Roster*, 321.

127. Union troops failed to break through the line of breastworks that spanned the narrow strips of dry land on both sides of the Teche at Bisland on April 13. They succeeded on the 14th because Taylor, realizing that he was outnumbered 3 to 1 on his front by the combined forces of Weitzel and Emory and also outmanned to the rear by Grover's brigade, had packed up his army and fled in the middle of the night. During the two days of fighting, Union casualties were 40 killed and 184 wounded. Winters, *Civil War*, 222–25.

128. On the morning of April 14 the Union gunboats *Estrella*, *Arizona*, and *Calhoun* sank the Confederate ram *Queen of the West* in nearby Grand Lake. Ninety men, including Captain E. W. Fuller, who was known as "King of the Swamp" according to Banks, were rescued from the sinking ram and taken prisoner, but at least thirty others drowned. Fuller was taken to Fort Delaware, where he died in prison. "A braver man," according to Taylor, "never lived." Ibid., 230; *War of the Rebellion*, XV, 303; Taylor, *Destruction*, 131.

129. The *Cornie* was a hospital transport.

130. The *Diana* had been seriously damaged during the battle for Bisland on April 13, and rather than see the formidable gunboat fall into Union hands,

General Taylor gave orders to abandon and burn it. These orders were carried out on April 14, but not before the crippled *Diana* had moved a little above the town of Franklin and provided protective cover for Taylor's retreating troops. Winters, *Civil War*, 224, 228–29.

131. The 290 figure in parentheses at the end of this entry is Kinsley's estimate of the number of Confederate prisoners brought into camp. Grover was not as decisive as Kinsley suggests. Rather, his slow and timid actions on April 14 at the Battle of Irish Bend, just above Franklin, allowed most of Taylor's vastly outnumbered army to escape. Union casualties were 49 killed, 274 wounded, and 30 missing. Taylor never filed a casualty report, but the fleeing Confederates left 21 dead and 35 wounded for Grover to deal with. One of those left behind was Captain Oliver J. Semmes, commander of the *Diana* and son of Rear Admiral Raphael Semmes. Like Kinsley, Banks tried to put a positive spin on an expedition that had failed to capture Taylor's army. On April 23, 1863, he wrote to Rear Admiral Farragut: "We have captured nearly 2,000 prisoners, more than 1,000 stand of small arms, twenty siege guns, including one field gun, considerable ammunition, and the chiefs of the three arms of the rebel service. . . . We have captured more than 10,000 head of cattle, and horses and mules sufficient for the entire service of the army. . . . They [the Confederates] were kept in entire ignorance of our purposes, and were not aware of our movement until we stood before their fortifications at Camp Bisland. Their surprise and their rout has been complete, and," Banks concludes this letter which he is writing from Opelousas after nine days of chasing Taylor's army through the bayous of southwestern Louisiana, "leaves us leisure for other operations." Taylor found many of Banks's claims ridiculously inflated, wryly noting after reading one of the general's prisoner reports that "it is rather startling to learn that we were all captured." Ibid., 224–29; *War of the Rebellion*, XV, 707–08; Taylor, *Destruction*, 132.

132. Slow to take up the chase, Banks's troops bivouacked near Jeanerette on the night of the 15th, while Taylor's forces spent the same night at Camp Pratt a few miles north of New Town (New Iberia). The next day the hard-driving Taylor pushed on to Vermilionville (Lafayette), and ultimately to Natchitoches.

133. Callithumpians were disturbers of elections in eighteenth-century England, but in nineteenth-century New England the appellation referred to members of a noisy, boisterous parade or shivaree.

134. After resting his troops in Opelousas from April 20 to May 5, Banks continued his chase after Taylor. Upon reaching Alexandria on the Red River on May 7, he learned that Taylor had fled north toward Natchitoches and that Acting Rear Admiral David Porter, after some involvement in Grant's failed expedition to open the Yazoo Pass and approach Vicksburg from the rear, had moved up the Red River and captured Alexandria. Now that he had cleared the Confederate forces out of southwestern Louisiana and Porter had opened the Red River, Banks felt confident about joining with Farragut in a campaign against Port Hudson. On April 18, 1863, he wrote that his successful march through the Teche "has so crippled the enemy, amounting almost to the annihilation of his Army and Navy, that it is hardly possible he can contemplate an attack on New Orleans in our absence." He wrote to General Grant about his plan to capture Port Hudson: "The

fleet of Admiral Porter above, that of Admiral Farragut below, and our forces in the rear, or so many of yours as you can spare, the fall of the post will be instant and certain." Farragut agreed, assuring Banks that "Porter above and my fleet below and a moderate army force in the rear, and Port Hudson must fall." *War of the Rebellion*, XV, 300–301, 703, 718, 720.

135. A corporal in Co. G of the Fourth Massachusetts Vols., Jeremiah C. Turner and his regiment were stationed at Brashear City from early April until the end of May 1863. In 1857 Turner and Kinsley, both printers, had boarded in the same house in Boston. Printers, including apparently those who worked with Kinsley at the *Massachusetts Life Boat*, liked to link themselves to Faust, the learned sixteenth-century German doctor who, after his mysterious death, became for Goethe and other intellectuals a symbol of humanity's heroic search for knowledge. Index to Compiled Service Records of Volunteer Union Soldiers, National Archives microcopy M544, reel 41; *Boston Directory for the Year 1857, Embracing the City Record, a General Directory of the Citizens, and a Business Directory* (Boston: George Adams, 1857), 352; *Massachusetts Life Boat*, February 23, 1853.

136. A native of Weston, Vt., Private Daniel B. Webster of Co. D, Sixteenth New Hampshire Vols., had been in the army for less than six months when he died at Brashear City. Luther Tracy Townsend, *History of the Sixteenth Regiment, New Hampshire Volunteers* (Washington, D.C.: Norman T. Elliott, 1897), 440.

137. Private George W. Scribner was a twenty-seven-year-old resident of Bakersfield, Vt., when he enlisted on December 20, 1861. He "died of disease" on May 2, 1863. Malaria and other diseases took a heavy toll on the Eighth Vermont; in July 1863 nearly 40 percent of the regiment was absent because of sickness. Carpenter, *Eighth Regiment*, 303; Benedict, *Vermont in the Civil War*, II, 135.

138. In January 1863 the War Department authorized General Daniel Ullmann (1810–1892), a Yale graduate, to raise a brigade of black soldiers in the Department of the Gulf. Although Banks offered him access to the thousands of blacks he had "liberated" during the Teche campaign, he resented Ullmann's meddling in his affairs and on May 1, 1863, announced a plan to raise his own Corps d'Afrique that would consist of nine brigades. Messner, *Freedmen*, 117–18; *War of the Rebellion*, XV, 716–17.

139. At dawn on May 27 Banks initiated a massive but poorly orchestrated attack on Port Hudson. The 13,000 Union troops suffered 1,995 casualties, including 293 killed, 1,545 wounded, and 157 missing. The Confederates lost only about 235 in killed, wounded, and missing out of 4,000 troops. Banks's failure to capture Port Hudson in the assault of May 27 resulted in a long and costly siege that lasted until July 9 when the Confederates finally surrendered. As Banks's forces included the First and Third Regiments, Louisiana Native Guards, the battle for Port Hudson had the distinction of being the first Civil War engagement of any magnitude that saw fighting between black and white troops. Winters, *Civil War*, chaps. 16–17.

140. Born in 1819, Cyrus H. Allen of Thetford, Vt., was commissioned assistant surgeon in the Eighth Vermont Vols. on October 1, 1862. He was promoted to surgeon in the Fifth Vermont Vols. on October 1, 1864. Allen died in Richmond, Vt., in 1876. Peck, *Revised Roster*, 305; Cyrus H. Allen Grave Registration.

141. Probably Private Nathaniel Tillotson of Co. A, Eighth Vermont Vols. A forty-four-year-old resident of Lowell, Vt., when he enlisted in October 1861, Tillotson was discharged in March 1864. Carpenter, *Eighth Regiment*, 288.

142. The Union command responded to the June 1 guerrilla attack on Berwick City, opposite Brashear City on Berwick Bay, by "moving our hospital as fast as possible." *War of the Rebellion*, vol. XXVI, pt. 1, p. 186.

143. Private Sylvester H. Avery of Co. D, Eighth Vermont Vols., died "of disease" on June 3, 1863. He was a twenty-nine-year-old resident of Topsham, Vt., when he enlisted in December 1861. Peck, *Revised Roster*, 315.

144. The hospital in which Kinsley was a patient was on an islet below Berwick Bay.

145. Private Armstrong, who was thirty-seven years old when he was mustered into the Forty-first Massachusetts Infantry on September 17, 1862, died of "Febris Typhoides" on June 5, 1863, in Brashear City. Adam Armstrong Compiled Military Service Record.

146. A collection of handsome buildings located at the lower limits of the city and fronting the Mississippi River, the New Orleans Barracks (sometimes referred to as the U.S. Barracks) were built during the presidency of Andrew Jackson to house the federal garrison at New Orleans. In 1849 the Barracks expanded to include a general military hospital that consisted of four two-story rectangular buildings and a free-standing, octagon-shaped operating room.

147. Only Privates Edward Ducharme and Peter Henchey of Co. F were killed in action during the battle for Port Hudson. Benedict, *Vermont in the Civil War*, II, 127; Peck, *Revised Roster*, 321–24.

148. Along the banks of the Mississippi River.

149. In 1853 and 1854 James S. Thomas was an "engineer" living in Algiers. *Cohen's New Orleans Directory . . . for 1853 . . .* (New Orleans: Office of the *Daily Delta*, 1852), 255; *New Orleans Directory . . . for 1854*, 232.

150. On June 18 a Confederate cavalry unit of about six hundred fifty men under the command of Colonel J. P. Major captured a small Union force and destroyed three Union steamers on Bayou Plaquemine. The attack was part of General Taylor's June campaign to reclaim the Teche and Lafourche districts while Banks was engaged in the siege of Port Hudson. In mid-June Taylor had ordered Major's cavalry to Morgan's Ferry on the Atchafalaya; from there it was instructed to march to Berwick Bay, where on June 23 it would join with another detachment Taylor had sent down the Teche in recapturing Brashear City. Taylor, *Destruction*, 134–38; Winters, *Civil War*, 284–85.

151. On the evening of June 21 a detachment from Colonel Major's cavalry attacked the roughly 800 Union men guarding the Lafourche railroad crossing. The Confederates, many of whom were drunk, made three frontal assaults on the Union stronghold before retiring. Official reports set Union losses at 8 killed and 41 wounded. As was so often the case, Confederate losses were shrouded in mystery, but conservative estimates report at least 50 killed, over 60 wounded, and 16 missing. Winters, *Civil War*, 286–87.

152. In the early morning of June 23 General Taylor's various detachments combined in a surprise attack at Berwick Bay. By ten o'clock they had captured the

Union garrison. Confederate losses were 3 killed and 18 wounded, while Union losses totaled 46 killed, 40 wounded, and 1,300 captured. The Confederates also confiscated 11 heavy guns, 2,500 rifles, 200 wagons, hundreds of tents, and huge quantities of other materials, which Kinsley estimated at "600,000 [dollars] worth of military stores." Apparently Kinsley did not know that the black troops stationed at Brashear City escaped during the battle. Ibid., 287–89; Table of Civil War Battles, Commanders, and Losses, Kinsley Papers.

153. Probably James Morton, a twenty-four-year-old Irish laborer who was living in Algiers in 1860. 1860 Manuscript Census, roll 415, p. 73.

154. There was intense fear of invasion in New Orleans because the city's defenses were grossly undermanned – on June 20 there were only two hundred fifty Union soldiers guarding New Orleans – and because Taylor's forces kept getting closer – on July 1 they occupied Boutte Station on the New Orleans, Opelousas, and Great Western Railroad, less than twenty-five miles from the city. *War of the Rebellion*, vol. XXVI, pt. 1, pp. 188, 213.

155. Official records state that Bonaparte J. Case "died June 30, '63, of disease." His father, Jerome Case, asked Kinsley to settle his son's debts in Louisiana and send him the balance of the young sergeant's savings. Six months later Case's father complained to Kinsley's father that all he had received so far was "a package of old letters on which [he] was charged 30 cts postage." Peck, *Revised Roster*, 321; Ben A. Kinsley to Rufus Kinsley, January 28, 1864, Kinsley Papers.

156. Kinsley may have written to Mr. Janes because Ezra E. Janes of Georgia, Vt., a fellow corporal in Co. F, had been wounded two weeks earlier, on June 14, 1863. Apparently, Mr. Janes was a friend of Kinsley's brother Edgar Kinsley Montague, who wrote in his diary on November 23, 1863: "Went to Georgia to see Mr Janes." Several farmers with the surname Janes appear in the 1860 federal census for Georgia, Vt. Peck, *Revised Roster*, 321; Montague Diary; 1860 Manuscript Census, roll 1321, pp. 3, 23, 26.

157. The proximity of Taylor's troops and the disabling of the transport *Iberville* greatly unsettled General W. H. Emory, who was in command of the defenses of New Orleans. On July 3 he wrote to Banks, who was still engaged in the siege of Port Hudson: "The enemy are in force at des [*sic*] Allemands Bayou, on the Vacherie road, and at Whitehall Saw-mill. The *Iberville* has been fired into and disabled, and is now coming down in tow of the *Sallie Robinson*. I do not think you have one moment to lose in sending re-enforcements [to New Orleans]." Emory's anxiety was exacerbated by his conviction that the ten thousand residents of New Orleans capable of fighting "will, at the first approach of the enemy within view of the city, be against us to a man." *War of the Rebellion*, vol. XXVI, pt. 1, pp. 49–50, 51, 615.

158. Kinsley was of course hoping that Grant would soon capture Vicksburg, which in fact fell on the Fourth of July, and that Banks would take Port Hudson, which surrendered five days later. These two capitulations, combined with Lee's defeat at Gettysburg on July 5, did indeed constitute a "turning point" in the war from which the Confederacy never recovered.

159. General John C. Pemberton's surrender on Independence Day brought Grant's brilliant Vicksburg campaign to an end. As Kinsley suggests, it assured

the fall of Port Hudson and thereby cut the Confederacy in half and turned the Mississippi into a highway for Union soldiers and goods.

160. General Franklin Gardner, Confederate commander of Port Hudson, received news of Vicksburg's capitulation on July 7, informed Banks he was "willing to surrender" on July 8, and formally surrendered on July 9. Although Confederate losses at Port Hudson during the siege from May 23 to July 8 totaled 176 killed, 447 wounded, and 6,340 captured, the victory was a costly one for Banks, who had 708 of his men killed, 3,336 wounded, and 319 captured or missing. *War of the Rebellion*, vol. XXVI, pt. 1, pp. 53, 144, 642.

161. In a letter to his brother William on May 10, 1865, Kinsley spells the widow's name McGeary. She may have been twenty-three-year-old Ellen McGarrey who in 1860 was married to Michiel McGarrey of Algiers. 1860 Manuscript Census, roll 415, p. 77.

162. After the surrender of Port Hudson, Banks ordered Union troops, under the command of Weitzel and Grover, to cross the Mississippi and head for Donaldsonville, where they were "to dislodge the enemy, who had temporarily obstructed our communication with New Orleans, and to drive his forces from the La Fourche district, where he was in considerable numbers." On July 11 and 12 they participated in successful minor skirmishes with the enemy. But on July 13, at the Battle of Cox's Plantation, about six miles below Donaldsonville on Bayou Lafourche, they did not whip the Confederates, as Kinsley states. Instead, Union troops were temporarily beaten back by a force a third their size and suffered a total loss of 56 killed, 217 wounded, and 186 captured or missing. *War of the Rebellion*, vol. XXVI, pt. 1, p. 55; Winters, *Civil War*, 292–93.

163. General George G. Meade repulsed General Robert E. Lee's bold venture into the North at Gettysburg in early July 1863, and General William S. Rosecrans conducted a brilliant campaign against General Braxton Bragg in Tennessee in late June 1863. It is difficult to imagine what Kinsley had in mind regarding General John A. Dix. Although he outranked all other volunteer officers in the Union army, Dix was considered too old to be a field commander and spent most of his time performing departmental and garrison duties. In fact one might argue that his most important contribution to the Union war effort was suppressing antidraft riots in New York City at precisely the time Kinsley was writing.

164. Soon after the fall of Port Hudson, General Taylor began pulling his forces back to Berwick Bay. Then, on July 21, Taylor writes in his Civil War memoir, "we ran the engines and carriages on the railway into the bay, threw in the heavy guns, and moved up the Teche, leaving pickets opposite Berwick's. The timidity manifested after the action of the 13th [at the Battle of Cox's Plantation] may be ascribed to the fertile imagination of the Federal commander, General Banks, which multiplied my force of less than three thousand of all arms into nine or twelve thousand." *Destruction*, 143.

165. In 1860 Charles W. Bingham, who was born on December 26, 1842, was living on his father's farm in Fletcher, close to where Kinsley was living with his aunt Elvira. After the war Kinsley would marry Bingham's first cousin, Ella Lenora Bingham. 1860 Manuscript Census, roll 1321, p. 7; Ballway, *A Genealogical Study*, 5–6.

166. Bingham had been mustered into the service as a private in Co. H of the Second Vermont Vols. on June 20, 1861, but he was discharged six months later on account of sickness. Hemenway, *Historical Gazetteer*, II, 412.

167. Kinsley's mother, Catherine Montague Kinsley, died on February 15, 1849, when he was seventeen. Although he was nearly twenty-three when his father remarried on September 26, 1854, Kinsley had a close relationship with his stepmother, Lucy Blair (1809–1881). Kinsley, "Fletcher," 312.

168. In 1833 Elvira Scott (1811–1894) married Kinsley's mother's brother Rufus Montague II. In 1860 Kinsley lived in Fletcher with his aunt Elvira and her adopted son, Edgar Kinsley Montague, who was also Kinsley's brother. 1860 Manuscript Census, roll 1321, p. 10; Ballway, *A Genealogical Study*, 54.

169. In 1860 Charles Bingham's mother, forty-one-year-old Alice M. Bingham, was living in Fletcher with her husband Benjamin F. Bingham, a forty-one-year-old farmer with property valued at $4,790. 1860 Manuscript Census, roll 1321, p. 7.

170. Kinsley is alluding to General Robert E. Lee's successful retreat to Virginia in the aftermath of his defeat at Gettysburg. Lincoln agreed with Kinsley. On July 14, 1863, he wrote to an overly cautious George G. Meade, the Union commander who allowed Lee's army to flee across the Potomac: "Again, my dear general, I do not believe you appreciate the magnitude of the misfortune involved in Lee's escape. He was within your easy grasp, and to have closed upon him would, in connection with our other late successes [in Louisiana, Mississippi, and Tennessee], have ended the war. As it is, the war will be prolonged indefinitely. . . . Your golden opportunity is gone, and I am distressed immeasurably because of it." Roy P. Basler, ed., *The Collected Works of Abraham Lincoln*, 9 vols. (New Brunswick, N.J.: Rutgers University Press, 1955), VI, 327–28.

171. Probably Huldah Bingham, who in 1860 was thirty-nine years old and living in the same house with Charles Bingham. 1860 Manuscript Census, roll 1321, p. 7.

172. Related to both the Kinsleys and the Montagues, Medad Parsons had three sons, Henry, Albert, and Charles. In the 1860 federal census he was listed as a fifty-six-year-old farmer living with his wife and two sons, aged twenty-six and eighteen. According to the census, his dwelling was just eleven houses away from Edgar Kinsley Montague's, where Rufus resided in 1860. Ballway, *A Genealogical Study*, 57–58; 1860 Manuscript Census, roll 1321, p. 8.

173. In 1850 thirteen-year-old Samuel W. Royce lived with his mother in Fletcher, near the Ben A. Kinsley household. Royce and Kinsley's brother Edgar were friends who visited back and forth until Edgar went off to war. On October 11, 1864, Royce married Sophia J. Armstrong. 1850 Manuscript Census, roll 924, p. 1; Montague Diary, November 18, 1860, March 18, 1863; Samuel W. Royce and Sophia J. Armstrong marriage certificate of October 11, 1864, Vital Records.

174. Probably Bonaparte Case's father, Jerome. In 1860 Jerome Case was forty-four years old, the father of eight children, and a farmer who owned property valued at four hundred dollars. 1860 Manuscript Census, roll 1321, p. 8.

175. Probably LeRoy Monroe Bingham (1845–1911), Charles Bingham's first cousin and brother of Kinsley's future wife, Ella Bingham. In the 1860 federal census he was listed as a fifteen year old without an occupation; ten years later he

was listed as a physician. 1860 Manuscript Census, roll 1321, p. 8; 1870 Manuscript Census, roll 1620, p. 19; LeRoy M. Bingham death certificate, Vital Records.

176. A resident of Portland, Conn., at the time of his enlistment as a first lieutenant in the Ninth Connecticut Vols., Alfred G. Hall was promoted to lieutenant colonel of the Second Regiment, Louisiana Native Guards, in October 1862. In January 1863 he was placed in command of three companies, A, E, and H, when they were detached for service at Fort Pike, which guarded the eastern entrance to Lake Pontchartrain. Although he was unpopular at Fort Pike and offered to resign in April 1863 because "great feeling has obtained among the officers of the regiment against me," Hall was nevertheless in early May given command of the regiment's remaining seven companies (B, C, D, F, G, I, and K), which had been stationed on Ship Island since mid-January 1863. He was later "dishonorably dismissed" from the service on October 27, 1865, for "'breach of arrest,' 'conduct unbecoming an officer and a gentleman,' 'and for neglect of duty.'" Hall to Captain Wickham Hoffman, April 16, 1863, and Field and Staff Muster Out Roll of November 14, 1865, in Alfred G. Hall Compiled Military Service Record; Adjutants-General, *Record of Service of Connecticut Men in the Army and Navy of the United States during the War of the Rebellion* (Hartford, Conn.: Case, Lockwood & Brainard Company, 1889), 362.

177. The Second Regiment Infantry, Corps d'Afrique, was originally organized as the Second Regiment, Louisiana Native Guards, at New Orleans on October 12, 1862. Its designation was changed to the Second Regiment Infantry, Corps d'Afrique, on June 6, 1863, and to the Seventy-fourth Regiment, USCI, on April 6, 1864. *OAR*, VIII, 248.

178. Kinsley is alluding to General Orders No. 60, which was issued by the Confederate War Department on August 21, 1862, and stated that any captured "commissioned officer employed in drilling, organizing or instructing slaves with a view to their armed service in this war . . . shall not be regarded as a prisoner of war but held in close confinement for execution as a felon at such time and place as the President shall order." *War of the Rebellion*, series 2, vol. IV, p. 857.

179. The day before, on October 1, 1863, Kinsley had written from the New Orleans Barracks Hospital to Major G. Norman Lieber, judge-advocate on Banks's staff: "I have the honor to respectfully request that I be discharged from my Regiment, in order that I may accept a Commission in the Corps d'Afrique." Rufus Kinsley Compiled Military Service Record.

180. Initially a sergeant in Co. C of the Eighth Vermont Vols., Augustine P. Hawley (1834–1905) was promoted to captain in the Second Regiment, Louisiana Native Guards, in August 1863. After his discharge in August 1864, Hawley returned to Vermont and attended reunions of the Eighth Vermont Vols. until his death. He is buried in Waterford. See Augustus Percy Hawley death certificate of March 20, 1905, Vital Records; Peck, *Revised Roster*, 719; Souvenir Scrapbook, 111.

181. Chaplain Elizur Andrus was mustered into the First Regiment, Michigan Heavy Artillery, on August 20, 1861. Kinsley's judgment of Union chaplains seems somewhat severe, but the army, especially in the early stages of the war, did have within its ranks a large number of intemperate, unethical, and uneducated

chaplains, and it is possible that the twelve apostles might not have lived up to Kinsley's standards. Nevertheless, the war yielded many courageous, hard-working, and upright chaplains who performed their duties under the most difficult circumstances. *OAR*, V, 277; Herman A. Norton, *The United States Army Chaplaincy: Struggling for Recognition, 1791–1865* (Washington, D.C.: Department of the Army, 1977), 85–90; Warren B. Armstrong, *For Courageous Fighting and Confident Dying: Union Chaplains in the Civil War* (Lawrence: University Press of Kansas, 1998), chaps. 3 and 6.

182. There were indeed many deaths at the Barracks Hospital in New Orleans. From January 1, 1863, to November 26, 1865, for example, roughly 1 out every 5 of the nearly 3,000 soldiers treated there for diarrhea or dysentery died. Although some complained bitterly about incompetence and corruption in the military hospitals of occupied New Orleans, Colonel N. A. Dudley, who inspected the hospital in August 1863 when Kinsley was there, praised the principal surgeon, Dr. John B. G. Baxter, and reported that "It is a pleasure to inspect a hospital in such admirable condition." U.S. War Department, Office of the Surgeon General, *The Medical and Surgical History of the War of the Rebellion. (1861–65)*, 3 parts (Washington, D.C.: Government Printing Office, 1875–88), pt. 2, vol. I, p. 14; Edward McMillan, "Military Medicine in Occupied New Orleans, 1863," *Louisiana History*, 8 (Spring 1967), 198–204; Inspection Report of Colonel N. A. Dudley, August 19, 1863, in Inspection Reports, pt. 1, entry 1826, Department of the Gulf, Records of United States Army Continental Commands, 1821–1920, Record Group 393, National Archives (cited hereinafter as Department of the Gulf, Army Commands).

183. Born on January 2, 1835, in Columbia, N.H., Noyes had married Annie E. Scott in 1860. At the time of his enlistment as a private in Co. C of the Eighth Vermont Vols., Noyes was living in Newbury, Vt. He was transferred to the Second Regiment Infantry, Corps d'Afrique, on December 31, 1862, and promoted to captain of Co. D on September 16, 1863. After the war Noyes moved to New Hampshire, where he served as a Methodist minister and, from 1886 to 1901, as superintendent of the New Hampshire Orphans' Home in Franklin. In 1887 he wrote in support of Kinsley's appeal for an increase in his government pension, and in 1899 he returned to Vermont to attend a reunion of the Eighth Vermont Vols. Noyes died on December 6, 1907. Henry E. Noyes and Harriette E. Noyes, comps., *Genealogical Record of Some of the Noyes Descendants of James, Nicholas and Peter Noyes*, 2 vols. (Boston, Mass.: n.p., 1904), I, 362–63; Peck, *Revised Roster*, 720; James Noyes affidavit, August 11, 1887, Rufus Kinsley Pension; Souvenir Scrapbook, 116; James Noyes Pension.

184. A resident of New Haven, Conn., at the time of his enlistment as a first lieutenant in the Thirteenth Connecticut Vols., William M. Grosvenor was promoted to colonel in the Second Regiment Infantry, Corps d'Afrique, on October 29, 1863. William M. Grosvenor Compiled Military Service Record; Adjutants-General, *Record of Service of Connecticut Men*, 532.

185. Hall served briefly in the One Hundred Seventy-sixth New York Vols. before resuming his command at Fort Pike. Alfred G. Hall Compiled Military Service Record.

186. An officer sent to inspect the post garrisoned by Kinsley's regiment was amazed at the quantity of whiskey that was being sold or issued on Ship Island. Special Report of Ship Island Inspection by Lieutenant Colonel W. D. Smith, January 3, 1865, cited in Edwin C. Bearss, *Historic Resource Study: Ship Island, Harrison County, Mississippi, Gulf Islands National Seashore, Florida/Mississippi* (Denver, Colo.: U.S. Department of the Interior, National Park Service, 1984), 294.

187. Botany Bay was the site of an early and infamous Australian convict settlement.

188. The large fort is Fort Massachusetts. Kinsley has greatly exaggerated here if Bearss is correct in his conclusion in *Historic Resource Study*, 271, that the last Confederate political prisoners incarcerated on Ship Island were released in the summer of 1863.

189. Doctors of Divinity. Since the average length of service among army chaplains was only one year, there were always regiments without formal religious guidance. Indeed, at times over half the regiments in the Union army had no chaplain. Norton, *United States Army Chaplaincy*, 108. Stephen A. Hodgman, the departed chaplain whose courage Kinsley questions here, is discussed in the Introduction.

190. Romans 6:23.

191. Under General Orders No. 76, issued on September 24, 1862, Butler announced that "All persons, male or female, within this department, of the age of eighteen years or upward, who have ever been citizens of the United States and have not renewed their allegiance before this date to the United States, or who now hold or pretend any allegiance or sympathy with the so-called Confederate States, are ordered to report themselves, . . . and each shall receive a certificate from the marshal of registration as claiming to be an enemy of the United States." *War of the Rebellion*, XV, 575.

192. Born in 1840, Lemuel I. Winslow enlisted in Co. H, Eighth Vermont Vols., on December 9, 1861. Previously a sergeant in the Eighth Vermont Vols., he was mustered into the Second Regiment Infantry, Corps d'Afrique, on December 20, 1863, and remained in the service until his discharge in October 1865. He died in Vermont on January 22, 1882. See Lemuel I. Winslow birth certificate of December 6, 1840, and death certificate of January 22, 1882, Vital Records; Lemuel I. Winslow Compiled Military Service Record; Peck, *Revised Roster*, 328.

193. Kinsley received an extra ten dollars per month "for responsibility of arms for the mos. of Nov. & Dec. 1863." Company Muster Roll for January & February 1864, in Rufus Kinsley Compiled Military Service Record.

194. A graduate of West Point, Joseph Jones Reynolds (1822–1899) was appointed a major general of volunteers in November 1862. In January 1864 he was put in charge of the New Orleans defenses, and in July he organized the campaign against Mobile. Warner, *Generals in Blue*, 397–98.

195. Born on January 1, 1842, in Salem, Mass., Zachariah Burchmore enlisted in Co. K, Twenty-sixth Massachusetts Vols., on September 14, 1861. He was mustered into the Second Regiment Infantry, Corps d'Afrique, on October 6, 1863. A clerk himself, Burchmore boasted that his father was a close friend of Nathaniel Hawthorne and "spoken of in the *Scarlet Letter* as the '*Model Clerk*.'" Zachariah

Burchmore Compiled Military Service Record; Burchmore to J. T. Dana, October 21, 1896, in Zachariah Burchmore Pension.

196. The reference is to "Some wee short hour ayont the twal," in Robert Burns's poem "Death and Doctor Hornbook." *The Poetical Works of Robert Burns with Notes, Glossary, Index of First Lines and Chronological List*, ed. J. Logie Robertson (1904; reprint, London: Oxford University Press, 1960), line 183, p. 67. I suspect that Kinsley picked up a copy of John Bartlett's *Familiar Quotations*, which first appeared in 1855, while he was living in Boston. Both the Burns quotation used here and another by Lord Byron used later are found in Bartlett's popular book. *A Collection of Familiar Quotations, with Complete Indices of Authors and Subjects*, new ed. (Cambridge, Mass.: John Bartlett, 1856), 224, 267. Kinsley, like many other abolitionists, was apparently inspired by the Romantic poetry of Burns and Byron. See Henry Mayer, *All on Fire: William Lloyd Garrison and the Abolition of Slavery* (New York: St. Martin's Press, 1998), 28, 34, 93, 114, 199, and John Stauffer, *The Black Hearts of Men: Radical Abolitionists and the Transformation of Race* (Cambridge: Harvard University Press, 2002), 150–51.

197. Kinsley is alluding to the Boston "Cotton Aristocracy" (and their functionaries in the Custom House) who despised radical antislavery disunionists like William Lloyd Garrison and sought to avoid war with the South because the fortunes of New England's textile industry depended upon the productivity of Southern cotton plantations. See Thomas H. O'Connor, *Lords of the Loom: The Cotton Whigs and the Coming of the Civil War* (New York: Charles Scribner's Sons, 1968).

198. James H. Schneider was chaplain of the Second Regiment, Infantry, United States Colored Troops. Organized in Virginia, the regiment laid over at Ship Island from December 8, 1863, to February 16, 1864, on its way to Key West, Fla. Surprisingly, Kinsley says nothing about a "mutiny" in the Second USCI that took place on Ship Island on December 27, 1863, when "a number of men from Companies I, C & G, defied the authority of the officers, and attacked them with brick-bats and other missiles." Following this initial outburst, "Some of the men brought their arms from their tents, and declared that no man should be punished in the Regiment." After subduing the "mutineers" with a strong show of force and investigating the uprising, Lieutenant Colonel Stark Fellows, commander of the regiment, concluded that "the outbreak was the result of a deeplaid [sic] conspiracy and it had for its object the complete overthrow of the authority of the officers of the Regiment." *OAR*, VIII, 170; S. Fellows to Zach Burchmore, January 4, 1864, "The Negro in the Military Service of the United States, 1639–1886," Bureau of Colored Troops, National Archives (microcopy 858, roll 3, frame 2303–2304).

199. Farragut was wrong about this. By the time Fort Massachusetts was completed in the 1880s, maritime technological advances had made it obsolete.

200. Major General William Tecumseh Sherman was indeed moving; but from his position at Vicksburg, he was heading east across Mississippi toward Meridian, not south toward Mobile. His mission was to strengthen the federal hold on Vicksburg by destroying the railroads and resources of central Mississippi. By

mid-February he had reached Meridian, where he spent five days destroying rail facilities; by early March he was headed for Nashville to prepare the Atlanta campaign.

201. First Lieutenant Frazer A. Stearns, of the Twenty-first Massachusetts Vols., was killed at Newburn, N.C., on March 14, 1862. *OAR*, I, 180.

202. The movement against Texas, begun in early March 1864 and popularly known as Banks's Red River campaign, ended in failure. Farragut's bombardment of Fort Powell in Grant's Pass was also timed to prevent Confederate troops stationed in Mobile from rushing north to help repulse Sherman's Meridian campaign. Farragut's expedition did little damage to Fort Powell, but it did teach the admiral that the entrance to Mobile Bay known as Grant's Pass was too shallow for his fleet to navigate. When the time to move against Mobile came, Farragut would, as Kinsley predicted on February 27, 1864, take the deeper channel guarded by Fort Gaines and Fort Morgan.

203. Second Lieutenant Frank L. Trask, an African American, had been mustered into the regiment on October 12, 1862, when he was twenty-four years old. He was in command of Co. C from June 30 until December 8, 1863, when Major C. C. Pike had him arrested for abandoning his post while on guard duty. He was subsequently court-martialed and dismissed from the service on February 25, 1864. Frank L. Trask Compiled Military Service Record.

204. In 1860 Charles Cephas Colton (1837–1873) was living on his father's farm in Georgia, Vt. Prior to being mustered into Co. F, Eighth Vermont Vols., on February 18, 1862, he had attended Harvard Law School and been admitted to the bar of Middlesex County, Mass. First Lieutenant Colton was discharged from the Second Regiment Infantry, Corps d'Afrique, on August 6, 1864. 1860 Manuscript Census, roll 1321, p. 351; Carpenter, *Eighth Regiment*, 302; Peck, *Revised Roster*, 321; *OAR*, VIII, 248; George W. Colton, *A Genealogical Record of the Descendants of Quartermaster George Colton, 1644–1911* (Lancaster, Pa.: Wickersham Printing Company, 1912), 356.

205. The Greek god of wine.

206. Slang for a woman of pleasure.

207. On April 8, 1864, Union forces were routed at Sabine Crossroads, forty miles south of Shreveport. Shortly thereafter Banks retreated, and his Red River campaign was over.

208. A West Point graduate and the adjutant general of the Union army, Lorenzo Thomas (1804–1875) played an important role in the recruitment, organization, and inspection of black troops. In early 1863 he was dispatched by Secretary of War Edwin M. Stanton to the Mississippi Valley to raise black regiments. By the end of the year he had enlisted nearly twenty-one thousand black soldiers from Arkansas, Tennessee, Mississippi, and Louisiana. By the end of the war Thomas had recruited close to seventy thousand black troops. After reviewing the Second Corps d'Afrique, Thomas declared: "It is in capital order and fine drill." Warner, *Generals in Blue*, 502–03; Ira Berlin, Joseph P. Reidy, and Leslie S. Rowland, eds., *Freedom: A Documentary History of Emancipation, 1861–1867*, series 2: *The Black Military Experience* (Cambridge: Cambridge University

Press, 1982), 113–22; Lorenzo Thomas to Colonel E. D. Townsend, April 8, 1864, "The Negro in the Military Service," roll 3, frame 2477.

209. Apparently, the men of the Second Corps d'Afrique took considerable pride in their appearance as well as their performance during drill. One resident of the island who had watched them march in 1863 noted that "they look very grand in their plumed cocked hats. They wear the plumes all the time." Quotation from the letter of John C. Palfrey to John G. Palfrey, October 18, 1863, John Gorham Palfrey Family Papers, Letters to John Gorham Palfrey, bMS 1704 (678), Houghton Library, Harvard University (Cambridge, Mass.), published by permission of Houghton Library, Harvard University.

210. During the spring of 1864, as agents of the Detroit Freedmen's Relief Association and at great personal risk, Laura Haviland (1808–1898) of Raisin, Mich., and Letitia Backus of Pittsford, Mich., delivered clothing, blankets, and other supplies to needy freedmen in Mississippi and Louisiana. A tireless worker in behalf of black Americans before, during, and after the war, Haviland gained considerable fame in antebellum America for working on the Underground Railroad and for establishing Raisin Institute, which admitted students irrespective of race. See Laura S. Haviland, *A Woman's Life Work: Including Thirty Years' Service on the Underground Railroad and in the War* (Grand Rapids, Mich.: S. B. Shaw, 1881); and Mildred E. Danforth, *A Quaker Pioneer: Laura Haviland, Superintendent of the Underground* (New York: Exposition Press, 1961).

211. Born the first child of an impoverished day laborer in Brookfield, Vt., in 1800, Orange Scott became one of the most important leaders of the antislavery movement before his death in 1847. Denouncing slavery as "*evil*, only evil, and that *continually*," Scott was a revolutionary evangelist who attacked not only Northern society but also the established Methodist Episcopal Church for tolerating the sin of slavery. Calling for a return to John Wesley's eighteenth-century abolitionist ideals, Scott and five other antislavery Methodists founded the Wesleyan Methodist Church in 1843. According to Haviland, when Mrs. Noyes learned that Haviland and Sister Backus were friends of her father as well as Wesleyan Methodists, the evangelist's daughter "laughed and cried at the same time" and "almost flew at us, placing her hands on our shoulders. 'I don't wonder you seemed so much like relatives.'" Lucius C. Matlack, *The Life of Rev. Orange Scott: Compiled From His Personal Narrative, Correspondence, and Other Authentic Sources of Information* (New York: C. Prindle & L. C. Matlack, 1848), pt. 2, chaps. 2–8; Donald G. Mathews, "Orange Scott: The Methodist Evangelist as Revolutionary," in Martin Duberman, ed., *The Antislavery Vanguard: New Essays on the Abolitionists* (Princeton, N.J.: Princeton University Press, 1965), 71–101 (quotation on 74); Haviland, *A Woman's Life Work*, 327.

212. Haviland wrote of her meeting with the prisoners: "Captain Noyce [Noyes] and wife took us to the barracks, where the prisoners were arranged in rows, six men deep, on both sides and at the end, leaving an aisle three feet in width between. In every berth there was a man in a horizontal position; and all were in irons, either in handcuffs with chain, or in a clog for the ankle, to which was attached the chain and ball. What a scene! The click of the irons at the least

move greeted our ears. We walked midway of the long aisle, and looked over the sad faces. . . . I exhorted them to come forth from this furnace of affliction with higher, nobler, and holier aspirations than ever before, and to lift up their heads in hope of better days, although the heavens might then seem as brass and the earth as bars of iron. I spoke a few minutes, and as I closed my remarks I turned to sister Backus, standing by, and asked her to say a few words of encouragement, but she declined. She said that all she could do was to weep with those who wept." *A Woman's Life Work*, 332.

213. Haviland also enjoyed the ten-mile, moonlit excursion, and her "long conversation with Lieutenant Kingsley [*sic*]." Kinsley had already made an impression upon Haviland by giving up his mattress and sleeping "on the bare tent floor" when she moved into the Noyes household. Further, she had been captivated by Kinsley's story-telling powers and recounted an evening spent listening "to Lieutenant Kingsley's thrilling description of the cruel irons he filed off from a number of slaves, who were too intelligent to be held without severe measures. He said these men made soldiers who hesitated not to brave the greatest dangers." Ibid., 327, 328.

214. William C. Abbe was mustered in as a first lieutenant in the Second Regiment Infantry, Corps d'Afrique, on April 15, 1864. *OAR*, VIII, 248.

215. Burchmore accused Grosvenor of intimidating him with "threatening and abusive language." An account of the charges brought against Grosvenor may be found in an anonymous pamphlet entitled *War Record of Col.? W. M. Grosvenor, Editor of the Missouri Democrat* (n.p., n.d.), 2.

216. Banks's army was not destroyed but suffered heavy losses at the Battles of Sabine Crossroads and Pleasant Hill, just above Grand Ecore on the Red River.

217. On April 12, 1864, Major General Nathan Bedford Forrest, who later gained notoriety as the reputed Grand Wizard of the Ku Klux Klan, commanded fifteen hundred Confederate cavalrymen in an attack on Fort Pillow, Tenn. After capturing the fort, according to Union officers, Forrest's troops brutally murdered up to three hundred black and white soldiers who had already surrendered. Instead of demoralizing black troops, the atrocities at Fort Pillow inspired greater effort and widespread retaliation by black soldiers and their officers. Berlin, et al., *Black Military Experience*, 520, 539–48; Joseph T. Glatthaar, *Forged in Battle: The Civil War Alliance of Black Soldiers and White Officers* (New York: The Free Press, 1990), 156–58.

218. Romans 12:19.

219. Kinsley is probably referring to Profit Island, which is about three miles below Port Hudson in the Mississippi River. When large numbers of runaway slaves began by their mere presence to interfere with Union forces during the siege of Port Hudson, they were removed to Profit Island. Given Kinsley's religious bent, it is not surprising that when he heard the name of this island, he thought of "prophet" rather than "profit." Cat Island lies about five miles west of Ship Island in Mississippi Sound. *War of the Rebellion*, vol. XXVI, pt. 1, pp. 72–74.

220. Hall assumed command of the regiment and post after Grosvenor's arrest. He remained in command until June 1864, when Colonel Ernest W. Holmstedt

relieved him. Alfred G. Hall Compiled Military Service Record; Ernest W. Holmstedt Compiled Military Service Record.

221. At his court-martial for "Conduct unbecoming an Officer and a Gentleman," Grosvenor pleaded guilty to the charge of keeping "in his quarters, a woman, not his wife, by the name of 'Belle Fisher,'" from "on or about the 3rd to the 8th of April, 1864." He was charged with keeping yet another woman, "not his wife," in his quarters from "on or about the 12th to the 17th day of April, 1864." *War Record of Col.? W. M. Grosvenor*, 3.

222. Mustered into the Second Regiment Infantry, Corps d'Afrique, on December 5, 1863, First Lieutenant George W. Foster, Jr., survived the attack by the regiment's surgeon, John H. Gihon. Gihon was often at the center of controversy during his tour of duty with the Second Corps d'Afrique. Lieutenant Foster's good friend, Captain James Noyes, accused Gihon of being corrupt and vindictive. Noyes declared that he would not consult the surgeon for medical attention for fear that "I should not come out alive." Another officer accused Gihon "of having attempted to create a 'mutiny' on the Island." *OAR*, VIII, 248; James Noyes to John C. Black, January 12, 1886, in James Noyes Pension; indictment of October 3, 1865, brought against Ernest W. Holmstedt, in Holmstedt Pension. See also *War Record of Col.? W. M. Grosvenor*, 2.

223. Kinsley's brother Edgar Kinsley Montague enlisted in the Second Vermont Vols. on December 14, 1863. The five-foot eight-inch private told his father that he had enlisted "because he thought his country needed his services & he had no right to withhold them." After being mustered into Co. H on December 31 he declared that the army offered "a good living & nothing to complain of." But according to his father Edgar's departure "made a sad change in his family," as his wife Annette and two-year-old son Rufus had to abandon their home and go live with Annette's widowed mother. Edgar was mustered out of the service on July 15, 1865. Montague Diary, December 14, 1863; Ben A. Kinsley to Rufus Kinsley, January 28, 1864, Kinsley Papers; Edgar Kinsley Montague Compiled Military Service Record; Edgar Kinsley Montague Pension; Ballway, *A Genealogical Study*, 42.

224. Alma R. Scott (1822–1895) gave her age as forty-seven and her occupation as servant in the 1870 federal census. A member of Edgar Kinsley Montague's household, she was the sister of Edgar's adoptive mother, Elvira Scott Montague, who also lived in the household. 1870 Manuscript Census, roll 1620, p. 17; Ballway, *A Genealogical Study*, 64.

225. Edgar's regiment participated in the campaign against Robert E. Lee that Ulysses S. Grant initiated in early May 1864. Through a series of ferocious battles at the Wilderness, Spotsylvania, and Cold Harbor, Union forces relentlessly drove Lee back into a defensive position at Petersburg, Va., where he remained until the final days of the war.

226. Joseph E. Johnston's forces did not defeat Sherman's army in the spring of 1864. Instead, beginning in May in Tennessee, Sherman steadily drove Johnston south toward Atlanta, which Sherman finally captured in September. Nor was Banks captured while chasing Richard Taylor up the Red River, but Banks's campaign to capture Shreveport and then use it as a springboard for the

invasion of Texas failed miserably. It failed in part because Banks was a poor field commander; moreover, after the fall of Vicksburg both Banks and Grant had wanted to move against Mobile, not Texas. It was Lincoln who ordered the Army of the Gulf to invade Texas.

227. The 1864 Louisiana Constitutional Convention, which met in New Orleans from early April until the end of July and voted to abolish slavery in Louisiana on May 11, had the blessing of Lincoln as well as Banks. The convention was not dominated by Yankee carpetbaggers who arrived in the wake of Butler's invasion, but it was largely controlled by Banks and his moderate followers. Kinsley was correct, however, in believing that the convention did not reflect the will of white Louisianans, the vast majority of whom did not vote in either the election for delegates to the convention or the election to ratify the constitution created by the convention. McCrary, *Abraham Lincoln*, esp. chaps. 8–9; Jean-Charles Houzeau, *My Passage at the New Orleans "Tribune,"* ed. David C. Rankin, trans. Gerard F. Denault (Baton Rouge: Louisiana State University Press, 1985), 44, 69–70.

228. The army played a vital role in the education of African Americans in the Department of the Gulf and throughout the South during the Civil War. See Messner, *Freedmen*, chap. 11; John W. Blassingame, "The Union Army as an Educational Institution for Negroes, 1862–1865," *Journal of Negro Education*, 34 (1965), 152–59; Robert S. Bahney, "Generals and Negroes: Education of Negroes by the Union Army, 1861–1865" (Ph.D. diss., University of Michigan, 1965).

229. Although Kinsley was clearly convinced that Northern philanthropists were doing "good" and that Southern freedmen were full of "gratitude," historians in recent years have often portrayed Yankee philanthropists as condescending cultural chauvinists attempting to impose Northern values on shrewd Southern peasants struggling to preserve a distinct world view. For a peerless introduction to the complex issues raised by Northern wartime philanthropy, see Willie Lee Rose, *Rehearsal for Reconstruction: The Port Royal Experiment* (New York: Oxford University Press, 1964).

230. Edited throughout most of the Civil War by either Henry Ward Beecher or the radical young abolitionist Theodore Tilton, the *Independent* was the nation's largest religious-political weekly. In the spring and summer of 1864 it joined the widely read *New York Tribune* in denouncing the labor system that Banks had implemented in Louisiana as unjust and oppressive. Published in Boston, *Zion's Herald* was the official organ of the New England Methodist Conference; before the war it published several articles by Orange Scott, the father of Captain James Noyes's wife, condemning the sin of slavery. A literary periodical that frequently published essays about slavery and its aftermath, the *Atlantic Monthly* was also published in Boston. The first chapters of what would become Thomas Wentworth Higginson's classic account *Army Life in a Black Regiment* began appearing in the *Atlantic* in the fall of 1864. *Harper's Monthly* was a popular magazine that in September 1864 published the first in a series of articles by John W. De Forest on fighting Rebels along Bayou Lafourche and other Confederate waterways. James M. McPherson, *The Struggle for Equality: Abolitionists and the Negro in the*

Civil War and Reconstruction (Princeton, N.J.: Princeton University Press, 1964), 290, 438–40; Mathews, "Orange Scott," 80–81; Christopher Looby, ed., *The Complete Civil War Journal and Selected Letters of Thomas Wentworth Higginson* (Chicago: University of Chicago Press, 2000), 7; De Forest, *A Volunteer's Adventures*, 53, 104, 204.

231. While Kinsley credited Colonel Grosvenor with improving the regiment's marching, Lieutenant Colonel Alfred Hall claimed that he was responsible for drilling the troops and bringing the Seventy-fourth USCI up to snuff. Hall to Major John Livering, June 7, 1864, in Alfred G. Hall Compiled Military Service Record.

232. The allusion is to Christ warning his disciples: "And every one that heareth these sayings of mine, and doeth them not, shall be likened unto a foolish man, which built his house upon the sand: And the rain descended, and the floods came, and the winds blew, and beat upon that house; and it fell: and great was the fall of it." Matthew 5:26–27.

233. Charles F. Dauchy was mustered into the Second Regiment Infantry, Corps d'Afrique, as a captain on September 15, 1863. *OAR*, VIII, 248.

234. Kinsley's brother Alonzo, who was mustered into Co. H of the Second Vermont Vols. on June 20, 1861, was mustered out of the service on June 21, 1864. His brother William was mustered out of the Eighth Vermont Vols. on June 22, 1864, but two months later he reenlisted, joining his brother Edgar in Co. H of the Second Vermont Vols. William was finally mustered out of the service on June 30, 1865. Alonzo Kinsley Compiled Military Service Record; William L. Kinsley Compiled Military Service Record; Edgar Kinsley Montague Compiled Military Service Record.

235. After his discharge from the army in December 1862, Charles Bingham attended a commercial college in Poughkeepsie, N.Y., from which he graduated in December 1864. Hemenway, *Historical Gazetteer*, II, 412.

236. A forty-nine-year-old farmer and sawmill proprietor with holdings valued at $3,534 in 1860, Royal Tyler Bingham had three daughters. In 1872 Kinsley would marry Ella Lenora, the middle daughter, who was nine years old when the war broke out. Bingham represented Fletcher in the state legislature in 1858 and later served as a judge in the Franklin County courts. 1860 Manuscript Census, roll 1321, p. 8; Lewis Cass Aldrich, *History of Franklin and Grand Isle Counties, Vermont, with Illustrations and Biographical Sketches of Some of the Prominent Men and Pioneers* (Syracuse, N.Y.: D. Mason & Co., 1891), 545, 548.

237. Albert Parsons, a son of Uncle Medad Parsons, was listed in the 1860 federal census as a twenty-six-year-old farmer living in his father's household in Fletcher. 1860 Manuscript Census, roll 1321, p. 8.

238. Susan Fleming is listed in both the 1850 and the 1870 federal census for the town of Fletcher. In 1870 she appears as a forty-year-old housekeeper living in a household headed by her twenty-eight-year-old brother Benjamin Fleming, a farmer with property valued at $6,850. She died in 1908. 1850 Manuscript Census, roll 924, p. 13; 1870 Manuscript Census, roll 1620, p. 18; Susan Fleming death certificate, Vital Records.

239. Probably John Fleming, who in 1870 is seventy-five years old and living in Fletcher with his daughter Susan and son Benjamin. 1870 Manuscript Census, roll 1620, p. 18; Benjamin S. Fleming death certificate, Vital Records.

240. Kinsley's mother's sister, Junia Robinson, was sixty-nine in 1860 and living with her son Demas Robinson, a thirty-three-year-old farmer. Kinsley and Demas Robinson were close friends as well as cousins, and in 1888 Robinson would submit an affidavit in support of Kinsley's efforts to get his pension payments increased. 1860 Manuscript Census, roll 1321, p. 265; Rufus Kinsley Pension.

241. Probably either Hetty Case, who was ninety-seven in 1860, or Emma Case, who was seventy-seven. Both lived with Jerome Case on his farm in Fletcher. 1860 Manuscript Census, roll 1321, p.8.

242. Much to the shock and dismay of his superiors, Commissary Sergeant Peter Fleming committed suicide in early May 1864. Joseph T. Wilson, *The Black Phalanx: A History of the Negro Soldiers of the United States in the Wars of 1775–1812, 1861–'65* (Hartford, Conn.: American Publishing Company, 1890), 176; Bearss, *Historic Resource Study*, 221.

243. Grosvenor was dismissed from the army on May 28, 1864. On August 8, 1864, however, he was informed by the War Department that "the President has removed the disability in your case, on the ground that the sentence (dismissal from the service) awarded by the General Court Martial before which you were tried, is not sustained by the evidence." After the war, Grosvenor became editor of the *St. Louis Democrat*, a regular contributor to the *New York Tribune*, and a leading anti-protectionist in the national debate over tariff reform. *War Record of Col.? W. M. Grosvenor*, 4; C. W. Foster to W. M. Grosvenor, August 8, 1864, in William M. Grosvenor Compiled Military Service Record; W. M. Grosvenor, *Does Protection Protect? An Examination of the Effect of Different Forms of Tariff upon American Industry* (New York: D. Appleton & Company, 1871), 362.

244. Several officers of the Second USCI, including Colonel Stark Fellows on May 23 and Chaplain James H. Schneider on April 26, died "of disease" at Key West, Fla., in the spring of 1864. *OAR*, VIII, 170.

245. Samantha Kinsley, fifteen years old and living with her parents and four sisters in Georgia, Vt., at the time of the 1860 federal census, was the daughter of Kinsley's Uncle Chellis. 1860 Manuscript Census, roll 1321, p. 24.

246. The firearms issued to the Seventy-fourth regiment had already been declared obsolete by an army inspector in March 1864. After a second inspector condemned them in June, the regiment was issued .57-caliber Enfield rifle-muskets. Bearss, *Historic Resource Study*, 225.

247. The Ninety-first USCI was consolidated with the Seventy-fourth USCI on July 7, 1864. *OAR*, VIII, 248.

248. Pastor of the Carondelet Street Methodist Episcopal Church, John P. Newman was an important but controversial figure in wartime New Orleans. A contemporary labeled Newman "the Luther of the churches of New Orleans during the rebellion" because of his defiant stand for liberty and Union. Anyone identified with his congregation ran the risk of being harassed by Confederate loyalists. During Reconstruction, Newman helped establish a normal school

for freedmen, served as director of a black orphanage, and published a religious newspaper, the *New Orleans Advocate*. *New Orleans Times*, March 26, 1864; *New Orleans Riots*, 428; Emily Hazen Reed, *Life of A. P. Dostie, or, the Conflict of New Orleans* (New York: W. P. Tomlinson, 1868), 240; Howard Ashley White, *The Freedmen's Bureau in Louisiana* (Baton Rouge: Louisiana State University Press, 1970), 79, 81–82, 191; Ted Tunnell, *Crucible of Reconstruction: War, Radicalism and Race in Louisiana, 1862–1877* (Baton Rouge: Louisiana State University Press, 1984), 148; *New Orleans Tribune*, January 11, 13, 1866.

249. Daniel Kinsley, who was working as messenger of the Worcester County courts in Massachusetts, and Guy Kinsley, who was farming in Iowa, were Ben Alva Kinsley's two sons who did not serve (five did serve) in the Union army.

250. At the time Kinsley made these observations, there was no reason to worry about Taylor, who had been relieved of his command by Kirby Smith and was sitting idly in Natchitoches with his wife and children, waiting for Jefferson Davis to decide his future. Winters, *Civil War*, 380–81; Taylor, *Destruction*, 194.

251. Actually, Massachusetts abolitionists like Wendell Phillips and Charles Sumner were disappointed in the 1864 Louisiana Constitution. In New Orleans the black press complained that the new constitution did virtually nothing to improve the status of African Americans beyond the abolition of slavery, which Lincoln's plan of Reconstruction had already mandated; even worse, it "restored power to the avowed as well as the secret enemies of our beloved Republic." Denouncing the election to ratify the constitution as "a sham and humbug," the black press further declared it "our duty to oppose all and every constitution which will be founded upon States Rights principles. . . ." McCrary, *Abraham Lincoln*, chaps. 8–9; Houzeau, *My Passage*, 44; *New Orleans Tribune*, August 20, September 6, 1864.

252. Daniel Edgar Sickles (1819–1914) was a fearless but controversial soldier who lost a leg at the Battle of Gettysburg. After his recovery, Lincoln ordered him to visit southern Louisiana and other former Confederate territory to report on the progress of the freedmen and the state of Reconstruction. Warner, *Generals in Blue*, 446–47.

253. Born in Bavaria, but a resident of New Orleans since childhood, Michael J. Hahn (1830–1886) had opposed secession and refused to take a Confederate loyalty oath. He had, however, held the office of notary under the Confederacy and made speeches and presented flags in support of Confederate troops. *New Orleans Riots*, 318, 388; Amos E. Simpson and Vaughn B. Baker, "Michael Hahn: Steady Patriot," *Louisiana History*, 13 (Summer 1972), 229–52.

254. Frank R. Chase was the superintendent of education in Louisiana for the Freedmen's Bureau. White, *Freedmen's Bureau in Louisiana*, 120, 177.

255. Organized in January 1863 and initially consisting of all troops in the Department of the Gulf, the Nineteenth Army Corps was originally under Banks's command. Most, but not all, of the regiments of the Nineteenth Army Corps headed north to Virginia in July 1864. The Eighth Vermont, embarking on the steamer *St. Mary* on July 5, was one of the first to go. Subsequently, the regiment saw heavy fighting under General Philip Sheridan at Opequon, Fisher's Hill, and Cedar Creek. The fighting days of the Eighth Vermont pretty much ended at

Cedar Creek, where 123 of the 164 men in the regiment were either killed or wounded. Peck, *Revised Roster*, 302.

256. John 20:28. The words of Thomas, who had doubted the resurrection, after he saw and touched the wounds of Christ.

257. Luke 22:48.

258. Mrs. Taylor taught in the New Orleans public schools until her dismissal in 1860 because of her loyalty to the Union. She was principal of the Washington School during the four years of Union occupation. She was dismissed again in September 1866, when conservative Confederate sympathizers took control of the city school board. Her offense, she told a congressional investigating committee, was taking the Union loyalty oath and making her students sing "Yankee Doodle," "Rally Round the Flag," "John Brown's Body," and other politically incorrect songs. *New Orleans Riots*, 392–93, 428.

259. Kinsley here erroneously contradicts what he had written in his diary on July 5 concerning the Eighth Vermont's destination. The regiment left Algiers on July 5 and reached Hampton Roads, Va., a week later.

260. Kinsley's sister Lucretia, who never married, was living in Iowa with her brother Guy Kinsley (1825–1921) and his wife Lucinda Ellsworth Kinsley (1830–1889). Ballway, *A Genealogical Study*, 41.

261. Originally mustered in on June 6, 1861, as a major in the Forty-first New York Vols., Ernest W. Holmstedt was later promoted to lieutenant colonel and fought at the Battle of Cross Keys in Virginia. After briefly leaving the service, he returned as a lieutenant colonel in the Seventy-sixth USCI on February 26, 1864. Four months later he was promoted to colonel in the Seventy-fourth USCI and sent to Ship Island. *OAR*, II, 481; Ernest W. Holmstedt Compiled Military Service Record.

262. On June 19, 1864, the *U.S.S. Kearsarge*, commanded by Captain John A. Winslow, sank the celebrated Confederate raider *Alabama* off Cherbourg, France, in what was the greatest ship-to-ship combat of the war in open seas. Since its launch in May 1862, the British-built *Alabama* had destroyed over sixty U.S. merchant vessels worth roughly six million dollars.

263. The regiment at Fort Pike, which guarded a strategic channel northeast of New Orleans that connected Lake Borgne and Lake Pontchartrain, was the Ninety-first USCI.

264. Although Major General Edward Richard Sprigg Canby (1817–1873) graduated next to last in his class at West Point, he had performed credibly in the regular army prior to the outbreak of civil war. On May 7, 1864, he was placed in command of the Military Division of West Mississippi, which included the Gulf states from Texas to Florida. After reorganizing Banks's troops in the aftermath of the disastrous Red River campaign, he planned the capture of Mobile and its forts. When this expedition, in which Kinsley participated, succeeded, he received official thanks and congratulations from President Lincoln. He was killed by Modoc Indians in Siskiyou Co., Calif., in 1873. Warner, *Generals in Blue*, 67–68.

265. A year later Holmstedt was court-martialed for, among other things, permitting the regiment's sutler to sell vast quantities of alcohol at exorbitant prices

to prisoners as well as soldiers. Holmstedt was mustered out of the regiment on October 11, 1865. See complaints filed in the Ernest W. Holmstedt Compiled Military Service Record.

266. Born on March 22, 1842, in Columbia, N.H., Parker J. Noyes was mustered into Co. C, Eighth Vermont Vols., as a musician on February 18, 1862. He was commissioned as a second lieutenant in the Second Regiment Infantry, Corps d'Afrique, in September 1863, and mustered out in October 1865. Noyes and Noyes, *Genealogical Record*, I, 363; Peck, *Revised Roster*, 720.

267. The allusion is to the brutal treatment of seamen in Richard Henry Dana's *Two Years before the Mast: A Personal Narrative of Life at Sea* (1840).

268. Like most volunteers, Kinsley was somewhat intimidated by the professional soldiers who made up the regular army, with its reputation for rigorous standards and iron discipline.

269. Kinsley did pass, and the examining board listed him among the officers judged "efficient and capable of performing the duties now assigned them." Captain John M. Wilson to Major C. T. Christensen, August 3, 1864, Applications for Commissions and Reports of Boards of Examiners for Officers in U.S. Colored Troops, pt. I, entry 1936, Department of the Gulf, Army Commands.

270. John Ericsson, the Swedish-born inventor, designed and built the Union ironclad *Monitor*, which fought the Confederate ram *Merrimac* in 1862 in a celebrated battle off the coast of Virginia. The *Monitor* subsequently served as a prototype for other Union ironclads, and the word "monitor" became a generic term for a small, shallow-draught warship with a central revolving gun turret.

271. David Glasgow Farragut (1801–1870) was the most celebrated naval commander of the Civil War. At the outbreak of the war he had already been in the navy for half a century. After his stunning victory at Mobile Bay, which left only Charleston and Wilmington as major Confederate ports, he was promoted to the rank of vice admiral. A year and a half later he became the first admiral in the history of the United States Navy.

272. Early on the morning of August 5, 1864, Farragut's fleet of four ironclads and fourteen wooden ships worked its way through the torpedo-laden channel guarded by Forts Gaines and Morgan and into Mobile Bay. It was during this daring passage that Farragut reportedly shouted the immortal words: "Damn the torpedoes! Full speed ahead!" Admiral Franklin Buchanan (1800–1874), the first superintendent of the U.S. Naval Academy and commander of the huge ironclad *Tennessee*, was wounded, but not mortally, during the ensuing Battle of Mobile Bay. Chester G. Hearn, *Mobile Bay and the Mobile Campaign: The Last Great Battles of the Civil War* (Jefferson, N.C., and London: McFarland & Company, 1993), chaps. 7–8.

273. Union losses in the battle for Mobile Bay were especially large compared to Confederate casualties. Confederate losses totaled 12 killed and 20 wounded, whereas Union losses amounted to 145 killed and 170 wounded. Union deaths included Commander Tunis A. M. Craven and the 92 other sailors who went down with him on the monitor *Tecumseh*. Farragut, who did indeed strap himself to the main rigging of the *Hartford* during the battle, agreed with Kinsley that

the victory was worth the cost. He wrote on April 12, 1864: "Notwithstanding the loss of life, particularly on this ship, and the terrible disaster to the *Tecumseh*, the result of the fight was a glorious victory, and I have reason to feel proud of the officers, seamen, and marines of the squadron under my command. . . . Regular discipline will bring men to any amount of endurance, but there is a natural fear of hidden dangers, particularly when so awfully destructive of human life as the torpedo, which requires more than discipline to overcome." Hearn, *Mobile Bay*, 91, 105, 115–17; Farragut report no. 343, *ORN*, XXI, 415.

274. Designed by Admiral John A. Dahlgren, America's premier naval ordinance expert at the outbreak of the Civil War, smoothbore as well as rifled Dahlgren cannons were used extensively throughout the war by the Union navy. Usually smoothbore weapons, Civil War mortars were typically short iron cannons designed to throw large, hollow projectiles at high elevations. Ripley, *Artillery and Ammunition*, chaps. 3 and 5.

275. Beginning on May 7, 1864, Sherman had advanced steadily on Atlanta, investing the city's northern and eastern suburbs by July 25. Confederate forces did not completely evacuate the city, however, until September 1, 1864.

276. On August 8, 1864, Major General Gordon Granger (1822–1876), commander of the Union land operations against Mobile, wrote to Major C. T. Christensen: "I have the honor to report that the old flag now floats over Fort Gaines, the entire garrison having surrendered to the combined forces of the Army and Navy this morning at 8 o'clock. By this surrender we have captured 818 prisoners of war. . . . " *ORN*, XXI, 524.

277. Kinsley is probably referring to the steamer *Savery*.

278. Christopher C. Pike had been a major in the Second Regiment Infantry, Corps d'Afrique, since September 1863. *OAR*, VIII, 248.

279. Burchmore was mustered out of the Seventy-fourth USCI by Special Orders No. 215 on August 15, 1864. Zachariah Burchmore Compiled Military Service Record.

280. Both Abram J. Nichols and Joseph Villeverde were discharged on August 15, 1864. Apparently found "deficient" in property and papers entrusted to him as commander of Co. G by the examining board, Villeverde, a hereditary free man of color, was discharged by Special Orders No. 89 on August 6, 1864. This order was subsequently revoked in 1878 by the secretary of war because Villeverde had been "subsequently, and before the execution of the above order, mustered out and paid. . . . " Augustine P. Hawley was discharged on August 6, 1864. Joseph Villeverde Compiled Military Service Record; Special Orders No. 89, Unit Record Books, Seventy-fourth Regiment, USCI, Records of the Adjutant General's Office, 1780s–1917, Record Group 94, National Archives (cited hereinafter as Unit Record Books, Seventy-fourth USCI); *OAR*, VIII, 248; Berlin, et al., *Black Military Experience*, 323. There are in these sources slight discrepancies in the dates of discharge for some of the officers who failed to survive the July 1864 examinations.

281. Charles F. Clark had been a first lieutenant in the Second Regiment Infantry, Corps d'Afrique, since October 10, 1863. First Lieutenant Theodule A.

Martin, a free man of color who was born in New Orleans in 1836, was discharged on August 15, 1864. Kinsley does not mention that First Lieutenant Charles C. Colton, his former fellow boarder with Captain Noyes, also failed the exam administered by the visiting board and was discharged from the army on August 6, 1864. *OAR*, VIII, 248; David C. Rankin, "The Origins of Black Leadership in New Orleans During Reconstruction," *Journal of Southern History*, 40 (August 1974), 423n, 438; Special Orders No. 89, Unit Record Books, Seventy-fourth USCI.

282. First Lieutenant S. Gardner Lewis was dismissed from the regiment on September 18, 1864; Second Lieutenant Austin W. Saunders was discharged on August 15, 1864. *OAR*, VIII, 248.

283. The reference is to "A change came o'er the spirit of my dream," in Lord Byron's poem, "The Dream." *Byron: Poetical Works*, ed. Frederick Page, 3rd ed., corrected by John Jump (Oxford: Oxford University Press, 1970), line 75, p. 92.

284. Designed by Sir Joseph Whitworth and used in small numbers by Confederate forces, the Whitworth was a remarkably accurate English rifled cannon made of steel in various calibers. Designed by the British officer Alexander Theophilus Blakely, the Blakely was also an English rifled cannon. The Confederacy purchased Blakelys in small numbers in several calibers, often employing the larger-caliber guns in coastal defenses. Ripley, *Artillery and Ammunition*, 142–59.

285. Robert E. Lee's first cousin and an officer in the U.S. Navy for most of his adult life, Richard Lucian Page (1807–1901) was appointed brigadier general in the Confederate army and commander of the outer defenses of Mobile Bay on March 1, 1864. Ezra J. Warner, *Generals in Gray: Lives of the Confederate Commanders* (Baton Rouge: Louisiana State University Press, 1959), 226–27.

286. General Page paid tribute to Kinsley and the other sharpshooters in his account of the battle for Fort Morgan: "During this heavy bombardment [of August 22] I found it useless to attempt to fire my guns, as the sharp-shooters could pick off my men as fast as they would appear at the guns." R. L. Page, "The Defense of Fort Morgan," in Robert U. Johnson and Clarence C. Buel, eds., *Battles and Leaders of the Civil War*, 4 vols. (1887; reprint, New York: Thomas Yoseloff, 1956), IV, 408–10.

287. According to official reports, Union losses in the battle for Fort Morgan were 1 killed and 7 wounded. Confederate losses stood at 1 killed and 3 wounded. Remembering that Union forces had bombarded the fort off and on for eighteen days, including the launching of some three thousand shells in the final twelve hours of fighting, General Page, like Kinsley, was surprised at the small number of Confederate casualties. R. L. Page to D. H. Maury, August 30, 1864, *ORN*, XXI, 574; Hearn, *Mobile Bay*, 131.

288. Given the horrible fate of the *Tecumseh*, Kinsley's fear of having his little skiff blown up by a torpedo was understandable. But because of design problems, most of the torpedoes in Mobile Bay were actually harmless after a few days in the water. Hearn, *Mobile Bay*, 39, 92.

289. Oscar W. Goodrich (also known as Oscar W. Goodridge) was born in Fletcher on September 25, 1839. His mother worked in the Kinsley household before the war and had known Rufus since he was an infant. Goodrich was a resident of Lowell, Vt., when he enlisted on October 19, 1861. Initially a sergeant

in Co. A, Eighth Vermont Vols., he was discharged from the Eighth in November 1862 for promotion to second lieutenant and later captain in the Third Regiment Infantry, Corps d'Afrique. This black regiment was originally organized at New Orleans on November 24, 1862, as the Third Regiment, Louisiana Native Guards. Its designation was changed to the Third Regiment Infantry, Corps d'Afrique, on June 6, 1863, and to the Seventy-fifth Regiment, USCI, on April 4, 1864. Goodrich, who suffered from diarrhea, dysentery, and gonorrhea for much of the fall and winter of 1863, submitted his resignation from the Third Corps d'Afrique in December 1863. His commanding officer approved the resignation, declaring that "This officer is worthless to the service." He died in poverty of kidney and heart disease in Craftsbury, Vt., on November 16, 1887. Carpenter, *Eighth Regiment,* 286; Peck, *Revised Roster,* 718; *OAR,* VIII, 250; Oscar W. Goodridge Grave Registration; 1850 Manuscript Census, roll 924, p. 1; 1860 Manuscript Census, roll 1322, p. 8; Oscar W. Goodrich birth certificate of September 25, 1839, and death certificate of November 16, 1887, Vital Records; Betsey Goodridge affidavit, April 16, 1889, Rufus Kinsley Pension; *OAR,* VIII, 250; Oscar W. Goodridge Compiled Military Service Record; Oscar W. Goodridge Pension.

290. The Wolf River flows into St. Louis Bay on the Mississippi coast, which is about ten miles from Cat Island.

291. Zechariah 4:10.

292. Harriet Newell Mudgett (1834–1900) was married to Kinsley's brother Daniel. Ballway, *A Genealogical Study,* 42.

293. Kinsley's brother Jason was born in Fletcher on October 25, 1833. In the 1850s he moved to McGregor, Iowa, where he became a teacher in a common school. In June 1861 the blue-eyed, fair-haired, five-foot six-inch Kinsley was enrolled as a private in Co. K, First Iowa Cavalry. He was mustered out of the service in Austin, Texas, on February 15, 1866. After the war he returned to McGregor, where he died on October 12, 1903. Jason W. Kinsley Compiled Military Service Record; undated Jason W. Kinsley obituary in unknown newspaper in possession of Reba Kinsley Hall.

294. Named after the French army Captain Claude E. Minié, the "minie ball" was a conoidal bullet designed for rifled guns.

295. Probably a reference to Harmon Warren, who was born in Fletcher on February 10, 1819, was married in Fletcher by Kinsley's future father-in-law, and, like Kinsley, was related by marriage to the Robinson and Montague families. Warren was listed in the 1860 federal census as a farmer worth twenty-five hundred dollars; his family included a wife, a son, and two daughters. In the 1870 federal census he is listed as having three daughters and property valued at sixty-five hundred dollars. Harmon Warren birth certificate, Harmon Warren and Valeria Shepardson marriage certificate, Vital Records; Ballway, *A Genealogical Study,* 66, 67; 1860 Manuscript Census, roll 1321, p. 18; 1870 Manuscript Census, roll 1620, p. 167B.

296. In the wake of Lincoln's landslide reelection, Benjamin F. Butler in a speech at the Fifth Avenue Hotel in New York City on November 14, 1864, presented a plan that offered full amnesty to all Confederates who laid down their arms by January 8, 1865. Those who rejected such a magnanimous offer

would face a "sharp, quick, decisive war" aimed at the "extinguishment" of those in rebellion and the permanent redistribution of their lands among invading Union soldiers. *New York Times*, November 15, 16, 1864.

297. Colonel Charles D. Anderson of the Twenty-first Alabama surrendered Fort Gaines on August 8, 1864. Anderson's superiors pronounced his decision to surrender "inexplicable," "disgraceful," and "shameful," and relieved him of his command. R. L. Page to Dabney H. Maury, August 8, 1864, D. H. Maury to J. A. Seddon, August 8, 1864, in *ORN*, XXI, 561–62.

298. The "Dead Line" was a boundary around the prisoners' encampment beyond which an inmate ventured at the risk of being shot.

299. Probably Martha Rood, a thirty-two-year-old schoolteacher in 1870, and her immediate neighbor, Harriet I. Riggs, a thirty-six-year-old book agent in 1870. Riggs was also vice president of the Ladies Green Mountain Soldiers Aid Society, which was organized in Kinsley's father's home and presided over by his step-mother, Lucy Blair Kinsley. 1870 Manuscript Census, roll 1620, p. 234; Ben A. [Kinsley] to Lucretia [Kinsley], February 14, 1864, Kinsley Papers.

300. Augusta Kinsley, a twenty-two-year-old teacher, was living with her parents and four sisters in Georgia, Vt., in 1860. She was the daughter of Kinsley's uncle Chellis. 1860 Manuscript Census, roll 1321, p. 24.

301. For a discussion of Lincoln's remarkably forgiving policy toward Tennessee, Kentucky, and Louisiana, see William C. Harris, *With Charity for All: Lincoln and the Restoration of the Union* ([Lexington]: University Press of Kentucky, 1997), esp. 17–19, 171–96, 212–28.

302. *Hamlet*, act 5, scene 2, lines 10–11.

303. Lieutenant Commander Charles H. Greene, who had been wounded at the Battle of Mobile Bay while commanding the gunboat *Octorara*, was made captain of the *Vincennes* in late August 1863. He also served as supervisor of repairs at the naval workshop on Ship Island. *ORN*, XXI, 81, 454, 643.

304. After the war Goodrich (or Goodridge) returned to Vermont, worked as a carpenter, and remarried in 1867. Oscar W. Goodridge and Alvira N. Goddard marriage certificate of May 12, 1867, Vital Records.

305. The acting assistant quartermaster on Cat Island at this time was Lieutenant John W. Harrison of Co. F, Seventy-fourth USCI. John W. Harrison Compiled Military Service Record.

306. At the time of this writing, Kinsley's brother Jason was in a military hospital in St. Louis, Mo., apparently suffering from tonsillitis. He remained there for several months. Jason W. Kinsley Compiled Military Service Record.

307. Lucretia was living at this time with her brother Guy and his family on the Iowa frontier.

308. Camp Dixie was a nickname for the Confederate prison camp on Ship Island.

309. In May 1865, according to the Louisiana Board of Education for Freedmen, there were 216 teachers and 13,462 students in the black public school system that had been put in place during Banks's tenure as commander of the Department of the Gulf. A few months later, when the Freedmen's Bureau took over the system, the numbers had jumped to 230 teachers and roughly 19,000

students, and the Bureau's national superintendent of education proclaimed Louisiana's experiment in black education without peer in terms of both size and quality. This achievement came, as Kinsley suggests, in the face of determined white opposition to black education. White, *Freedmen's Bureau in Louisiana*, chap. 8; Messner, *Freedmen*, chap. 11; and C. Peter Ripley, *Slaves and Freedmen in Civil War Louisiana* (Baton Rouge: Louisiana State University Press, 1976), chap. 7.

310. In Parton's account of Butler's administration of the Department of the Gulf, Mrs. Lee and her husband appear as the owners of Lee's Boarding House in Pass Christian, Miss. Mrs. Lee is depicted as an inveterate Yankee hater. Parton, *General Butler*, 218.

311. After the war Lieutenant Colton did not take Alice Taylor back to Vermont. Instead he married Alice Candee and moved to Alabama, where he died of yellow fever on October 20, 1873. Colton, *Quartermaster George Colton*, 356.

312. Kinsley is alluding to the conspiracy to assassinate Vice President Andrew Johnson, Secretary of State William Seward, and Secretary of War Edwin Stanton as well as President Abraham Lincoln. Seward was stabbed several times but survived.

313. During the month of April 1865 roughly forty-three hundred Confederate soldiers – the vast majority of them captured in the battle for Mobile – were imprisoned on Ship Island. Bearss, *Historic Resource Study*, 315–19.

314. On April 30, 1865, there were 4,070 Confederate prisoners on Ship Island; a month later, on May 31, there were 10. The last prisoners left the island on June 8. Nearly all those released were sent to Vicksburg, where they were to be exchanged for Union soldiers held by Lieutenant General Richard Taylor, the Confederate commander of the Department of Alabama, Mississippi, and East Louisiana. Ibid., pp. 319–24.

315. Kinsley was not excused from duty, but according to his company captain he was so lame during his final months of service "that field duty would have been absolutely impossible.... " James Noyes affidavit, August 11, 1887, Rufus Kinsley Pension.

316. James Redpath's wildly popular *The Public Life of Capt. John Brown* appeared in January 1860. Filiopiestic and full of errors, it contributed mightily to the John Brown legend. Given Kinsley's admiration for John Brown, perhaps the Henry Ward Beecher that he mentions reading in conjunction with Redpath was a copy of the celebrated pastor's famous sermon of October 30, 1859, in which he expressed his hope that Brown would go to the gallows for his raid on Harpers Ferry and thereby become a martyr for freedom. Paul Finkelman, "Manufacturing Martyrdom: The Antislavery Response to John Brown's Raid," in Paul Finkelman, ed., *His Soul Goes Marching On: Responses to John Brown and the Harpers Ferry Raid* (Charlottesville: University of Virginia Press, 1995), 51–57; Stephen B. Oates, *To Purge This Land with Blood: A Biography of John Brown* (New York: Harper & Row, 1970), 318–19.

317. Rufus Kinsley Compiled Military Service Record.

318. In his letter of resignation Noyes emphasized that he had already served nearly four years in the army and that his wife was in "very feeble health such as requires an immediate change of climate in order to save life and restore health."

Noyes to Lieutenant Colonel J. Schuyler Crosby, July 22, 1865, in James Noyes Compiled Military Service Record. Noyes had expressed anxiety about his wife's health before. Laura Haviland wrote of Mrs. Noyes in April 1864: "She had been on the island a long time with her husband, and in poor health, sick and tired of army life, and longing for her Northern home. Yet she would not consent to leave her husband so long as he could stay in one place a sufficient time for her to be with him. But he was fearful it was impairing her health." *A Woman's Life Work*, 328.

319. The transformation of the Medical College of Alabama into a schoolhouse for freed slaves must have been especially galling for Dr. Joseph C. Nott, who was not only the director of the college but also a leading defender of slavery and proponent of black inferiority. But by March 1866 Mobile had seven black public schools educating nearly 1,000 students, as well as private and Sabbath schools that offered instruction to hundreds of other children. Elsewhere in postwar Alabama black education progressed slowly, however. In October 1866 the Alabama superintendent of education for the Freedmen's Bureau knew of only thirty-five black public schools in the entire state, and they were attended by only 3,338 students. Walter L. Fleming, *Civil War and Reconstruction in Alabama* (New York: Columbia University Press, 1905), 456–70; Peter Kolchin, *First Freedom: The Responses of Alabama's Blacks to Emancipation and Reconstruction* (Westport, Conn.: Greenwood Press, 1972), 80–92, 101.

320. By the time Noyes was finally mustered out of the army on October 11, 1865, Kinsley was long gone. On August 24, twelve days after making the final entry in his diary, Kinsley was in Cairo, Ill., booking passage to Boston. Peck, *Revised Roster*, 720; Rufus Kinsley Compiled Military Service Record.

Index